# In Your Mouth and
# In Your Heart

# In Your Mouth and
# In Your Heart

A Study of Deuteronomy 30:12–14 in Paul's
Letter to the Romans in Canonical Context

## Colin J. Smothers

PICKWICK *Publications* · Eugene, Oregon

IN YOUR MOUTH AND IN YOUR HEART
A Study of Deuteronomy 30:12–14 in Paul's Letter to the Romans in Canonical
Context

Pickwick Publications
An Imprint of Wipf and Stock Publishers
199 W. 8th Ave., Suite 3
Eugene, OR 97401

www.wipfandstock.com

PAPERBACK ISBN: 978-1-6667-3620-5
HARDCOVER ISBN: 978-1-6667-9422-9
EBOOK ISBN: 978-1-6667-9423-6

*Cataloguing-in-Publication data:*

Names: Smothers, Colin J. [author]

Title: In your mouth and in your heart : a study of Deuteronomy 30:12–14 in Paul's letter to the Romans in Canonical Context / by Colin J. Smothers.

Description: Eugene, OR: Pickwick Publications, 2022 | Includes bibliographical references and index.

Identifiers: ISBN 978-1-6667-3620-5 (paperback) | ISBN 978-1-6667-9422-9 (hardcover) | ISBN 978-1-6667-9423-6 (ebook)

Subjects: LCSH: Bible.—Romans—Criticism, interpretation, etc. | Bible.—Romans, X—Criticism, interpretation, etc. | Bible.—Romans—Theology | Bible.—Old Testament—Relation to Romans | Bible.—Romans—Relation to Deuteronomy | Bible.—Deuteronomy—Relation to Romans | Deuteronomy, XXX, 12–14—Criticism, interpretation, etc

Classification: BS2665.52 S66 2022 (print) | BS2665.52 (ebook)

08/10/22

To my wife, Elise,
whose loving companionship is evidence of
God's overwhelming kindness to me;
and to our children, Lydia, Isaac, Laurel, John, and James
who bring immeasurable joy to my life.
*Soli Deo Gloria*

# Contents

*List of Tables and Figures* | ix

*Preface* | xi

*List of Abbreviations* | xiii

1    Introduction | 1

2    Deuteronomy 30:11–14 in Its Immediate Literary Context | 27

3    Deuteronomy 30:11–14 in Its Old Testament Context | 92

4    Deuteronomy 30:11–14 in Paul's Letter to the Romans | 152

5    Conclusion | 212

*Bibliography* | 217

*Ancient Document Index* | 231

# List of Tables and Figures

## Tables

1. S. R. Driver's diachronic structure of Deuteronomy | 29

2. Deuteronomy as ANE treaty formula | 31

3. Structural introductory formulae in Deuteronomy | 33

4. Proposed parallel literary structure of Deuteronomy | 33

5. Translation landscape of the כי chain in Deuteronomy 30:9–14 | 65

6. Verbless clause constructions in Deuteronomy 30:11–14 | 71

7. Mood swings and changing agents in Isaiah 51 | 98

8. Verbal parallels in the heart theology of
    Jeremiah and Deuteronomy | 110

9. Jeremiah recapitulates the promise of Deuteronomy | 113

10. Structure of Jeremiah's Book of Consolation | 114

11. Parallelism in Jeremiah 31:33 | 122

12. Citations and allusions to Deuteronomy in Romans | 153

# Figures

1. Syntactical flow of Deuteronomy 6:1–3 | 44

2. שוב chiasm in Deuteronomy 30:1–10 | 54

3. Key words chiasm in Deuteronomy 30:1–10 | 55

4. לבב chiasm in Deuteronomy 30:1–14 | 56

5. Main-clause discourse analysis of *weqatal* and imperfect verbal forms in Deuteronomy 30:1–14 | 57

6. Translation distribution of כי in the LXX | 67

7. Present or Future? Translating the verbless clauses in Deuteronomy 30:11–14 | 76

8. N. T. Wright's chiastic structure of Romans 9–11 | 154

# Preface

THE LORD'S FAITHFULNESS AND steadfast love toward me in Christ is overwhelming. His kindness to me during the completion of the dissertation on which this book is based and the Ph.D. degree has been mediated through those he has placed around me—the many without whose love, encouragement, and support I would have failed to succeed, including the initial encouragement to pursue a Ph.D. from my pastor and doctoral supervisor, Dr. Jim Hamilton; the generous financial support from my father- and mother-in-law, Robert and Audrey Hyman; the never-diminished enthusiasm of my own father and mother, Stephen and Cathleen Smothers; and not least, the unfailing love of my wife, Elise, whose constant presence by my side as an encourager and companion has provided a precious source of life. She has made a loving home for our family through her tireless self-giving, and I am eternally thankful to God for bringing us together in his kind providence.

Too many are owed thanks to name here, but I would like to express publicly my gratitude to Dr. Jim Hamilton for the copious pushback and feedback he graciously provided on earlier drafts of this project. His knowledge of and love for the Bible is as infectious as it is unmatched. I would also like to thank Dr. Peter Gentry for the many spirited conversations we had over Deuteronomy 30:11–14, heart circumcision, and the brilliant singularity that is the new covenant. Here is a man well acquainted with God's faithfulness and steadfast love.

I pray the work herein will bring glory to God by exalting the Lord Jesus through the proclamation of the good news that "if you confess with your mouth that Jesus is Lord and believe in your heart that God raised him from the dead, you will be saved" (Rom 10:9)—our only hope in life and in death. This gospel has been brought near in the mission of Christ, who has inaugurated the new covenant and is even now communicating salvation by the Spirit to all who believe the word of faith "in your mouth and in your heart."

**Colin James Smothers**
Wichita, Kansas
December 2021

# List of Abbreviations

ANE      Ancient Near East

*ANF*      *The Ante-Nicene Fathers: Translations of the Writings of the Fathers Down to A.D. 325.* Edited by Alexander Roberts and James Donaldson. 10 vols. 1885–1887

BDB      Francis Brown, S. R. Driver, and Charles A. Briggs, ed., *Hebrew and English Lexicon of the Old Testament*

BDAG      Bauer, W., F. W. Danker, W. F. Arndt, and F. W. Gingrich. *Greek-English Lexicon of the New Testament and Other Early Christian Literature.* 3rd ed.

*BHS*      *Biblia Hebraica Stuttgartensia*

*DCH*      *Dictionary of Classical Hebrew*

ET      English Text

*HALOT*      *Hebrew and Aramaic Lexicon of the Old Testament*

LXX      Septuagint

LNTS      Library of New Testament Studies

MT      Masoretic Text

NICOT      The New International Commentary on the Old Testament

| | |
|---|---|
| *NPNF* | *A Select Library of Nicene and Post-Nicene Fathers of the Christian Church.* Edited by Philip Schaff and Henry Wace. 28 vols. in 2 series. 1886–1889. |
| NSBT | New Studies in Biblical Theology |
| JPS | Jewish Publication Society |
| JSNTSup | Journal for the Study of the New Testament: Supplement Series |
| JSOTSup | Journal for the Study of the Old Testament: Supplement Series |
| SNTSMS | Society for New Testament Studies Monograph Series |
| *WTJ* | *Westminster Theological Journal* |
| WUNT | Wissenschaftliche Untersuchungen zum Neuen Testament |

—— 1 ——

# Introduction

A RENEWED INTEREST IN biblical theology[1] has led to a resurgence of studies on the cohesion of the biblical canon, especially among evangelical interpreters operating within the confessional bounds of biblical inspiration and inerrancy. At the center of biblical theology is the relationship between the Old Testament (OT) and New Testament (NT),[2] which includes how the NT authors understood and used the OT. Paul's use of Deuteronomy 30:11–14 in Romans 10:5–13 has featured prominently in the academic discussion surrounding the NT's use of the OT.[3] Indeed,

1. For a recent summary of the various approaches to biblical theology extant today, see Klink and Lockett, *Understanding Biblical Theology*. The Southern Baptist Theological Seminary has carved out an impressive position contributing to the contemporary discipline of biblical theology. See Hamilton, *God's Glory in Salvation through Judgment*; Gentry and Wellum, *Kingdom through Covenant*; Schreiner, *The King in His Beauty*. For non-evangelical approaches to biblical theology, see Childs, *Biblical Theology of the Old and New Testaments*; Feldmeier and Spieckermann, *God of the Living*.

2. See James K. Mead's helpful discussion of various approaches to the relationship (or lack thereof) between the OT and NT: Mead, *Biblical Theology*, 61–68.

3. Jonathan Lunde, summarizing Andy Naselli's approach, condenses the issues surrounding the NT's use of the OT into five questions: "Is *sensus plenior* an appropriate way of explaining the NT use of the OT? How is typology best understood? Do the NT writers take into account the context of the passages they cite? Does the NT writers' use of Jewish exegetical methods explain the NT use of the OT? Are we able to replicate the exegetical and hermeneutical approaches to the OT that we find in the writings of the NT?" Lunde, "An Introduction to Central Questions in the New

this passage has been variably viewed as a silver bullet,[4] a Gordian knot,[5] or a *locus classicus*[6] in answering questions regarding how NT authors appropriated the OT.

In Romans 10:5–13, Paul cites two OT passages to ground his previous assertion that Christ is the τέλος of the law in 10:4. The second citation, Deuteronomy 30:12–14, is a veritable museum of problems that are encountered in the NT's use of the OT. In this passage, there is (1) an atypical introduction formula; (2) a text differing from both the MT and LXX, including both transformations and omissions;[7] (3) additional commentary interspersed; and (4) an original context that, at first glance, seems contrary to the NT application. These realities have led many interpreters to conclude that Paul cannot be quoting from Deuteronomy

---

Testament Use of the Old Testament," 11–12. Article V of the *Chicago Statement on Biblical Inerrancy* states, "We deny that later revelation, which may fulfill earlier revelation, ever corrects or contradicts it."

4. Richard Hays bases much of his approach to understanding the NT use of the OT on Paul's citation of Deut 30:12–14 in Rom 10:6–8. "Even passages that might have seemed perspicuous, such as Deut. 30:11–14, turn out to have concealed a meaning manifest only in Paul's inspired reading, a meaning that neither Moses nor Ezra could have guessed and that Paul himself could never have imagined before his own turning. Now, however, that latent meaning turns out to be the hermeneutical key that unlocks all the mysteries and God's revelation in the past. 'The word is near you, in your mouth and in your heart,' (That is, the word of faith which we preach) (Rom. 10:8). . . . Consequently, for Paul, original intention is not a primary hermeneutical concern. If Paul's intertextual readings are metaphorical in character, the reader of Paul's letters is assigned the same active responsibility that falls on readers of all figurative discourse: to articulate semantic potentialities generated by the figures in the text. Such potentialities can far exceed the conscious design of the author. The scriptural text as metaphor speaks through the author; whether such speaking occurs with or without the author's knowledge is a matter of little consequence, for Paul's readings of Scripture are not constrained by a historical scrupulousness about the original meaning of the text." Hays, *Echoes of Scripture in the Letters of Paul*, 155–56.

5. The following interpreters rule out the possibility of an organic relationship between these texts: Dodd, *The Epistle of Paul to the Romans*, 1949, 166; Schmidt, *Der Brief Des Paulus an Die Römer*, 176; Rhyne, "*Nomos Dikaiosynēs* and the Meaning of Romans 10:4," 496.

6. Black calls Paul's quotation of Deut 30:12–14 "one of the boldest, and most individualistic, of Pauline peshers." Black, "The Christological Use of the Old Testament in the New Testament," 1. Greg Beale indicates that this passage has been used as a "classical example" of the "Rhetorical" use of the OT in the NT in Beale, *Handbook on the New Testament Use of the Old Testament*, 78–79.

7. I am convinced by Gentry's arguments regarding the textual history of the Old Testament, particularly the relationship between the MT and LXX, presented in Gentry, "The Text of the Old Testament," 19–45.

30:12–14 in Romans 10.[8] Others have accused Paul of being willfully arbitrary,[9] and still others of using a "drastic and unwarranted allegorizing" that "must have exposed him to attack,"[10] or of employing a specially crass typological method of interpretation.[11] But as Anthony Hanson has wisely noted, "[P]roof texts that have been arbitrarily tampered with are ineffective as proofs."[12] And those slower to impugn the methods and motivations of Paul have exercised more patience in trying to understand Paul's use of Deuteronomy in Romans 10. Herein lies the fundamental question of this study: why does Paul turn to Deuteronomy 30:12–14 in Romans 10:5–13?

Speaking at a session of the 2015 meeting of the Evangelical Theological Society, G. K. Beale gave the illustration of a beautiful, green meadow that represents the NT's use of the OT. In this green meadow, however, are a number of weeds, representing difficult texts that pose a problem to the interpreter. One could take a mower and cut them down all at once, which would represent a broad-brush approach to the NT's use of the OT. But Beale prefers to wait for a PhD dissertation to tackle each individual textual "weed" in order that it might be dealt with properly at the root. This study is an attempt at tackling the "weed" of Deuteronomy 30:12–14 in Romans 10:5–13.

## Thesis

My thesis is that when Paul quotes Deuteronomy 30:12–14 as the content of the message of the righteousness based on faith over against Leviticus 18:5 and the righteousness based on the law in Romans 10:6–8,[13] he

---

8. Sanday and Headlam argue for a tenuous proverbial allusion, not a quotation, in Rom 10:6–8. Sanday and Headlam, *A Critical and Exegetical Commentary on the Epistle to the Romans*, 289. Cf. Davies, *Paul and Rabbinic Judaism*, 153–55; Longenecker, *The Epistle to the Romans*, 853–54.

9. Hays calls this quotation "deliberately provocative" as "[i]t would not be easy to find another text in the Old Testament that looks less promising for Paul's purposes." Hays, *Echoes*, 79.

10. Kirk, "The Epistle to the Romans," 225.

11. Cf. Gaugler, *Der Epheserbrief*, 214.

12. Hanson, *Studies in Paul's Technique and Theology*, 147.

13. For a thorough treatment of Paul's quotation of Lev 18:5 in Rom 10:5, see Sprinkle, *Law and Life*. While Sprinkle's project focuses on Lev 18:5 in its canonical (and Jewish) context, I aim to provide the corollary to his project by focusing on Deut 30:12–14 in canonical context. For a concise, compelling argument on Paul's use of Lev 18:5 in Gal 3:12, see Hamilton, "The One Who Does Them Shall Live by Them," 10–12.

understands this text to be fulfilled in the mission of Christ in accord with the original meaning of the text written by Moses. More precisely, Paul reads Deuteronomy 30:11–14 as an extension of the after-exile restoration foretold in Deuteronomy 30:1–10, which points forward to the new covenant experience of faith-empowered obedience, or heart circumcision, a reality that includes the internalization of the Word of God—the eschatological *torah*—by the Spirit of God. What Paul finds in Deuteronomy 30:11–14 is a promise of righteousness which he declares fulfilled in the gospel of the Lord Jesus, which is the message of the righteousness of faith.[14]

I begin this study below by categorizing the various approaches taken by interpreters in the history of research. In chapter 2, I exegete Deuteronomy 30:11–14 in its immediate literary context, with careful attention paid to chapter 30 as well as the narrative and literary structure of the book of Deuteronomy.[15] Then in chapter 3, I investigate inner-biblical allusions[16] to Deuteronomy 30:11–14 in the Prophets and the Writings in order to explore how this passage might have been understood, used, and developed in the rest of the OT. In so doing, I am pursuing the "canonical, genetic-progressive (or organically developmental, as a flower develops from a seed and bud), exegetical, and intertextual" task of biblical-theological exegesis.[17] Then in chapter 4, I engage in an exegesis of Romans 10:5–10, which includes unraveling Paul's citation of Deuteronomy 30:12–14, with special attention to the flow of chapters 9–11 and the greater literary structure of the book of Romans, as well as its dependence on the narrative flow of the book of Deuteronomy—particularly chapters 29–32. In the final chapter, I sum up my conclusions and end with some theological reflections.

---

14. One assumption this project attempts to test is set forth by Doug Moo and Andy Naselli: "The NT writers do not casually appeal to the OT or argue merely by analogy. They repeatedly assert that we must believe and do certain things *because* of what is said in specific OT texts. The NT authors suggest that their teachings are grounded in the OT." Moo and Naselli, "The Problem of the New Testament's Use of the Old Testament," 704.

15. L. Michael Morales sets forth a compelling model of this approach in his treatment of the narrative and literary structure of the book of Leviticus in Morales, *Who Shall Ascend the Mountain of the LORD?*

16. This phrase is self-consciously drawn from Beale: "[I]t may be better to use the phrase 'inner-biblical exegesis' or 'inner-biblical allusion' instead of 'intertextuality,' since the former two nomenclatures are less likely to be confused with postmodern reader-oriented approaches to interpretation, where the term 'intertextuality' had its origin." Beale, *Handbook on the New Testament Use of the Old Testament*, 40.

17. Beale, *A New Testament Biblical Theology*, 15.

## History of Research

There have been numerous attempts at explaining Paul's quotation of Deuteronomy 30:12–14 in Romans 10. Virtually every commentator on the book of Romans has had to take a position on the passage; many Pauline theologies and studies of Deuteronomy have weighed in;[18] and several articles have been dedicated to this citation.[19] Only one monograph to date has dealt exclusively with Paul's Deuteronomy citation in Romans 10, which I interact with extensively below.[20] Instead of enumerating and examining each individual approach to this quotation in the history of interpretation, which would require nearly one section per interpreter due to the uniqueness and eclectic nature of each approach, I have attempted to sum up the major approaches to this passage in five categories: (1) Rhetorical, (2) Metaphorical/Allegorical, (3) Jewish Exegetical, (4) Analogical/Typological, and (5) Contextual-Canonical.[21] In the Rhetorical approach, I have placed interpreters who argue that Paul is not intending to quote, cite, or even allude to Deuteronomy 30:12–14. Instead they contend he is—intentionally or unintentionally—merely appropriating the language of Deuteronomy 30:12–14 to make an

18. See, for example, McConville, *Grace in the End*, 150–57; Braulik, *The Theology of Deuteronomy*, 162–64; Westerholm, *Perspectives Old and New on Paul*, 326–30; Barclay, *Paul and the Gift*, 326, 542–43.

19. For example, Coxhead, "Deuteronomy 30:11–14 as a Prophecy of the New Covenant in Christ," 305–20; Seifrid, "Paul's Approach to the Old Testament in Romans 10:6–8," 3–37.

20. Bekken, *The Word Is Near You*.

21. Doug Moo and Andy Naselli offer a taxonomy of nine popular approaches to the problem of the New Testament's use of the Old Testament: Fideism, Subjectivism, Jewish Exegetical Methods, Dual Authorship, Theological Exegesis, Intertextuality, Typology, *Sensus Plenior*, and Canonical. Moo and Naselli, "The Problem of the New Testament's Use of the Old Testament," 711. G. K. Beale similarly surveys several categories in the form of "classical debates" that surround the NT use of the OT in Beale, *Handbook on the New Testament Use of the Old Testament*. These include Jewish Interpretation Influence, Testimony Book, Christocentric, Rhetorical, Postmodern, and Typology. My categories correspond in the following ways to those offered by Moo/Naselli and Beale: my Metaphorical/Allegorical approach is a mix between Moo/Naselli's Subjectivism and Intertextuality approaches and Beale's Postmodern category; my Jewish Exegetical approach is the same as Moo/Naselli's Jewish Exegetical Methods approach and Beale's Jewish Interpretation Influence category; my Analogical/Typological is a mix between Moo/Naselli's Typology and Canonical approaches and Beale's Typology category; and my Contextual-Canonical category overlaps with Moo/Naselli's Theological Exegesis and Canonical categories and Beale's own approach to the NT's use of the OT.

unconnected point about the righteousness of faith.[22] This approach has been considered and rejected by the vast majority of interpreters who acknowledge Paul's engagement with Deuteronomy 30:12–14 at some significant level in Romans 10:6–8. As a result, the Rhetorical approach is not considered below.[23]

At root in each of the other four approaches—Metaphorical/Allegorical, Jewish-Exegetical, Analogical/Typological, and Contextual-Canonical—is the *context* within which an interpreter proposes Paul's citation is best fundamentally understood. For the Metaphorical/Allegorical approach, interpreters propose Paul's contemporary situation as the primary context for interpreting his Deuteronomy quotation in Romans 10. In the Jewish Exegetical approach, the writings and hermeneutical practices of Second-Temple Judaism are primary. In the Analogical/Typological approach, an old/new covenant dichotomy or the overarching *heilsgeschichte* of Scripture is primary. In the Contextual-Canonical approach, the immediate literary context of Deuteronomy and its subsequent development in the canon is primary.

The aim of this study is not to provide a comprehensive hermeneutic to explain every use of the OT in the NT. Nor is the aim of this study to suggest a summary position on Paul's general use of the OT.[24] While each of the approaches mentioned above may have legitimate claims in other NT quotations of the OT—I am especially sympathetic to the Analogical/Typological approach—the goal of this study is to better understand, specifically, Paul's use of Deuteronomy 30:12–14 in Romans 10:6–8.

Below, I have chosen a noteworthy exemplar to represent each of these four categorical approaches taken in the history of research by interpreters trying to understand Paul's use of Deuteronomy 30:12–14

22. Several scholars have argued that Paul is using the language of Deut 30:11–14 but not quoting: Lagrange, *Saint Paul: Épitre Aux Romains*, 256; Robertson, *Word Pictures in the New Testament*, 4:388; Godet, *Commentary on Romans*, 378. Some scholars have argued that Paul is accessing a common proverb behind both the Deuteronomy and Romans text: Sanday and Headlam, *A Critical and Exegetical Commentary on the Epistle to the Romans*, 289; Davies, *Paul and Rabbinic Judaism*, 153–55; Barrett, *A Commentary on the Epistle to the Romans*, 129; Longenecker, *Biblical Exegesis in the Apostolic Period*, 114–21.

23. Schreiner dismantles what I am calling the Rhetorical approach in Schreiner, *Romans*, 556–57.

24. I applaud such efforts, and commend the work of my colleague Aubrey Sequeira as he attempts to do just this for the book of Hebrews. Perhaps the conclusions of this study might be incorporated into a similar work for the book of Romans, or for a complete Pauline hermeneutic on his use of the OT.

in Romans 10:6–8. Agreement among significant interpreters is noted where present.

## Metaphorical/Allegorical Approach: Richard Hays

In many ways, Richard Hays's seminal work *Echoes of Scripture in the Letters of Paul* serves as a wellspring for contemporary discussion on the NT's use of the OT. Hays's methods have become paradigmatic for the discipline,[25] and his exegetical conclusions have been adopted by many. Significantly, Paul's composite quotation of Deuteronomy in Romans 10 functions for Hays as a quintessential test case for understanding the Pauline OT hermeneutic and, in turn, for understanding the NT's use of the OT in general. For these reasons, Hays's interpretation of Paul's use of Deuteronomy 30:12–14 in Romans 10 is very important in the history of research.

### *Summary*

Hays sums up his view of Paul's use of Deuteronomy 30 in Romans 10 when he writes, "What Paul has in fact done is, simply, to read the text of Deuteronomy 30 as a *metaphor* for Christian proclamation. . . . Paul is reading the ancient scriptural text as a trope, which speaks by indirection about his own message and ministry."[26] In other words, Paul quotes Deuteronomy 30:12–14 not for the meaning he finds hidden in the text for support of his arguments, but for the meaning he may hide himself and then reveal.

In a provocatively titled section, "Paul as Reader and Misreader of Scripture," Hays refers to Paul's quotation of Deuteronomy and his subsequent interpretation as a "revisionary reading,"[27] a "theologically generative reappropriation,"[28] and an "audacious *rereading*."[29] The introductory paragraph to Hays's exegesis of Paul's quotation deserves quotation in full:

25. For example, Hays's criteria for detecting OT allusions in the NT have influenced the criteria of Beale, who writes, "Probably the most referred-to criteria for validating allusions is that offered by Richard Hays." Beale, *Handbook on the New Testament Use of the Old Testament*, 32.

26. Hays, *Echoes*, 83. Emphasis original.

27. Hays, *Echoes*, 1.

28. Hays, *Echoes*, 2.

29. Hays, *Echoes*, 4. Emphasis added.

In an apparently capricious act of interpretation, the reader will
recall, Paul seizes Moses' admonition of Israel, warning them to
obey the law without rationalization or excuse (Deut. 30:11–14),
and turns it into an utterance of The Righteousness from Faith, a
character who *contravenes the manifest sense of Moses' words* by
transmuting them into cryptic prophecy of the Christian gospel
as preached by Paul.[30]

According to Hays, Paul's use of Deuteronomy 30 is "deliberately provocative" for "[i]t would not be easy to find another text in the Old Testament that looks less promising for Paul's purposes" in Romans 10.[31] Paul
has intentionally transformed the meaning of Deuteronomy 30:12–14 to
serve his own purposes which are seemingly untethered from the original
context. In quoting Deuteronomy 30:12–14—with an introduction from
Deuteronomy 8:17 and/or 9:4—Paul engages in "subversive exegesis,"[32]
while he triangulates by metalepsis[33] and intertextuality[34] the contexts of

30. Hays, *Echoes*, 73–74. Emphasis added.

31. Hays, *Echoes*, 79. Hays seems to suggest that Paul did not pick Deut 30:12–14
to quote for the meaning that he found in the text, but actually in spite of it. In this
sense, Hays finds an unlikely ally in Luther: "Moses writes these words in Deut. 30:12,
and he does not have the meaning in mind they have here, but his abundant spiritual
insight enables the apostle to bring out their inner significance. It is as if he wanted to
give us an impressive proof of the fact that the whole Scripture, if one contemplates
it inwardly, deals everywhere with Christ, even though in so far as it is a sign and a
shadow, it may outwardly sound differently. This is why he says: 'Christ is the end of
the law' (Rom. 10:4); in other words: every word in the Bible points to Christ. That
this is really so, he proves by showing that this word here, which seems to have nothing whatsoever to do with Christ, nevertheless signifies Christ." Luther, *Lectures on
Romans*, 288. Luther, however, ends up interpreting this passage very similar to the
fourth view surveyed below, which understands Deut 30:12–14 to be speaking of the
effect of the gospel in the heart of the believer, after which God's "commandment will
become neither difficult nor too distant." Luther, *Lectures on Deuteronomy*, 278.

32. Hays, *Echoes*, 79.

33. The idea of metalepsis is central to Hays's understanding of Pauline hermeneutics in *Echoes*. This term Hays borrows from the world of literary criticism, specifically
from Hollander, *The Figure of Echo*. Hays explains, "Allusive echo can often function as
a diachronic trope to which Hollander applies the name of *transumption,* or *metalepsis.*
When a literary echo links the text in which it occurs to an earlier text, the figurative effect of the echo can lie in the unstated or suppressed (transumed) points of resonance
between the two texts. . . . Allusive echo functions to suggest to the reader that text B
should be understood in light of a broad interplay with text A, encompassing aspects
of A beyond those explicitly echoed." Hays, *Echoes*, 20.

34. Hays defines intertextuality at first as "the imbedding of fragments of an earlier
text within a later one" but then expands the definition to include both allusion, which

Deuteronomy 8 and 9, Deuteronomy 30, and Jewish Wisdom tradition to produce a Christological reading that affirms Paul's Christian *kerygma*.

Hays argues that the law-oriented text of Deuteronomy is forced, seemingly against its will, to bear witness to the grace-oriented spirit of the gospel. "Paul exposits Deuteronomy in such a way that its latent sense is *alleged to be identical* with the manifest claims of his own proclamation."[35] For Hays, this "historically outrageous reading" has "poetic plausibility" when intertextuality, metalepsis, and "sheer force of assertion" are the hermeneutical keys.[36] In this way, Paul has read Deuteronomy 30 as a "*metaphor* for Christian proclamation."[37]

Paul's quotation of Deuteronomy in Romans 10 serves as a unifying hermeneutical thread throughout Hays's *Echoes*. Not only does Hays introduce *Echoes* with this text as an exemplar and subsequently spend a large portion of the book on its exegesis, in the summary chapter he returns to it again where he homes in on the phrase "the word is near you, in your mouth and in your heart." This phrase, according to Hays, gives the believer hermeneutical warrant to follow Paul in taking "the risks of interpretive freedom."[38]

> We are authorized to perform imaginative acts of interpretation because as people of the new covenant we find the Law written on our hearts, and we discover in our own corporate life a letter from Christ whose import is open to all, whose message is in the deepest sense congruent with the message of Scripture.[39]

For Hays, this hermeneutical freedom is constrained by three substantive—as opposed to methodological—constraints. A reading must (1) affirm the faithfulness of God to his covenant promises, (2) bear witness to the gospel of Jesus Christ, and (3) shape the reader into Christlikeness and love for God.[40]

---

he defines as conscious textual citation by an author, and echo, which occurs either in the sub-conscience of an author or is a meaning-significant event created by the reader's own textual associations. Hays, *Echoes*, 14.

35. Hays, *Echoes*, 83. Emphasis added.

36. Hays, *Echoes*, 82.

37. Hays, *Echoes*, 82. Emphasis original.

38. Hays, *Echoes*, 189.

39. Hays, *Echoes*, 190.

40. Hays, *Echoes*, 191.

Thus, in Romans 10, Hays not only finds Paul performing the sort of exegesis Hays advocates in his book, but he also finds a hermeneutical warrant for reading Scripture unbound from its original context.

## Similar Interpreters

Many interpreters in the history of interpretation have employed a Metaphorical/Allegorical approach to Paul's quotation of Deuteronomy 30 in Romans 10, including E. Käsemann,[41] F. Watson,[42] R. M. Grant,[43] W. Barclay,[44] and A. Nygren.[45] For these interpreters, the original meaning of Deuteronomy 30:12–14 is not the primary context for interpreting Paul's use of this text. Rather, Paul's own situation and application is primary—an application that may actually directly oppose the meaning of the original text.

## Evaluation

Hays's exegesis of Romans 10:5–8 serves, in his own words, as "a crucial text for [his] enterprise."[46] Responding in a subsequent work to one of the critics of his hermeneutical method in *Echoes*, Hays doubles down on his exegesis of Paul's quotation of Deuteronomy 30:12–14.

> Rom 10:5–10 remains a vexing passage because Paul so daringly coopts the voice of Moses. Paul's rhetorical strategy is one of revision rather than rejection. Despite our discomfort about his reading, we cannot escape acknowledging that Paul is subjecting Deuteronomy to a hermeneutical transformation that makes the Law bear witness to the gospel.[47]

41. Käsemann, *Perspectives on Paul*, 155.

42. Francis Watson concurs with Hays that it is only a "facile harmonization" that would attempt to explain Paul's citation in harmony with Moses' original meaning. For Watson, Paul cannot accept the ostensible teaching of Moses, so he "rewrites the passage as the utterance of the Righteousness of faith." Watson, *Paul and the Hermeneutics of Faith*, 437–38.

43. According to Grant, "This is pure allegorization." Grant, *The Letter and the Spirit*, 51.

44. Barclay, *The Letter to the Romans*, 148.

45. Nygren, *Commentary on Romans*, 38.

46. Hays, *The Conversion of the Imagination*, 184.

47. Hays, *The Conversion of the Imagination*, 185–86.

If Hays is correct that Paul does subject Deuteronomy to a hermeneutical transformation via a revisionary reading, then surely Jack Suggs
is right in his comments about interpreters who, like Hays, suggest Paul
misused Deuteronomy 30 when he says, "The apostle's adversaries would
have found him guilty of an irresponsible use of scripture, which would
have undone every effort to persuade either friend or foe."[48] The issue
with Hays's approach to this passage is the issue with most postmodern
approaches to Scripture: the absence of validity and, in turn, objectivity.[49]
Simply put, if what Paul appeals to in Deuteronomy 30:12–14 is merely
meaning he himself placed there, then any meaning that contradicts Paul
which may be found by others is irrefutable, and arguing from or according to the Scriptures—a practice Paul and the other apostles based their
ministries on—is futile (Acts 18:24–28; 1 Cor 15:3–4).

Ironically, Hays's hermeneutical approach establishes uneven
ground. He is left unable to critique definitively the validity of other
interpretations, while others are presuppositionally grounded to offer a
negative judgment on his.[50] What Hays has found in his quest for Paul's
hermeneutic may in fact be a pale reflection of himself. Has Hays constructed Paul in his own postmodern image?[51]

## Jewish-Exegetical Approach: Per Jarle Bekken

I have chosen Per Jarle Bekken to represent the Jewish-Exegetical approach. Bekken has written the only monograph to date dedicated to

48. Suggs, "The Word Is Near You," 299.

49. Cf. Moo, "Paul's Universalizing Hermeneutic in Romans," 83.

50. To his credit, Hays does recognize this problem. "The dilemma is this: if we
read Scripture with the same imaginative freedom Paul employed, will we not inevitably contradict his particular construals of it? Will we not, in fact, produce readings of
Paul's own letters that cut across the grain? . . . Indeed, Paul's own example would lead
us to expect that the community, under the guidance of the Spirit, will remain open
to fresh readings of the same text, through which God will continue to speak. While
we continue to recognize Paul's readings of Scripture as abidingly valid figurations, we
will also create new figurations out of the texts that Paul read." Hays, *Echoes*, 186–87.
By this logic, the reading offered in my thesis—insofar as it affirms the faithfulness of
God to his promises, bears witness to the gospel of Jesus Christ, and shapes readers
into a community that embody the love of God in Christ—is unassailable from Hays's
hermeneutical position.

51. As Moo puts it, "Hays's proposal, along with other similar intertextual methods, is influenced not a little by postmodern views of meaning and interpretation."
Moo, "Paul's Universalizing Hermeneutic in Romans," 83.

Paul's quotation of Deuteronomy 30:12–14 in Romans, a work that stems from his dissertation completed at the Norwegian University of Technology and Science under Peder Borgen. In *The Word Is Near You: A Study of Deuteronomy 30:12–14 in Paul's Letter to the Romans in a Jewish Context*, Bekken attempts to situate Paul's quotation within a Jewish context, including both Jewish exegetical methods such as *pesher* interpretation and the literature of Second-Temple Judaism.[52] While others have posited Jewish exegesis and literature as the primary background to interpreting Paul's use of Deuteronomy 30 in Romans 10, Bekken's work contains the most thorough treatment according to this approach.

### Summary

According to Bekken, Paul's quotation of Deuteronomy 30:12–14 is best understood in light of Jewish exegetical methods and literature.

> It is the hypothesis of this study that an understanding of Paul's treatment of Deut 30:12–14 on the basis of the method of exegetical paraphrase can not only explain aspects of Paul's rendering of the Jewish Scripture, but also clarify the exegetical reasoning and arguments in and behind Rom 10:4ff., and thus to some extent justify his fresh exposition of Deut 30:12–14. . . . Thus the whole analysis aims at substantiating the thesis that Paul's christological treatment of Deut 30:12–14 can be placed within a Jewish exegetical context of his day with respect to the wording of the quotation, exegetical methods, structures and terminology.[53]

Bekken identifies four major Jewish texts that deal explicitly with Deuteronomy 30:12–14: *Targum Neofiti*, Baruch, and Philo's *De Virtutibus* and *De Praemiis et Poenis*. In these last two works, Bekken finds the most promising background to Paul's quotation in Romans 10, and he spends two very thorough chapters examining the literary contexts of Philo's interaction with Deuteronomy 30:12–14. In *De Virtutibus*, Bekken observes two similarities between Paul and Philo: they both speak about conversion from Deuteronomy 30:12–14, and both apply this passage to the entry of Jews and Gentiles into the true people of God.[54] Bekken finds

---

52. Interestingly, Bekken pursued this project in response to Richard Hays's call to "attend to certain traditions of scriptural interpretation within Judaism that might thicken our perception of Paul's readings of Scripture." Bekken, *The Word Is Near You*, 9.

53. Bekken, *The Word Is Near You*, 53–54.

54. Bekken, *The Word Is Near You*, 83–114.

in *De Praemiis et Poenis* a foil for Paul's gospel in Philo's exclusionary concept of the people of God, which is rooted in law observance.[55] Consequently, when Bekken turns in a third chapter to Paul's quotation of Deuteronomy 30:12–14, he aims to interpret Paul's exegesis in Romans 10:6–8 mainly in light of Philo's understanding of the same passage.[56]

In the end, Bekken argues that Paul's quotation of Deuteronomy 30:12–14 is an "exegetical paraphrase" comparable to the interpretations of the same text in Baruch and Philo.[57] But as Bekken elaborates on this conclusion, it appears that Paul's "exegetical paraphrase" is less an exegesis of the original passage in the book of Deuteronomy and more an exegesis of and response to the reigning Jewish reading of Deuteronomy 30:12–14, as represented in Baruch and Philo's two works. In step with advocates for the so-called New Perspective on Paul (NPP), Bekken understands Paul's main concern in Romans 10:6–8 to be countering those Jewish interpretations that perpetuated Jew-Gentile antipathy through law obedience.[58] According to Bekken, what Paul has in mind when he quotes Deuteronomy 30:12–14 is the contemporary Jewish application of the passage, which Paul seeks to overturn with a christologically-oriented "transfer" of its meaning in an attempt to "broaden the significance of the Law from what he perceived to be a too narrowly defined understanding."[59]

> In light of Christ as the "goal" of the Law, [Paul] transfers Deut 30:12–14 to the "righteousness of faith" (Rom 10:6), Christ (Rom 10:6–7), the "word of faith" (Rom 10:8) and the "word of Christ" (Rom 10:17) as the Law properly understood. The distinctive marks of the eschatological people of God are then no longer "works of the law" but the inclusive marker of faith in Christ (Rom 10:11–13). In this way Paul redefined the conception of

---

55. Bekken, *The Word Is Near You*, 115–52.

56. Bekken, *The Word Is Near You*, 153–221.

57. Bekken, *The Word Is Near You*, 224.

58. Though a fluid, multiform movement, this is summary of the *sine qua non* concern of proponents of the NPP. See Dunn's seminal 1983 essay for a summary of the NPP: Dunn, "The New Perspective on Paul (1983)," 99–120. Dunn's essay gave a name to an interpretive movement associated with Sanders, *Paul and Palestinian Judaism.* Cf. Westerholm, *Perspectives Old and New on Paul*; Carson, O'Brien, and Seifrid, *Justification and Variegated Nomism.* For a thorough engagement with and refutation of a key "stone" in the NPP edifice, see Hamilton, "N .T. Wright and Saul's Moral Bootstraps," 139–55.

59. Bekken, *The Word Is Near You*, 227.

the Jewish people of God in terms of Christ as the "end"/"goal" of the Law.[60]

In short, Bekken argues that Paul quotes Deuteronomy 30:12–14 in Romans 10 to support the preaching of his gospel not necessarily for the meaning located in the passage itself and in its immediate literary context, but for the chance to engage the contemporary reigning Jewish interpretation of this significant text.

### Similar Interpreters

It is not surprising that Bekken's conclusions are similar to those reached by James Dunn, who argues much the same way in his article, "Righteousness from the Law":

> Paul's interpretation would have all the greater credibility since there was already a widespread recognition that the language of Deut 30:11–14 pointed to something more mysterious, more ultimate. Whereas Lev 18:5 pointed up a narrow and particularist view of the law as Israel's alone, in both Baruch and Philo Deut 30:11–14 was seen as expressing something which everyone of good will was open to and eager for—divine Wisdom, the good. Of course Baruch and Philo both see that more universal ideal to be focused in the law. But by developing such an apologetic line they opened Jewish thought to the recognition that what Deuteronomy spoke of was capable of more universal expression. Whereas Lev 18:5 expressed Israel's claim to a national monopoly of God's righteousness, Deut 30:11–14 could better express the eschatological breadth of God's covenant purpose.[61]

In addition to Bekken and Dunn, several scholars posit an essentially Jewish background for understanding Paul's use of Deuteronomy

---

60. Bekken, *The Word Is Near You*, 227.

61. Dunn, "'Righteousness from the Law' and 'Righteousness from Faith,'" 224.

30:12–14, including M. J. Suggs,[62] D. Georgi,[63] H. Vollmer,[64] J. A. Fitzmyer,[65] and P. J. Achtemeier.[66]

## Evaluation

Absent in Bekken's interpretation of Paul's use of Deuteronomy 30:12–14 in Romans 10:6–8 is a chapter on the original literary context of the quoted text itself—namely an exposition of Deuteronomy 30. Bekken deals with the literary context of Deuteronomy 30 in passing in a section summarizing the current state of research, which amounts to two paragraphs in the entire book. As a result, is Bekken able to evaluate Paul's use of Deuteronomy 30:12–14—not to mention Baruch's and Philo's use—in a substantive way?

## Analogical/Typological Approach: John Calvin

Most common among evangelical interpreters is an analogical or typological approach to understanding Paul's quotation of Deuteronomy 30:12–14 in Romans 10. Among interpreters who take this approach, John Calvin stands tall. Calvin's view of Deuteronomy 30 and Paul's quotation in Romans 10 can be gleaned from three sources: (1) his *Commentaries on the Epistle of Paul the Apostle to the Romans*, written in 1539; (2) his *Sermons on Deuteronomy*, which he delivered between 1555 and 1556 and were first published in English in 1583; and (3) his *Commentaries on the Four Last Books of Moses: Arranged in the Form of a Harmony*, a four-volume harmony of Exodus, Leviticus, Numbers, and Deuteronomy, which Calvin wrote the year before he died in 1563.[67]

---

62. Suggs, "The Word Is Near You" 289–312.

63. Georgi, *The Opponents of Paul in Second Corinthians*, 180.

64. Vollmer, *Die Alttestamentlichen Citate Bei Paulus*, 52.

65. Fitzmyer, "The Use of Explicit Old Testament Quotations in Qumran Literature and in the New Testament," 297–333.

66. Achtemeier, *Romans*, 169.

67. I find it noteworthy that Calvin attempted a harmony of these four books which he believed to be written by the same author, Moses. Calvin no doubt felt the need to defend the validity of such a project when he wrote his introduction: "If I do not at once begin by stating my reasons for the plan I have adopted in the composition of this Work, it will undoubtedly incur the censures of many. Nor will it be attacked only by the malevolent and the envious, (a matter of little consequence,) but some will perhaps

## Summary

Calvin's approach to Deuteronomy 30:11–14 is intriguing. In his *Harmony*, Calvin treats Deuteronomy 30 in two separate sections. He considers the majority of the chapter, Deuteronomy 30:1–10 and 15–20, in Volume III of his *Harmony* under the section title "The Sanction of the Law contained in the Promises and Threats." But Calvin treats 30:11–14 separately in volume I of his *Harmony*, apart from its immediate literary context, under the section title "The Preface to the Law." Because he separates these passages in his *Harmony*, Calvin reflects on them in isolation from one another.

In his interpretation of Deuteronomy 30:11–14, which, again, is in isolation from his interpretation of Deuteronomy 30:1–10 and 15–20, Calvin argues that Moses is speaking of the comprehensible yet humanly unattainable nature of the law. Moses "declares that the Law is not hard to be understood, so as to demand inordinate fatigue in its study; but that God there speaks distinctly and explicitly, and that nothing is required of them but diligent application." But according to Calvin, "the power of performance is a very different thing from understanding."[68] When he goes to explain Deuteronomy 30:12–14 within the larger message of the Pentateuch, Calvin pivots to how Paul employs this passage in Romans. For Calvin, when Paul uses Deuteronomy 30:12–14 in Romans 10,

---

be found, who, with no other cause of disapproval, and without any malignity, will still think that I have inconsiderately, and therefore unnecessarily, altered the order which the Holy Spirit himself has prescribed to us. Now, there cannot be a doubt that what was dictated to Moses was excellent in itself, and perfectly adapted for the instruction of the people; but what he delivered in Four Books, it has been my endeavor so to collect and arrange, that, at first sight, and before a full examination of the subject, it might seem I was trying to improve upon it, which would be an act of audacity akin to sacrilege. I pass by those critics with indifference whose object is to frame causes of detraction out of nothing, and whose greatest pleasure it is to invent occasions of railing; but there will be no difficulty in conciliating those who are only unfavorable through misunderstanding, if they will but listen calmly to the course I have pursued. For I have had no other intention than, by this arrangement, to assist unpracticed readers, so that they might more easily, more commodiously, and more profitably acquaint themselves with the writings of Moses; and whosoever would derive benefit from my labors should understand that I would by no means withdraw him from the study of each separate Book, but simply direct him by this compendium to a definite object; lest he should, as often happens, be led astray through ignorance of any regular plan." Calvin, *Commentaries on the Four Last Books of Moses*, 1:x.

68. Calvin, *Commentaries on the Four Last Books of Moses*, 1:413.

he "accommodates this passage to the Gospel"[69] via the connection of a theological doctrine: man's inability to do the law.

In Calvin's view, which he admits is formed in part by reading Paul's citation of Deuteronomy 30:12–14 in Romans 10, Moses cannot be talking about man's ability to do the law, for "it is clear that men's hearts are strongly and obstinately opposed to the Law; and that in the Law itself is contained only a dead letter."[70] Noteworthy is Calvin's recourse to a systematic explanation rather than an exegetical explanation in his attempt to explain Deuteronomy 30:11–14. Perhaps this is because he interprets it apart from its original context in Deuteronomy 30. Calvin concludes his interpretation of Deuteronomy 30:11–14 saying that if "God, by the Spirit of regeneration, corrects the depravity of the heart and softens its hardness, this is not a property of the Law, but of the Gospel."[71] And this reality, he concedes, is a new covenant reality:

> But this is the peculiar blessing of the new covenant, that the Law is written on men's hearts, and engraven on their inward parts; whilst that severe requirement is relaxed, so that the vices under which believers still labour are no obstacle to their partial and imperfect obedience being pleasant to God."[72]

In a sermon Calvin delivered from the same passage, Deuteronomy 30:11–14, he arrives at a similar conclusion, but this time he appears to stand on surer exegetical ground.[73] Noteworthy again is Calvin's impulse to consider this passage through the lens of and not in isolation from Paul's quotation in Romans 10.

> At the first sight, it would seem that S. Paul took it contrary to the meaning of Moses. And for the proof thereof, does not Moses in this place speak of the Law? He says: *The commandment which I ordain for thee this day.* In saying, *this day,* he speaks of his office. Now his office was to bring the Law and to publish it. It is said in the First of John, that *the Law was given by Moses, but grace and truth were given by Jesus Christ* (John 1:17): It seems not then that this can in any way agree with the Gospel. But if we mark it well; we shall find it good reason, that Saint Paul says, that this point is not verified, until we come through to

---

69. Calvin, *Commentaries on the Four Last Books of Moses,* 1:413.

70. Calvin, *Commentaries on the Four Last Books of Moses,* 1:413.

71. Calvin, *Commentaries on the Four Last Books of Moses,* 1:413.

72. Calvin, *Commentaries on the Four Last Books of Moses,* 1:413.

73. This may be due to his just having preached Deut 30:1–10.

Christ. And why? Let us take Moses to witness without going any further. We have seen here afore, that in forty years' space after the setting forth of the Law, the people had profited nothing in it. The reason thereof is this: *For thy God hath not given thee an understanding heart, even unto this day* (Deut. 29:4). We have the Law beaten into our ears, and yet in the mean while we are still dull-headed, and conceive not the meaning of God's speech. This (as I have said afore) proceeds not of any fault . . . in the Law; but of our own wretched blindness.[74]

In this sermon, Calvin wrestles with the difficulty of Paul's use of Deuteronomy in Romans 10. But he finds Paul's exegetical warrant in the surrounding context of Deuteronomy where Moses laments the state of Israel's heart in Deuteronomy 29:3 (ET 29:4). Calvin's individual application of this passage is striking. He relates this passage to the experience of the unconverted man when confronted with the word of God, not to corporate Israel.

When Calvin arrives at Romans 10:6–8 in his *Romans* commentary, he again wrestles with the seemingly improper application and "different meaning" Paul assigns these words.[75] Nevertheless, Calvin contends that Paul sees in Deuteronomy 30:12–14 not just a reference to the law but also a reference to the "remarkable kindness of God." Moses commends this kindness to the Israelites throughout the book of Deuteronomy, especially in chapters 4 and 30. And God's kindness includes the promise of heart circumcision after the exile in Deuteronomy 30:6, the "main truth" that undergirds Paul's understanding of Deuteronomy 30:11–14.[76]

---

74. Calvin, *Sermons on Deuteronomy*, 1059. Some spelling updated from the Old English.

75. Calvin, *Commentaries on the Epistle of Paul the Apostle to the Romans*, 388.

76. Calvin's nineteenth-century translator disagrees with Calvin's appeal to the context of Deuteronomy in order to explain Paul's use of Deut 30:12–14. "It seems not necessary to have recourse to the distinctions made in the foregoing section. The character of the quotation given is correctly described in the words of Chrysostom, as quoted by Poole, 'Paulus ea transtulit et aptavit ad justitiam fidei—Paul transferred and accommodated these things to the righteousness of faith.' He evidently borrowed the words of Moses, not literally, but substantially, for the purpose of setting forth the truth he was handling. The speaker is not Moses, but 'the righteousness of faith,' represented as a person. Luther, as quoted by Wolfus, says, that 'Paul, under the influence of the Spirit, took from Moses the occasion to form, as it were, a new and a suitable text against the justiciaries.' It appears to be an application, by way of analogy, of the words of Moses to the gospel, and not a confirmatory testimony. Chalmers hesitates on the subject; but Pareus, Wolfus, Turretin, and Doddridge, consider the words as applied by way of accommodation." Calvin, *Romans*, 388.

In sum, Calvin argues that the word of faith that Paul proclaims in Romans 10—a word about the kindness and graciousness of God—was first declared by Moses in Deuteronomy 30, signaling agreement, not disagreement, between Moses' original meaning in Deuteronomy 30:12–14 and Paul's application in Romans 10:6–8. In this way, Calvin finds what we might call an analogy of grace in Paul's appeal to Deuteronomy 30:12–14 in Romans 10:6–8.

### *Similar Interpreters*

Most evangelical interpreters take an analogical or typological approach to Paul's quotation of Deuteronomy 30:12–14 in Romans 10. This includes:

- J. Murray,[77]

- C. Cranfield,[78]

- R. Badenas,[79]

- M. Seifrid,[80]

77. Murray, *The Epistle to the Romans*, 2:52.

78. Cranfield states, "[T]here is real inward justification for what Paul is doing here. It is not arbitrary typology but true interpretation in depth. Between the fact that God's law was addressed directly to the Israelite's heart, requiring faith and obedience, and was not something esoteric to be first discovered by human searching, and the fact that the Son of God has now become incarnate, so that there can be no question of man's needing to bring Him down, there is an intimate connexion; *for behind both the gift of the law and the incarnation of the Son of God is the same divine grace— that grace, the primary and basic initiative of which was God's election of man in Jesus Christ.*" Cranfield, *A Critical and Exegetical Commentary on the Epistle to the Romans*, 2:524–25. Emphasis added.

79. Badenas writes, "[A]lthough Paul may seem to pass beyond the conscious intentions of the OT text, it cannot be said that he gives an entirely new meaning to the OT quotation. In a comprehensive and creative way, he is just developing the theme suggested by the text itself. Since the original passage was already dealing with the accessibility of God's word of grace to his people, it cannot be said that Paul was misapplying a 'law-righteousness' text to a 'faith-righteousness' purpose. He could see his concept of 'righteousness by faith in Christ' with 'the word which is near' (Deut 30:14) because the basic idea underlying both concepts is the same: God bringing life by grace." Badenas, *Christ the End of the Law*, 130.

80. Seifrid explicitly names Paul's approach: "To name this Pauline usage as one of the numerous typological NT uses of the Old does not seem at all out of order." Seifrid, "Paul's Approach to the Old Testament in Romans 10:6–8," 36. He writes elsewhere, "This is precisely the thrust of Deut. 30:11–14: God has conferred the law as

- T. Schreiner,[81]

- D. Moo,[82]

- F. Thielman,[83]

- J. Hamilton,[84]

- A. Das,[85] and

- J. Meyer.[86]

This view is also clear in historic interpretations, such as Chrysostom's.[87] All these interpreters see Paul's citation of Deuteronomy 30:12–14 rooted

---

a *gift* to Israel. The 'commandment' (i.e., the whole of the law) is not beyond Israel's comprehension ('not too difficult, wonderful for you' [*niplē't*]). It is not beyond Israel's reach. They need not seek someone to attempt the impossible ascent into heaven to obtain and learn the law. Nor need they attempt what seemed to them the equally impossible task of crossing the Great Sea in order to obtain the law. Through Moses, the LORD had *given* them the law; it was now in their mouth and heart. Thus they were able to observe 'the commandment'—even if in fact they never would do so." Seifrid, "Romans," 657.

81. While Schreiner directly engages and dismisses the possibility this text is a "future prophecy," he does leave room for contextually rooted "fulfilment," much like the view Thielman takes. Schreiner argues that "Moo is correct that strictly speaking the text is not a future prophecy. Yet its placement in the narrative of Deuteronomy (after the prophecies of chaps. 29–30) and Paul's understanding of salvation history led him to see it as fulfilled in his day." Schreiner, *Romans*, 558n17.

82. Moo considers the possibility that Deut 30:11–14 is future-oriented, but he ends up dismissing it based on, surprisingly, S. R. Driver's text-critical divisions of the book of Deuteronomy, which I engage below. Moo, *The Epistle to the Romans*, 652–53.

83. Thielman, *Paul & the Law: A Contextual Approach*, 209–10.

84. Hamilton, *God's Glory in Salvation through Judgment*, 112–13.

85. Although he sticks to an analogical approach ultimately, Das has a noteworthy footnote where he states that Paul "must see in Deut 30:12–14 a promise of the new age of Christ." Das, *Paul, the Law, and the Covenant*, 261n117.

86. Meyer, *The End of the Law*, 227.

87. Chrysostom writes on Rom 10:6–8, "For this, which he here says of faith, Moses says to them of the commandment, so showing that they had enjoyed at God's hand a great benefit." Notably, Chrysostom's interpretation of Paul's dual citation from Leviticus and Deuteronomy in Rom 10:5–8 serves as a sound rebuttal of those who charge the Reformers, particularly Luther, of innovating in their understanding of Paul's teaching on the law and the gospel. Listen to how Chrysostom frames Paul's citation of Lev 18:5 and Deut 30:12–14: "What he means is this. Moses showeth us the righteousness ensuing from the Law, what sort it is of, and whence. What sort is it then of, and what does it consist in? In fulfilling the commandments. 'He that doeth these things,' He says, 'shall live by (or in), them.' (Lev. xviii. 5.) *And there is no other way of becoming righteous in the Law save by fulfilling the whole of it.* But this has not been possible for any one, and therefore this righteousness has failed them. (διαπέπτωκεν).

in the narrative context of Deuteronomy 29–30 by an analogical or typological connection, which points to a coming age of fulfillment. But they stop short of calling it prophetic or promissory.

## Evaluation

The analogical/typological approach to Paul's quotation of Deuteronomy 30:12–14 in Romans 10 is appealing, as there are many examples of NT authors using the OT in just this way.[88] While not all of the interpreters above would label their approach to this quotation as analogical or typological, the fact is that the hermeneutical warrant they identify Paul to be using is an appeal that falls short of promise/fulfillment or prophecy. Instead, they argue that Paul finds the message of the righteousness of faith in a common theological concept such as God's kindness or grace, or a divine gift or initiative in Deuteronomy 30:12–14, which can be gleaned from the broader context of Deuteronomy 30 and/or the salvation-historical development across the testaments.[89]

My critique of this approach has less to do with what it asserts and more to do with what it does not. I am in whole-hearted agreement that what Paul finds in Deuteronomy 30 is a picture of God's grace, kindness,

---

But tell us, Paul, of the other righteousness also, that which is of grace. What is that then, and of what does it consist? . . . To prevent the Jews then from saying, How came they who had not found the lesser righteousness to find the greater? he gives a reason there was no answering, that this way was easier than that. For that requires the fulfillment of all things (for when thou doest all, then thou shalt live); but the righteousness which is of faith doth not say this, but what? 'If thou confess with thy mouth the Lᴏʀᴅ Jesus, and believe in thy heart that God hath raised Him from the dead, thou shalt be saved.'" Chrysostom, *Hom. Rom.*, 1/11:473. Emphasis added.

88. Caution must be used with the analogical approach, as it is further away from the "fallibilism" test that Kevin Vanhoozer champions, which incorporates questions such as the following: Does the NT interpretation of the OT make sense? Does it make better sense than the interpretation of the OT found in Jewish literature? Vanhoozer, "Christ and Concept," 99–145. I return again to Moo and Naselli's summary of the NT use of the OT, "The NT writers do not casually appeal to the OT or argue merely by analogy. They repeatedly assert that we must believe and do certain things *because* of what is said in specific OT texts. The NT authors suggest that their teachings are grounded in the OT." Moo and Naselli, "The Problem of the New Testament's Use of the Old Testament," 704.

89. This view can sound as if Paul misunderstood the verses of Deut 30:12–14 while understanding the overall context of Deuteronomy correctly, e.g., Via, who argues, "Paul misinterpreted Deut. 30:11–14, but his global understanding of Deuteronomy is correct." Via, *Kerygma and Comedy in the New Testament*, 62.

and divine initiative. But I also think that Paul finds so much more in Deuteronomy 30, namely the promise of the eschatological *torah* that accompanies a circumcised heart, which Paul understands is the message of the righteousness that comes by faith. This view is similar to the fourth and final approach below.

## Contextual-Canonical Approach: Steven Coxhead

Steven Coxhead has recently challenged the notion that Deuteronomy 30:11–14 demands interpreters read it as a return to a present timeframe on the plains of Moab in isolation from Moses' future-oriented promise in 30:1–10. Coxhead's exegesis offers a promising way forward to understanding Paul's quotation of Deuteronomy 30:12–14 in Romans 10 as exegetically rooted not only in the surrounding text of Deuteronomy 30, but in the actual text of 30:11–14.

### *Summary*

In an article that appeared in the *Westminster Theological Journal*, Coxhead argues that Deuteronomy 30:11–14 is best understood as a continuation of 30:1–10 as part of "the grand restoration prophecy" found in those verses. This interpretive option is a possibility because of the timeless nature of the verbless clauses in Deuteronomy 30:11–14.[90] Coxhead offers three exegetical grounds for this interpretation: (1) the כי in verses 11 and 14 should be understood as causally parallel with the three other instances of כי in verses 9–10; (2) the symbolism of the idea of God's word in the mouth and in the heart is everywhere associated with knowledge of God's law (cf. Exod 13:9; Deut 6:6–7; Josh 1:8; Ps 119:43; Mal 2:6–7) and obedience to that law (Ps 40:8; Mt 15:18–19); and (3) the apparent contrast between the *torah* mentioned in Deuteronomy 30:11–14 and the *torah* received by Moses at Sinai.[91] Thus, Deuteronomy 30:11–14 does not speak to the people's ability to "do" the law *now*, in their current state lacking the "heart" to obey (cf. Deut 29:3 [ET 29:4]), but instead speaks of the enabled obedience of a circumcised heart, which experiences the law internally, not merely externally.

---

90. Wolde, "The Verbless Clause and Its Textual Function," 333.
91. Coxhead, "Deuteronomy 30:11–14," 305–11.

According to Coxhead, this is what Paul finds in Deuteronomy 30 as coterminous with the message of the righteousness of faith: an announcement of the "eschatological torah." This eschatological *torah* is "the form that God's law would take in the new covenant age, . . . the torah that would be written by the Spirit of God on the hearts of eschatological Israel (Jer 31:31–34; Ezek 36:26–27), which is also the *torah* that the nations would come to Zion to learn and keep (Isa 2:1–4)."[92] In this sense, Paul declares a promise or prophecy fulfilled in his quotation of Deuteronomy 30:12–14 in Romans 10, not merely an analogical or typological relationship between the new covenant Christ and the old covenant law.

### Similar Interpreters

Though he holds the minority position, Coxhead is not alone in his interpretation of Paul's quotation of Deuteronomy 30:12–14 in Romans 10:6–8. Similar interpreters include:

- N. T. Wright,[93]

- J. Sailhamer,[94]

92. Coxhead, "Deuteronomy 30:11–14," 316n33.

93. Wright could be placed in the Jewish Exegetical category, but at the end of the day his interpretation lands him in this one. Wright sees the Second Temple literature, particularly 4QMMT, Baruch 3, Pseudo Philo 19, *Testament of Moses*, 4 Ezra, as proof that Deut 30, including 30:11–14, was being read eschatologically as pointing forward to a post-exilic covenant renewal. Paul concurs by interacting with this text at exactly this point, but he does so emphasizing that it is Jesus Christ who brings about the eschatological renewal. "Paul's exegesis of Deuteronomy 30 thus explains what he means by the Messiah's being the goal of Torah: this covenant renewal, this promised life for those who discover that the word is not far off, but very near to them, this status of being God's people, evidenced by faith in God's Messiah—this is what Torah envisaged all along, but in and of itself could not perform. . . . I suggest that Paul intends his fresh reading of Deut 30:11–14 to say: 'the covenant has been renewed, following the devastation of exile, through the Messiah's coming from God and his resurrection from the dead. This has meant that God has brought his "word" near to you, placing it on your lips as you confess Jesus as LORD, writing it on your heart as you believed that he was raised from the dead.'" Wright, "The Letter to the Romans," 663–64.

94. Sailhamer writes, "In explaining the nature of the new covenant which he envisions in these chapters, Moses compares it to the covenant at Sinai (Dt 30:11–14). In the covenant given at Sinai, the Law was written on tablets of stone which Moses had to go up the mountain to receive and then take back to proclaim to the people, . . . in the new covenant the Law would not be given again on tablets of stone but written on circumcised hearts (as in Eze 36:26)." Sailhamer, *The Pentateuch as Narrative*, 473.

- P. Gentry,[95]
- J. Meade,[96]
- K. Wells,[97]
- Paul Barker,[98] and
- W. Strickland.[99]

G. Braulik summarizes this position effectively in an essay on Deuteronomy:

> Israel, whose heart was circumcised by YHWH (cf. Rom 2:28–29), is able to follow the deuteronomic social order, not only because the change of heart brought about by YHWH disposes Israel to act in this way, but also because, according to verses 30:11–14, the law is "very near to you, upon your lips and in your heart, so that you can keep it" (verse 14). Here the deuteronomic Torah, according to the explicit witness of Rom 10:6–10, which rightly quotes this passage, expresses "the righteousness that comes by faith" (Rom 10:6). The truly internalized deuteronomic law is "a word of faith" (Rom 10:8), that is, "gospel" (Rom 10:16).[100]

95. Gentry argues, "According to Deuteronomy 30:1–10, Israel will obtain a circumcised heart at a future time, and that is why 30:11–14 refers to the future and not to the present. Paul in his exposition in Romans was right." Gentry, "The Relationship of Deuteronomy to the Covenant at Sinai," 52.

96. Meade states, "In Deuteronomy, the connection between internal transformation and obedience to the Torah is not made explicit in 30:6. However, if 30:11–14 continues the thought in 1–10 as a subordinate clause explaining the future implications of the circumcised heart, then 30:11–14 clarifies that the internal transformation of heart circumcision leads to keeping the Torah commanded by Moses in Moab." Meade, "Circumcision of the Heart in Leviticus and Deuteronomy," 78.

97. Wells contends, "[T]he section could easily bear the translation: 'this commandment *will not be* too difficult for you, . . . it *will be* on your mouth.' Verses 11–14, then, would encourage the present generation concerning the things YHWH's future saving action will accomplish. While this reading may seem strained, what is important is that it is possible." Wells, *Grace and Agency in Paul and Second Temple Judaism*, 38.

98. Barker, *The Triumph of Grace in Deuteronomy*, 198.

99. Strickland, "The Inauguration of the Law of Christ with the Gospel of Christ," 250–52.

100. Braulik, *The Theology of Deuteronomy*, 164.

*Evaluation*

In my view, the interpretation followed by Coxhead, Sailhamer, Gentry, and others offers the best way forward to understanding Paul's use of Deuteronomy 30:12–14 in Romans 10. However, there are a few loose ends, as it were, that need to be tied up in order for this interpretation to become fully convincing. One challenge to this interpretation is the exact referent of "this command" מצוה (sg.) in 30:11. Relatedly, the referent of the "word" דבר in 30:14 and its relationship to the command in 30:11 are unclear, which Paul applies to the message of the gospel in Romans 10. Another challenge, which interpreters must wrestle with in every approach to this text, is Paul's interspersed commentary throughout the quotation related to the descent and ascent of Christ. Even in a future-oriented reading of Deuteronomy 30:12–14, Paul's application of this passage to Christ must be accounted for. These, along with an exploration of possible canonical developments in the Prophets and Writings, are in need of thorough examination if this reading is to be convincing.

## Methodology

As one engaged in the discipline of biblical theology, I am seeking to "understand and embrace the interpretative perspective of the biblical authors."[101] This involves an irreducibly historical dimension.[102] In order to understand and embrace the perspective of the biblical authors, I will attempt to understand Moses in Deuteronomy on his own terms, which involves literary analysis of the book of Deuteronomy as a whole. With this in place, I will turn to the rest of the Old Testament in order to see how later biblical authors, who had textual access to the Pentateuch and, specifically, Deuteronomy 30:11–14, may have understood and developed the meaning of this text. Finally, I will turn to Paul's quotation of Deuteronomy 30:11–14 in Romans 10, where its fullest meaning is culminated in the proclamation of Christ, the τέλος of the law (Rom 10:4), and its significance in the biblical canon.[103]

---

101. Hamilton, *With the Clouds of Heaven*, 21.

102. Vos distinguished biblical and systematic theology in terms of organizing principles: biblical theology is organized historically, and systematic theology, logically. Vos, *Biblical Theology*, 16.

103. This project could be described as an evangelical appropriation of Brevard Childs's canonical approach to biblical theology, which would necessarily be based on

The methodology outlined above is self-consciously dependent on that proposed and modeled by Greg Beale, who defines biblical-theological interpretation as an attempt "to interpret texts in light of their broader literary context, their broader redemptive-historical epoch of which they are a part, and to interpret earlier texts from earlier epochs, attempting to explain them in the light of progressive revelation to which earlier scriptural authors would not have had access."[104]

By examining not only the flower (Rom 10:5–8) but also the stem (e.g., Pss 37; 40; 119; Isa 51; Jer 31) and the root (Deut 30:1–14), I hope to provide a full botanical diagram of the beautiful, divinely authored truth on display in these texts: the righteousness of faith that includes a torah-infused, Spirit-filled, circumcised heart in all those united to Christ by faith.

---

the foundation of the doctrines of inspiration and inerrancy. Childs, *Biblical Theology*. For a defense of the evangelical perspective on Scripture, see Hamilton, "Still *Sola Scriptura*: An Evangelical Perspective on Scripture," 215–40.

104. Beale, *The Erosion of Inerrancy in Evangelicalism*, 104n41.

---
2
---

# Deuteronomy 30:11–14 in Its
# Immediate Literary Context

THE CENTRAL QUESTION IN view in this chapter is whether or not the experience described in Deuteronomy 30:11–14—"the word" (דבר) "in your mouth and in your heart"—points to a non-contingent, present reality[1] when Moses addressed the Israelites on the plains of Moab, or to a reality contingent on divine intervention and related to the promise of return from exile and heart circumcision in Deuteronomy 30:1–10.[2]

---

1. Craigie is representative of this view: "The emphasis returns once again to the present, the renewal ceremony being enacted on the plains of Moab." Craigie, *The Book of Deuteronomy*, 364. Nelson concurs: "Moses abruptly stops portraying the future and returns to the present 'Moab moment.'" Nelson, *Deuteronomy*, 349.

2. As noted above, a future-oriented interpretation of Deut 30:11–14 as tied to the prophetic promises of 30:1–10 has been hinted at by many interpreters in the history of interpretation of this passage. For example, Martin Luther interprets this passage as speaking of the effect of the gospel in the heart of the believer, after which God's "commandment will become neither difficult nor too distant." Luther, *Lectures on Deuteronomy*, 278. Only recently, however, have a handful of interpreters made exegetical arguments toward this interpretation, such as Sailhamer, *The Meaning of the Pentateuch*; Barker, *The Triumph of Grace in Deuteronomy*; Wells, *Grace and Agency in Paul and Second Temple Judaism*; Coxhead, "Deuteronomy 30:11–14 as a Prophecy of the New Covenant in Christ"; Starling, *Hermeneutics as Apprenticeship*, 44–45; Gentry, "The Relationship of Deuteronomy to the Covenant at Sinai"; Meade, "Circumcision of the Heart in Leviticus and Deuteronomy."

How one answers this question significantly affects not only the interpretation of this passage in Deuteronomy but also the larger message of Deuteronomy, as well as the interpretation of the Mosaic covenant and new covenant.

This chapter will examine Deuteronomy 30:11–14 in its immediate literary context, the book of Deuteronomy. Before exegeting this text in depth, attention will first be paid to the literary structure of Deuteronomy in order to delimit the bounds of the section that contains Deuteronomy 30:11–14. Focusing in on this section, the overarching narrative of Deuteronomy will be established as well as themes pertinent to the passage in view. With this preliminary work complete, a detailed exegesis of Deuteronomy 30:11–14 will commence. Ultimately, I will make the case that Deuteronomy 30:11–14 is best understood as a continuation of the future-oriented prophecy of 30:1–10, which outlines an eschatological hope for Israel after exile that is centered on the promise of divine intervention in the heart in the context of a new covenant.

## The Structure of Deuteronomy

The structure of a book shapes how it is read. Reading a book according to an imposed structure often results in readings not rooted in the text, while reading a book according to its inherent structure guides the reader into an understanding that grows from the text. Such reading means paying attention to the conjunctives, disjunctives, parallelisms, and other literary features of a text.

Many structures have been proposed for the book of Deuteronomy. For heuristic purposes, I have organized these structures into three categories, though these categories are not mutually exclusive: Redaction-critical, ANE treaty form, and literary structures of Deuteronomy.

### Redaction-Critical Structures

Redaction-critical structures of Deuteronomy are based on the JEDP documentary hypothesis advanced by Julius Wellhausen and are aimed at discerning the textual layers that are believed to have been diachronically developed into the book we now know as Deuteronomy. These proposals attempt to understand the structure of Deuteronomy in light of its historical reconstruction. S. R. Driver provides a structure in his Deuteronomy commentary that is representative of this school, assigning individual passages, verses, and even sometimes verse fragments to three origins: JE (Yahwist-Elohist), D and D² (two iterations of Deuteronomists), and P (Priestly).

| JE | D | D² | P |
|---|---|---|---|
| | 1:1–2 | | |
| | | | 1:3 |
| | 1:4—3:18 | | |
| | | 3:14–17 | |
| | 3:18—4:28 | | |
| | | 4:29–31 | |
| | 4:32–40 | | |
| | | 4:41–49 | |
| | 5:1—26:19 | | |
| | | 27:1–4 | |
| 27:5–7a | | | |
| | | 27:7b–8 | |
| | 27:9–10 | | |
| | | 27:11–26 | |
| | 28; 29:1–8 | | |
| | | 29:9—30:1–10 | |
| | 30:11—31:18 | | |
| 31:14–15 | | | |
| | | 31:16–22 | |
| 31:23 | | | |
| | 31:24–27 | | |

| JE | D | $D^2$ | P |
|---|---|---|---|
|  |  | 31:28–44 |  |
|  | 32:45–47 |  |  |
| 33:1—34:5a |  |  | 34:1a |
|  |  |  | 34:5b–9 |
| 34:10 |  |  |  |
|  |  | 34:11–12 |  |

**Table 1. S. R. Driver's diachronic structure of Deuteronomy**

Noteworthy in Driver's structure for the purpose of this book is his insistence on driving a source-critical wedge between Deuteronomy 30:1–10 and 30:11–14, texts that he argues originate from two different authors writing from two different perspectives at two different times. He drives a similar source-critical wedge between a related passage in 4:29–31 and 4:32–40 for the same reason.[3]

## ANE Treaty Form Structures

Interpreters who posit ancient Near Eastern (ANE) treaty form structures to the book of Deuteronomy argue that the book reflects suzerain-vassal treaties in the ANE, most commonly those of the Hittites. These ANE treaty-form structures seek to understand Deuteronomy in light of contemporary ANE historical documents, specifically covenant or treaty documents. G. E. Mendenhall's work, "Covenant Forms in Israelite Tradition," broke ground for a cottage industry on ANE suzerain-vassal

---

3. Driver writes, "4:29–31 and 30:1–10 are the only two passages of Dt. in which the ultimate repentance and restoration of Israel *after* its apostasy and exile are contemplated. They are assigned here—not without hesitation—to D2, not on account of the incompatibility of such a prospect with the general point of view of Dt.,—for the author writes not merely as a legislator, but also as a prophet, announcing like other prophets Jehovah's counsels for His people's welfare; and the promise of ultimate restoration would not neutralize the motive to obedience which the prospect of such a disaster as antecedent exile would bring with it,—but on account of their imperfect connexion with the context." Driver, *A Critical and Exegetical Commentary on Deuteronomy*, lxxvi.

treaty studies that still has great influence on interpreters today.[4] ANE treaty-form structures can be approached both diachronically and synchronically, that is, either from the foundation that Deuteronomy is a literary collection of sources written by multiple people at various times (diachronic), or from the foundation that Deuteronomy was written by one individual at or around the same time (synchronic).

| | |
|---|---|
| 1. Preamble | 1:1–5 |
| 2. Historical Prologue | 1:6—4:44 |
| 3. Stipulations | |
| a. General | 4:45—11:32 |
| b. Specific | 12:1—26:19 |
| 4. Document Clause | 17:1–10 |
| 5. Appeal to Witness | 27:11–26 |
| 6. Blessings and Curses | 28:1–69 (ET 29:1) |
| 7. Solemn Oath Ceremony | 29:1 (ET 29:2)–30:20 |

**Table 2. Deuteronomy as ANE treaty formula**

Steven Guest suggests a structure of Deuteronomy based on ANE suzerain-vassal treaties that approaches the text synchronically, which is reproduced in table 2 above.[5]

---

4. Mendenhall, "Covenant Forms in Israelite Tradition," 50–76.

5. Guest, "Deuteronomy 26:16–19 as the Central Focus of the Covenantal Framework of Deuteronomy," 55. Guest does not include Deut 31–34 because he says, "it is generally agreed that the addresses of Moses are limited to the text of Deuteronomy 1:6–3:20." He goes on to write in a footnote that "[t]his decision does not imply a denial that Moses spoke after 30:20, but rather it is an acknowledgement of the definite change in style from hortatory address in 1:6—3:20 to a more narrative based report of speech." Guest, 51, 51n85. Gentry proposes a very similar structure in Gentry and Wellum, *Kingdom through Covenant*, 358.

## Literary Structures

Though not mutually exclusive to the other structure categories, interpreters who favor literary structures in Deuteronomy seek to understand the book's architecture in light of the its final form. With the rise of discourse and literary analysis came a more concerted attention to the final form of the text.[6] This attention has led many interpreters to notice the unique literary markers of Deuteronomy that divide the book into several sections. Rejecting the inevitable subjectivism of the diachronic, redaction-critical approach represented by interpreters like Georg Fohrer,[7] Brevard Childs opts for a more objectively-grounded literary approach:

> [I]t seems to me very doubtful that one can distinguish the different levels of development as sharply as Fohrer suggests. The strikingly different theories of other scholars regarding the original stages of material which Fohrer rejects in his treatment only emphasize the subjectivity of his proposal.[8]

In his dissertation on the literary structure of Deuteronomy using discourse analysis, Neal Huddleston has convincingly argued that Deuteronomy is subdivided into three major sections by a common grammatical construction.[9] Each major section of Deuteronomy (Deut 1:1—4:44; 4:45—28:68 [ET 29:1]; 28:69 [ET 29:1]–34:12) begins with the plural demonstrative אלה that heads a nominal clause[10] followed by the relative particle אשר heading a clause with a speaking subject—Moses in the first two discourses and Yahweh in the third—and a ב preposition heading a clause that situates the discourse in a geographical location. This common construction is followed by a sentence that introduces a direct quote from the mouth of Moses. Interestingly, each section introduction also mentions the defeat of the regional kings Sihon and Og (1:4;

---

6. See, for example, Longacre, *The Grammar of Discourse.*

7. Fohrer, *Das Alte Testament*, 177ff.

8. Childs, *Introduction to the Old Testament as Scripture*, 212. Evangelical interpreters can follow Childs in his rejection of the subjectivity of the diachronic approach for a literary approach with better theological warrant: the divine inspiration of Scripture and the Mosaic authorship of the Pentateuch, which necessitate a synchronic, literary organization to Deuteronomy.

9. Huddleston, "Deuteronomy as Mischgattung," 149.

10. Huddleston refers to these as "Deictic Nominal" clauses in "Deuteronomy as Mischgattung," 149.

4:46–47; and 29:6 [ET 29:7]). Table 3 illustrates this macro structure of Deuteronomy.[11]

| Introduction of Direct Speech | ב *Locative Clause* | *Object Clause* | *Relative Clause* | אלה *Nominal Clause* | *Section* |
|---|---|---|---|---|---|
| הואיל משה באר את־התורה הזאת לאמר | בעבר הַיַרדן | אל־כל־ישראל | אשר דבר משה | אלה הדברים | 1:1ff |
| ויקרא משה אל־כל־ישראל ויאמר אלהם | בעבר הירדן | אל־בני ישראל | אשר דבר משה | אלה והחקים והמשפטים | 4:45ff |
| ויקרא משה אל־כל־ישראל ויאמר אלהם | בארץ מואב | את־משה את־בני ישראל | אשר־צוה יהוה | אלה דברי הברית | 28:69ff (29:1) |

**Table 3. Structural introductory formulae in Deuteronomy**

## Proposing a New Parallel Literary Structure

Taking up Huddleston's structural formulae that form these three larger sections—what some recognize as three distinct discourses—I suggest the following structure in table 4 that highlights the parallelism between Deuteronomy 1:1—4:4 and 28:69 (ET 29:1)—30:20.

| | | Literary Section 1: Deut 1:1 (אלה הדברים) —4:44 |
|---|---|---|
| | 1:1—3:29 | a. Covenant remembrance: Yahweh's faithfulness and Israel's unfaithfulness |
| A | 4:1–28 | b. Covenant warning: unfaithfulness results in exile |
| | 4:29–31 | c. Covenant hope: heart change in exile results in covenant reconciliation |
| | 4:32–44 | d. Covenant exhortation: keep the commandments |

11. Table 3 is adapted from Huddleston, 149.

**34**     In Your Mouth and In Your Heart

| | | |
|---|---|---|
| | Literary Section 2: Deut 4:45 (אלה והחקים והמשפטים) —28:28 | |
| B | 4:45—26:19 | Covenant stipulations: Obedience to the Ten Words (4:45—11:32) and Application of the Ten Words (12:1—26:19) |
| | 27:1–26 | Covenant curses: unfaithfulness results in curses |
| | 28:1–14 | Covenant blessings: faithfulness results in blessings |
| | 28:15–68 | Covenant warning: unfaithfulness results in destruction and exile |
| | Literary Section 3: Deut 28:69 (ET 29:1, אלה דברי הברית) —30:20 | |
| A' | 28:69(29:1)– 29:8(9) | a'. Covenant remembrance: Yahweh's faithfulness and Israel's unfaithfulness |
| | 29:9(10)– 28(29) | b'. Covenant warning: unfaithfulness results in exile |
| | 30:1–14 | c'. Covenant hope: heart change in exile results in covenant reconciliation |
| | 30:15—30:20 | d'. Covenant exhortation: keep the commandments |
| | Literary Section 4: Deut 31:1—34:12 | |
| C | 31:1–15 | Transfer of leadership from Moses to Joshua |
| | 31:16–23 | Yahweh's prophetic pronouncement: Israel's unfaithfulness today and tomorrow |
| | 31:24–30 | Moses' prophetic pronouncement: Israel's unfaithfulness today and tomorrow |
| | 32:1–47 | Song of Moses: (a") Covenant remembrance: Yahweh's faithfulness and Israel's unfaithfulness (32:1–14); (b") Covenant warning: unfaithfulness results in destruction and exile (32:15–43); (c[d"]) Covenant exhortation: keep the commandments (32:44–47) |
| | 33:1–29 | Mosaic blessing |
| | 34:1–12 | Historical epilogue |

**Table 4. Proposed parallel literary structure of Deuteronomy**

The advantage of the structure proposed in table 4 is that it pays close attention to the literary markers in the text, which result in a parallelism between Deuteronomy 1:1—4:44 and 28:69 (ET 29:1)—30:2. This parallelism is similar to that noted by Duane Christensen in his chiastic structure of Deuteronomy.[12] In these two sections, the following thematic parallels occur: (a, a') covenant remembrance which outlines Yahweh's faithfulness and Israel's unfaithfulness to the covenant (Deut 1:1—3:29; 28:69 [ET 29:1]—29:8 [ET 29:9]); (b, b') covenant warning that connects disobedient idolatry directly with exile from the land (4:1–28; 29:9 [ET 29:10)–28 [ET 29:29]); (c, c') covenant hope that promises reconciliation with Yahweh on the basis of heart change (4:29–31; 30:1–14); and (d, d') covenant exhortation to keep the commandments (4:32–44; 30:15–20). The section (B) between these two parallel sections (A, A') contains the covenant stipulations (4:45—26:19), blessings and curses (27:1—28:14), and then a covenant warning that does not result in covenant hope (28:15–68)—a reality shared with the Song of Moses (32:15–43).

## Deuteronomy 29 and the Coming Exile

The macro structure of Deuteronomy proposed by Huddleston and the one outlined above suggest that 28:69 (ET 29:1)—which contains the Deuteronomic introduction formula אלה דברי הברית—stands as the superscript of a new section, not a subscript of the previous section.[13] Thus Deuteronomy 30:11–14 belongs in a larger section that begins in 28:69 (ET 29:1) and runs through 30:20.

Most critical scholars argue against the unity of chapters 29 and 30. Various evidence is cited in support of this conclusion, including the supposed divergence of perspectives on Israel's ability to keep the law in

---

12. Duane Christensen proposes a more formally chiastic structure with similar parallelism in Christensen, *Deuteronomy 1:1—21:9*, lviii.
    A. The Outer Frame: A Look Backward (Deut 1–3)
      B. The Inner Frame: The Great Preoration (Deut 4–11)
        C. The Central Core: Covenant Stipulations (Deut 12–26)
      B'. The Inner Frame: The Covenant Ceremony (Deut 27–30)
    A'. The Outer Frame: A Look Forward (Deut 31–34)

13. For a detailed defense of Deut 28:69 (ET 29:1) as superscript, see Lohfink, "Dtn 28,69—Überschrift Oder Kolophon?," 40–52. So also Rofé, "It is my opinion that the text of 'The Covenant in the Land of Moab' begins in Deut 28:69 with the inscription 'These are the Words of the Covenant which the LORD commanded Moses to make with them at Horeb' and the conclusion is to be found in Deut 30:20." Rofé, "The Covenant in the Land of Moab," 269. Contra Lundbom et al., who argue 28:69 (ET 29:1) is a subscription to the previous section, in Lundbom, *Deuteronomy*, 798. Lenchak thinks 28:69 (ET 29:1) has a dual function as both a subscription and superscription. Lenchak, *Choose Life!*, 172–73.

30:1–10 from the rest of the section[14] and an uncommon vocabulary between 29 and 30 with a plural address in 29 and a singular address in 30, which, it is argued, better matches the singular address at the end of chapter 28.[15] But Barker has it right: "All these approaches are in large part attempts to resolve the tension between the pessimism of chapter 29 and the optimism of chapter 30."[16] Against the supposed disjunction that has been suggested by various diachronic approaches to this text, this passage can be shown to cohere as one discourse both rhetorically and theologically.[17]

## The Covenant at Moab: Sinaitic or New?

In Deuteronomy 28:69 (ET 29:1) through to 30:20, Moses facilitates the cutting of a covenant at Moab with the new wilderness generation. While the covenant stipulations are nearly identical to the covenant cut at Horeb, Moses' pessimistic expectations for this covenant after shepherding Israel through the wilderness for forty years—expectations shared by Yahweh—seem to overshadow this covenant ceremony. Moses expresses a pessimism not about the righteousness of the law, but about the righteousness of the people. He has come face-to-face with the inadequacy of the hearts of the people of Israel, and he understands that heart change is required for a lasting covenant.

14. Driver argues that "30:11–20 has the genuine Deuteronomic ring; but 30:1–10 (the passage which speaks of Israel's penitence after apostasy) connects so imperfectly with 30:11ff., that no doubt it is either (if written by D) misplaced, or is to be attributed to a different hand. . . . The paragraph [containing 30:11–20] is loosely connected with v. 1–10. V. 11–14 ('For' . . . ) clearly states the reason for a *present* duty; in view of the contents of the four verses, it is exceedingly unnatural to suppose that they explain why Israel should find it easy to return to Jehovah in the future contingency contemplated in v. 10. It is next to impossible, therefore, that v. 11–20 can have been originally the sequel of v. 1–10." Driver, *A Critical and Exegetical Commentary on Deuteronomy*, lxxv, 331.

15. For example, Rofé writes, "But what about the relation of [Deut 30:1–10] to its context? Here we have a problem. indeed, Deut 29:27 speaks about uprooting and dispersion and Deut 30:1–10—about gathering and return, but the diction of this passage clearly demonstrates that it is not a following to Deuteronomy 29, but to Deuteronomy 28." Rofé, "The Covenant in the Land of Moab," 271. Cf. Nicholson, *Deuteronomy and Tradition*, 35.

16. Barker, *The Triumph of Grace in Deuteronomy*, 109.

17. For an argument on the unity of Deut 28:69—30:20 via rhetorical analysis, see Lenchak, *Choose Life!*

As with the other two discourses in Deuteronomy 1:1—4:44 and 4:45—28:68, Deuteronomy 28:69ff (ET 29:1ff) is set in the land of Moab where Israel is poised opposite the land of Canaan, on the other side of the Jordan, waiting to enter the land. As such, this verse introduces the content that follows in chapters 29–30 as "the words of the covenant which the LORD commanded Moses to cut with the sons of Israel in the land of Moab, besides (מלבד) the covenant which he cut with them at Horeb."[18]

As Peter Gentry points out, מלבד is crucial to understanding this covenant ceremony and, I would add, to understanding the book of Deuteronomy as a whole.[19] Is this covenant—a covenant which is clearly to be distinguished in some way from the Sinai covenant—merely an addition to the Sinai covenant? Or, as Gentry suggests, is it a sort of addendum or codicil that acts as a covenant supplement? Or more radically, is the Moab covenant to be understood as an altogether different covenant which points toward a new covenant?[20] Sailhamer argues the for this last option:

> It is not entirely correct to speak of a "renewal" of the covenant in this introductory verse. It states quite clearly that the covenant which Moses now speaks of is "in addition to the covenant he had made with them at Horeb [Sinai]." With these words, Moses deliberately sets up a contrast between the covenant at Sinai and the covenant he envisions for Israel in the future.[21]

After a close examination of the text below, I will suggest another possibility that combines these positions: The centrality of the love command in the *Shema* of Deuteronomy 6:4–5 and the certainty of man's

18. My translation. All translations are from the English Standard Version unless otherwise noted. As Gentry writes, "Deuteronomy 29–30 indicates that in the book of Deuteronomy, Moses is adding something in continuity with the Covenant at Sinai. Moses is making a covenant to keep the Covenant at Sinai. This is why only the expression *kārat běrît*, 'to cut a covenant,' is the only one appropriate for this situation. And this time the covenant is made not only with the Israel present but with all future generations of Israel so that the children cannot argue that covenant at Sinai was with their parents, and not with them. Deuteronomy is best seen as a renewal and expansion of the Sinai Covenant." Gentry, "The Relationship of Deuteronomy to the Covenant at Sinai," 55.

19. Gentry and Wellum, *Kingdom through Covenant*, 378. According to J. G. Millar, "The revelation at Moab is presented not as *replacing* Horeb in the life of Israel, but as *augmenting and upgrading* it for the new conditions of life in the land of Canaan." Millar, Now Choose Life, 92.

20. Gentry and Wellum, *Kingdom through Covenant*, 378.

21. Sailhamer, *The Pentateuch as Narrative*, 471.

inability to uphold the covenant stipulations, which are summed up in
the command to love God from a whole heart, are additional elements
of the covenant at Moab not found explicitly in the covenant at Horeb.
These new elements do indeed point forward to the necessity of a future,
divine intervention and the cutting of a new covenant, but they function
within the covenantal structures of the covenant cut at Horeb.[22]

## The Dilemma in Deuteronomy 29:3

Summoning Israel before him, Moses begins the covenant ceremony in
Deuteronomy 29:1–2 (ET 29:2–3) by recounting the signs and wonders
of the deliverance from Egypt and subsequent provision that Yahweh has
worked on their behalf, before their eyes, which their eyes saw (cf. Deut
4:34; 7:19). But in the face of this remembrance of Yahweh's faithfulness
to Israel, and in spite of the acknowledgement that Israel has seen the
great salvation of Yahweh, Moses passes quickly to why Israel still finds
themselves on the plains of Moab and will enter the land under the certainty of failure (cf. 31:16–29): "But Yahweh has not given you a heart to
understand or eyes to see or ears to hear to this day" (ולא־נתן יהוה לכם לב
לדעת ועינים לראות ואזנים לשמע עד היום הזה, 29:3 [ET 29:4]).[23] "To this day,"
which means up to and including "this day," Yahweh has not supplied
Israel with the missing component—a heart to know and respond rightly
to Yahweh and his self-revelation—that will make covenanting with him
sustainable. Moses has already explained in Deuteronomy 8:2 that the
forty years of wilderness wandering and Yahweh's miraculous provisions
were for the purpose of (למען) humbling Israel to test them to know what
was in their hearts (ענתך לנסתך לדעת את־אשר בלבבך). And what the wilderness wandering revealed was Israel's lack of heart to respond to divine
revelation.

Jeffrey Tigay disputes the translation of עד היום as "to this day" in
Deuteronomy 29:3 (ET 29:4) in his JPS commentary, even though this
translation is nearly identical to the one in the JPS text on which he is
commenting. Instead, Tigay argues that the correct translation of this

---

22. This is a modification of the position held by Georg Braulik, who understands
the covenant stipulations at Horeb to include only the Ten Commandments and the
covenant stipulations at Moab to include further requirements fleshed out in Deut
5–26. Braulik, "Die Ausdrücke für 'Gesetz' im Buch Deuteronomium," 43–45.

23. My translation.

verse is "But the LORD did not give you a mind to understand . . . until today." He goes on to explain,

> The NJPS translation implies that even now Israel lacks the capacity to understand its experiences properly. If that were Moses' meaning, his appeal that Israel observe the covenant would be hopeless. Verses 6–7 indicate that now, after forty years, Israel has shown that it finally does understand and trust in God's power.[24]

Tigay's argument is unpersuasive not only because it is semantically improbable, but also because it does not square with the message of the rest of Deuteronomy, as I will argue below. The expression "to this day" (עד היום הזה) used here in Deuteronomy 29:3 (ET 29:4) is used elsewhere in the Pentateuch not to imply that a condition that was true in the past will change on "this day," but instead that a past condition continues even up to "this day," with the expectation that it will continue in that condition into the foreseeable future (cf. Gen 19:37; 26:33; 32:33[32]; 47:26; 48:15; Exod 10:6; Num 22:30; Deut 2:22; 3:14; 10:8; 11:4; 34:6).[25]

Moses has seen the unfaithfulness of Israel in the past, and he has been shown the state of their hearts even "to this day" and into the foreseeable future. In Deuteronomy 31:26–29, Moses expands on this pessimistic outlook on Israel's rebellious nature, declaring his knowledge of their hearts openly: "For I know how rebellious and stubborn you are. Behold, even today while I am yet alive with you, you have been rebellious against the LORD. How much more after my death!" (Deut 31:27). Moses knows Israel's heart has not been changed yet, and he knows that it will not be changed even in the near future. As he says in Deuteronomy 31:29, "I know that after my death you will surely act corruptly and turn aside from the way that I have commanded you."

Deuteronomy 29:3 (ET 29:4) has been rightly identified as the dilemma of the covenant at Moab, which turns out to be the dilemma of Deuteronomy and the entire Pentateuch.[26]

---

24. Tigay, *Deuteronomy*, 275.

25. Exod 10:6 may be the one instance where the meaning somehow indicates a change "on this day," but it seems more likely that it is referring to the condition that has been in the past and still continues. See Hamilton, *God's Glory in Salvation through Judgment*, 125n129.

26. Link asserts, "We claim that the pericope's dilemma of Deut 29:3 is one of the human heart and that this quandary is also the Pentateuch's dilemma. As such, we contend that the Horeb-Moab covenant of laws is not addressed to overcoming this dilemma but in minimizing its repercussions until the heart's future circumcision in

In proclaiming that Yahweh has not given Israel a heart to know, Moses invites Israel to reflect on why they are still in the wilderness and not yet in the land. Israel's stubborn heart is what caused Yahweh to bar them entrance into the land in the first place, a reality Moses recounts in the structurally parallel section in Deuteronomy 1:1—4:4. In that passage, Moses also briefly rehearses the history of Israel from the time of the Exodus to the present on the plains of Moab, a history marked by Israel's unfaithfulness and Yahweh's faithfulness. Instead of listening to the words of Yahweh when he said they would be able to take the promised land (Deut 1:21), they listened to the words of their brothers that said they could not (1:28), words that melted (מסס) their hearts (לבב). Israel's failure was a heart failure, which was a failure of faith. They did not believe the words of Yahweh and instead believed the words of man. The promise of the words of Yahweh was not their hope; the apprehension in the words of their brothers became their fear. Fundamentally, Israel "did not believe (אמן) Yahweh [their] God" (1:32), which led directly to forty years of wilderness wandering. For this reason, Israel stands in Moab, opposite the promised land, across the Jordan in Deuteronomy 29.

The dilemma of Deuteronomy 29:3 (ET 29:4) recalls the heart of Deuteronomy (Deut 6:4–9), which at its center is concerned with the heart of man—a major thread within the book of Deuteronomy.

### The Heart in Deuteronomy and the Heart of Deuteronomy

The heart and love from the heart are major themes in the book of Deuteronomy. Fifty-one of the 122 occurrences (42 percent) of "heart" (לב/לבב) and eighteen of the thirty-six occurrences (50 percent) of "love" (אהב) in the Pentateuch occur in the book of Deuteronomy.[27] The Shema in Deuteronomy 6:4–9, which commands whole-hearted love for Yahweh, "is arguably the key text of the Old Testament."[28] Mentioned elsewhere in the Pentateuch only in Exodus 20:6, the concept of loving Yahweh is first developed in the book of Deuteronomy, and it is directly

---

the promised return as described in Deut 30:6." Link, "A Composition Criticism of Deut 28:69—30:20," 447.

27. Myers points out that the "term 'love' occurs more frequently in Deuteronomy than in any other book of the Old Testament." Myers, "Requisites for Response," 29.

28. Gentry and Wellum, *Kingdom through Covenant*, 357.

linked to the heart in Deuteronomy 6:5.[29] Loving Yahweh from a whole heart is the central command of Deuteronomy, and the central concern of Deuteronomy is how a sinful people could ever do so. I argue below that this radical command of whole-hearted love for Yahweh is only enabled by a prior love extended from Yahweh that imparts a new heart, a heart that is circumcised and thus enabled to love Yahweh.[30] What is more, heart circumcision is the metaphor employed in Deuteronomy for true covenant loyalty[31]—true covenant love—which can only come about by radical divine intervention.[32]

To substantiate this assertion and relate it to the dilemma in Deuteronomy 29:3, I take up three passages in Deuteronomy that uniquely target the heart: (1) a rhetorical question raised by Yahweh in Deuteronomy

29. Hamilton, *God's Glory in Salvation through Judgment*, 119.

30. So Hamilton: "[C]ircumcision of the heart does seem to result in the *ability* to love God and live (Deut 30:6). This spiritual circumcision (circumcised heart and ears) *enables* people to incline to Yahweh." Hamilton, *God's Indwelling Presence*, 47.

31. According to Meade, "Deuteronomy presents circumcision of the heart as [an] important means for attaining the Deuteronomic vision of loyalty from a devoted heart." Meade, "Circumcision of the Heart in Leviticus and Deuteronomy," 70–71.

32. In his comprehensive survey of the meaning of "heart" in the OT, Wolff suggests that heart circumcision is connected to divine intervention in a man in order to create in him a willing obedience: "This view of the heart is put in pictorial terms in the prophetic demand for circumcision for Yahweh's sake and for the removal 'of the foreskin of your hearts' (Jer. 4.4). This illustrates the new return— indeed the surrender— to Yahweh. Deut. 10.16 explains the expected event still further by indicating that the people's previous 'stubbornness' will now be ended: 'Circumcise therefore the foreskin of your heart, and be no longer stubborn.' Jer. 3.10 contrasts a deceptive, hypocritical or merely outward conversion (*beseqer*) with one which takes place 'with the whole heart' (*bekol-l.*), with a sincere devotion that could also stand up to an examination of the hidden intentions. Thus Joel (2.12) calls for 'a return with all your heart', that is to say for a change brought about by a clear decision of will (cf. Jer. 29.13). The Deuteronomist is continually charging the people to fear God and serve him sincerely 'with the whole heart'—exhorting them, that is, to a conscious surrender of the will (cf. I Sam. 12.24). The prophet Ezekiel recognizes that man cannot renew his heart by himself. He promises in the name of his God (11.19; cf. 36.26). . . . The rest of the passage shows that here *l.* also probably means perception and a sense of spiritual direction—indeed conscience; but it means more than that. For 11.20 (cf. 36.27) goes on: 'that they may walk according to my statutes and keep my ordinances and obey them.' The heart of stone is the dead heart (cf. I Sam. 25.37), which is unreceptive and makes all the limbs incapable of action. The heart of flesh is the living heart, full of insight, which is at the same time ready for new action. The new *rūah* brings to the perception and will of the heart the new vital power to hold on steadfastly in willing obedience. . . . [T]he invitation to get a new heart is an exhortation to accept the offer of a purposeful willingness for new obedience." Wolff, *Anthropology of the Old Testament*, 53–54.

5:29; (2) the central call to love Yahweh from the heart in the *Shema* of Deuteronomy 6; and (3) the heart circumcision commanded in Deuteronomy 10:16.

*Who will give them a heart like this?* In Deuteronomy 5:1–33, Moses recounts Israel's experience at the covenant ceremony at Mount Sinai when Yahweh spoke to Israel "out of the midst of the fire, the cloud, and the thick darkness, with a loud voice" (Deut 5:22). In response to this direct address from Yahweh after seeing the spectacular display, the people of Israel were afraid and told Moses, "Go near and hear all that the LORD our God will say, and speak to us all that the LORD our God will speak to you, and we will hear and do it" (5:27).

But in Deuteronomy 5, the reader is granted a privileged perspective behind the scenes, as it were, with Moses and Yahweh, a perspective not revealed in the book of Exodus where the same event is documented (Exod 19:1–25). In Deuteronomy 5, one is able to overhear a conversation that took place between Moses and Yahweh at the covenant ceremony at Sinai. After hearing the response of the people to Moses, Yahweh says, "I have heard the words of this people, which they have spoken to you. They are right in all that they have spoken" (Deut 5:28). But though Yahweh commends Israel for desiring to hear and to do all the words of the covenant in Deuteronomy 5:28, in 5:29 Yahweh voices a concern to Moses. "Who will give them a heart like this (מי־יתן והיה לבבם זה להם), to fear me and to keep all my commandments always (כל־הימים)?"[33]

Most English translations interpret מי־יתן as a Hebrew idiom and translate Deuteronomy 5:29, "Oh that they had such a heart as this always."[34] But underlying this idiom is the literal phrase "who will give?" that conveys a volitional longing and hope for change. The LXX opts for a more literal translation which preserves the force of the Hebrew idiom (τίς δώσει οὕτως εἶναι τὴν καρδίαν αὐτῶν ἐν αὐτοῖς ὥστε).

While Yahweh praises Israel's desire to obey, he recognizes their lack of ability to obey continually (כל־הימים). Yahweh has foreseen Israel's inevitable failure because he knows their heart, and he wonders aloud to Moses who will give them what it takes to succeed. This is a question Moses revisits in Deuteronomy 29:3 (ET 29:4) and Yahweh finally answers in chapter 30. In 29:3 (ET 29:4), Moses declares that Yahweh has

---

33. My translation.

34. Wevers writes, "The collocation מי יתן is a Hebrew idiom expressing desire 'O that, would that,' and the Greek τίς δώσει can only be understood as a Hebraism." Wevers, *Notes on the Greek Text of Deuteronomy*, 108.

not given (נתן) Israel a heart (לבב) to know, which implicitly answers the rhetorical question posed in 5:29: "Who will give them a heart like this?" The implication of 29:3 (ET 29:4) is, "Yahweh will, but he has not 'to this day.'" The final answer to the question comes only in chapter 30. Yahweh will give them "a heart like this" in the restoration after exile.

*Obeying the* Shema *from the heart.* In Deuteronomy 6:4–5, at the center of the center of the Old Testament,[35] Moses commands Israel to love Yahweh with their whole being: heart, soul, and strength. At the center's center, we find under the microscope the center of man, the heart.[36]

Deuteronomy 6:1 begins a new subsection (וזאת המצוה, "Now this is the commandment") within the covenant stipulations, a subsection that conveys distinct material from the revelation given at Sinai record-ed in Exodus. Syntactically, 6:1–3 is held together by the *weqatal* Qal perfect ושמעת in 6:3, which continues the result clause (למען) begun in 6:2, instead of starting a new paragraph as an imperative as most translations suggest.[37]

If figure 1 below reflects the proper syntactical structure of Deuter-onomy 6:1–3, then something similar to the following translation would best reflect the underlying syntax:

> Now this is the commandment—the statutes and judgements—
> which Yahweh your God commanded to teach you to do in the
> land, which you are crossing there to possess it, in order that
> you will fear Yahweh your God to keep all his statutes and com-
> mandments which I am commanding you and your sons and
> your sons' sons all the days of your life, and in order that your
> days will be long, and [in order that] you will hear, oh Israel, and
> be careful to do what will be good for you and what will multiply
> you greatly, as Yahweh the God of your fathers said to you, a
> land flowing with milk and honey.[38]

35. So Gentry and Wellum: "The book of Deuteronomy is the centre of the entire Old Testament, in terms of both metanarrative and theology" and "Deuteronomy 6:4–5 [is the] centre of the book of Deuteronomy." Gentry and Wellum, *Kingdom through Covenant*, 363, 365.

36. Gentry and Wellum argue, "In Hebrew, the word 'heart' refers to the core of who you are, the centre of each person." *Kingdom through Covenant*, 366.

37. Most translations follow the LXX, which renders the beginning of 6:3 with imperatives. Wevers calls the LXX translation "unusual" but possible. Wevers, *Notes on the Greek Text of Deuteronomy*, 113. Lohfink identifies a chiastic structure that binds 6:1–3 with 5:27–32. Lohfink, *Das Hauptgebot*, 67–68.

38. My translation.

In Deuteronomy 6:1, Moses references a singular command (זאת המצוה) which is immediately defined by apposition as "the statutes and judgments" (החקים והמשפטים). What is the singular command? If 6:1–3 are indeed syntactically coordinated with *weqatals*, as demonstrated in the syntactical diagram below and translation above, then the singular command points forward to the *Shema* in 6:4–5, which stands as a synecdoche for the whole of the commandments. This reference to a singular command standing for the whole of the commandments is a noteworthy pattern followed in Deuteronomy (Deut 5:31; 6:25; 7:11; 11:22; 15:5; 17:20; 19:9; 30:11).

**Figure 1. Syntactical flow of Deuteronomy 6:1–3**

Deuteronomy 6:4 begins with a clear imperative. "Hear, O Israel: The LORD our God, the LORD is one. You shall love the LORD your God with

all your heart and with all your soul and with all your might." This imperative, referred to as a commandment in 6:1, is fleshed out by other statutes
and rules (החקים והמשפטים, 6:1). All the rest of the commandments flow
from this fundamental command (cf. 19:9, where to "keep all this commandment" is "to love the LORD your God and walk in his ways").

Love for Yahweh from a whole heart is what is required, and the
fundamental means by which this love is encouraged is the word of Yahweh. "These words, which I am commanding you today, shall be on (על)
your heart" (Deut 6:6; cf. 11:18; 32:46).[39] Love for Yahweh is enabled
by a love of his word. This call to internalize the word is developed in
Deuteronomy right along with the focus on the need for heart change.

In Deuteronomy 29:3 (ET 29:4), Moses says Israel has not been
given a heart to know (לדעת לבב), eyes to see (לראות עינים), or ears to hear
(אזנים לשמע). In 6:4–5, Israel is commanded to "hear" (שמע) and "love"
(אהב) Yahweh with a whole heart (לבב). But without a heart to know and
ears to hear, how will Israel fulfill the *Shema* of Deuteronomy 6?

*Obeying the* Shema *from a circumcised heart.* In Deuteronomy
10:12–13, Moses again revisits the *Shema*. "And now, Israel, what does
the LORD your God require of you, but to fear the LORD your God, to
walk in all his ways, to love him, to serve the LORD your God with all
your heart and with all your soul, and to keep the commandments and
statutes of the LORD." This command to fearfully, lovingly keep Yahweh's
commandments is a restatement of the *Shema* in Deuteronomy 6:4–5:
Moses commands Israel to fear (ירא, Deut 10:12, cf. 6:2) Yahweh, to walk
(הלך, 10:12, cf. 6:7) in all his ways, to love (אהב, 10:12, cf. 6:5) him, to
serve (עבד, 10:12, cf. 6:13) him with their whole heart (לבב, 10:12, cf. 6:5)
and soul (נפש, 10:12, cf. 6:5), and to keep (שמר, 10:13, cf. 6:2) his statutes.

But in Deuteronomy 10:16, Moses adds an additional command,
"Circumcise the foreskin of your heart" (לבבכם ערלת את מלתם) and "no
longer stiffen your neck" (תקשו לא וערפכם עוד). Remarkably, this is the
only place where Israel is commanded to perform circumcision (מול)

---

39. Meade summarizes the deuteronomic command to put the law on the heart
thusly: "The verb שִׂים functions as a command in [Deut] 11:18 and in 32:46, which
communicates that it is desirable for the people to place or set Moses' instructions on
their heart and soul, that is, for them to internalize the Torah or instruction of Moses.
In 6:6, the verb form הָיָה ('to be') indicates that the words Moses commanded the
people *shall* be upon (על) their hearts. The people are to place the Torah on the part
of them that controls their feelings, reason, desires, and will. Moses envisions nothing less than a people fully constrained and controlled by the Torah from the heart."
Meade, "Circumcision of Flesh to Circumcision of Heart," 134.

in the whole book of Deuteronomy, a central rite in the covenant with Abraham and the Mosaic covenant cut at Sinai. But physical circumcision is not Moses' concern here. In fact, the only two places מול occurs in Deuteronomy—here and in 30:6—are in reference to heart circumcision, not the physical circumcision of the covenant sign.[40] Moses has spent forty years seeing the circumcised act like the uncircumcised, and he understands the impossibility of obedience without a changed heart.

In his study on the meaning of heart circumcision in Leviticus and Deuteronomy, John Meade points to several texts in Deuteronomy that have performative verbs paired with an instrumental use of the preposition ב + heart (לבב): "to love" (אהב, Deut 6:5; 13:4; 30:6), "to serve" (עבד, 10:12; 11:13), "to do" (עשה, 26:16), "to obey" (שמע, 30:2), and "to seek" (שדר, 4:29). These texts "demonstrate the goal for a people to be devoted to Yahweh with all their heart."[41] But there is an impediment to this devotion. Israel has a heart defect that prevents them from whole-hearted covenant devotion—the kind that Moses calls them to in Deuteronomy 6:4–5 and again in 10:12—and the remedy prescribed here is heart circumcision. Moses has located a metaphorical foreskin[42] that impedes the function of love and covenant devotion from a whole heart. Only when the foreskin is removed will Israel be enabled to fear, love, obey, and serve Yahweh with all their heart and soul. In short, heart circumcision would enable Israel to fulfill the central requirement in the OT, the *Shema* of Deuteronomy 6:4–5. As Meade concludes, "Deuteronomy presents circumcision of the heart as [an] important means for attaining the Deuteronomic vision of loyalty from a devoted heart."[43]

### Dilemma and Dissonance in Deuteronomy 29:3

Thus, returning to the problem in Deuteronomy 29:3 (ET 29:4), the book of Deuteronomy has set the reader up to wonder when Israel will be given "a heart like this" (Deut 5:29), when they will have hearts that are circumcised (10:16) to obey the *Shema* (6:4–5), or whether Israel will be left in exile where Yahweh will give them failing hearts (28:65–68).

---

40. So Wells, *Grace and Agency*, 157.

41. Meade, "Circumcision of the Heart in Leviticus and Deuteronomy," 70.

42. Moses is simply following the lead of Yahweh in Lev 26:41, where Yahweh refers to Israel's "uncircumcised heart."

43. Meade, "Circumcision of the Heart in Leviticus and Deuteronomy," 70–71.

Even though Israel has not yet been given a heart to know, eyes to see, or ears to hear (Deut 29:3 [ET 29:4]), it is not as though they have not had opportunity to gain a heart of understanding. The fault is not with Yahweh's revelation. The fault is with the people. In fact, the expressed purpose of Israel's wilderness wandering was so that they might learn "to know." In Deuteronomy 29:4 (ET 29:5), Moses' voice blends with Yahweh's as he reminds Israel how he led them for forty years through the wilderness and how they were miraculously provided both clothing that did not wear out (29:4, [ET 29:5]) and otherworldly food (29:5, [ET 29:6]). This was done "so that you may know (יְדַע) that I am the LORD your God."[44]

The dissonance created in Deuteronomy 28:69—29:3 (ET 29:1–4) is a dissonance threaded throughout the book of Deuteronomy: Israel is supposed to gain a heart of understanding from Yahweh's revelation, but Yahweh has not given them a heart of understanding. Only in 30:1–14 is this dissonance resolved.

## Covenant Ceremony at Moab

In spite of Israel's heart problem revealed in Deuteronomy 29:3 (ET 29:4), Moses proceeds with cutting the covenant on the plains of Moab. After recounting the works of Yahweh on behalf of Israel in 29:1–2, 4–7 (ET 29:2–3, 5–8), including the plagues in Egypt leading to the Exodus, miraculous provision in the wilderness, and the defeat of Sihon the king of Heshbon and Og the king of Bashan—this last bit of history is a feature in every major section of Deuteronomy (Deut 1:4; 4:46–47; and 29:6 [ET 29:7])—Moses declares that Yahweh's wondrous works demand a response from Israel. He commands Israel: "Keep the words of this covenant and do them, that you may be wise in all that you do" (29:8 [ET 29:9]).

In Deuteronomy 29:9–14 (ET 29:10–15), Moses establishes the two parties of the covenant, Israel—including sojourner and slave (Deut

---

44. In Deut 8, the other place in Deuteronomy where Israel is reminded of Yahweh's miraculous provisions of clothes that did not wear out and manna from heaven in the wilderness, it is also clear that these things were done in order that Yahweh might "make them know (הוֹדִעֲךָ, *Hiphil* 3ms + 2ms pronominal suffix) that man does not live by bread alone, but man lives by every word that comes from the mouth of God" (8:3). And in the same context, Yahweh likewise reminds them of their stubbornness "from the day you came out of the land of Egypt until you came to this place" (9:7).

29:10 [ET 29:11])[45]—and Yahweh. Israel has been summoned together to cross over (עבר) into the covenant of Yahweh, Israel's God, and into his oath (בברית יהוה אלהיך ובאלתו).[46]

Moses states this covenant with the standard covenant formula[47] in Deuteronomy 29:11 (ET 29:12), "that he may establish you today as his people, and that he may be your God," and grounds it in Yahweh's sworn promise to the patriarchs, just as he does in 4:31. The covenant at Moab incorporates the new generation and future generations—sojourners and slaves included—into the people of God, and Yahweh declares himself to be their God and them his people.

Is the covenant at Moab thus (1) a new covenant, to be completely distinguished from the Sinai covenant; (2) the Sinai covenant for the new generation, or (3) an updated covenant, a kind of Sinai 2.0, with no subtractions and a few additions and upgrades? In Deuteronomy 4, which comes at the end of the first section (Deut 1:1—4:44) that serves to introduce the major themes of the Book of Deuteronomy—a section that contains many parallels to 29–30, as noted in the proposed structure above—Moses calls the Moab generation to remember the Sinai covenant (4:23, 31), the requirements of which are summarized in the Ten Words (4:13). There Moses defines the Moab generation's relationship to the Sinai covenant in Deuteronomy 5:2–3: "The LORD our God made a covenant with us in Horeb. Not with our fathers did the LORD make this covenant, but with us, who are all of us here alive today." Thus, it cannot be that the Moab covenant is meant to completely replace the Sinai covenant. But it is also not the case that the Moab covenant is merely a restatement of the Sinai covenant.

---

45. This is an interesting detail added to the covenant at Moab—sojourners and foreigners (hewers of wood and drawers of water, cf. Josh 9:3–27) are included in the covenant ceremony. Their inclusion may hint at a more inclusive covenant to come in the same way the promise of heart circumcision in Deut 30 hints at a new covenant.

46. The אלה of Deut 29:11 (ET 29:12) could be in reference to the negative aspect, the curses, of the covenant. The LXX renders it with ἀρά, which is usually a negative oath. Mayes likewise detects a negative aspect to this formula, which he calls a "self-cursing formula to guard against disobedience." Mayes, *Deuteronomy*, 363.

47. Childs, *Biblical Theology*, 421. Rendtorff, *The Covenant Formula*, 13–32.

## The Curse of Covenant Disobedience

In Deuteronomy 29:15–27 (ET 29:16–27), Moses warns the Israelites of the consequences of breaking the covenant they are entering. This warning is similar to and recalls the warnings found in Deuteronomy 4:15–31 and 28:15–68 (cf. 31:16–18, 24–29; 32:15–43) which I will take up briefly below.

### *Deuteronomy 4:15–31*

In Deuteronomy 4:15–31, Moses spells out what will happen if the Israelites "act corruptly" and fall into idolatry, either through idol worship (Deut 4:16–18, 23, 25) or worship of the creation (4:19). The consequence is utter destruction (4:26), exile among the nations (4:27), and a handing over to idolatry (4:28). But a kernel of hope is contained in 4:29–31. In exile Israel will seek Yahweh and "find" (מצא) him, when they seek with all their heart and soul (4:29). In their distress, "all these things/words" (דברים) will "find" (מצא) them, and they will "turn" (שוב) to Yahweh and "hear" (שמע) his voice (4:30). This promise is grounded in the character of Yahweh: He is merciful, and he will not forget his sworn covenant with the patriarchs (4:31).

### *Deuteronomy 28:15–68*

In Deuteronomy 28, Moses returns again to the consequences of covenant disobedience, but in this section there is no hope held out to the people of Israel. Israel's disobedience to the voice of Yahweh, which stems from a failure to serve Yahweh from a joyful and good heart (לבב, Deut 28:47) and a misplaced trust (בטח) in fortified walls (28:52), will lead to the curses of the covenant falling on Israel (28:15–24). The Israelites will find themselves suffering like the Egyptians at the Exodus and the Canaanites at the conquest: disease ridden (28:27, 35, 60–61), blinded by darkness (28:29); defeated and pillaged by their enemies (28:25, 29b–31, 33; 49–52), enslaved (28:32, 41, 68), exiled (28:36, 64), given over to idolatry (28:36, 64), and in utter hopelessness and despair (28:53–57, 65–67). In the end, they will be back where they started, back in captivity in the land of Egypt (28:68). Instead of giving them a heart to know and eyes to see to keep the covenant—in answer to Yahweh's rhetorical lament in 5:29 and in keeping with what we have seen is required to fulfill the stipulations of this covenant—Yahweh will give (נתן) them a trembling heart (רגז לב), darkened eyes (כליון עינים), and a languishing soul (דאבון נפש) (28:65). In contrast with chapter 4, Deuteronomy 28:68 does not end on a note of hope:

> And the LORD will bring you back in ships to Egypt, a journey that I promised that you should never make again; and there you shall offer yourselves for sale to your enemies as male and female slaves, but there will be no buyer.

### Deuteronomy 29:15–27 (ET 29:16–28)

Thus, when it comes to the consequences for covenant disobedience in chapter 29, Israel's future seems indeterminate. Moses again warns against the sins of idolatry (Deut 29:17a, [ET 29:18a]) and heart disobedience (29:17b–18, [ET 29:18b–19]). Significantly, Moses' warnings focus on the heart as the root of both sins that will lead to exile:

> Deuteronomy 29:17a (ET 29:18a): "Beware lest there be among you a man or woman or clan or tribe whose heart (לבב) is turning away from the LORD our God to go and serve the gods of those nations."

> Deuteronomy 29:17b–18 (ET 29:18b–19): "Beware lest there be among you a root bearing poisonous and bitter fruit, one who, when he hears the words of this covenant oath, blesses himself in his heart (לבב) saying, 'Peace will be with me, though I walk in the stubbornness of my heart (לבב).'"[48]

---

48. My translation, with dependence on the language of the ESV. This language of internal dialogue within a person's heart crops up numerous times in Deuteronomy. Deut 7:17: "If you say in your heart (לבב) 'These nations are greater than I. How can I dispossess them?'" Deut 8:17: "Beware lest you say in your heart (לבב), 'My power and the might of my hand have gotten me this wealth.'" Deut 9:4: "Do not say in your heart (לבב), after the LORD your God has thrust them out before you, 'It is because of my righteousness that the LORD has brought me in to possess this land.'" Deut 29:17–18 (ET 29:18–19): "Beware lest there be among you a root bearing poisonous and bitter fruit, one who, when he hears the words of this covenant oath, blesses himself in his heart (לבב) saying, 'peace will be with me, though I walk in the stubbornness of my heart (לבב).'" This is also the language Paul accesses in Rom 10 when he introduces the quotation of Deut 30:12–14, which I return to below in chapter 4.

The imagery in Deuteronomy 29:17b–18 (ET 29:18b–19) is of a root that grows to bear poisonous fruit, and when the anger of Yahweh comes, his jealousy will burn against it and will "sweep away the moist and dry alike" in accord with the curses written in this book. The one who is disobedient will be singled out from the tribes to bear the curses (Deut 29:20 [ET 29:21]), but this punishment will affect all of Israel. The sin of one turns out to be the sin of Israel, as later generations are told that "they abandoned the covenant of the LORD, the God of their fathers . . . and went and served other gods and worshiped them" (29:24–25 [ET 29:25–26]). And as in chapter 28 and the plagues of the Exodus, the punishment reserved for the enemies of God's people will be meted out against God's own people. This time the punishment against Israel is likened to the destruction of Sodom and Gomorrah (29:22 [ET 29:23]). And as was true in Deuteronomy 4 and 28, Israel's fate is exile, an uprooting and casting out to another land. With the threat of the curse of exile, this passage in Deuteronomy 29 leaves one wondering if hope will be extended, as in chapter 4, or withheld, as in chapter 28.

## Things Hidden and Revealed

At this point, Moses says one of the most enigmatic things in all of the OT in Deuteronomy 29:28 (ET 29:29), "The hidden things are for Yahweh our God, but the revealed things are for us and our sons forever, to do all of the words of this *Torah*."[49] The significance of the location of this statement is picked up by several commentators.[50] The fact that it occurs at the seam of chapters 29 and 30, between exile foretold in Deuteronomy 29 and restoration promised in Deuteronomy 30, indicates that Deuteronomy 29:28 (ET 29:29) acts as a kind of meta-comment to the entire section.[51]

But what is the referent of "the hidden things" (הנסתרת) that are for Yahweh and "the revealed things" (והנגלת) that are for Israel? Do the hidden and revealed things refer to Israel's sin and covenant

---

49. My translation.

50. See, for example, Turner, *The Death of Deaths in the Death of Israel*, 156. "With 29:28, we can perceive a transition from the generally negative attitude of chapter 29 to the more optimistic tone of chapter 30." See also Lenchak, *Choose Life!*, 153, 174.

51. So Gentry, "The Relationship of Deuteronomy to the Covenant at Sinai," 51.

conformity,[52] God's word and the torah,[53] God's will and counsel,[54] or something else?[55]

Looking at the immediate context, Moses has just warned Israel to beware two manifestations of disobedience to the covenant: in Deuteronomy 29:17a (ET 29:18a) Israel is warned against the one whose heart turns away from Yahweh to serve idols; and in Deuteronomy 29:17b–18 (ET 29:18b–19) Israel is warned against the one who would bless himself in his heart despite walking in the stubbornness of his heart. These two sins, idolatry and stubbornness of heart, both lead to covenant curses and ultimately result in exile (Deut 29:26–27 [ET 29:27–28]). For Israel to beware the idolater is one thing—it would be relatively easy to detect when someone was worshipping other gods by the presence of alternate forms of worship. But for Israel to beware the one whose internal dialogue is

---

52. According to Biddle, "The concluding proverb-like statement continues the theme of secret apostasy. YHWH knows the secrets of an individual's heart. Abandonment of the covenant cannot be kept secret. The Torah and its requirements, on the other hand, are public knowledge. Israel's responsibility is simply 'to do all the words of this Torah.'" Biddle, *Deuteronomy*, 442. The Jewish commentator Rashi concurs: "And if you say, 'But what can we do?' "Thou threatenest the many (the whole community) with punishment because of the sinful thoughts of one individual as it is said, (v. 17): 'Lest there should be among you a man, [or a woman or a family . . . whose heart turneth away this day from the LORD . . .]'", and afterwards it states, (v. 21) 'And they will see the plagues of that land'. But surely no man can know the secret thoughts of his fellow! Now, I reply: I do not threaten to punish you because of secret thoughts for these belong to our LORD our God and He will exact punishment from that individual; but those things which are revealed belong to us and to our children that we may put away the evil from our midst; and if we do not execute judgment upon them, the whole community will be punished." Rashi, *Pentateuch with Targum Onkelos, Haphtaroth and Prayers for Sabbath and Rashi's Commentary*, 148.

53. Cairns claims that "[Deut] 30:11–14 [is] a useful clue to the interpretation of 29:29. The emphasis of 30:11–14 is that Yahweh's torah is not some obscure secret knowledge but guidance open and accessible, easily understood and practiced." Cairns, *Word and Presence*, 262.

54. Keil and Delitzsch argue, "That which is revealed includes the law with its promises and threats; consequently that which is hidden can only refer to the mode in which God will carry out in the future His counsel and will, which He has revealed in the law, and complete His work of salvation notwithstanding the apostasy of people." Carl Keil and Delitzsch, *Biblical Commentary on the Old Testament*, 451.

55. John Currid notes that above the words "to us and to our sons" in the Hebrew text appear *puncta extraordinara*, which, according to Emanuel Tov, are meant by the Masoretes to indicate text that should be omitted. Such an omission would dramatically alter the interpretation of this passage. Currid, *A Study Commentary on Deuteronomy*, 464.

disobedient to Yahweh, who spurns the words of the covenant and blesses himself in his stubborn heart, is quite another.

In Deuteronomy 29:28 (ET 29:29), Israel is aware of both outward and inward manifestations of conformity to the covenant and their seeming helplessness with regard to the latter—both in their own hearts and in the hearts of their neighbors. There is external conformity to the law and there is internal conformity to the law. External conformity to the law, "the revealed things," is what belongs to Israel, both the practicing of the law and the meting out of the sanctions that are prescribed against those who fail to uphold the law. But internal conformity to the law, "the hidden things," is what belongs to Yahweh as he exercises his sovereignty over the heart of man and judges man according to his heart.[56]

Deuteronomy 29:28 (ET 29:29) may function the same way in chapters 29–30. The infinitive construct לעשות את־כל־דברי התורה הזאת and the adverbial clause עד־עולם could be read with both independent clauses at the beginning of the verse, to הנסתרת ליהוה אלהינו and ולבנינו לנו והנגלת, which would yield "The hidden things belong to Yahweh our God to do forever all the words of this law" and "the revealed things belong to us and to our sons to do forever all the words of this law." In the context, Yahweh has just promised to visit the curses of the covenant against the "stubborn hearted" (Deut 29:19 [ET 29:18], 27 [ET 26]). He will discern the state of the heart and act according to all the words of this law. Thus, the internal state of a person is for Yahweh to judge in order to carry out the blessings and curses of this covenant; whereas the outward state of a person is for man to judge in order to carry out the blessings and curses of this covenant. In particular focus, then, in 29:28 (ET 29:29) moving into chapter 30, especially 30:11–14, is Yahweh's unilateral ability to exercise sovereignty over the hidden things and judge a man according to the secrets of his heart.

---

56. This interpretation is similar to the one taken by Rofé, "The Covenant in the Land of Moab," 272. Many contemporary commentators have noted an allusion to Deut 29–30 in Rom 2:25–29. See, for example, Rendtorff, *The Covenant Formula*, 13–32.; Lincicum, Paul and the Early Jewish Encounter with Deuteronomy, 150. In that passage, Paul makes clear that being a Jew is not in outward appearances (φανερός, cf. LXX Deut 29:28) which can be discerned by men, e.g., circumcision, but being a Jew is an inward, hidden (κρυπτός, cf. LXX 29:28) reality that can only be discerned by God, for true circumcision is of the heart (Rom 2:29).

## Deuteronomy 30 and the Promised (Re)turn

Deuteronomy 30 has been variably broken up into multiple sections. The majority of interpreters take 30:1–10 as a unit and 30:11–20 as a unit,[57] while some interpreters take 30:11–14 to be its own section or a hinge between the two.[58] I will argue instead that 30:1–14 should be interpreted together as a unit, whereas 30:15–20 forms a separate pericope.

Several chiastic structures have been posited for the first section of Deuteronomy 30. One common chiastic structure proposed is organized around the seven[59] occurrences of שוב in verses 1–10 (figure 2).[60] Finding this chiasm unpersuasive, Jack Lundbom offers an alternative chiasm organized around key words in the passage (figure 3).[61]

| | | |
|---|---|---|
| A | Israel will (re)turn (שוב) to their heart all these words and (re)turn (שוב) to Yahweh and obey (vv. 1–2) | vv. 1–2 |
| B | Yahweh will (re)turn (שוב) to Israel's (re)turning (שוב) | vv. 3–4 |
| C | Yahweh will circumcise Israel's heart and Israel will (re)turn (שוב) and obey | vv. 6–8 |
| B' | Yahweh (re)turn (שוב) to rejoice over Israel | v. 9 |
| A' | Israel will (re)turn (שוב) to Yahweh | v. 10 |

**Figure 2. שוב chiasm in Deuteronomy 30:1–10**

57. Merrill is representative, titling a section covering Deut 30:11–20 together as "The Appeals for Covenant Obedience," in Merrill, *Deuteronomy*, 390.

58. So Wright: "This short interlude [in Deut 30:11–14] before the final appeal reassures Israel that God's law *can* be kept." Wright, *Deuteronomy*, 290.

59. There are eight occurrences if it is the case that the noun שבית in Deut 30:3 stems from שוב. BDB notes this noun may derive from שבה, "to take captive," instead. BDB, s.v. "שבה." Holladay notes either translation, "bring about the restoration of" or "return the captivity of," is a viable option, but he opts for the prior. Holladay, *The Root שוב in the Old Testament*, 110–12.

60. So Tigay, *Deuteronomy*; Nelson, *Deuteronomy*, 347; Wells, *Grace and Agency*, 32.

61. Lundbom, *Deuteronomy*, 816.

| A | return . . . obey . . . heart and soul | v. 2 |
|---|---|---|
| B | the land . . . do you more good . . . your fathers | v. 5 |
| C | circumcise your heart . . . that you may live | v. 6 |
| B' | your soil . . . for good . . . for good . . . your fathers | v. 9 |
| A' | obey . . . return . . . heart and soul | v. 10 |

**Figure 3. Key words chiasm in Deuteronomy 30:1–10**

But if the section is expanded to include Deuteronomy 30:11–14 with 30:1–10, as I am inclined to do for a host of reasons listed below, the chiasm Georg Braulik detects related to the seven occurrences of לֵב, which is corroborated by Eckart Otto,[62] becomes more convincing (figure 4).[63]

62. Otto, *Deuteronomium*, 4:2041–42.

63. Braulik suggests two interlocking chiasms with keyword שׁוב in Deut 30:1–10 and לבב in 30:1–14, with the second belonging to a later redaction layer. As we are interested in the canonical form of the text, this "final layer" is most important to our project. "Das »Prinzip Hoffnung« hängt zwar an der Umkehr, hat aber seinen letzten Grund darin, daß Gott »das Herz beschneidet« (6). *lebāb* »Herz« und *šûb* »umkehren« (in der EÜ je nach Kontext verschieden übersetzt) werden hier wie sonst nirgends im Dtn gehäuft, nämlich siebenmal, verwendet und dienen dem Aufbau zweier palindromischer Strukteren, die 30 1–14 bzw. 1–10 umfassen und ineinander verschränkt sind. Im literarischen und theologischen Zentrum beider Figuren stehen die Herzensbeschneidung und die Gottesliebe (6). 30 1–10 muß deshalb im Rahmen der (wohl erst redaktionellen) Einheit von 1–14 interpretiert werden. Hier bestehen die folgenden Stichwortbezüge: 1 »diese Worte . . . dir zu Herzen nimmst« (A) — 2 »zum Herrn, deinem Gott, zurückkehrst . . . mit ganzem Herzen und mit ganzer Seele" (B) — 6 »der Herr, dein Gott, wird dein Herz und das Herz deiner Nachkommen beschneiden. Dann wirst du den Herrn, deinen Gott, mit ganzem Herzen und mit ganzer Seele lieben können« (C) — 10 »zum Herrn, deinem Gott, mit ganzem Herzen und mit ganzer Seele zurückkehrst" (B') — 14 »das Wort . . . in deinem Herzen« (A'). Braulik, *Deuteronomium II: 16,18–34,12*, 128. Braulik's chiasm is reproduced and followed in Turner, *The Death of Deaths*, 162.

| A | return the word(s) to your לבב | v. 1 |
| B | return and obey with all your לבב and all your soul | v. 2 |
| C | circumcision of your לבב and the לבב of your seed, which enables love with all your לבב and all your soul | v. 6 |
| B' | return and obey with all your לבב and all your soul | v. 10 |
| A' | the word in your לבב | v. 14 |

**Figure 4. לבב chiasm in Deuteronomy 30:1–14**

Deuteronomy's emphasis on the heart, which was highlighted in foregoing sections, provides good evidence for accepting Braulik's chiasm organized around לבב. This chiastic structure crucially puts Deuteronomy 30:1 in parallel with 30:11–14, which will in turn affect the interpretation of 30:11–14. To anticipate, Israel must take these words to heart (Deut 30:1), and this is possible when the word is divinely placed in their heart (30:14).

## Promise of a Circumcised Heart in Deuteronomy 30:1–10

Virtually all interpreters are in agreement about the prophetic, predictive, future-oriented nature of Deuteronomy 30:1–10.[64] At the center of this prophetic announcement is found the solution to the dilemma of Deuteronomy 29:3 (ET 29:4). Deuteronomy 30:1–10 is the most optimistic portion of the entire book—an optimism that is closely matched by 4:29–31—because it contains blessings that *presuppose* failure. In exile, at the apex of the curses of the covenant, Israel is promised another chance, and this time failure is not held out as an option.

---

64. Von Rad is representative: "These verses turn our eyes to the future and, like 29.20–29, assume that the threatened judgment has already been carried out. . . . In fact, our text can no longer be called an exhortation; it contains no admonitions, but, with regard to Israel's future, simple affirmative propositions, that is, it is clothed altogether in the style of prophetic predictions." Von Rad, *Deuteronomy*, 183.

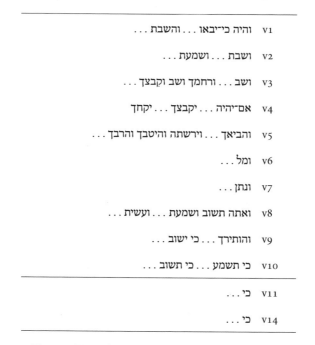

והיה כי־יבאו ... והשבת ...    v1

ושבת ... ושמעת ...    v2

ושב ... ורחמך ושב וקבצך ...    v3

אם־יהיה ... יקבצך ... יקחך    v4

והביאך ... וירשתה והיטבך והרבך ...    v5

ומל ...    v6

ונתן ...    v7

ואתה תשוב ושמעת ... ועשית ...    v8

והותירך ... כי ישוב ...    v9

כי תשמע ... כי תשוב ...    v10

כי ...    v11

כי ...    v14

**Figure 5. Main-clause discourse analysis of *weqatal* and
imperfect verbal forms in Deuteronomy 30:1–14**

Deuteronomy 30:1a forms the beginning of a protasis: "And it will
happen *when* the words (דברים) of the covenant, blessing and curse, have
come upon you." But where the protasis ends and the apodosis begins
is not immediately clear. Following in 30:1b is a series of *weqatal* verbs
that carries the main-clause discourse, which continues to verse 4 where
a conditional clause (אם) plus an imperfect verb begins another *weqatal*
series that runs through the end of verse 7. In verse 8, another imperfect
verb picks up the main-clause discourse, which is again followed by another series of *weqatal* verb forms through to verse 9b, at which point a
series of כי clauses continues the discourse, in my view, through the end
of verse 14 (see figure 5 above).

Many interpreters suggest the apodosis starts at Deuteronomy
30:3, an interpretation reflected in most translations: "*then* Yahweh will
return."[65] But this is an interpretive conclusion that is not clearly delin-
eated in the text, and this interpretation makes it sound like Yahweh's

65. So Vanoni, "Der Geist und der Buchstabe," 73–79; Lohfink, "Der Bundesschluss im Land Moab," 41.

"return" to the people is contingent on their prior "return" to Yahweh.[66] Instead, it is grammatically possible for the apodosis to start at 30:1b with the first *weqatal* verb form ושבת, which would make the events spelled out in 30:1–10 dependent solely on the end of the exile.[67] This interpretation is preferred by Wells: "The contingency here lies purely in the condition of the curses taking effect."[68]

If Wells' interpretation is correct, *when* the words (דברים)[69] of the covenant, blessings and curses, have come upon Israel (Deut 30:1a; cf. 4:30 where the דברים "find" them), *then* they will return these words to their heart (והשבת אל-לבבך 30:1b; cf. 4:39 where this exact phrase occurs, even matching the *Hiphil* stem) and return to Yahweh and hear/obey his voice with their whole heart and soul (30:2); and Yahweh will return to them and have compassion on them and gather them up (30:3)—even from the outer reaches of heaven (30:4)—and will bring them back into the land to multiply them (30:5). Lohfink emphasizes this divine priority:

> Nicht Israel wird Jahwe finden, sondern Jahwes Worte werden
> Israel finden. Israel muß nicht umkehren, damit Jahwe sich ihm

---

66. Some interpreters who understand the priority belonging to Israel's repentance in Deut 30:1–10 rather than Yahweh's divine intervention pit Scripture against Scripture. See, for example, Meyers and Meyers: "One biblical tradition (Deut 30:1–10) regarded the people's repentance in the exile as the basis for reestablishing the proper relationship with Yahweh. Another view (Ezek 36:24–31) leaves all initiative to Yahweh, who brings the people back to himself and to the land through his own divine actions and spiritual cleansing. In the latter view, God's actions will cause the people to repent of their evil ways and so return to Yahweh." Meyers and Meyers, *Haggai, Zechariah 1–8*, 99.

67. So Craigie, "And it shall be that when all these things come upon you, the blessing and the curse which I have set before you, then you shall return . . . (emphasis added)." Craigie, *The Book of Deuteronomy*, 361. So also Wells, "The location of the apodosis is also uncertain. Following the clause introduced by כי והיה comes a string of weqatal verbs. The only indication that the apodosis begins in verse 3 is the change in subject. But a change in subject does not mandate a shift from protasis to apodosis. In fact, on that basis the apodosis should begin in verse 1b where the subject changes from 'all these things' to 'you,' resulting in a substantially different sense." Wells, *Grace and Agency*, 29. Cf. Brettler, "Predestination in Deuteronomy 30.1–10," 174–79.

68. Wells, *Grace and Agency*, 29. Von Rad corroborates: "[30:1–10] contains no admonitions, but . . . is clothed altogether in the style of prophetic predictions." Von Rad, *Deuteronomy*, 183.

69. Peter Gentry remarked to me that perhaps there is a play on the word דברים in this context, which can mean "words," "events," "matters," etc.

> wieder zuwendet, sondern wenn Jahwes Worte Israel finden,
> dann wird Israel die Gnade der Umkehr gewährt werden.[70]

But why the optimism towards Israel's obedience? How will this time be any different than before? The answer is located at the center of the chiasm: divine intervention in the heart (לבב, Deut 30:6).

### The Divine Gift of Heart Circumcision

In Deuteronomy 30:6, the chiastic center of this passage, Yahweh promises to circumcise the hearts of Israel and their seed. "And the LORD your God will circumcise (מול) your heart (לבב) and the heart (לבב) of your offspring (זרע), so that you will love the LORD your God with all your heart (לבב) and with all your soul, that you may live." The use of זרע here in 30:6 is most likely an allusion to the Abrahamic covenant and Yahweh's promise to the patriarchs (cf. זרע in Gen 3:15; 9:9; 12:7; 13:15, 16; 15:5, 13, 18; 17:7, 8, 9, 10, 12, 19),[71] which is fulfilled in this divine promise—land (Deut 30:5), seed (30:6), and blessing (30:3, 5, 9). As Dempster puts it, "[t]his salvation is based not on Sinai but on the covenant with the patriarchs" (cf. 4:31).[72]

The center of the center of the OT in Deuteronomy 6:4–5—the call to love Yahweh with a whole heart in the *Shema*—is finally and only enabled by divine attention to man's center. Yahweh's question in 5:29, command in 10:16, and diagnosis in 29:3 (ET 29:4) are found to function rhetorically, driving toward the ultimate solution in 30:6. It is Yahweh who will affect the heart change necessary in order for Israel to do what the law requires, which is to love Yahweh with a whole heart.

As noted above, the only two places circumcision is mentioned in the book of Deuteronomy are in 10:16 and 30:6, both of which refer to heart circumcision, not physical circumcision. The sign of the Mosaic covenant has a corollary in this covenant ceremony at Moab, but it is not

70. Lohfink, *Höre, Israel!*, 113.

71. In the book of Deuteronomy, זרע appears fourteen times: four times referencing agricultural seed (Deut 11:10; 14:22; 22:9; 28:38); five times referencing the seed of the patriarchs (1:8; 4:37; 10:15; 11:9; 34:4); and five times referencing the seed of the current generation (28:46, 59; 30:6, 19; 31:21). To see how integral the theme of God's promise of a "seed" to Abraham is in biblical theology, see Hamilton, "The Seed of the Woman and the Blessing of Abraham," 253–73; Hamilton, "The Skull Crushing Seed of the Woman: Inner-Biblical Interpretation of Genesis 3:15," 30–54.

72. Dempster, *Dominion and Dynasty*, 121.

physical circumcision. While the rite of physical circumcision has not been done away with, its typological function is now revealed: pointing to the need of spiritual circumcision. Kline rightly notes, "What had been externally symbolized in circumcision . . . would be spiritually actualized by the power of God."[73] The covenant at Moab includes within it—even here at the ceremony that marks its inauguration—a prediction of its own dissolution on account of the human party and its necessary renewal by the divine party, thus foreshadowing the need for a new covenant.[74]

This divine heart circumcision in Deuteronomy 30:6 will result in (ל) Israel's ability to love Yahweh with a whole heart. Significantly, everywhere else in the book of Deuteronomy the verb אהב ("to love") appears with Yahweh as its object, it is expressed as a commandment (Deut 6:5; 11:1), as an infinitive construct dependent on a command (10:12; 11:13, 22; 19:9; 30:16, 20), or as a participle similarly dependent on a command (13:4).[75] Only in Deuteronomy 30:6 is אהב an indicative and not an imperative. Here love is not a command, but a gift. The impediment to covenant love, which is the metaphorical foreskin of a disobedient heart, will be divinely cut away, revealing a new heart with new affections. But love is not the only result of heart circumcision: life (חיים) itself results. In Deuteronomy, life (חיים) is associated with "goodness" (30:15) and "blessing" (30:19). Significantly, Yahweh (30:20) and his word (32:47) are equated with life (חיים). Heart circumcision results in life because the circumcised heart can rightly receive Yahweh and his word.

### Covenant Curses Turned to Covenant Blessings

The benefits that flow from a divinely-wrought heart circumcision are manifold, and all the consequences of covenant disobedience are overturned:[76] the covenant curses will be visited on Israel's enemies instead of on them (Deut 30:7; cf. 28:45; 29:27); they will obey the voice of Yahweh and keep all his commandments (30:8; cf. 28:15, 45, 58; 29:24

---

73. Kline, *Treaty of the Great King*, 132.

74. So Dempster: "It is almost as if another covenant is needed, one in which the heart is transformed to conform to the demands of the law." Dempster, *Dominion and Dynasty*, 121.

75. This point is also noted by Barker, *The Triumph of Grace in Deuteronomy*, 162.

76. So also Braulik: "The curses of 28:62b-64a are changed into blessings in 30:3b-10a." Braulik, "The Destruction of the Nations and the Promise of Return," 59.

[ET 29:25]), and they will prosper abundantly in the land (30:9a; cf. 28:64–68; 29:27 [ET 29:28]).[77]

In Deuteronomy 30:9b–10, there are three clauses that begin with the particle כִּי. Below, this particle is closely examined, as it occurs twice in 30:11–14 and plays a significant role in the interpretation of that passage. I argue below that this chain of כִּי particles grounds the foregoing information in 30:1–9a. Where exactly the apodosis begins in 30:1–4 can affect how one interprets these כִּי particles. The best options are either causal or circumstantial, "for" or "when," as variably reflected in some translations (see table 5 below). I suggest "for," which would accord with the interpretation of the protasis/apodosis in 30:1a–7 above:[78]

> *For* Yahweh will return to rejoice over you for your good, as he rejoiced over your fathers, *for* you will hear/obey the voice of Yahweh your God, to keep his commandments and his statutes that are written in this book of the Law, *for* you will turn to Yahweh your God with all your heart and with all your soul. (Deut 30:9b–10)[79]

But how will it be different this time? How will Israel not fall back into their old patterns of sin? I believe this is the question Moses seems to answer in Deuteronomy 30:11–14. Obedience will not be too difficult because the words of the covenant come to be internalized. The virtue demanded by the word of Yahweh becomes the same virtue of the heart of Israel that finally motivates obedience. The words of the covenant will be returned to their heart (Deut 30:1) because of the internalization of the Word that accompanies circumcision of the heart (30:6, 14).

## Deuteronomy 30:11–14: Future Promise?

Barker summarizes the fundamental question in Deuteronomy 30:11–14 as follows:

> There is general agreement that vv11–14 deal with Israel's capacity to obey the covenant commands of Yahweh. However

---

77. See Wells, *Grace and Agency*, 33ff. for a discussion on the priority of divine agency in this passage.

78. This is in line with Lundbom, who argues, "The כִּי . . . כִּי construction [in v. 10] should be translated "for . . . for," "when . . . when," or "because . . . because," not "if . . . if," since the statement is wholly positive, not conditional." Lundbom, *Deuteronomy*, 821.

79. My translation.

the grounds of that capacity need clarification. One view is that Israel's capacity to obey derives from having received, learnt, and understood the torah which has been given to it. That is, the grounds are external to Israel, and involve both the easiness of the torah and its revelation. The second view is that Israel's capacity to obey rests on a change of heart which enables obedience. In this case, the grounds are internal to Israel.[80]

The interpretive majority understands Deuteronomy 30:11–14 to be speaking of a non-contingent, present motivation for obedience on the plains of Moab just before entering the land, and not a continuation of the future-oriented promise of 30:1–10. McConville is representative of this view when he argues that 30:11–14 "contains the most explicit statement in the whole book of *their ability* to obey [Yahweh's] commands."[81] Merrill's comments likewise summarize the view that 30:11–14 is a return to the Moab present:

> Having set forth the results of covenant disobedience (29:16–19) and the blessings of covenant reaffirmation even in the midst of judgment and exile (30:1–10), Moses return[s] to the reality of the present situation and plead[s] for Israel's obedience to the LORD.[82]

Interpreters give several reasons in support of a change in the temporal framework from future time in Deuteronomy 30:1–10 to present time in 30:11–14: the occurrence of the "urgent 'today'" (היום) in 30:11;[83] the switch from *weqatal* and imperfect verbal forms in 30:1–10 to verbless clause constructions in 30:11–14; and a supposed shift in perspective

---

80. Barker, *The Triumph of Grace in Deuteronomy*, 187.

81. McConville goes on to note, however, that Deut 30:11–14 must "be read in light of both 9:4–6 (which 30:11–14 formally contradict) and of 30:1–10." McConville, *Grace in the End*, 137–38. In the view articulated below, it is not necessary to admit a formal contradiction between 30:11–14 and 9:4–6.

82. Merrill, *Deuteronomy*, 390. So also Craigie, *The Book of Deuteronomy*, 364; Driver, *A Critical and Exegetical Commentary on Deuteronomy*, 330–31; Currid, *A Study Commentary on Deuteronomy*, 470; Von Rad, *Deuteronomy*, 184; Brueggemann, *Deuteronomy*, 268; Labuschagne, *Deuteronomium*, 155.

83. McConville writes, "The relationship between 30:6 and 30:11–14 is not a simple one. The former is part of Deuteronomy's glimpse into the future (from the standpoint of those who are assembled on the plains of Moab), its vision of a new hope for Israel on the other side of the failures of its history from settlement to exile. But vv. 11–14 come back to the Mosaic present, with the typical urgent 'today' (v. 11; the point is obscured by the NIV translation), repeated in vv. 15–16." McConville, *Grace in the End*, 137. So also Von Rad, *Old Testament Theology*, 231.

of Israel's ability to obey from 30:1–10 to 30:11–14.[84] S. R. Driver goes so far as to categorically reject any connection between 30:1–10 and 30:11–14 and suggests this material originally did not belong together and was instead (erroneously?) juxtaposed by a later redactor. According to Driver,

> The paragraph [30:11–14] is loosely connected with v. 1–10. V. 11–14 ("For" . . .) clearly states the reason for a *present* duty; in view of the contents of the four verses, it is exceedingly unnatural to suppose that they explain why Israel should find it easy to return to Jehovah in the future contingency contemplated in v. 10. It is next to impossible, therefore, that v. 11–20 can have been originally the sequel of v. 1–10.[85]

Driver's historical-critical suggestions have been immensely influential in the literature, even infiltrating evangelical commentaries as a foregone conclusion.[86] But instead of disjunction, I think Deuteronomy 30:11–14 makes better sense coordinated with and even subordinated to 30:1–10. This view is summed up by Barker: "It is our contention that both structurally and theologically, vv11–14 are dependent on, and must be read in light of, vv1–10."[87] In the sections that follow, I argue that

84. According to McConville, "The perspective of Moses' speech appears to revert to 'present time', in Moab, an impression supported by the continuation in vv. 15–20, which is clearly addressed to the people who are about to go into the land for the first time." McConville, *Deuteronomy*, 429. So also Nelson: "Moses abruptly stops portraying the future and returns to the present 'Moab moment.'" Nelson, *Deuteronomy*, 349.

85. Driver, *A Critical and Exegetical Commentary on Deuteronomy*, 330–31.

86. Moo rejects a future reading of Deut 30:11–14 based on Driver's exegesis. "One possibility would be to find in Deut. 30:11–14 a continuation of the prophecy in Deut. 30:1–10 about God's restoration of Israel after the Exile. . . . While an attractive alternative, this way of explaining Paul's use of Deut. 30:12–14 cannot be accepted: at v. 11 in this chapter, there is a clear transition from the prophecy of future restoration in vv. 1–10 to the situation of Israel as she prepares to enter the promised land." For support of this interpretation, Moo turns to Driver's commentary: "Deuteronomy 30:11–14 returns to the theme of 29:29, as Moses lays the basis for his appeal to the Israelites to obey the law that God gave the people (vv. 11–15). The future time orientation of vv. 1–10, with its *waw* + perfect verbs, is dropped in v. 11. See S. R. Driver." Moo, *Romans*, 652. Citing Moo, Schreiner rejects a future reading of 30:11–14 but holds out the possibility of a future interpretation in the narrative flow of Deuteronomy: "Moo is correct that strictly speaking the text is not a future prophecy. Yet its placement in the narrative of Deuteronomy and Paul's understanding of salvation history led him to see it as fulfilled in his day." Schreiner, *Romans*, 558n17.

87. Barker, *The Triumph of Grace in Deuteronomy*, 183. Coxhead likewise argues, "[T]he first reason supporting the reading of Deut 30:11–14 in the future tense relates

30:11–14 is best interpreted as a continuation of 30:1–10 for the following reasons, which are in addition to and reinforce the chiasm identified in 30:1–14: (1) the כי that heads 30:11 continues the chain of subordinating כי clauses that begins in 30:9b–10 and concludes in 30:14; (2) the verbless clauses in 30:11–14 are atemporal and thus must gain tense from the context; and (3) the narrative flow nudges the reader to a future-oriented interpretation of 30:11–14.

## Subordinating כי Chain in Deuteronomy 30:11–14

Deuteronomy 30:11 is headed by the particle כי, which also appears once in 30:9, twice in 30:10, and once more in 30:14. Understanding the function of כי in this passage is crucial to understanding the literary flow of 30:1–14. Some who posit a disjunction between 30:1–10 and 30:11–14 stress an emphatic sense of כי in 30:11,[88] while the few interpreters who posit conjunction stress a subordinate/conjunctive sense.[89]

The particle כי is commonly regarded as one of the most versatile words in the Hebrew language.[90] Occurring just under 4,500[91] times in the Hebrew Bible, it is second only to *waw* in frequency.[92] Depending on how one translates this particle, a passage's meaning can vary widely. Commenting on the state of Bible translations today, Harry Orlinsky and Robert Bratcher point to כי as a central challenge for modern interpreters seeking to understand the original meaning of the biblical text:

---

to the כי in v. 11 that subordinates the thought of vv. 11–14 to v. 10. The כי in v. 11 ties vv. 11–14 in with vv. 1–10." Coxhead, "Deuteronomy 30:11–14," 308.

88. Cf. NIV "Now . . ."; NRSV "Surely . . ." So Lundbom, "The verses [vv. 11 and 14] are tied together by an inclusion containing an asseverative כִּי ("Indeed")." Lundbom, *Deuteronomy*, 821.

89. As Barker argues, "In light of the other arguments for the association of vv. 11–14 with the preceding, it seems fair to treat the particle as causal or evidential, that is, giving further reason for the expected blessing and restoration expressed in v9a." Barker, *The Triumph of Grace in Deuteronomy*, 186. Cf. Braulik, *Deuteronomium II*, 216–17.

90. Gross, Irsigler, and Seidl, *Text, Methode Und Grammatik*, 97. According to Muilenberg, of all the words appearing in the Old Testament, כי has "the widest and most varied range of nuance and meaning." Muilenburg, "The Linguistic and Rhetorical Usages of the Particle Ky in the Old Testament," 136.

91. According to the *DCH*, כי occurs 4,488 times in the Hebrew Bible. Clines, *The Dictionary of Classical Hebrew*, 383.

92. Follingstad, "Deictic Viewpoint in Biblical Hebrew Text," 2.

In the wide range of meaning and nuances commanded by it, the common conjunction כי is probably next to ו in hardly having been exploited in the traditional translations and not yet fully enough in the modern ones. . . . [F]uture revisions of the modern versions that may come into being will have to do greater justice to the various nuances of כי; it will not do to "play it safe" by relying on "for" or "because" or the like.[93]

I contend that the way כי is deployed in Deuteronomy 30:1–14 suggests that 30:11–14 is coordinated with the future time prophecy in 30:1–10, which would make greater sense of the narrative arc of the book of Deuteronomy.

| | v. 9 | v. 10a | v. 10b | v. 11 | v. 14 |
|---|---|---|---|---|---|
| LXX | ὅτι | ἐάν | ἐάν | ὅτι | -- |
| Vulgate | *enim* | *si tamen* | *et* | -- | *sed* |
| KJV | for | if | and if | For | but |
| RSV | for | if | if | For | but |
| NRSV | For | when | because | Surely | No |
| ESV | For | when | when | For | but |
| NASB | for | if | if | For | but |
| NIV 84 | -- | if | -- | Now | but |

**Table 5. Translation landscape of the כי chain in Deuteronomy 30:9–14**

The current translation landscape of the כי in Deuteronomy 30:1–14 seems to be largely influenced by the LXX. Table 5 above shows how the five occurrences of כי in Deuteronomy 30:1–14 are interpreted in various translations. As table 5 makes clear, the LXX translates the first כי in Deuteronomy 30:9 with the conjunction ὅτι, and the other translations follow

93. Orlinsky and Bratcher, *A History of Bible Translation and the North American Contribution*, 295–97. Though Orlinsky and Bratcher are advocates for the dynamic equivalency translation theory, to which I am philosophically and theologically opposed, their point about the particle כי stands for those who want to understand the original intentions of the biblical authors.

semantical suit: the Latin Vulgate uses *enim*, glossed "for" or "therefore," and all English translations use "for" (except the NIV, which omits it).

The LXX renders both instances of כי in 30:10 with the conditional/temporal conjunction ἐάν, and for the most part the Vulgate and English translations follow suit—the exception being the NRSV, which translates the second כי with the causal subordinating conjunction "because." The LXX translates כי in 30:11 as it did in 30:9 with ὅτι, and again the English translations follow suit, except for the NIV, which translates it with the emphatic adverb "Now," and the NRSV, which translates it with the emphatic adverb "Surely." Important to note here is the fact that the LXX does not use an emphatic or disjunctive such as δέ in 30:11, but by using ὅτι the LXX leaves open the possibility of coordinate subordination. The Vulgate omits translating כי in 30:11. The final כי in 30:14 is not translated by the LXX, but the Vulgate and the English translations opt for semantic equivalents, the adversative conjunction "but." In order to decide between these interpretive possibilities, it is necessary to drill down on the core function of כי.

*Core Function of* כי

In his thorough work on the particle כי, Carl M. Follingstad looks at the numerous ways interpreters have understood כי to function in the Hebrew language. It has been variously classified as some form of conjunction, adverb, emphatic particle, or an assorted combination.[94] Depending on what is understood to be the core function of the particle, interpreters have assigned כי a variety of meanings. *DCH* summarizes the function of כי as fundamentally a conjunction, glossed "for," with fifteen possible meanings.[95] *HALOT* is in agreement with *DCH* as to each of these fifteen

---

94. Follingstad writes, "Throughout its history of grammatical interpretation, כי has been classified as a member of various word classes." Follingstad, "Deictic Viewpoint in Biblical Hebrew Text," 22. Follingstad's survey of the diachronic development of כי as well as the various classifications and meanings that have been assigned to כי is illuminating, as it highlights just how much in flux the function of this particle is even today. Follingstad, 15–63.

95. Clines, *The Dictionary of Classical Hebrew*, 4:383–91. "The Dictionary of Classical Hebrew is a completely new and innovative dictionary. Unlike previous dictionaries, which have been dictionaries of biblical Hebrew, it is the first dictionary of the classical Hebrew language to cover not only the biblical texts but also Ben Sira, the Dead Sea Scrolls and the Hebrew inscriptions. This Dictionary covers the period from the earliest times to 200 CE. It lists and analyses every occurrence of each

possible meanings for כי, but differs in understanding its fundamental function to be a demonstrative particle and secondarily a conjunction.[96]

The translators of the LXX generally reflect the possible meanings for כי given in *DCH* and *HALOT*. While frequently left untranslated (49 percent!), the clear preference for כי in the LXX is the Greek conjunction ὅτι (31 percent), followed by a not-so-close second, ἐάν (4 percent).[97]

| כי, 4488 | untranslated (2206, 49%), ὅτι (1413, 31%), ἐάν (192, 4%), δέ (107, 2%), ἀλλά (102, 2%), γάρ (100, 2%), ἤ (61, 1%), καί (60, 1%) |
|---|---|

**Figure 6. Translation distribution of כי in the LXX**

More recently, scholars in search for the core function of כי have suggested an emphatic-deictic classification of this particle. A. Schoors, T. Muraoka, and C. Follingstad all argue that an emphatic-deictic classification of כי points to a macro-syntactical function, as opposed to the logical, connective function of past understandings of כי.[98] But other scholars are not convinced. While conceding that כי may have originated from a non-connective or demonstrative particle, Anneli Aejmelaeus argues that "[a] brief survey of the use of כי in the OT suffices to make it clear that, in the stage of development of the Hebrew language represented in the OT text, כי mainly serves as a connective, a conjunction to join clauses to one another."[99] Aejmelaeus goes on to assert,

> The solution of the translators in the case of apparently superfluous particles is usually to omit them; also in cases where כי is claimed to be emphatic it is often not rendered at all. I regard

---

Hebrew word that occurs in texts of that period, with an English translation of every Hebrew word and phrase cited. Among its special features are: a list of the non-biblical texts cited (especially the Dead Sea Scrolls)." https://www.logos.com/product/29300/the-dictionary-of-classical-hebrew-dch. According to Follingstad, "The *Dictionary of Classical Hebrew* has the most complete entry on כי to date." Follingstad, "Deictic Viewpoint in Biblical Hebrew Text," 37.

96. Köhler et al., *The Hebrew and Aramaic Lexicon of the Old Testament*, 470–71.

97. Analysis completed using Tov and Polak, *The Parallel Aligned Text of the Greek and Hebrew Bible*.

98. Schoors, "The Particle Ki"; Muraoka, *Emphatic Words and Structures in Biblical Hebrew*, 159–64; Follingstad, "Deictic Viewpoint in Biblical Hebrew Text." Follingstad argues כי is a "discourse deictic" that switches the viewpoint of a passage with epistemic modal side effects.

99. Aejmelaeus, "Function and Interpretation of כי in Biblical Hebrew," 195.

it as more appropriate—at least the lesser evil of the two—to remain with the causal interpretation of כי, that is, causal in the broadest sense of the word—even where the logical connection is imperceptible—and to regard כי as a connective rather than an emphatic or assertive particle.[100]

In his dissertation on the particle כי, Barry Bandstra examines every occurrence of כי in the Pentateuch and the Psalms and, in the end, rejects this trend toward understanding כי as a fundamentally emphatic, demonstrative, or deictic particle. Bandstra argues that these approaches fall prey to the etymological fallacy in an attempt to explain כי in relationship to its origin in the language. Instead, Bandstra begins his investigation with an agnostic position with respect to the etymology of כי and analyzes the actual uses in the text.[101] He contends that interpreters who understand כי to function mainly as an emphatic or deictic particle do not take it seriously enough, often eliding it in their translations, as Aejmelaeus corroborates above. Bandstra's conclusion, which is immanently pertinent for Deuteronomy 30:11–14, is that כי is a "syntactic relator particle in all of its semantic functions. Its primary function is to relate two clauses together in a dependency relation to form a sentence."[102]

Bandstra proposes two rules for determining the nature of the semantic relationship between the כי clause and the rest of the sentence: "(1) if the order of clauses is main clause followed by כי clause then the semantic relationship is one of complementation, consequence, adversion or causation," and (2) "if the order of clauses is כי clause followed by main clause then the semantic relationship is one of temporal circumstance, condition or concession."[103]

Significantly for the present study, Bandstra categorizes both כי clauses in Deuteronomy 30:11–14 as following their main clauses. Therefore, according to Bandstra's classification system, both כי clauses in 30:11 and 14 would have to be one of four types of clause: complementation, consequence, adversion, or causation. In verse 11, Bandstra specifically labels the כי clause a "cause grounds" clause and offers the gloss "for," which would support the argument that 30:11–14 should be read as a

---

100. Aejmelaeus, "Function and Interpretation of כי in Biblical Hebrew," 205.

101. Bandstra, "The Syntax of Particle 'Ky' in Biblical Hebrew and Ugaritic," 8.

102. Bandstra, "The Syntax of Particle 'Ky' in Biblical Hebrew and Ugaritic," 407.

103. Bandstra, "The Syntax of Particle 'Ky' in Biblical Hebrew and Ugaritic," 408.

continuation of 30:1–10.[104] Even if Bandstra's specific labels are not adopted and only his classification system is received, the results of his study point toward the view that 30:11 is logically subordinate to 30:1–10 and does not begin a new section, as is almost universally assumed by interpreters. In 30:14, Bandstra labels the כי clause an "adversative" clause and offers the gloss "but."[105] As Bandstra points out, however, this is conceptually close to and derivative of causal כי. "The semantic development from cause to adversion is fairly straight-forward: x is not the cause <u>because</u> y is the case, because not x <u>but</u> y. The two meanings are so close at times that they are difficult to distinguish."[106] Whether the כי in 30:14 is adversion or another "cause grounds" clause as in 30:11 makes no difference in the following interpretation.

Initially, then, the introductory כי in Deuteronomy 30:11 would point toward understanding this passage to be logically subordinate to Deuteronomy 30:1–10, which would link the כי clauses in 30:11–14 with the כי clauses in 30:9b–10. Telford Work sees connective significance in the כי of 30:11–14 when he writes, "the conjunction *ki* (for) suggests a connection with the preceding verses and their eschatological scenario."[107] Braulik likewise argues that the כי in 30:11 continues and further grounds 30:10:

> Das dreifache satzeinleitende כִּי in 30:10f, das die EÜ zweimal mit »wenn« übersetzt (10), einmal nicht weiter berücksichtigt (11), wird wohl besser mit »denn« wiedergegeben. Dann stehen am Ende mehrere parallele Begründungssätze, die immer wieder das gleiche Urdatum von verschiedenen Seiten her ins Auge fassen, aber keine Bedingungen.[108]

What is apparent in Deuteronomy 30:9–14 is a כי cluster, or "כי chain," that serves to ground the prophetic vision in 30:1ff.[109] The implica-

---

104. Bandstra, "The Syntax of Particle 'Ky' in Biblical Hebrew and Ugaritic," 286.

105. Bandstra, "The Syntax of Particle 'Ky' in Biblical Hebrew and Ugaritic," 286.

106. Bandstra, "The Syntax of Particle 'Ky' in Biblical Hebrew and Ugaritic," 150. Even those who argue against the fundamental causal function of כי admit this close relationship, e.g., Schoors, "The Particle Ki," 252.

107. Work, *Deuteronomy*, 269.

108. Braulik, *Deuteronomium II*, 216–17.

109. Barker likewise recognizes the significance of this כי chain, what he refers to as "a sequence of כִּי clauses in vv9–11. . . . Yahweh will make Israel prosperous (v9a) for (כִּי evidential, v9b) he will restore Israel's fortunes when (כִּי temporal, v10a) Israel obeys and when (כִּי evidential, causal, v11) the word is in Israel's heart." Barker, *The Triumph of Grace in Deuteronomy*, 185–86.

tions of this conclusion are revisited below after examining other textual features that point toward the view that 30:11–14 is a continuation of 30:1–10.

## Verbless Clauses in Deuteronomy 30:11–14

The five main clauses in Deuteronomy 30:11–14 are verbless clauses.[110] It should not be surprising to see כי paired with verbless clauses in 30:11–14; as Revell writes, "The vast majority of the verbless clauses are coordinate (introduced by the conjunction *waw*), or כי clauses (introduced by the particle כי)."[111]

In an analysis of the use and function of the verbless clause in biblical Hebrew, Cynthia Miller defines a verbless clause as "represent(ing) a predication by means of the collocation of nominal elements apart from a fully inflected verbal form."[112] As such, verbless clauses are atemporal, which means their temporal framework is determined by the surrounding context. The exact syntactical function of the verbless clause in biblical Hebrew is contested, but Ellen van Wolde attempts a summary description: "Their function is . . . a positive one, namely the presentation of *background* information in which a situation, circumstance, or event is depicted that occurs simultaneously with the sequence of actions expressed in the *preceding foreground clause*."[113] If van Wolde is correct, the verbless clauses in Deuteronomy 30:11–14 provide *background* information to the *preceding* context.

The five main clauses in Deuteronomy 30:11–14 are verbless clauses composed of two of the following nominal elements: pronouns, nouns, substantival participles, substantival adjectives, or prepositional phrases. The pronoun הוא appears in four of the five verbless clauses, and while the

---

110. It should be noted that the term "verbless clause" is a debated one. As Miller points out, "Among Hebraists and linguists, there is little agreement about what to call predications lacking a finite verb. Some Hebraists prefer *nominal clause*, others *verbless clause*. Some linguists use the term *small clause*; others reject the category entirely." Miller, "Pivotal Issues in Analyzing the Verbless Clause," 6. I will not use the term "nominal clause" due to its potential confusion with the term "nominal sentence."

111. Revell, "Thematic Continuity and the Conditioning of Word Order in Verbless Clauses," 297.

112. Miller, "Pivotal Issues in Analyzing the Verbless Clause," 3.

113. Van Wolde, "The Verbless Clause and Its Textual Function," 330. Emphasis added.

relationship between המצוה הזאת (Deut 30:11a), הוא (30:11b, c, 12, 13), and הדבר (30:14) is not immediately clear, the Masoretic vowel pointing on הוא is worthy of comment. It is pointed as a 3fs pronoun, but the Hebrew consonants could just as well be a 3ms pronoun. If it is indeed a 3fs pronoun, as the Masoretic vowel points indicate, the natural antecedent is the feminine noun "this command" (המצוה הזאת) in verse 11, which is probably the reason the Masoretes added feminine vowel points to match the 3fs participle in 30:11.[114] But without the Masoretic vowel points, it could be construed as a 3ms pronoun, which might point forward to the הדבר of verse 14 or stand in as a summary pronoun for a larger idea. Most likely it is a 3fs pronoun referring to the command.

"This command," as represented by the pronoun הוא, has four predicate attributes expressed negatively in Deuteronomy 30:11–13, the first two metaphorical-qualitative and final two metaphorical-spatial: (1) לא־נפלאת ממך, (2) לא רחקה (3), לא בשמים, and (4) לא־מעבר לים. After these four negative predicates in 30:11–13, the subject switches in 30:14 to הדבר, which is attributed two positive predicates.

| Predicate | Subject | Clause Structure | |
|-----------|---------|------------------|---|
| לא־נפלאת ממך | הוא | Pronoun-[היה]-participle | v. 11b |
| לא רחקה | הוא | Pronoun-[היה]-adjective | v. 11c |
| לא בשמים | הוא | Pronoun-[היה]-prepositional phrase | v. 12 |
| לא־מעבר לים | הוא | Pronoun-[היה]-prepositional phrase | v. 13 |
| קרוב אליך מאד | הדבר | Noun-[היה]-adjective | v. 14 |

**Table 6. Verbless clause constructions in Deuteronomy 30:11–14**

114. For an in-depth look at this phenomenon known as *qre perpetuum*, see Rendsburg, "A New Look at Pentateuchal HW'," 351–69. According to BDB, "In the Pent., הוא is of common gender, the fem. form היא occurring only 11 times, viz. Gn 14:2; 20:5; 38:25 (v. Mass here), Lv 11:39; 13:10, 21; 16:31; 20:17; 21:9 Nu 5:13, 14. The punctuators, however, sought to assimilate the usage of the Pent. to that of the rest of the OT, and accordingly wherever הוא was construed as a fem. pointed it הִוא." BDB, s.v. "הוא."

*"Not too difficult; not out of reach."*

The first verbless clause in Deuteronomy 30:11a has the third singular pronoun הוא as its subject and the negative adverb לא plus a 3fs *Niphal* participle from the root פלא as its predicate (לֹא־נִפְלֵאת). In the *Niphal* stem, פלא can mean "too difficult to comprehend or do," "beyond one's power," or "exceedingly wonderful."[115] In a verbless clause construction, a participle has no inherent tense; it can be used to refer to past, present, or future time.[116] Thus, the interpreter must supply some form of copulative verb in translation. This verb פלא is used nearby in the *Hiphil* in 28:59, where Moses describes the plagues that Yahweh will pour out on Israel in response to their covenant disobedience: "Yahweh will make extraordinary/difficult/unbearable (הפלא) your plagues and the plagues of your seed."[117] In contrast to the plagues, this command is described as not too difficult or unbearable.

The second verbless clause in Deuteronomy 30:11b has the same pronoun הוא for its subject and לא plus a feminine singular noun as its predicate. "This command" is described as not "far beyond" or "distant" (לא רחקה).[118] That is, the command is portrayed as within reach, most probably referring to a figurative distance, not a physical one (cf. Ps 119:155; Isa 46:12).[119]

*"Not in heaven; not across the sea."*

The third and fourth verbless clauses in Deuteronomy 30:12 and 13 share an identical construction, both having the same pronoun הוא for their subject and prepositional phrases for predicates, בשמים and עברם לים, respectively. Once again, these constructions are inherently timeless, and some form of copulative verb must be supplied.

---

115. BDB, s.v. "פלא."

116. Driver writes about the possibility of a future meaning for participles: "The ptcp. is used, lastly, of future time, which it represents as already beginning: hence, if the event designated can only in fact occur after some interval, it asserts forcibly and suggestively the certainty of its approach. In the latter case, however, its use is pretty much restricted to announcements of the Divine purpose." Driver, *A Treatise on the Use of the Tenses in Hebrew and Some Other Syntactical Questions*, 168.

117. My translation.

118. BDB, s.v. "רָחַק."

119. So BDB, s.v. "רָחַק."

| | | | | |
|---|---|---|---|---|
| ויקחה לנו וישמענו אתה ונעשנה | מי יעלה־לנו השמימה | לאמר | לא בשמים הוא | v. 12 |
| ויקחה לנו וישמענו אתה ונעשנה | מי יעבר־לנו אל־עבר הים | לאמר | לא־מעבר לים הוא | v. 13 |

In these two parallel constructions, the command is depicted in a place of accessibility, not in heaven or across the sea that it must be said, "Who will go up for us to heaven (Deut 30:12a), who will cross for us to the other side of the sea (30:13a), and take it for us and cause us to hear it and do it? (30:12b, 13b)."[120] The vocabulary similarities between Deuteronomy 30:11–14 and 30:1–10 are noteworthy. In 30:2, 9, and 10, שמע appears in *Qal* imperfect form "hear/obey." Additionally, 30:8, עשה appears together with שמע as a collocation, a pattern repeated here in 30:12 and 13. But in 30:12 and 13, שמע appears as a *Hiphil* imperfect, denoting a causative function, "cause to hear." How will Israel "hear/obey" as foretold in 30:2, 9, and 10? They will be caused to "hear/obey" by Yahweh. Barker further elaborates,

> Obedience is obviously a central issue to both sections. Verses 11–14 extrapolate on vv1–10 showing how the obedience expected in v8 may happen. The hiphils of שָׁמַע reflect this. We are told that Israel will hear (שָׁמַע *Qal*, vv2, 8 and 10). This is now shown to be because Yahweh will make Israel hear (שָׁמַע hiphil, vv12, 13). This is not by a messenger going and getting the commandment and making Israel hear. That is denied by vv12, 13. Rather, Yahweh himself makes Israel hear by putting the word in its heart and mouth (v14).[121]

John Sailhamer argues that this description of "the command" in Deuteronomy 30:11–14 is set over against Deuteronomy's description of the Sinai covenant.[122] At Sinai, God spoke to Israel "from heaven" (Deut

120. My translation.

121. Barker, *The Triumph of Grace in Deuteronomy*, 184.

122. Sailhamer writes, "In explaining the nature of the new covenant which he envisions in these chapters, Moses compares it to the covenant at Sinai (Dt 30:11–14). In the covenant given at Sinai, the Law was written on tablets of stone which Moses had to go up the mountain to receive and then take back to proclaim to the people. Thus when he says in the present chapter: 'This commandment . . . is not up in heaven, so that you have to ask, "Who will ascend into heaven to get it and proclaim it to us so we may obey it?"' he means that in the new covenant the Law would not be given again on tablets of stone but written on circumcised hearts (as in Eze 36:26). . . . Furthermore, his reference to 'going across the sea to get [the commandment]' (30:13) also appears, in the larger context of the Pentateuch, to be an allusion to Moses' leading the people

4:36) out of a fire that burnt "to the heart of heaven" (4:11). The people were afraid, so they told Moses to "go near and hear all the LORD our God will say, and speak to us all that the LORD our God will speak to you, and we will hear and do it" (5:27). In contrast, "this command" is described as not being in heaven, in need of someone to retrieve it. Likewise, the command is described as not being across the sea, in need of someone to "cross over" to retrieve it. "Crossing the sea" is associated with the crossing of the Red Sea at the Exodus elsewhere in the OT (cf. Neh 9:11; Ps 78:13; Zech 10:11; Isa 43:2; 51:10; Josh 4:23). Thus "this command" is contrasted with the commands associated with Sinai. Instead of being too difficult, out of reach, in heaven, or across the sea, "this command" is portrayed as accessible. In drawing this parallel, Israel is invited to ask who the corollary is to Moses in this arrangement, an invitation already made explicit in Deuteronomy 18:15–20. Who is the prophet like Moses who will mediate this (new?) covenant? Discerning the identity of the coming prophet seems to be a concern that is reflected in *Targum Neofiti* on Deuteronomy 30:11–14:

> For this precept which I command you this day is not hidden from you, neither is it far away. The law is not in the heavens, that one should say: "Would that we had one *like Moses the prophet* who would go up to heaven and fetch it for us, and make us hear the commandments that we might do them!" Nor is the Law beyond the Great Sea, that one should say: "Would that we had one *like Jonah the prophet* who would descend into the depths of the Great Sea and bring it up for us, and make us hear the commandments that we might do them!" For the word is very near to you, in the word of your mouths and in your hearts, that you may do it.[123]

The tension between Barker's understanding of the divine passives in Deuteronomy 30:12–14 to be pointing to Yahweh and Sailhamer's understanding of the search in 30:12–14 to hint at the coming of a prophet like Moses in the new covenant may find a satisfying resolution in Paul's application of this text to Christ in Romans 10:5–8.

---

across the Red Sea and to Sinai. Thus in contrast to the giving of the Law in the Sinai covenant, in the covenant of which Moses speaks here, 'the word is very near you; it is in your mouth and in your heart to do it' (v. 14)." Sailhamer, *The Pentateuch as Narrative*, 473–74.

123. McNamara, *Targum Neofiti 1: Deuteronomy*, 141. Emphasis added.

## *"In your mouth and in your heart."*

The fifth and final verbless clause in Deuteronomy 30:14 has the definite masculine noun הדבר for a subject and the masculine adjective קרוב as a predicate. No longer is the singular pronoun הוא used in reference to "this command," instead the דבר takes its place as actor. "This command" transforms into a word, which is described as so near as to be "in your mouth and in your heart" (בפיך ובלבבך).

J. Ridderbos argues that the nearness in Deuteronomy 30:14 does not describe a physical nearness: "It is very near you, not because it has been written down for you, but because it is 'in your mouth and in your heart.'"[124] But he goes on to say that the expression "in your mouth and in your heart" refers to the memory, akin to our expression "you know it by heart." Ridderbos writes, "Moses apparently thinks of a future situation where the people will have been instructed in the law to the extent that they can recite its main contents from memory."[125] But I find this unconvincing. In Deuteronomy 6:6, Israel is commanded to put these commandments "on the heart" (על-לבב). This surely refers in part to memorization of and meditation on the *torah*, but this action is not an end unto itself but is a means toward Israel's conformity with and obedience to the word of Yahweh (cf. Deut 6:12–15). Just as Israel is commanded to circumcise their hearts in Deuteronomy 10:16 and Yahweh subsequently promises to accomplish this very feat for them in 30:6, so also does Yahweh promise to grant in 30:14 what he commands in 6:6.[126] As Coxhead argues,

> The concept of *God's law in the heart* appears only a few times in the OT, but it is a highly significant expression used in describing a person who is covenantally righteous. The righteous person is distinguished from the wicked person by having "the law of his God . . . in his heart" (Ps 37:31; Isa 51:7).
>
> Also relevant at this point is the idea of the new covenant in Jer 31:33, where the new covenant is defined in terms of God writing the law on the hearts of the people of Israel, which would cause eschatological Israel not to break the covenant with

124. Ridderbos, *Deuteronomy*, 271.

125. Ridderbos, *Deuteronomy*, 271.

126. Contra Barker, who attempts to distinguish between something being "on" the heart, referring to something memorized and thus still "external," and something "in" (ב) the heart, referring to something fully internalized so that it becomes motivation for obedience. Barker, *The Triumph of Grace in Deuteronomy*, 189.

God again (Jer 31:32). Thus, *God's law in the heart* is in effect an
idiom for *obedience* (see Ps 40:8). The thinking underlying the
idiom seems to be that God's law, which comes from outside
through external revelation, needs to be internalized within the
heart, and as it becomes internalized in the heart—given that
all actions naturally proceed from the heart (Matt 15:19)—the
person with God's law in the heart acts in obedience to God.[127]

In the next chapter, I will take up these other places in the OT where
"God's law in the heart" seems to be present.

In Deuteronomy 30:14, this nearness of the word results in, or occurs for the purpose of, the ability "to do it" (לעשתו). What causes Israel
to hear and do this command? The word (דבר). "These words" which
Yahweh commands Israel to "return" to their hearts in 4:39 (הֲשֵׁבֹתָ, *Hiphil*) and "these words" which Yahweh promises will return to their heart
in 30:1 (הֲשֵׁבֹתָ, *Hiphil*) are surely related to the "word" which in 30:14 is
described as "in" the heart "to do it."[128]

### Future Prophecy?

In any translation of Deuteronomy 30:11–14, a copulative verb must be
supplied in the atemporal verbless clauses, and the tense of these clauses
could be construed in past, present, or future time. No interpreter argues
for a past tense timeframe in 30:11–14, but both present and future tense
timeframes are grammatically possible, as shown in figure 7.

---

Translating the verbless clauses in Deut 30:11–14 in a present timeframe

---

For this commandment, which I command to you today, *is* not too difficult for
you and it *is* not far off. It *is* not in heaven saying, "Who will go up for us to
heaven and retrieve it for us and cause us to hear it so we will do it?" And it *is*
not across the sea saying, "Who will cross for us to the other side of the sea and
retrieve it for us and cause us to hear it so we will do it?" For the word *is* exceedingly near you, in your mouth and in your heart to do it."

---

127. Coxhead, "Deuteronomy 30:11–14," 309. Emphasis original.

128. Cf. Barker: "The words, then, are not fundamentally a demand for obedience
of the law. כָּל־הַדְּבָרִים הָאֵלֶּה prompt repentance and are Yahweh's means of effecting a
reconciled relationship with his people. In a sense they are a call to rely on Yahweh's
enabling grace. They are an invitation to and promise of conversion." Barker, *The
Triumph of Grace in Deuteronomy*, 151. See also Lohfink, "Der Neue Bund Im Buch
Deuteronomium?," 121. Contra Otto, *Deuteronomium*, 4:2071–73.

Translating the verbless clauses in Deut 30:11–14 in a future timeframe

For this commandment, which I command to you today, *will not be* too difficult for you and it *will not be* far off. It *will not be* in heaven saying, "Who will go up for us to heaven and retrieve it for us and cause us to hear it so we will do it?" And it *will not be* across the sea saying, "Who will cross for us to the other side of the sea and retrieve it for us and cause us to hear it so we will do it?" For the word *will be* exceedingly near you, in your mouth and in your heart to do it."

**Figure 7. Present or future? Translating the verbless
clauses in Deuteronomy 30:11–14**

Gentry goes to the heart of the interpretive dilemma in Deuteronomy 30:11–14 when he writes, "A major part of correctly grasping the tension in the plot structure is interpreting the time of Deuteronomy 30:11–14. Is it present or future? . . . Both positions are anchored in the data of the text. How do we decide?" After considering both options, Gentry appeals to the surrounding context and states, "According to Deuteronomy 30:1–10, Israel will obtain a circumcised heart at a future time, and that is why 30:11–14 refers to the future and not to the present."[129] Gentry goes on to write that Moses believes this future may be "today, i.e., his present, hence the force of his appeal for the present."[130] Nonetheless, as I argue below, the presence of "today" (היום) in 30:11 does not necessarily require a present force for Moses' appeal. In fact, it may actually serve as another link between 30:11–14 and 30:1–10.

## FUTURE-ORIENTED VERBLESS CLAUSES IN DEUTERONOMY

Interpreting the verbless clauses in Deuteronomy 30:11–14 to refer to the future would not be unprecedented, even in the book of Deuteronomy. There are a handful of cases in Deuteronomy where a verbless

---

129. Cf. Barker, who seems to hold on to present tense constructions while at the same time arguing for a future sense of Deut 30:11–14. "[V]v11–14 may be understood proleptically as being addressed to those who have experienced the circumcision of the heart by Yahweh." Barker, *The Triumph of Grace in Deuteronomy*, 185. Braulik argues that "this command" is something that will be commanded in the future. Braulik, *Deuteronomium II*, 218–19. While a few interpreters argue for a future emphasis and even fulfillment of 30:11–14 as it relates to 30:1–10, to my knowledge Coxhead and Wells are the only interpreters who explicitly suggest a future *translation* of 30:11–14. Coxhead, "Deuteronomy 30:11–14"; Wells, *Grace and Agency*, 37.

130. Gentry, "The Relationship of Deuteronomy to the Covenant at Sinai," 52.

clause headed by the particle כי can be translated with the future tense. In Deuteronomy 4:6, the verbless clause כי הוא חכמתכם ובינתכם לעיני העמים follows two grammatically imperfect *weqatal* verbs. The ESV renders this verbless clause in the future tense, "for that *will be* your wisdom and your understanding in the sight of the peoples."[131] In Deuteronomy 7:16, the verbless clause כי־מוקש הוא לך follows two grammatically imperfect imperatives. The NIV translates this phrase in the future tense, "for that *will be* a snare to you," while the ESV and NASB translate it as a subjunctive, "for that would be a snare to you." In Deuteronomy 8:7, the verbless clause כי יהוה אלהיך מביאך אל־ארץ טובה follows a grammatically imperfect imperative. While all translations opt for a present, imperfective tense, Yahweh's action of "bringing" Israel to a good land has yet to be completed and anticipates a future fulfillment. In Deuteronomy 9:5, the verbless clause כי ברשעת הגוים האלה יהוה אלהיך מורישם מפניך follows another verbless clause. The NIV translates this phrase in the future tense, "but on account of the wickedness of these nations, the LORD your God *will* drive them out before you." In Deuteronomy 20:1, the verbless clause כי־יהוה אלהיך עמך המעלך מארץ מצרים follows an imperfect verb. The NIV translates this phrase in the future tense, "because the LORD your God, who brought you up out of Egypt, *will be* with you."

## MEDIEVAL TESTIMONY

In his commentary on the Pentateuch published circa AD 1270, Ramban argues for a future interpretation of Deuteronomy 30:11–14 on grammatical grounds, appealing to the presence of these verbless clauses.[132]

Commenting on Deuteronomy 30:11–14, Ramban writes, "It is said in participle form to hint in the form of a promise that the thing will

---

131. The NIV and RSV concur, while the NASB and KJV translate this clause in present tense. This example illustrates the interpretive possibilities which must be adjudicated by context.

132. Elman writes, "Moses ben Nahman (Lat. Nahmanides, often called by the acronym RaMBaN), was one of the most influential scholars that Spanish Jewry produced, one whose versatility and scope still astonish. He was a penetrating Talmudist and legalist, a mystic whose early training in medieval Jewish philosophy nevertheless remained a living influence in his thought, an accomplished courtier and communal leader. Withal, he was a prolific writer, producing some 50 works or more, including talmudic *novella*, legal and ritual treatises, biblical commentaries, occasional poetry and sermons." Elman, "Moses Ben Nahman / Nahmanides (Ramban)," 416. See also Sæbø, *Hebrew Bible / Old Testament*, 1075.

take place in the future"[133] (כן להיות הדבר עתיד כי בהבטחה זלרמו הבינוני
וזשבל ונאמרה). My translation of Ramban's commentary differs from the
one offered by Chavel: "It is stated in a future tense [rather than in the
imperative] to suggest, in the form of a pledge, that it is destined [that Israel will repent]."[134] In his translation, Chavel obscures Ramban's employment of the technical term בינוני, which functions as a grammatical term
for participles in Medieval Hebrew.[135] But Ramban clearly singles out the
participle constructions of 30:11–14, which I refer to as a verbless clause
construction above, and argues that it "hints" at a future fulfillment of
Deuteronomy 30:11–14. Hence, Ramban's commentary lends medieval
support to the argument of the present book that 30:11–14 should be
interpreted as a continuation of the redemptive restoration program outlined in 30:1–10.[136]

## Narrative Flow and Thematic Unity in Deuteronomy 30:1–14

To summarize my argument thus far, the chiastic structure of Deuteronomy 30:1–14, the subordinating כי particle in Deuteronomy 30:11, and
the nature and presence of the verbless clauses in 30:11–14, which act
to provide background information for the preceding context, lean the
evidence toward understanding 30:11–14 as a continuation of the prophetic material in 30:1–10. In my view, the narrative flow and thematic

133. My translation.

134. Nachmanides, *Commentary on the Torah*, 342.

135. This term comes from ון + בֵּין ("denoting some general idea or concept with
reference to the noun to which it is added") + י. Klein, *A Comprehensive Etymological
Dictionary of the Hebrew Language for Readers of English*, 72, 191, 253.

136. While some interpreters are not convinced that Deut 30:11–14 should
be translated with future verbs, they nevertheless argue that the reality detailed in
30:11–14 is related to and contingent on 30:1–10, and specifically the heart circumcision promise of 30:6. This is the approach taken by Barker, who argues that "30:11–14
comes to reality only when Yahweh circumcises Israel's heart. The present tense of
vv11–14 is not in contrast to vv1–10 but rather highlights rhetorically the certainty
of this future event and its effects for obedience." Barker, *The Triumph of Grace in
Deuteronomy*, 193. A better way forward for these interpreters could be in what I will
call a "gnomic" timeframe for Deut 30:11–14, which would be grammatically possible
in the following way: If one interprets the כי clause in 30:14 as a temporal conjunction, "when," then only "when" the "word is in your mouth and in your heart to do
it," i.e. when 30:1–10 takes place and your heart is circumcised, is the commandment
"not too difficult." But this reading would necessarily reject Bandstra's כי classification
system, which is why I default to a future reading.

continuity of the book of Deuteronomy further reinforce this interpretation of 30:11–14.

In this section, I provide further evidence from the surrounding context in support of the interpretation that understands Deuteronomy 30:11–14 to be a continuation of the promise in 30:1–10, a promise that refers to a future reality that is contingent on divine intervention and not to a present, non-contingent reality at the time of cutting of the covenant of Moab.

### "Today"

McConville is representative of the majority interpretation when he argues that the presence of the word "today" (היום) in Deuteronomy 30:11 resets the temporal framework from future time in 30:1–10 to the present in 30:11–14. He writes,

> The relationship between 30:6 and 30:11–14 is not a simple one. The former is part of Deuteronomy's glimpse into the future (from the standpoint of those who are assembled on the plains of Moab), its vision of a new hope for Israel on the other side of the failures of its history from settlement to exile. But vv. 11–14 come back to the Mosaic present, with the typical urgent "today" (v. 11; the point is obscured by the NIV translation), repeated in vv. 15–16.[137]

But the presence of היום does not necessitate a temporal reset to the present, and in fact the immediate context presents two examples where this exact expression appears and interpreters universally recognize that the context refers to a time when what Moses commands *today* will be obeyed *in the future*.[138]

---

137. McConville, *Grace in the End*, 137.

138. J. G. Millar, following Von Rad, argues that the ambiguity of the time referents in Deuteronomy, especially surrounding the word היום, is a feature of the book. "Once more, *hayyôm* is an important term. On the day when Yahweh intervenes to change the human heart, all Israel will be able to obey wholeheartedly what Moses has proclaimed 'today' (verse 2 and 9). The time reference is a little ambiguous—it is difficult to tell if *hayyôm* refers to the day *after* Yahweh's intervention, or the day of Moses' preaching at Moab." Millar, *Now Choose Life*, 94.

30:2 ושבת עד־יהוה אלהיך ושמעת בקלו ככל <u>אשר־אנכי מצוך היום</u> אתה ובניך בכל־לבבך ובכל־נפשך

30:8 ואתה תשוב ושמעת בקול יהוה ועשית את־כל־מצותיו <u>אשר אנכי מצוך היום</u>

30:11 כי המצוה הזאת <u>אשר אנכי מצוך היום</u> לא־נפלאת הוא ממך ולא רחקה הוא

In Deuteronomy 30:2 and 8, where Moses prophesies Israel's future return to Yahweh, Moses expands on the reality of this future promise. When all these words (דברם) come upon them (30:1), Israel "will return (imperfective *weqatal* ושבת) to Yahweh and hear/obey (imperfective *weqatal* ושמעת) his voice in everything *which I command you today*" (אשר־אנכי מצוך, Deut 30:2) and "will return (imperfective *yiqtol* ובשת) and hear/obey (imperfective *weqatal* ושמעת) the voice of Yahweh and do (imperfective *weqatal* ועשית) all his commandments *which I command you today* (אשר־אנכי מצוך, 30:8)." What Moses foretells in 30:2 and 30:8 is that Israel will be able to obey *in the future* what Moses commands *today*. Moses uses what Norbert Lohfink calls "der Promulgationssatz,"[139] or the Promulgation Formula (אשר אנכי מצוך היום), in 30:2, 8, and 11 not to reset the temporal framework but, as Simon deVries says, "to provide an identifying characterization of the general parenetical situation." DeVries continues,

> In every individual passage the promulgation formula with *hayyôm* remains subsidiary to the central appeal (4:40, 6:2, 6, 7:11, 8:1, 11, 10:13, 11:8, 27:1, 4, 10) or the wider characterization (11:13, 22 LXX, 27, 28, 13:19, 15:5, 19:9, 28:1, 13, 14, 15, 30:2, 8, 11, 16) to which it happens to be attached.[140]

Instead of resetting the temporal framework, the repetition of the phrase אשר־אנכי מצוך in 30:2, 8, and 11 may instead point toward understanding 30:11–14 as a continuation of the promise of 30:1–10.[141]

---

139. Lohfink, *Das Hauptgebot*, 59–63.

140. De Vries, *Yesterday, Today, and Tomorrow*, 186–87.

141. So Barker: "Thus הַיּוֹם in v11 has the function of identifying the commandment under discussion and does not have the function of stressing the present tense any more than הַיּוֹם in vv2, 8. Rather than creating a tension with the preceding, the 'today' of v11, and the relative clause in which is occurs, are links of similarity between the paragraphs rather than markers of contrast." Barker, *The Triumph of Grace in Deuteronomy*, 185. Strickland similarly contends that "if Deuteronomy 30:1–10 is future and includes the phrase 'which I am giving you today,' it is equally possible for Deuteronomy 30:11–14 to be further discussion of the future, furnishing the possibility and

If this is correct, then the logic of Deuteronomy 30:1–14 would be as follows: Israel will return to Yahweh and hear/obey his voice *in the future* according to all Moses commands *today* (Deut 30:2) and Israel will return and hear/obey Yahweh's voice and do *in the future* all the commands which Moses commands *today* (30:8). For (כי, 30:11) this command, which Moses commands *today*, will not be too difficult or out of reach *in the same future time* as 30:1–10. For (כי, 30:11) the word will be in their heart and mouth to do it *in the same future time* as 30:1–10. Barker makes a similar point:

> [The chiastic structure of 30:1–14] suggests not only that vv11–14 belong with vv1–10, but also how they are to be understood in relation to that section. The optimistic expectation that Israel is able to obey, reflected in vv11–14, thus derives from the circumcision of the heart in v6. So the word is placed in the heart by the circumcision of the heart.[142]

This may be more satisfying than the interpretation offered by McConville, who says that "Deuteronomy 30:11–14 state a truth in principle, but one that is negated by the character of Israel."[143] Barker offers an improvement on this statement by McConville when he writes, "We would prefer to say that 30:11–14 states a truth *yet to be effected by Yahweh*."[144] As Barker points out, perhaps this is what McConville suggests when he writes, "The exhortation [in 30:11–14] remains absolute, though we know that it can only ever have validity in a new arrangement that lies beyond both sin and judgment."[145]

Commentators who invoke היום in Deuteronomy 30:11 as a temporal reset to the present tend to overlook the היום of 30:15, which does not occur in a relative clause, and thus actually does function to reset the temporal framework to the present along with the *Qal* imperative ראה.[146]

---

reason for the fulfillment of the commands God was giving them." Strickland, "The Inauguration of the Law of Christ," 251.

142. Barker, *The Triumph of Grace in Deuteronomy*, 187.

143. McConville, *Grace in the End*, 138.

144. Barker, *The Triumph of Grace in Deuteronomy*, 193.

145. McConville, *Grace in the End*, 138.

146. Sailhamer, who interprets Deut 30:11–14 as a continuation of the prophecy in 30:1–10, writes, "As the word 'today' shows (Dt 30:15), at this point in the chapter the perspective and focus of Moses' words are no longer that of the future time after the captivity. This word brings us back to Moses and to the people who are about to enter the land." Sailhamer, *The Pentateuch as Narrative*, 474.

In other words, Israel has a genuine choice before them *today*, but it is only in the *future* that Yahweh will guarantee they make the right one.

## Present Duty or Future Motivation?

The argument that Deuteronomy 30:11–14 "clearly states the reason for a present duty" led S. R. Driver to conclude that this passage was not originally written to follow 30:1–10, but was subsequently placed there by the hand of a redactor. But rejecting this redactional-critical conclusion and looking at the final form of the canonical text reveals a thematic unity that unveils a deeper truth about God's faithfulness in the midst of Israel's faithlessness.

As we have seen, the narrative flow of Deuteronomy 29–30 begins with Moses gathering Israel together on the plains of Moab to make a covenant besides the covenant made at Horeb (Deut 28:69 [ET 29:1]). But this covenant ceremony begins on an ominous note which sprouts into a warning that grows into a prophetic announcement. Israel has seen the wonders of Yahweh, but he has not given them "a heart to understand or eyes to see or ears to hear" (29:3 [ET 29:4]). Yahweh enters into a covenant with them, promising to be their God and to make them his people, just as was promised to Abraham, Isaac, and Jacob (29:12 [ET 29:13]). But he does so with a warning. The roots of idolatry and pride will lead to covenant curses being leveled against Israel, which will land them in exile (29:17–27 [ET 29:18–28]). The way this passage progresses, there is a seamless movement from a disobedient individual (29:17–20 [ET 29:18–21]) to a disobedient Israel (29: 21–27 [ET 29:22–28]), and from a contingent warning (29:17–20 [ET 29:18–21]) to a prophetic announcement (29: 21–27 [ET 29:22–28]), which continues into 30:1–10. Therefore, when the reader arrives at the promised restoration in 30:1–10, and specifically the divine circumcision in 30:6, he is invited to reflect again on the problem of 29:3 (ET 29:4)—the problem of Israel's heart—and to see 30:6 as the divine solution.

With this narrative flow in mind, if Deuteronomy 30:11–14 is read as referring to Israel's present, non-contingent ability to obey the law—which is the logical conclusion of a solely present timeframe[147]—we can

147. As noted above, some interpreters who recognize the dissonance between Deut 28:69 (ET 29:1)—30:10 and 30:11–14 but nevertheless want to interpret the narrative synchronically instead of diachronically, opt for a kind of gnomic interpretation of 30:11–14. Turner recognizes the validity of both a future and present reading in

understand Driver's inability to see how this text fits with the divine diagnosis in 29:3 (ET 29:4) and the necessity of divine intervention in 30:6. If the command is "not too difficult" for Israel and "not out of reach," but indeed already the word is "in their mouths and in their hearts" for them "to do it," then the command in Deuteronomy 6:4–5 could be seen as redundant, the diagnosis in 29:3 (ET 29:4) could be seen as misleading, the promise in 30:1–10 could be seen as unnecessary, and the rest of chapters 31–32 could be seen as alarmist.

Instead, reading Deuteronomy 30:11–14 as a continuation of the prophetic promise of reconciliation after exile, which includes divine intervention into the state of Israel's heart, makes better sense of the overall message of Deuteronomy.

---

30:11–14, but ultimately he decides that "it is not clear to the present writer that one must necessarily choose between them. . . . The proposal here, then, is that both positions are valid. On the one hand, verse 11–14 speak to the present (and every pre-exilic) generation as a motivation for obedience. They have God's word and it is clear what he wants of them. The only obstacle they face is themselves! On the other hand, verse 11–14 proleptically describe the striking reality resulting from the circumcision of the heart, in which this one obstacle has been removed." Turner, *The Death of Deaths*, 162. Significantly for this study, Turner says in a footnote that this second angle seems to be the one "Paul takes in Romans 10, where he cites portions of Deut 30:11–14." Turner, 162n269. McConville takes a similar position: "The accessibility of the law runs counter to the theme of Israel's inability to keep it, met in 9:4–6, and the golden-calf narrative more broadly (9–10). And it is, at first sight, curious that such a passage such as 30:11–14, addressed to the Moab generation, should come only now, after the blessings and curses (chs. 28–29) and a promise of Yahweh's special action to enable a disobedient people (30:1–10). The placing of these verses is essential, however. As we noticed, the time distinction between the future generation, restored from exile, and the present Moab generation, was blurred in 30:8, where the immediate relevance of Moses' sermon to the latter broke through the other perspective. The words in v. 8 ('with which I am charging you today') are now echoed in v. 11, showing that there is unity of conception between the two parts of the chapter. This means that the affirmation of the accessibility of the commands comes directly under the influence of the promises of 30:3–7, with v. 6 at their heart. The appeal to the Moab generation has its own integrity; but ultimately the realization of an obedient people will depend on Yahweh's new act in compassion." McConville, *Deuteronomy*, 429. He writes elsewhere, "The renewed exhortations in 30:11–14 must certainly be read in light of both 9:4–6 (which 30:11–14 formally contradict) and of 30:1–10. Deuteronomy 30:11–14 state a truth in principle, but one that is negated in history by the character of Israel. The exhortation remains absolute, though we know that it can only ever have validity in a new arrangement that lies beyond both sin and judgment. When it finally gains this validity, it is a work of God's grace—'grace in the end.'" McConville, *Grace in the End*, 138.

## A Pessimistic Perspective

If there remains any doubt about Yahweh's view of Israel's ability to "do" all that is commanded at this point in the book, in Deuteronomy 31:16–21 Yahweh shares with Moses one final time his expectations for the people of Israel once they are in the land:

> Behold, you are about to lie down with your fathers. Then *this people will rise and whore after the foreign gods among them in the land that they are entering, and they will forsake me and break my covenant that I have made with them.* Then my anger will be kindled against them in that day, and I will forsake them and hide my face from them, and they will be devoured. And many evils and troubles will come upon them, so that they will say in that day, "Have not these evils come upon us because our God is not among us?" And I will surely hide my face in that day because of all the evil that they have done, because they have turned to other gods. (Deut 31:16–18)[148]

> Now therefore write this song and teach it to the people of Israel. Put it in their mouths, that this song may be a witness for me against the people of Israel. For when I have brought them into the land flowing with milk and honey, which I swore to give to their fathers, and they have eaten and are full and grown fat, *they will turn to other gods and serve them, and despise me and break my covenant.* And when many evils and troubles have come upon them, this song shall confront them as a witness (for it will live unforgotten in the mouths of their offspring). *For I know what they are inclined to do even today, before I have brought them into the land that I swore to give.* (Deut 31:19–21)[149]

This is a perspective Moses shares with Yahweh. Moses reveals his pessimistic perspective to the people in his final farewell address in Deuteronomy 31:26–29:

> Take this Book of the Law and put it by the side of the ark of the covenant of the LORD your God, that it may be there for a witness against you. *For I know how rebellious and stubborn you are. Behold, even today while I am yet alive with you, you have been rebellious against the LORD. How much more after my death!* Assemble to me all the elders of your tribes and your officers, that I may speak these words in their ears and call heaven and

148. Emphasis added.
149. Emphasis added.

earth to witness against them. *For I know that after my death you will surely act corruptly and turn aside from the way that I have commanded you.* And in the days to come evil will befall you, *because you will do what is evil in the sight of the LORD*, provoking him to anger through the work of your hands"[150]

Even embedded in the song Moses writes for Israel to sing in the days to come—a song commissioned by Yahweh to stand as witness against the people when they disobey (Deut 31:19)—Israel's unfaithfulness and Yahweh's impending punishment are treated as foregone conclusions. Note the perfective aspect of things yet to come: Israel "dealt corruptly" with Yahweh (שָׁחֵת, 32:5); they "forsook him" and "scoffed at him" (וַיְנַבֵּל, וַיִּטֹּשׁ, 32:15). Because of their unfaithfulness, Yahweh "saw" and "spurned" them (וַיִּנְאָץ, וַיַּרְא, 32:19); and he promises to hide his face from them, embrace another, foolish people (32:21), and heap disasters upon them (32:23). The one glimmer of hope comes after judgment, "For the LORD will vindicate his people and have compassion on his servants, when he sees that their power is gone and there is none remaining, bond or free" (32:36). Their salvation comes only through total judgment.[151]

The overarching narrative of Deuteronomy, with particular acceleration in chapters 29 and on, reveals that Israel lacks the capacity to do the commandments of the law; they lack righteousness (cf. Deut 9:4–6).[152]

150. Emphasis added.

151. As Hamilton poetically puts it, "Yahweh's glory is the central reality of Deuteronomy. It is Yahweh who has saved Israel through judgment of their enemies (Deuteronomy 1–3). It is ultimately Yahweh whose compelling existence is to motivate obedience (Deuteronomy 4) to the law he revealed when Israel heard his voice out of the midst of the fire on the mountaintop (Deuteronomy 5). It is Yahweh that Israel is to love (Deuteronomy 6–11), Yahweh Israel is to serve (Deuteronomy 12–28), and it is Yahweh who must give them the heart they need (29:3, ET 4; 30:6). . . . Israel will break Yahweh's covenant (30:1; 31:16—32:42), but Yahweh will restore them through the judgment he visits upon them (30:2–10; 32:43). There is none like Yahweh, God of Jeshurun (33:26), who is glorified in salvation through judgment in the manifestation of his justice and mercy." Hamilton, *God's Glory in Salvation through Judgment*, 132.

152. As I note in chapter 4 below on Paul's citation of Deut 30:12–14 in Rom 10, Deut 9:4–6 is a passage Paul seems to allude to by incorporating some of its words in the introduction of Deut 30:12–14. "Do not say in your heart, after the LORD your God has thrust them out before you, 'It is because of my righteousness that the LORD has brought me in to possess this land,' whereas it is because of the wickedness of these nations that the LORD is driving them out before you. Not because of your righteousness or the uprightness of your heart are you going in to possess their land, but because of the wickedness of these nations the LORD your God is driving them out from before you, and that he may confirm the word that the LORD swore to your fathers, to Abraham, to Isaac, and to Jacob."

Yes, the law had been given to them (5:29). Yes, they had been instructed to put it on their hearts (6:6). But it seems evident that in Moab, it was not yet the case that Moses' words were "not too difficult" or "not out of reach" for them to do. What Deuteronomy 30:11–14 hints at instead is a divinely-created reality when this *torah*, this Word, no longer stands over against Israel as judge of their unfaithfulness but is written on their hearts as the grounds of their faithfulness.[153]

## "This Command" and "the Word"

If it is correct to read Deuteronomy 30:11–14 as a continuation of 30:1–10, what are the referents of "this command" and "the word" in this passage? In Deuteronomy 30:11–13, "this command" is described as not too difficult, not out of reach, not in heaven and not across the sea. But then the subject changes in 30:14 to "the word," which is described as "in your mouth and in your heart to do it." Are we to understand "this command" and "the word" to have the same referent? Or does "the word" refer to something besides or in addition to "this command"?

### The Greatest Commandment

The majority of those who interpret Deuteronomy 30:11–14 as referring to a present, non-contingent reality for the generation on the plains of Moab generally understand both "this command" and "the word" to be some variation of the law delivered to Israel by Moses, either the oral or written law as it existed when Moses completed the book of Deuteronomy.[154] The LXX adds the words ἐν ταῖς χερσίν σου to verse 14, most likely to make clear the connection to the written *torah*.[155]

Some interpreters have insisted on a connection between "this command" and "the word" and the repentance and heart circumcision

153. See Starling's chapter "'In Your Mouth and in Your Heart': Deuteronomy and the Hermeneutics of Law" for how a future reading of Deuteronomy 30:11–14 fits into the larger message of Deuteronomy and could guard against Pelagian and Marcionite interpretations of Deuteronomy's message about the law in Starling, *Hermeneutics as Apprenticeship*, 35–46.

154. Cf. Cairns, *Word and Presence*, 264–65; Thompson, *Deuteronomy*, 286;

155. Importantly, when Paul quotes Deut 30:11–14, he does not include ἐν ταῖς χερσίν σου, which is an argument for Paul's use of the Hebrew text and not just the LXX, as some have argued.

described in Deuteronomy 30:1–10. Ramban comments on 30:11–14: "This command refers to the commandment of repentance aforementioned, for the verses 'and thou shalt bethink thyself; and thou shalt return unto the Eternal thy G-d' constitute a commandment, wherein he commands us to do so."[156] But there are no linguistically compelling reasons to find the commandment limited to the repentance in 30:1–10. And if the interpretation of 30:1–10 offered above is correct, the repentance therein is a promise, not a command.

Matthew Poole interprets Deuteronomy 30:11–14 in light of 30:1–10, and he suggests "this command" refers to the sum of the law—that is, love of God.

> He seems to speak of the law, or of that great command of loving and obeying God, mentioned here in ver. 2, 6, 10, 16, which is the sum of the law, of which yet he doth not here speak simply, or as it is in itself, but as it is mollified and accompanied with the grace of the gospel, whereby God circumciseth men's hearts to do this, as is expressed in ver. 6.[157]

Poole's argument is compelling. As I argued above, the references to the singular command in Deuteronomy 6:1–3 and again here in 30:11 may refer to the summary commandment to love Yahweh with a whole heart as proclaimed in the *Shema* of Deuteronomy 6:4–5 and reiterated throughout the book (cf. Deut 5:10; 7:9; 10:12–13; 11:1, 13, 22; 13:3; 19:9; 30:6, 16). This command subsumes all others beneath it: to love God is to obey God. And the love of God is ultimately and only possible from a repentant and circumcised heart.

---

156. Nachmanides, *Commentary on the Torah*, 342–43. Ramban goes on to explain the word as the torah, which is imminently doable: "And the sense thereof is to state that *if thy outcasts be in the uttermost parts of heaven* and you are under the power of the nations, you can yet return to G-d and do *according to all that I command thee this day*, for the thing is not hard, nor far off from you, but rather *very nigh unto thee* to do it all times and in all places. This is the sense of the expression, *in thy mouth, and in thy heart, that thou mayest do it* meaning that they *confess their iniquity, and the iniquity of their fathers* by word of their mouth, and return in their heart to G-d and accept the Torah upon themselves this day to perform it throughout all generations, as he mentioned, *thou and thy children with all thy heart*, as I have explained."

157. Poole, *Annotations upon the Holy Bible*, 1:395.

## The Word of Life

What, then, is the word (דבר) in Deuteronomy 30:14? The word must in some way be related to "the command," otherwise the flow of 30:11–14 is disrupted. "This command" is described as not too difficult, not out of reach, not in heaven or across the sea. Why? Because (כי) the word is described as "in your mouth and heart," and this "to do it" (לעשתו). This infinitive construct has a 3ms pronominal suffix that in context refers to דבר and functions either as the purpose of or result of the word being "in the mouth and in the heart." The דבר, then, must be something that can be "done."

In a search for the referent of דבר in Deuteronomy 30:14, one first notices that the "word" (דבר/דברים) in Deuteronomy is closely associated with Yahweh himself, as established from the beginning of the book. In Deuteronomy chapter 1, Moses recasts the sins of Israel as a fundamental failure to believe Yahweh and his word (דבר). Yahweh had told them not to fear or be dismayed (Deut 1:21), and Moses had told them to remember the great acts of salvation God had accomplished on their behalf at the Exodus (1:30) and in the wilderness (1:31). But instead of heeding "this word" (זה דבר) they did not believe (אמן) Yahweh (1:32, ובדבר הזה אינכם מאמינם ביהוה אלהיכם). It is not just that Israel did not believe the "word." As is clear from the syntax—the object of אמן is יהוה—the failure to act according to the word was a failure to believe Yahweh. And Yahweh responded to this unbelief by banishing an entire generation to wilderness wandering outside of the promised land (1:34).

Another intertextual clue to the referent of דבר in Deuteronomy 30:14 may be seen in 18:15–19. This is the only place in Deuteronomy besides 30:14 where דבר and פה occur together, and here the location of the דבר is in (ב) the mouth (פה), just as it is described in 30:14. In 18:15–19, Moses foretells of a prophet like himself who will arise from among the brothers (מקרבך מאחיך) of Israel.[158] This prophet will function in the place of Moses as a mediator between Yahweh and the people (Deut 18:16–17), and Yahweh will put (נתן) his words (דברים) in the prophet's mouth. The prophet will speak in the name of Yahweh and those who fail to listen to the prophet will be punished by Yahweh.

Closer in context to the דבר in Deuteronomy 30:14 is the announcement of the דברים of the covenant at Moab in 28:69 (ET 29:1) that, if not

---

158. This phrase is nearly identical to the description of the king in Deut 17:15 (מקרב אחיך).

kept (Deut 29:7 [ET 29:8]), will lead to destruction. Both hidden and revealed realities play a part in the fulfillment of these דברים (29:27 [ET 29:28]), and after all these words (דברים) come upon Israel—both blessing and curse—they will be returned to the heart (30:1).

With this as background, I am inclined to describe the contents and function of "the word" in Deuteronomy 30:14 without delimiting exclusively the referent of "the word"—a task ultimately taken up under the inspiration of the Holy Spirit by Paul in Romans 10. The דבר in 30:14 and the chiastically parallel דברים in 30:1 bind together the gift promise of a whole heart to love Yahweh (Deut 30:6), which fulfills the command to love Yahweh from a whole heart ("this command," the *Shema* of 6:4–5; cf. 30:2, 8, 11)—a promise that presupposes the faithless failure of Israel in chapter 29. In this way, the דברים "returned to the heart" in 30:1 and the דבר "in the heart" in 30:14 function as change-agents that precipitate repentance (30:2), reconciliation (30:3), and ultimately a motivated capacity for obedience (30:6) to the *Shema* to love Yahweh. This is nothing short of "das »Evangelium« für ein schuldig gewordenes Volk"[159]—the gospel for a guilty people. Understood this way, it is the דבר in the circumcised heart that creates love for Yahweh and guarantees salvation even out of the midst of judgment.

## Chapter Summary

I am in agreement with virtually all interpreters in understanding that Deuteronomy 30:11–14 does speak to "Israel's capacity to obey the covenant commands of Yahweh."[160] But in the view I have articulated above, the capacity described in 30:11–14 can only be achieved through divine intervention in the heart, and not merely by the external written, oral, or even memorized word of the *torah*. Yahweh must prepare the heart in circumcision, removing the impediment of the heart foreskin, and the word must be divinely implanted. Then, and only then, will Israel be able to "do it" (Deut 30:14). Here is J. G. Millar's diagnosis of the covenant at Moab:

> This covenant at Moab, then, is about theology more than about ritual. The advances on Horeb are in the content of the laws, now applied to the incipient occupation, and in the admission

159. Braulik, "Gesetz als Evangelium: Rechtfertigung und Begnadigung Nach der Deuteronomischen Tora," 155.

160. Barker, *The Triumph of Grace in Deuteronomy*, 187.

that laws do not change people. Both the Horeb and Moab covenants are fatally flawed, because they can do nothing about the problem of human nature.[161]

The "problem" of the covenant at Moab lies not in a deficiency of the commandments. What is described everywhere in Deuteronomy is a deficiency of the people—recall again the dilemma of Deuteronomy 29:3 (ET 29:4). Only when this deficiency is dealt with can there be true covenant keeping on the part of the people, and I believe this is what is promised in Deuteronomy 30:1–14: Yahweh, acting out of love for his people, giving the people the capacity for loving obedience—heart circumcision and Word implantation—so that his people may love him in return.

A unified, future-oriented reading of Deuteronomy 30:1–14 may serve to undergird interpretations such as Luther's that see fulfillment in the future preaching of the gospel:

> But why does he say, "in the mouth" before he says, "in the heart," since it is in the heart before it is in the mouth and is loved before it is taught? He does this to indicate that the manner of fulfilling the commandment of God will be through the Word of the Gospel, which is first preached by the mouth and then believed as a result of hearing. So by this text Moses directs the people to another Word to come, which, when received in the heart, causes His commandment to be loved. It is as if he said: "You will not fulfill My commandment when you hear it, but only if you love it with the heart. This you will not do unless the Word has been preached with the mouth and believed in the heart. So My commandment will become neither too difficult nor too distant."[162]

Before we get to Paul's use of Deuteronomy 30:12–14 in Romans 10:6–8 in chapter 4 below, in the next chapter I explore all of the places where the OT seems to speak of God's law on the heart, this internalized *torah*: Isaiah 51:7, Jeremiah 31:31–33, and Psalms 37:31, 40:8, and 119:11.

---

161. Millar, *Now Choose Life*, 174.

162. Luther, *Lectures on Deuteronomy*, 9:278.

# Deuteronomy 30:11–14 in Its
# Old Testament Context

IF THE ANALYSIS IN the chapter above is correct—namely that Deuteronomy 30:11–14 speaks of the internalization of an eschatological *torah* associated with heart circumcision and the new covenant—then it could be expected that other OT texts which speak similarly of the internalized *torah* are likewise associated with the new covenant. I will argue below that the book of Jeremiah provides the clearest and most extended interaction with the text of Deuteronomy 30:11–14 through textual allusion in what is commonly called the Book of Consolation (Jer 30–33), which will naturally receive the most attention in this chapter.[1] There are, however, possible allusions to and developments of Deuteronomy 30:11–14 in the following passages which reference in some way God's law in the heart: Psalm 37:31; Psalm 40:8; Psalm 119:11; and Isaiah 51:7.[2]

---

1. In the evangelical view of Scripture, assuming Mosaic authorship of the Pentateuch, the Old Testament books after the Pentateuch were written chronologically after the Pentateuch. In these books there is the possibility of allusion to, quotation of, and even elaboration upon the text in the Pentateuch. Underpinning the following analysis is the assumption that the Prophets and the Writings are essentially inspired commentary and application of the Pentateuch for the people of God. I owe this seemingly basic insight to my doctoral supervisor, Jim Hamilton, an insight that was transformative in my own reading of the Old Testament.

2. I will not be examining those texts where the internalization of the word is

Each of these passages are taken up below in the order of how they appear in the Hebrew Bible.

I identified textual allusions by looking for texts where it is possible that the reality described in Deuteronomy 30:11–14—namely an internalization of the word of Yahweh—is similarly described. The verbal possibilities include various descriptions of the divine Word—God's special revelation—such as דבר, אמרה, and תורה, coupled with a description of the internal seat of man's will, including לב, and מעה.

## Deuteronomy 30:11–14 and the Book of Isaiah

In Isaiah 51:7, the prophet Isaiah addresses a people who appear to have internalized the *torah,* providing a possible allusion to Deuteronomy 30:11–14: "Listen to me, you who know righteousness, the people in whose heart is my law; fear not the reproach of man, nor be dismayed at their revilings."

In the following section, I situate this passage within the larger structure of the book of Isaiah and then attempt to interpret it in context in order to understand the identity and nature of this *torah*-internalized people.

### The New Things in Isaiah

A general structure of the book of Isaiah divides the book into two halves: chapters 1–39 and chapters 40–66.[3] Peter Gentry has recently challenged

---

commanded, such as in Prov 3:3 and 7:3, as they have parallels more with Deut 6:6 and are related in the same way as the command to circumcise your heart in Deut 10:16 is related to the promise of heart circumcision in Deut 30:6.

3. The critical consensus since Duhm that the book of Isaiah should be interpreted as three distinct books is cracking up and even giving way to support for a unified reading of Isaiah. So Beuken: "In the last decades opinion concerning the origin of the book of Isaiah (BI), as almost universally accepted since B. Duhm (1892), has begun to waver. Some scholars no longer consider the book a combination of three more or less independent documents, Proto-Isaiah (PI), Deutero-Isaiah (DI) and Trito-Isaiah (TI), which have each experienced their own redaction history. The book is, rather, the result of a complicated process, in which extensive *Vorlagen* of what now are called the three principal parts, have been joined together by means of a sweeping redaction, which has attuned all the materials to each other." Beuken, "The Main Theme of Trito-Isaiah, 'the Servants of YHWH,'" 67. For a survey of how this critical consensus changed, see Childs, *Isaiah*, 1–5. Contra Childs, however, this study does

the view that chapter 40 begins a new section, instead locating the beginning of a new section in what he calls the "Historical prologue: Hezekiah's fatal choice" in Isaiah 38:1—39:8.[4] But regardless of whether chapters 37-38 belong to the former or latter half of the book of Isaiah, Brevard Childs' identification of these two halves as the "former things" (Isa 1–37) and the "new things" (Isa 40–66) is a theme embedded in the logic of the book of Isaiah itself (cf. 43:18–19; 48:3–8).[5] The "former things" of chapters 1–37 generally address a people not yet in exile but headed for judgment, while the "new things" of chapters 40–66 generally assume a people in exile. It is the second half of the book of Isaiah, the "new things" in chapters 40–66, which contains the three passages under consideration—specifically the "Book of the Servant" in Isaiah 40–55.

John Oswalt, assuming the Isaianic authorship of Isaiah 40–66, contends that "[Isaiah] had a knowledge of the future that was more detailed than that displayed by other OT prophets. Furthermore, . . . these chapters are speaking *to* people in the future, not merely *about* them."[6] Lohfink similarly observes, "From chapter 40 on the book devotes itself fully to this future."[7] Gentry delimits this future orientation to some sections of 40–66: "Isaiah 38–55 looks farther into the future, beyond the judgment of exile to the comfort and consolation of Israel, that is, the return of the people from exile," while in Isaiah 56–66 he notes that "some parts focus on the people of God in Isaiah's time and some focus on the distant future."[8] Though some of the contents of Isaiah 40–55 appear to be set in the past or appear to be addressing the author's present—the

---

indeed assume "the eighth-century prophet" Isaiah to be "a clairvoyant of the future." Childs, *Isaiah*, 3–4. For an excellent overview of the state of Isaianic studies from an evangelical viewpoint, see Schultz, "The Origins and Basic Arguments of the Multi-Author View of the Composition of Isaiah," 7–31.

4. Gentry, "The Literary Macrostructures of the Book of Isaiah and Authorial Intent," 249. According to Gentry, "Hebrew literature typically encases poetry in prose settings. We observe these structures in macro-sections as well as in micro-sections. The norms of Hebrew literature do not support interpreting Isa 40 as the beginning of a new section." Gentry, "The Literary Macrostructures of the Book of Isaiah and Authorial Intent," 249n32.

5. Childs, *Isaiah*, 296. Poulsen follows Childs in this general framework. Poulsen, *God, His Servant, and the Nations in Isaiah 42:1–9*, 212.

6. Oswalt, *The Book of Isaiah*, 5.

7. Lohfink and Zenger, *The God of Israel and the Nations*, 45.

8. Gentry, "The Literary Macrostructures of the Book of Isaiah and Authorial Intent," 249, 251.

perfective verbs in the Servant Song of Isaiah 53 are almost universally interpreted as future-predictive—Christopher North's explanation of the prophetic perfect and the future-oriented nature the servant songs may apply to the whole of Isaiah 40–55:

> Even if the Hebrew perfect and imperfect exactly corresponded to our past and future—which they do not—there is no need for us to make quite such a bogey of them as we often do in this connexion. The whole of the last Song is future to the first, which itself is already future. Within it the sufferings of the Servant are described, though not consistently, in past "tenses." Moreover, the sufferings in the last Song are set within the framework of Yahweh's declaration concerning his future exaltation. They are described by Gentiles whose eyes are now opened. It is, therefore, in relation to the future that the death of the Servant is past, not in relation to the present of the writer.[9]

That the prophet Isaiah addresses a future people in these chapters of his book is a point that will undergird the analysis below.[10]

In addition to the turn from the "former things" in Isaiah 1–39 to the "new things" in Isaiah 40–66, John Oswalt argues that there is a general chronological movement to the second half of the book of Isaiah. In Isaiah 40–48, the prophet addresses questions about God's character against the backdrop of Israel's (yet-future) exile in Babylon: Yahweh is the Creator God who reigns supreme over all so-called gods (Isa 40:18–20; 44:6–9; 45:20–21; 46:1–5); he is still for his people as their redeemer and savior who will not leave his people in exile (41:8–9, 14; 43:1–21; 44:21–28; 48:20–22); he is orchestrating history for his own purposes as sovereign LORD over the nations (40:15–17, 23–24; 41:2–4; 48:14–16); and he is raising up individuals on the world stage to this end (45:1–7),

---

9. North, *The Suffering Servant in Deutero-Isaiah*, 211.

10. Calvin detects a turn from the present to the future in his commentary on Isa 40:1ff. "The Prophet introduces a new subject; for, leaving the people on whom no favourable impression was made either by threatenings or by admonitions, on account of their desperate wickedness, he turns to posterity, in order to declare that the people who shall be humbled under the cross will experience no want of consolation even amidst the severest distresses. . . . What will afterwards follow will relate to the future Church, the revival of which was effected long after his death; for he will next lay down a perpetual doctrine, which must not be limited to a single period, and especially when he treats of the commencement and progress of the reign of Christ." Calvin, *Commentary on the Book of the Prophet Isaiah*, 197. Calvin goes on to emphasize the future nature of the imperfect verb יאמר in Isaiah 40:1 in order to make clear Isaiah's intended audience is set in the future.

even naming future events and individuals by name (41:26; 45:4; 48:3–5) for the sake of his own name. Then in Isaiah 49–55, the prophet addresses Yahweh's dealings with the people's sins. Oswalt summarizes this section with a series of questions, "What will God do about the sin that precipitated the exile in the first place? Will he ignore it, acting as though it did not occur? In short, how can sinful Israel become servant Israel?"[11] In these chapters, we see that Yahweh's final solution for sin is related to the coming of his servant. Gentry argues that embedded in the structure of this section is the hint of a two-stage redemption plan in Isaiah 40–55.[12]

In Isaiah 56–66, the prophet Isaiah seems to turn to address life in the land after exile, the future beyond the future return. This future includes the nations among the people of God (56:1–8; 60:1–3; 62:2; 66:20), a new heavens and new earth (65:17–25, 66:22), and a new Jerusalem (62:1–12).

One of the main themes, if not the main theme, of Isaiah 40–66 is the servant of Yahweh and his mission, which von Rad describes as a predictive, future-oriented reality:

> The picture of the Servant of Jahweh, of his mission to Israel and to the world, and of his expiatory suffering, is prophecy of the future, and, like all the rest of Deutero-Isaiah's prophecy, belongs to the realm of pure miracle which Jahweh reserved for himself.[13]

11. Oswalt, *The Book of Isaiah*, 9.

12. The following outline of Isa 38–55 that Gentry borrows and slightly alters from Motyer is illuminating:

   A. Historical prologue: Hezekiah's fatal choice (38:1—39:8)
      B. Universal consolation (40:1—42:17)
         1. The consolation of Israel (40:1—41:20)
         2. The consolation of the Gentiles (41:21—42:17)
      C. Promises of redemption (42:18—44:23)
         1. Release from Babylon (42:18—43:21)
         2. Forgiveness of Sins (43:22—44:23)
      C'. Agents of redemption (44:24—53:12)
         1. Cyrus: liberation (44:24—53:12)
         2. The Servant: atonement (49:1—53:12)
      B'. Universal proclamation (54:1—55:13)
         1. The call to Zion (54:1–17)
         2. The call to the world (55:1–13)

Gentry, "The Literary Macrostructures of the Book of Isaiah and Authorial Intent," 249. Cf. Motyer, *The Prophecy of Isaiah*, 289.

13. Von Rad, *Old Testament Theology*, 2:260. Contra Baltzer, "In what follows I shall try to interpret the text . . . in light of the supposition that Moses is the Servant of God." Baltzer, *Deutero-Isaiah: A Commentary on Isaiah 40–55*, 126. Von Rad

With the general contours of Isaiah 40–66 in mind—a future-oriented redemption from exile—the next section examines Isaiah 51:7 in context in order to determine the referent and nature of the people "in whose heart is my law" (Isa 51:7).[14]

## A People "in Whose Heart Is My Law"

Isaiah 51:7 is addressed to a people "in whose heart is my law." Who are these people? Is this a remnant of faithful Israelites from among Isaiah's contemporaries? Is this the remnant of faithful Israel throughout time and space? Or is this the people of God whose identity is bound up with the servant? Are these mutually exclusive possibilities? In order to answer these questions, it is necessary to explore the context of Isaiah 51.

Isaiah 51:1 begins with a speaker, presumably Yahweh or one who is closely identified with him,[15] addressing a plural audience through a plural imperative: "Listen (pl.) to me" (שמעו אלי). This is followed by five more plural imperatives in 51:2–8: "Look to Abraham," "Give attention to me," "give ear to me," "Lift up your eyes," and again, "Listen to me."

---

distinguishes the Servant of Yahweh from Moses as an antitype. Von Rad, *Old Testament Theology*, 2:261.

14. Lessing's outline points in the same direction: "Isaiah 51–55 depicts Yahweh's rescue of Israel through a new exodus accomplished by the Suffering Servant. Four major units make up these chapters: (1) Yahweh's promise of salvation (51:1—52:12); (2) the Fourth Servant Song (52:13—53:12); (3) the epilogue of the Fourth Servant Song (54:1–17); and (4) the epilogue of chapters 41–54 (55:1–13)." R. Lessing, *Isaiah 40–55*, 541.

15. The identity of this speaker is relayed through a series of first-person assertions: he is the one who called Abraham (Isa 51:3); to whom the people and nation of Israel belong (51:4a); from whom a law will go out (51:4b); whose justice is a light to the peoples (51:4b); whose righteousness draws near, whose salvation has gone out, and whose arm will judge the peoples (51:5); whose salvation will be forever and whose righteousness will never be dismayed (51:6); whose law is in the people's heart (51:7); and whose righteousness will be forever and whose salvation to all generations (51:8). But this speaker also refers to Yahweh in the third person in 51:1 and 51:3—where either the voice of the prophet is intermingled with Yahweh's or Yahweh refers to himself in the third person.

| vv. | Mood | Speaker | Addressee | Subject | Predicate |
|---|---|---|---|---|---|
| 51:1–2 | Imp. | 1cs (Yahweh?) | 2mp (People) | -- | -- |
| 51:3 | Ind. | -- | -- | 3ms (Yahweh) | 3fs (Zion) |
| 51:4–8 | Imp. | 1cs (Yahweh) | 2mp (People) | -- | -- |
| 51:9 | Imp. | 1cs (Prophet) | 2fs (Arm of Yahweh) | -- | -- |
| 51:10 | Ind. | -- | -- | 2fs (Arm of Yahweh) | 3mp (Redeemed) |
| 51:11 | Ind. | -- | -- | 3mp (Redeemed) | -- |
| 51:12a | Ind. | -- | -- | 1cs (Yahweh) | 2mp (People?) |
| 51:12b | Ind. | -- | -- | 1cs (Yahweh) | 2fs (Jerusalem?) |
| 51:13 | Ind. | -- | -- | 1cs (Yahweh) | 2ms (Israel?) |
| 51:14 | Ind. | -- | -- | 3ms (Individual?) | -- |
| 51:15–16 | Ind. | -- | -- | 1cs (Yahweh) | 2ms (Israel?) |
| 51:17 | Imp. | 1cs (Prophet) | 2fs (Jerusalem) | -- | -- |
| 51:18 | Ind. | -- | -- | 3fs (Jerusalem) | -- |
| 51:19–20 | Ind. | -- | -- | 2fs (Jerusalem) | -- |
| 51:21 | Imp. | 1cs (Prophet) | 2fs (Jerusalem) | | |
| 51:22a | Ind. | -- | -- | 3ms (Yahweh) | 2fs (Jerusalem) |
| 51:22b–23a | Ind. | -- | -- | 1cs (Yahweh) | 2fs (Jerusalem) |
| 51:23b | Imp. | 1cp (Tormentors) | 2fs (Jerusalem) | -- | -- |
| 51:23c | Ind. | | | 2fs (Jerusalem) | -- |

Table 7. Mood swings and changing agents in Isaiah 51

The speaker changes in Isaiah 51:9–11, where the imperatives change from masculine plural to feminine singular and are addressed to the "arm of the LORD" (cf. Isa 51:5). Instead of a first-person perspective, we have a second-person address about the "arm of the LORD" (51:9b–10) and third-person assertions about the redeemed (51:11).

In Isaiah 51:12a, the speaker changes again back to the first person, again presumably Yahweh, once again addressing a plural group. But the addressee quickly changes in 51:12b to a 2fs—perhaps referring to Jerusalem in anticipation of the feminine addressee of 51:17ff—and then changes once more to a new addressee, this time a 2ms in 51:13, which continues through to 51:16—minus the interjection in 51:14 where we are introduced to an individual who is "bowed down" but will "speedily be released"; who will "not die and go down to the pit" or have lack of bread. Table 7 above summarizes the changing mood (imperative or indicative) and agents (speaker/subject or addressee/predicate) in Isaiah 51.

Who is this people (masc. pl.) "who know righteousness, the people in whose heart is my law" in Isaiah 51:7? Seeking a masculine plural antecedent, one first observes that the 2mp pronouns and the 2mp imperative, "Listen to me," in 51:7 match the 2mp imperative and 2mp addressees of 51:1, where one finds a people "who pursue righteousness" and "who seek the LORD." This grammatical relationship points to a similar referent in 51:7 and 51:1. If the lens is zoomed out to include the surrounding context, a question is found on the lips of either the prophet or the servant in the immediate context in Isaiah 50 asking, "Who among you (2mp) fears the LORD and obeys the voice of his servant?" (Isa 50:10a). This search for God-fearers who would obey the voice of the servant of Yahweh in 50:10 finds resolution in and terminates on those who pursue and know righteousness, who seek Yahweh, and in whose heart is his law (cf. Isa 51:1, 7).[16] Those who respond to the servant in obedience have the law of God in their hearts.

According to Childs, this development is part of the "new things" of Isaiah 40–66: "The new element in the divine response to the prayer in [Isaiah 51:9ff] lies precisely in the new role assigned to those who have

16. Cf. Oswalt: "In 50:10 those who feared the LORD were described as those who listened to the voice of the Servant. Here [in 51:1,] persons who are *pursuers of righteousness and seekers of the LORD* are called to *listen to me,* that is, to God. The same group of people is clearly being addressed in both places, persons who when they listen to and obey the voice of the Servant are also listening to and obeying the voice of God." Oswalt, *The Book of Isaiah,* 334.

responded to the LORD by following in the footsteps of the servant (vv. 1ff.). They are the people in whose heart is God's law (v. 7)."[17] Though Poulsen does not argue that the identity of the servant is future-predictive, contra von Rad above, he similarly relates the identity of the faithful in 51:7 with the identity of the servant:

> [T]he servant's truthful witness to God creates a decisive divide between believers and opponents, that is, between those individuals who embrace the message that he brings and respond to him and those who continue to resist the offer of redemption and taunt him (50:10–11; cf. Isa 56–66). In other words, 50:10–11 presents the call to realize one's true identity in the encounter with the servant. 51:1—52:12 accordingly addresses those faithful within the nation of Israel who have responded to the servant; those who "pursue righteousness" and "seek YHWH" (51:1).[18]

In Isaiah 51:15–16, a few verses removed from the previous text but sharing in the same context, the passage is addressed a 2ms individual:

> And I have put my words in your (sg.) mouth
> and covered you (sg.) in the shadow of my hand, establishing the heavens
> and laying the foundations of the earth,
> and saying to Zion, "You (sg.) are my people."

The 2ms pronoun in these verses could refer back to the 2ms addressee in Isaiah 51:13 or to the individual introduced by Isaiah 51:14.

---

17. Childs, *Isaiah*, 404.

18. Poulsen, *God, His Servant, and the Nations in Isaiah 42*, 218. Childs interprets the people addressed in Isa 51:1ff as those who identify with the Servant of Yahweh as a new people of God: "In v. 4 the addressee is named 'my people,' 'my nation.' The referent is thus clearly the faithful within Israel who have responded to the servant. They are to listen when the nature of God's salvation is described as the same goal that was first set forth to the servant Israel in 42:11ff. God's torah will go forth, for which the coastlands wait (51:4, 5//42:4), and his justice will be for 'a light to the nations' (51:4//42:6; 49:6). The effect of this promise is that the sharp line once separating Israel from the nations has been overcome, and the new people of God emerges as encompassing those responding in faith to God. Often the appeal to look to the heavens serves to remind Israel of the creative sovereignty of God, but here the divine power is excercised in apocalyptic judgment. The heavens and earth—the gracious setting for God's rule—will disappear as part of the old, corrupt order, but God's true salvation will endure forever, as was always in accord with divine purpose in his creation. The final imperative to listen in vv. 7ff further defines the heart of God's people. . . . The imagery is again taken from 42:4, 5. God's new people, like Israel of old (10:24), is not to fear the scorn of others." Childs, *Isaiah*, 402–3.

Either way, the phrase "shadow of my hand" (בצל ידי) in 51:16 is a phrase that appears once elsewhere in Isaiah in the context of the first servant song in Isaiah 49:2 (בצל ידו). This inner-textual reference points the evidence toward understanding this individual as the servant of Yahweh described everywhere else in the book of Isaiah. As J. Blenkinsopp argues,

> Putting words in an individual's mouth (v 16b) is a familiar prophetic designation and endowment formula (Num 22:38; Jer 1:9: Isa 59:21), and comparison with 49:2 and 50:4 show that the statement is addressed to the prophetic servant whose voice we have just heard (50:4–9). If v 16a is an insertion, the initial confusion in suffixes (masc. pl. 12a; fem. sing. 12b; then masc. sing. throughout, except 14, which speaks of the servant in the third person) would suggest an editorial attempt to read the entire passage as addressed to the prophetic servant of 50:4–9.[19]

In Deuteronomy 18, Yahweh promises to raise up a prophet like Moses in whose mouth Yahweh will place his words (Deut 18:18)—a phrase that is appropriated here in Isaiah 51:16 to describe the servant of Yahweh in Isaiah 51:16.

Further support for identifying the people in whose heart is Yahweh's *torah* (51:7) with the identity of the servant of Yahweh is found in the description of the *torah* that is in the heart of this people. The *torah* described in 51:7 is a *torah* with a new animation: it will proceed from Yahweh ("a law will go out from me," 51:4) when he sets his "justice for a light to the people" (51:4). Isaiah identifies this light elsewhere with the servant of Yahweh (cf. Isa 42:6; 49:8). This all takes place in tandem when Yahweh's righteousness draws near (קרב, 51:5).[20] Interestingly, this *torah*

---

19. Blenkinsopp, *Isaiah 40–55*, 334–35.

20. Justin Martyr interpreted the new promulgation of the law from Yahweh as a new covenant: "The law promulgated on Horeb is now old, and belongs to yourselves alone; but this is for all universally. Now, law placed against law has abrogated that which is before it, and a covenant which comes after in like manner has put an end to the previous one; and an eternal and final law—namely Christ—has been given to us, and the covenant is trustworthy, after which there shall be no law, no commandment, nor ordinance. Have you not read this which Isaiah says: 'Hearken unto Me, hearken unto Me, My people; and you kings, give ear unto Me: for a law shall go forth from Me, and My judgment shall be for a light to the nations.'" Martyr, *Dialogue with Trypho* (*ANF* 1:200). Lessing highlights the fact that this new covenant is accompanied by a new vindication (justification?): "Speaking about the coming Savior, Balaam says, 'I see him, but not now; I behold him, but not near' (Num 24:17). In contrast, Yahweh here announces that his righteousness and salvation *are near* . . ." In "Is 50:8 the Servant likewise asserts, 'Near is my Vindicator!'" Lessing, *Isaiah 40–55*, 545.

animation is anticipated in hope by the peoples of the coastlands (51:5), potentially an allusion to the expansion of the covenant people of God, signaling a new covenant.[21]

J. Muilenburg draws out the implications of this text when he writes, "the prophet is thinking of the new covenant with its *tôrāh* or revelation written on the heart."[22] This new covenant will reverse the state of things under the old covenant, which produced a people who "draw near with their mouth and honor me with their lips, while their hearts are far from me, and their fear of me is a commandment taught by men" (Isa 29:13). By this announcement, Yahweh promises to "again do wonderful things with this people" (29:14).

Lohfink similarly sees in Isaiah 51:7 a connection to the new covenant promise as developed in the book of Jeremiah:

> The reader of the prophets, when coming later upon Jer 31:33 and then looking back on this passage [Isaiah 51:7], will perhaps notice talk about the "new covenant" already here. For what this passage is about is the moment in which God forgives and turns once again toward God's people in exile. That is precisely the time, according to Jeremiah 31, when God writes the torah on their hearts.[23]

In Isaiah 51:7, the prophet speaks of a people who respond in obedience to the servant of Yahweh, whose coming brings about a reality similar to that foreshadowed by Deuteronomy 30.

The new covenant context of Isaiah 51 can be triangulated by another passage related to Isaiah 51:7 through a verbal and thematic connection to 51:16. In Isaiah 59:21, Yahweh addresses another 2ms individual with reference to a 3mp group of people. Yahweh declares,

> And as for me, this is my covenant with them (3mp). . . . My Spirit that is upon you, and my words that I have put in your (2ms) mouth, shall not depart out of your (2ms) mouth, or out of the mouth of your (2ms) offspring, or out of the mouth of your (2ms) children's offspring . . . from this time forth and forevermore.

---

21. I am indebted to a conversation with Peter J. Gentry for this observation.

22. Muilenburg, "The Book of Isaiah: Chapters 40–66 (Exegesis)," 595. Cf. North, *The Second Isaiah*, 211.

23. Lohfink and Zenger, *The God of Israel and the Nations*, 46n37.

The referent of the individual in whose mouth Yahweh has put his words is almost certainly the servant of Yahweh described in the Servant Songs.[24] Two verbal connections point in this direction: the Spirit is upon him (cf. Isa 42:1; 44:3; and 11:2; 32:15; 61:1) and his offspring prosper because of him (cf. 53:10).[25] The covenant described in Isaiah 59:21 is identified with the coming of an individual, the divine warrior of Isaiah 59:15b–21, who is the redeemer of 59:20.[26] In Isaiah 42:6 and 29:8 the covenant is identified *as* the servant in 42:6 and 49:8; in 59:21 the covenant is identified as the coming of the Spirit and the word(s): "my Spirit that is upon you" and "my words that I have put in your mouth"—these "will not depart" (cf. Ezek 36:26–27).[27]

The coming of the redeemer, the divine warrior, the servant of Yahweh, will bring the Spirit of Yahweh and the word(s) of Yahweh to put

24. The language of putting the words of Yahweh ("my words") in the mouth of an individual is also allusive to the servant like Moses in Deut 18, where Yahweh promises to raise up a prophet like Moses saying, "I will put my words in his mouth" (Deut 18:18).

25. So Beuken, "The Main Theme of Trito-Isaiah, 'the Servants of YHWH,'" 70.

26. A chiastic arrangement of Isa 56–66 is proposed by John Oswalt which situates 59:21 within the "Divine Warrior" motif:

56:1–8 Foreign worshipers
  56:9—59:15a Ethical righteousness
    59:15b–21 Divine Warrior
      60–62 Eschatological hope
    63:1–6 Divine Warrior
  63:7—66:17 Ethical righteousness
66:18–24 Foreign worshipers

Oswalt, *The Book of Isaiah: Chapters 40–66*, 465. Oswalt's chiasm was brought to my attention in Hamilton, *God's Glory in Salvation through Judgment*, 210.

27. Isaiah describes this new covenant through a description of Israel as a people and as an individual who is identified as the Messiah. This individual and people are interchangeable throughout Isa 40–65 and thus express a corporate solidarity. So North: "The idea of the Servant of Jehovah . . . is rooted in Israel. It is, to put it briefly and clearly, a Pyramid: its lowest basis is the whole of Israel; its middle section, Israel not merely κατά σάρκα but κατά πνευμα; its summit is the person of the Redeemer. Or to change the figure: the conception consists of two concentric circles with a common centre. The wider circle is the whole of Israel, the narrower Jeshurun (xliv. 2), the centre Christ." North, *The Suffering Servant in Deutero-Isaiah*, 44. So also Blenkinsopp: "While the identity of the prophet and disciples will probably always elude us, the second major section of the book provides a few clues, apart from 59:21, to their hidden presence. At the outset (40:1–8), the six imperatives in the plural and one in the singular attest to a mission confided to an individual prophet together with a prophetic plurality." Blenkinsopp, *Isaiah 56–66: A New Translation with Introduction and Commentary*, 202.

finally to rest the people of God's struggle against sin.[28] Lohfink connects
Isaiah 59:21 to Deuteronomy 30:11-14 when he writes:

> With the people of Jacob YHWH makes a new covenant, which
> consists in the gift of the Spirit and the gift of words put in the
> mouth, gifts that shall never depart, even in the coming genera-
> tions (59:20-21). . . . One is tempted to think of the torah here
> (cf. Deut 30:14). But the word does not occur. And even if it
> did occur, it would not be one lived out by Israel but, counter to
> Israel's own behavior, a torah given in the Spirit and only as such
> able to be handed on.[29]

At the very least, the book of Isaiah presents the people "in whose
heart is my law" as a people to be distinguished from the rest of Israel
who do not seek Yahweh or his righteousness. But if the analysis above
is correct, this people is related to the promise of a new covenant as well
as to the catalyst of this covenant: the coming of the servant of Yahweh.
An exploration of the implications of this interpretation is put off to the
concluding chapter as I turn now to the most significant development of
Deuteronomy 30:1-14 in the OT: Jeremiah 31:31-34.

---

28. Oswalt expands on this theme when he argues, "These words [in Isa 29:21]
serve to conclude not only 58:1—59:21 but also 56:1—59:21. God is depicted as the
mighty warrior who comes to defeat Israel's enemies as he first did Amalek and the
Canaanites so many years before (Exod. 17:8-13; Josh. 5:13-15). But who are those
enemies now? There is no reference to Assyria, Babylon, or Persia, or even the nearer
neighbors, the Philistines, Moabites, or Ammonites. What is it that is defeating Israel,
that is preventing its light from dawning on the world? It is no longer Babylon, for
from a literary point of view that threat has been dealt with. Yet Israel is still in need of
deliverance; it is still defeated. By what? By its inability to live the life of God, to do justice and righteousness (56:1) in the world. Here is the true enemy against which God
has come to make war. It is not the Canaanites who are the enemies of God's people,
and thus of God; rather, it is the sin that the Canaanites represent. This is the ultimate
development of the Divine Warrior motif in the Bible: God comes to destroy the final
enemy of what he has created: not the monster Chaos, but the monster Sin. This understanding of the passage is supported by what has been noted of the structure of chs.
56-59. The repetition of the call to righteousness (56:1-8; 58:1-14), the description of
Israel's inability to do righteousness (56:9—57:13; 59:1-15a), and the announcement
of the delivering power of God (57:14-21; 59:15b-21) lead to this climactic point. Just
as in the conquest of the land of Canaan, so it will be in the conquest of sin: the power
of God alone makes such a conquest possible. When it does so, the mouth of God's
people will be a clean vehicle for the Spirit of God to speak through to reveal himself
to the watching world (v. 21). In short, the vocation that came to the man of unclean
lips for his nation in ch. 6 will now have come to the nation of unclean lips (6:5) for the
world." Oswalt, *The Book of Isaiah*, 527.

29. Lohfink and Zenger, *The God of Israel and the Nations*, 55.

## Deuteronomy 30:11–14 and the Book of Jeremiah

In my view, the book of Jeremiah provides the most significant interaction with Deuteronomy 30:1–14 in the Old Testament. Similarities between the books of Jeremiah and Deuteronomy are universally noted.[30] These similarities have led scholars to one of two divergent conclusions: The critical consensus maintains that the similarities between the two are due to the same hand(s) at work shaping and composing the books of Deuteronomy and Jeremiah. Fretheim summarizes this view:

> Scholars have observed that a number of Jeremiah passages have a style, vocabulary, and perspective similar to that of the book of Deuteronomy and the Deuteronomistic History (=Joshua, Judges, Samuel, Kings; often referred to as Dtr). . . . It seems likely . . . that editors that had been at work on other literature (such as Dtr) have had their hand in Jeremiah.[31]

Most evangelical scholars, however, maintain that the similarities between the books of Deuteronomy and Jeremiah reflect a heavy dependence on the book of Deuteronomy on the part of the author or editor[32] of the book of Jeremiah. McConville articulates this view:

> This theology is arrived at as a result of Jeremiah's reflection on his own message throughout his ministry, as well as on Deuteronomy, the prophetic tradition (especially Hosea, but not exclusively so), and on parts at least of DtH. The mature Jeremiah knows that Judah could not have avoided the exile because of her inability to be other than apostate. He sees the exile as a necessary purifying judgment, and holds out hope of a wholly

---

30. Since the publication of Mowinckel's *Zur Komposition des Buches Jeremia*, studies have noted the similarities between the book of Jeremiah and the so-called deuteronomistic literature, which includes the books of Deuteronomy, Joshua, Judges, Samuel, and Kings. In an intriguing theory, Holladay suggest that parts of the book of Jeremiah would have been written with the public recitation of the Book of Deuteronomy before the people of Israel in view. Holladay, *Jeremiah*, I:197.

31. Fretheim, *Jeremiah*, 26. There is a minority opinion in critical scholarship that maintains the book of Jeremiah represents a dissenting opinion to what is recognized as the "centralization of the cult in Jerusalem." For a summary and engagement of this view, see Cazelles, "Jeremiah and Deuteronomy," 90. The majority in critical scholarship follow Wellhausen who concludes that Jeremiah "has contributed to the enactment of Deuteronomy." Wellhausen, *Israelitische und Jüdische Geschichte*, 94.

32. Some scholars who take a more conservative position on the authorship of the book of Jeremiah nevertheless argue that "[t]he book of Jeremiah is a redaction" by an editor or editors. McConville, *Judgment and Promise*, 24.

new kind of covenantal arrangement, in which the people will be enabled to live in harmony with YHWH in the ancient land.[33]

The following analysis assumes the Mosaic authorship of Deuteronomy and the subsequent authorship of the book of Jeremiah by the hand of the eponymous prophet[34] with the help of his friend and scribe, Baruch, as Jeremiah personally experienced and reflected on the unfolding history of Israel in light of earlier inspired revelation, namely the Pentateuch.[35] There is speculation that Hilkiah, Jeremiah's father (Jer 1:1), was the same high priest who rediscovered the *torah* during the reign of Josiah mentioned in 2 Kings 22:8. If true, this would further solidify Jeremiah's connection to and concern for the book of Deuteronomy.[36]

---

33. McConville, *Judgment and* Promise, 24.

34. The material recorded in the book of Jeremiah spans much of the adult life of a prophet who lived through one of the most tumultuous times in Israel's history. Nearly a century after the northern kingdom fell to the Assyrians in 722 BC, the word of Yahweh came to Jeremiah in 627 BC, commissioning him as a prophet of God to warn the nations, particularly the southern kingdom of Judah, of an impending fate similar to that experienced by her sister to the north if they failed to repent of their wickedness. The people did not heed Yahweh's warnings through his prophet, and Jeremiah's prophetic ministry witnessed the fall of the southern kingdom and eventually the destruction of Jerusalem in 586 BC at the hands of the Babylonians. The last event recorded in the book of Jeremiah takes place in Babylon in 561 BC when the exiled king of Judah, Jehoiachin, receives a place of honor in the court of the Babylonian king (Jer 52:31–34). For a defense of the dates given here, see Hamilton, *God's Glory in Salvation through Judgment*, 212–13.

35. Shead expands the possible authors of the book of Jeremiah to include a small community gathered around in support of the prophet Jeremiah. "[T]he book of Jeremiah is unique in the extent and significance of its biographical material. While some of this is presented as autobiography, the bulk is written about Jeremiah by a biographer, named in the book as Baruch a scribe for Jeremiah. . . . Not only was Baruch a scribe for Jeremiah; he was that rare thing in Jeremiah's life, a trusted ally (as may be inferred from 36:8, 19; 43:3). Actually, despite his marginalization, Jeremiah was not completely without friends and supporters, of whom the family of Shaphan, the court secretary, was the most significant politically (cf. 2 Kgs 22:8–14; Jer 26:24; 29:3; 36:10–13; 39:14). . . . It was from within the support of this group that the words of Jeremiah were written down, collected, assembled and (probably) disseminated." Shead, *A Mouth Full of Fire*, 118.

36. While some interpreters, such as Keil, dismiss this familial connection as an impossibility, others, like Hamilton, hold out the possibility. Cf. Keil and Delitzsch, *Biblical Commentary on the Old Testament*, 3:25; Hamilton, *God's Glory in Salvation through Judgment*, 212n150; Shead, *A Mouth Full of Fire*, 117.

## The Macro-Structure of Jeremiah

The structure of the book of Jeremiah is loosely chronological and can be summarized generally as two parts, chapters 2–24 and 25–51, that reflect two dispensations of Jeremiah's ministry. These two parts are framed by chapter 1, which details the call of Jeremiah and is headed by "the words of Jeremiah" (ירמיהו דברי, Jer 1:1), and chapter 52, which records the destruction of the temple after signaling the end of "the words of Jeremiah" (ירמיהו דברי, Jer 51:64). The first half of the book of Jeremiah, chapters 2–24, is largely devoted to Jeremiah's prophetic call to repentance and warnings of coming exile, what Shead refers to as "the tearing down of the nations by the word of the LORD." The second half of the book of Jeremiah in chapters 25–51, what Shead calls "the triumphant vindication of the word of the LORD among all the nations," turns from warning against exile to assuming the inevitability of the exile.[37]

For our purposes, we will be looking in detail at a few chapters in the second half of the book of Jeremiah—specifically, Jeremiah 29, which contains a letter that Yahweh commissioned Jeremiah to write to the exiles; and Jeremiah 30–33, where Jeremiah's prophetic words turn to a note of hope even in the midst of Israel's seemingly inevitable exilic judgment.

## Jeremiah's Deuteronomic Vision

The note of hope struck in Jeremiah 30–33 is of particular interest to the current thesis. In this section, I will argue that Jeremiah sets forth a new covenant hope in these chapters *primarily* through a deuteronomic lens, particularly the prophetic vision encountered in Deuteronomy 30:1–14.

---

37. Shead, *A Mouth Full of Fire*, 73. For a literary diagram in defense of this structure of Jeremiah, see ibid., 69. The book of Jeremiah can also be subdivided by a variation of the heading, "The word that came to Jeremiah from the LORD" (Jer. 7:1; 11:1; 18:1; 21:1; 25:1 [lacks "from the LORD"]; 30:1; 32:1; 34:1, 8; 35:1; 40:1; 44:1 [lacks "from the LORD"]). John Bright argues that the book of Jeremiah contains three smaller "books" stitched together mostly by biographical material arranged topically with no discernable literary structure. The three "books" Bright suggests are the oracles of doom (Jer 1–25), the message hope (30–33), and the oracles against foreign nations (46–51). Bright, "Book of Jeremiah," 259–78. But Shead has convincingly shown the presence of a more sophisticated literary structure in the book of Jeremiah. Shead, *A Mouth Full of Fire*, 65–106. While LXX Jeremiah contains significantly less text than MT Jeremiah, there is good reason to suppose the LXX text represents an incomplete edition of Jeremiah. For a detailed discussion on the differences between the LXX and MT, see Gentry, "The Septuagint and the Text of the Old Testament," 217.

Specifically, my aim is to demonstrate how Jeremiah's language of *torah* written on the heart that accompanies the prophetic vision of the new covenant in Jeremiah 31:31–34 stems directly from Deuteronomy 30:11–14 and its relationship to Deuteronomy 30:1–10.[38] But before looking at Jeremiah 31:31–34 in parallel with Deuteronomy 30:1–14, I will first establish what I will refer to as Jeremiah's deuteronomic orientation in the Book of Consolation (Jer 30–33), specifically, but also in the book more generally. I will do this by highlighting verbal, thematic, and structural connections between the two texts.

## Thematic and Verbal Connections to Deuteronomy in Jeremiah 1–28

Throughout his appeal to Israel leading up to chapters 30–33, Jeremiah uniquely appropriates the theological vocabulary and perspective of Deuteronomy to draw attention to the root problem that is careening Israel toward exile: their own hearts. As McConville put it, "*Jeremiah* mirrors the train of thought ... in Deuteronomy."[39] I believe Jeremiah's treatment of the following themes particularly exhibits a dependence on Deuteronomy's heart theology: (1) Israel's stubborn heart, (2) Yahweh's gift of a heart to know, and (3) the (un)circumcised heart.

### Israel's Stubborn Heart

Whereas in Deuteronomy 29:18 [ET 29:19] Israel is warned to beware of the one who would walk in the stubbornness of his own heart, in the book of Jeremiah a prime descriptor of Israel's rebellious nature is that they are stubborn of heart (Jer 3:17; 7:24; 9:13 [9:14 ET]; 11:8; 13:10; 16:12; 18:12; 23:17). This appeal to deuteronomic vocabulary is more significant when we observe with Gentry that "[t]he Hebrew expression 'the stubbornness of his/their heart' occurs ten times in the Old Testament:

38. In their *Handbook on Jeremiah*, Newman and Stine note the potential allusion to Deut 30:11–14 in Jer 31:31–33 when they write, "Put my law within them and write it upon their hearts mean essentially the same thing ... in Hebrew psychology within them would represent the seat of emotions, while heart would be the equivalent of 'mind' in the modern world. Another way to express this is 'I will make my law part of their thinking and feeling.' See Deut 6.6; 30.11, 14." Newman and Stine, *A Handbook on Jeremiah*, 652.

39. McConville, *Judgment and Promise*, 82–83.

the one instance in Deuteronomy (Dt. 29:18 [ET 29:19]) is picked up by Jeremiah, who uses the phrase a total of eight times (Jer. 3:17; 7:24; 9:13 [9:14 ET]; 11:8; 13:10; 16:12; 18:12; 23:17)."[40]

### *Yahweh's Gift of a Heart to Know*

One finds another allusion to Deuteronomy's theology of the heart in Jeremiah 24:7 where Yahweh promises to "give [Israel] a heart to know" after exile because (כי) they will "return to [Yahweh] with their whole heart."[41] In this text, Jeremiah recalls the dilemma in Deuteronomy 29:3 [ET 29:4] where Moses tells Israel that Yahweh has not yet given them a "heart to know," and he develops it through a promise. As Wells argues, "[t]his gift anticipates Jeremiah's descriptions of a new and eternal covenant" that is found in the Book of Consolation.[42]

### *The (Un)circumcised Heart*

The metaphor of heart circumcision plays a prominent role in the books of Deuteronomy and Jeremiah. Outside these two books, the metaphor of heart circumcision is only twice explicitly referenced in the OT: Leviticus 26:41 and Ezekiel 44:7. In both occurrences, the metaphor appears negatively, "uncircumcised hearts." The books of Jeremiah and Deuteronomy each mention heart circumcision twice: Deuteronomy 10:16 and 30:6, which were considered in a previous chapter, and Jeremiah 4:4 and 9:24–25 (ET 9:25–26; cf. 6:10). Echoing Deuteronomy 10:16, Israel is commanded in Jeremiah 4:4 to "circumcise" their hearts.

---

40. Gentry and Wellum, *Kingdom through Covenant*, 503. The other place where this phrase occurs is Ps 81:13. If the search is expanded to include the Hebrew lemma סרר, which is phonetically and conceptually similar to שׁרר, one more reference to a "stubborn heart" is located in Jer 5:23.

41. Contrary to Hans Walter Wolff, who argues that "knowledge of Yahweh" refers to a cognitive capacity that knows by heart the salvation tradition, Brueggemann suggests that "'knowledge of Yahweh' means affirmation of Yahweh as sovereign LORD with readiness to obey the commands for justice that are the will of Yahweh." Brueggemann, *A Commentary on Jeremiah*, 293. So also Unterman, *From Repentance to Redemption*, 76–80; Fretheim, *Jeremiah*, 347.

42. Wells, *Grace and Agency in Paul and Second Temple Judaism*, 43.

| | | | Jer 3:17 | שררות לבם |
|---|---|---|---|---|
| | | | Jer 7:24 | בשררות לבם |
| | | | Jer 9:13 (ET 9:14) | שררות לבם |
| stubborn heart | Deut 29:18 [ET 29:19] | בשררות לבי | Jer 11:8 | בשרירות לבם |
| | | | Jer 13:10 | בשררות לבם |
| | | | Jer 16:12 | בשררות לבו |
| | | | Jer 18:12 | בשררות לבו |
| | | | Jer 23:17 | בשררות לבו |
| gift of a heart to know | Deut 29:3 [ET 29:4] | ולא־נתן יהוה לכם לב לדעת | Jer 24:7 | ונתתי להם לב לדעת |
| (un)circumcised heart | Deut 10:16 | ומלתם את ערלת לבבכם | Jer 4:4 | המלו ליהוה והסרו ערלות לבבכם |
| | Deut 30:6 | ומל יהוה אלהיך את־לבבך ואת־לבב זרעך | Jer 9:25 (ET 9:26) | ערלי־לב |

**Table 8. Verbal parallels in the heart theology of Jeremiah and Deuteronomy**

Then in Jeremiah 9:24–25 (ET 9:25–26), Jeremiah polemicizes against a circumcision of the flesh that has failed to lead to heart change by comparing Israel to the surrounding nations.

> Behold, the days are coming, declares the LORD, when I will punish all those who are circumcised merely in the flesh—Egypt, Judah, Edom, the sons of Ammon, Moab, and all who dwell in the desert who cut the corners of their hair, for all these nations are uncircumcised, and all the house of Israel are uncircumcised in heart. (Jer 9:24–25 [ET 9:25–26])

Particularly noteworthy in this text is Judah's inclusion among the list of pagan nations. Carroll gets to the significance of this inclusion when he writes, "In spite of the fact that the group of nations referred to all practised circumcision, they would be the object of Yahweh's punishment."[43] Circumcision in the flesh will not save from the coming wrath of Yahweh. In fact, it fails even to set Israel apart from her surrounding neighbors who also practice circumcision. Yahweh could not be clearer: the sign without the thing signified is meaningless, and "all the house of Israel" lacks the significant reality: a circumcised heart.

The verbal similarities between these concepts in the books of Jeremiah and Deuteronomy—Israel's stubborn heart, Yahweh's gift of a heart to know, and the (un)circumcised heart—are summarized in table 8 above. These observations are merely the first in a series of shared imagery and vocabulary between Jeremiah and Deuteronomy.

## Heart Circumcision and Writing the Law on the Heart

Turning from broad themes to specific texts in Jeremiah 29–33, it is clear that Jeremiah's theology continues to mirror the book of Deuteronomy. Although heart circumcision is mentioned explicitly only twice in Deuteronomy, Stephen Dempster notes the similarities between Jeremiah's description of the heart in the new covenant and the deuteronomic heart circumcision in Deuteronomy 30:6:

> There is a strong link between this "Little Book of Comfort" and portions of the Torah, particularly Deuteronomy. Repentance in exile, restoration and a change in heart echo deuteronomic language. The law written on the heart is conceptually similar to the deuteronomic "circumcision of the heart", which is also found in other parts of Jeremiah (Jer. 4:4; cf. 9:25–26 [MT 9:24–25]). Jeremiah expands on the deuteronomic concepts and sees things happening as a complex of events "in the latter days".[44]

As I argue below in agreement with Dempster, Jeremiah's imagery of the law written on the heart in the context of a new covenant is similar to and a development of the circumcision of the heart introduced by Deuteronomy in 10:16 and promised in 30:6. According to Lundbom, the newness of Jeremiah's covenant is addressed to the deuteronomic recognition of the law's inability to penetrate the human heart *per se*:

> The new covenant is new because Yahweh's *torah* will be written on the human heart. The Sinai covenant was written on tablets of stone (Exod 24:12; 31:18; et passim). In the homiletical

43. Carroll, *Jeremiah*, 250.
44. Dempster, *Dominion and Dynasty*, 166.

rhetoric of Deuteronomy, however, the *torah* was supposed to find its way into the human heart (Deut 6:6; 11:18). But Deuteronomy knows—as does Jeremiah—that the heart is deceitful and layered with evil (Deut 10:16; 11:16; Jer 4:4). Jeremiah . . . believes that the people have not the ability within themselves to make their relationship with Yahweh right again (2:25; 13:23). Nevertheless, prior "heart talk" in Deuteronomy and Jeremiah is background for and determines the articulation of the new covenant promise. If the law did not penetrate the human heart before, and this might still be debated (Ps 119:11), it will with the new covenant in place, because Yahweh promises to make it happen (cf. Isa 51:7).[45]

## Thematic and Verbal Connections in Jeremiah's Letter to the Exiles.

The Book of Consolation comes on the heels of a letter commissioned by Yahweh in chapter 29 that Jeremiah writes to those who had been taken captive to Babylon. In the flow of the book of Jeremiah, this letter sets the reader/listener up to think in deuteronomic categories ahead of the chapters 30–33.

In this letter, Yahweh doubles down on a promise he made to Israel: "For thus says the LORD: When seventy years are completed for Babylon, I will visit you, and I will fulfill to you my promise and bring you back to this place" (Jer 29:10). Where/when exactly did Yahweh promise to bring Israel back to this place? This promise is spelled out most explicitly in Deuteronomy. In fact, as table 9 demonstrates below, Jeremiah uses deuteronomic language to convey this hope.

Nathan Mastnjak's work on the literary connections between Jeremiah and Deuteronomy supports this inter-canonical allusion: "The connections between Jer 29:13–14a and Deut 4:29 are strong. . . . The lexical correspondence is dense and unparalleled elsewhere. As such, a literary relationship appears highly probable."[46]

45. Lundbom, *Jeremiah*, 2:468. Though Lundbom clearly views the books of Jeremiah and Deuteronomy to share a perspective on the condition of the human heart and its, to say the least, complicated relationship with the *torah* under the Old Covenant, he goes on right after this quotation to cite Deut 30:11–14 as supporting the exact opposite conclusion: "Even in the later chapters of Deuteronomy, which may be contemporary with Jeremiah, the law is said to reside in human mouths and hearts, enabling people to carry it out without difficulty."

46. Mastnjak, *Deuteronomy and the Emergence of Textual Authority in Jeremiah*, 196.

When Israel seeks Yahweh with their whole heart (Jer 29:13; cf. Deut 4:29), Yahweh will restore their fortunes (Jer 29:14; cf. Deut 30:3). This last phrase, "restore fortunes" (שוב שבות) first appears in the OT in Deuteronomy 30 and serves in the rest of the canon as a kind of technical term for Yahweh's post-exilic, redemptive blessing (cf. Job 42:10; Ps 14:7; 53:6; 85:1; 126:1, 4; Lam 2:14; Ezek 16:53; 29:14; 39:25; Hos 6:11; Joel 3:1; Amos 9:14; Zeph 2:7; 3:20). As the reader moves into the Book of Consolation, the book of Jeremiah seems to intend for Deuteronomy to give color to its interpretation.

| Jeremiah 29:13–14a | Deuteronomy 4:29 | Deuteronomy 30:3 |
|---|---|---|
| ובקשתם אתי <u>ומצאתם כי</u> <u>תדרשני בכל־לבבכם</u>: <br><br> <u>ונמצאתי</u> לכם נאס־יהוה <u>ושבתי</u> את־שביתכם <u>וקבצתי</u> אתכם | <u>ובקשתם</u> משם את־יהוה אלהיך <u>ומצאת כי תדרשנו</u> בכל־לבב ובכל־נפשך | ושב יהוה אלהיך <u>את־שבותך</u> ורחמך ושב <u>וקבצך</u> מכל־ העמים אשר הפיצך יהוה אלהיך שמה: |
| You will seek me and <u>find me</u>, <u>because you will seek me with all your heart</u>. I will be <u>found</u> by you, declares the LORD, and I will <u>restore your fortunes</u> and <u>gather you</u> . . . | But from there <u>you will seek</u> the LORD your God and <u>you will find</u> him, <u>because you will seek him with all your heart</u> and with all your soul. | then the LORD your God will <u>restore your fortunes</u> and have mercy on you, and he will <u>gather you</u> |

Table 9. Jeremiah recapitulates the promise of Deuteronomy

## Thematic, Verbal, and Structural Links to Deuteronomy in Jeremiah's Book of Consolation

Jeremiah's use of the phrase, "restore fortunes" (שוב שבות), a phrase which occurs uniquely in the Pentateuch in Deuteronomy 30:3 and rather infrequently in the OT, stitches together the letter to the exiles in chapter 29 and the Book of Consolation in chapters 30–33. It also serves to punctuate in deuteronomic terms Yahweh's promise to bless Israel in the context of the return from exile and a new covenant (Jer 30:18; 31:23; 32:44; 33:7, 11, 26). This is the first strong link between Jeremiah's Book of Consolation and Deuteronomy 30. McConville similarly notes,

The orientation of *Jeremiah* to Deuteronomy 30 is proved by a further point of contact, namely the phrase, "then the LORD your God will restore your fortunes." This phrase, used only here in Deuteronomy 30:3, occurs with slight variants, eleven times in *Jeremiah*, eight referring to the restoration of Judah. Once again *Jeremiah* has taken its cue from Deuteronomy, but, as we shall see, develops the idea in its own away.[47]

| Stanza | vv. | Audience | Opening | Theme |
|--------|-----|----------|---------|-------|
| Preamble | 30:1–4 | -- | -- | The hope of restored fortunes (שוב שבות) |
| Song 1 | 30:5–11 | male | -- | Forgiveness is not enough |
| Song 2 | 30:12–17 | female | -- | Justice is not enough |
| Song 3 | 30:18—31:1 | male | -- | Meditation is not enough |
| Song 4 | 31:2–6 | female | -- | God's unquenchable love . . . |
| Song 5 | 31:7–14 | male | -- | . . . is shown to the judged |
| | 31:15–17 | female | | |
| Song 6 | 31:18–20 | male | -- | Mourning turns to joy |
| | 31:21–22 | female | | |
| Epilogue | 31:23–26 | the land | -- | Fortunes restored (שוב שבות) |
| Promise 1 | 31:27–30 | -- | "Behold, days are coming" | A new Israel |
| Promise 2 | 31:31–34 | -- | "Behold, days are coming" | A new heart and covenant |
| Guarantee | 31:35–37 | -- | "Thus says the LORD" | A hope as solid as the earth |
| Promise 3 | 31:38–40 | -- | "Behold, days are coming | A new life with God |

**Table 10. Structure of Jeremiah's Book of Consolation**

47. McConville, *Judgment and Promise*, 83.

The careful structure of the first two chapters of the Book of Consolation also serves to drive home Jeremiah's deuteronomic orientation. According to Shead, the Hebrew phrase שוב שבות, which occurs prominently in both the preamble (Jer 30:1–4) and epilogue (31:23–26) of the songs in the carefully structured Book of Consolation presented in table 10 above, "announces the subject of the Book of Consolation: the restoring of fortunes."[48] The fact that this phrase's *font* is Deuteronomy 30:1–14 should trigger an inter-canonical awareness.[49] What Jeremiah announces in this detailed section is an expanded vision of the deuteronomic promise of restoration in Deuteronomy 30:1–14.

Other vocabulary similarities further cement the connection between Jeremiah's Book of Consolation and Deuteronomy 30. In both passages, Yahweh promises to gather (צבק Jer 31:8, 10; cf. Deut 30:3) Israel from far away where he scattered them (צפו Jer 30:11; cf. Deut 30:3), and to return them (שוב Jer 30:3, 10; 31:8, 16, 17, 18[x2], 21[x2]; cf. Deut 30:2)[50] to the land of their fathers so that they may possess it (שיר Jer 30:3; cf. Deut 30:5). There Yahweh will have compassion on them (רחם Jer 30:18; 31:20; cf. Deut 30:3) and will multiply them (רבה Jer 30:19; cf. Deut 30:5).

In Deuteronomy 30:1–14, the themes of "repentance," "return," and "restoration" are all summarized by the productively versatile שוב. And in Deuteronomy 30:1–10, שוב is a central verb in the prophetic reconciliation:

> And when all these things come upon you, the blessing and the curse, which I have set before you, then you will *return* (שוב) them to heart among all the nations where the LORD your God has driven you, and will *return* (שוב) to the LORD your God, you and your children, and obey his voice in all that I command you today, with all your heart and with all your soul, and the LORD your God will *restore* (שוב) your fortunes and have mercy on you, and he will *return* (שוב) and gather you again from all the peoples where the LORD your God has scattered you. . . . And you shall *return* (שוב) to obey the voice of the LORD and keep all his commandments that I command you today. The LORD

48. Shead, *A Mouth Full of Fire*, 188.

49. Table 10 is adapted from Shead, *A Mouth Full of Fire*, 189. Shead is following closely the work of Bozak in *Life Anew*.

50. As noted in chapter 2, שוב plays an integral part to Deut 30:1–14, occurring seven times in that passage. This word is also integral to the Book of Consolation (Jer 30–33), occurring twenty times.

your God will make you abundantly prosperous in all the work of your hand, in the fruit of your womb and in the fruit of your cattle and in the fruit of your ground. For the LORD will *return* (שוב) to taking delight in prospering you, as he took delight in your fathers, when you obey the voice of the LORD your God, to keep his commandments and his statutes that are written in this Book of the Law, when you *turn* (שוב) to the LORD your God with all your heart and with all your soul. (Deut. 30:1–3; 8–10)[51]

It could be said, then, that the prayer of Ephraim in captivity in Jeremiah 31:18 is a summary prayer for the prophetic promise in Deuteronomy 30:1–14 to be made a reality: "Bring me back (שוב) that I may be restored (שוב)." Turning attention now to Jeremiah 31:31–34, an awareness that not only the book of Deuteronomy but Deuteronomy 30:1–14 specifically is in the background helps make sense of Jeremiah's metaphorical imagery.[52]

## Deuteronomy 30:1–14 in Jeremiah 31:31–34

Jeremiah 31:31–34 is the second of three oracles that span Jeremiah 31:27–40 and are all similarly headed by the prophetic declaration, "Behold, the days are coming, declares the LORD" (Jer 31:27; 31; 38), which also occurs at Jeremiah 30:3.[53] The elaborate structure of Jeremiah 30–31, along with the thematic unity of the eschatological vision of reconciliation telling of the coming days to behold (Jer 30:3; 31:27, 31, 38), bind these passages together and demand a mutually informing interpretation.[54]

51. My translation, adapted from the ESV.

52. As Dempster says, "Repentance in exile, restoration and a change in heart echo deuteronomic language. The law written on the heart is conceptually similar to the deuteronomic 'circumcision of the heart' . . . Jeremiah expands on the deuteronomic concepts and sees things happening as a complex of events 'in the latter days.'" Dempster, *Dominion and Dynasty*, 166.

53. Gentry notes that these three "prophetic oracles" come at the end of the direct divine address which took place as Jeremiah was sleeping (Jer 31:26). Perhaps these oracles are to be understood as a continuation of the word of the LORD that came to Jeremiah in 30:1, which would explain the divine first-person address and the repetition of the phrase "declares the LORD." Or, as Gentry suggests, these three oracles are appended to the end of the Book of Consolation not as a continuation of the vision but as thematically similar revelations that further fill out the vision. Gentry and Wellum, *Kingdom through Covenant*, 494.

54. Contra Buis, who argues, "It is more difficult to situate Dt. 30:1–10, which is fairly commonly attributed to the Deuteronomist edition of Deuteronomy when it is

## The First Oracle: Replacing the Mosaic Covenant

In the first oracle (Jer 31:27–30), Yahweh's commissioning word to Jeremiah in Jeremiah 1:10 is assumed by Yahweh to reveal that Jeremiah's work has been the work of Yahweh: "And it shall come to pass that as I have watched over them to pluck up and break down, to overthrow, destroy, and bring harm, so I will watch over them to build and to plant, declares the LORD" (Jer 31:28). While Jeremiah was temporarily set over nations to pluck up and break down, to overthrow and destroy, to build and to plant, Yahweh reveals here that he has been behind the scenes all along, as it were, sovereignly conducting the orchestra of these events. Yahweh's commissioning of Jeremiah was intentionally ordered: the plucking up and the breaking down, the overthrowing and the destroying—these chronologically precede the building and the planting in history. But Yahweh's promise is emphatic: though he has stood against Israel in the past for their destruction, days are coming when he will build and plant. Not only will Yahweh turn his energies from bringing harm to building up, but the very covenantal structures that uphold the current paradigm will be shaken in the process: "In those days they shall no longer say:

---

not assigned a later date. This text is therefore probably more recent than Jr. 31. Does it follow that it depends on it? That would be a far too quick conclusion. The two texts have little in common (Dt. 30:8 and Jr. 31:33); Dt. 30 would be closer to Jr. 24 (Dt. 30:3, 4, 9 and Jr. 24:6; Dt. 30:6 and Jr. 24:7). And it is distinguished from all other oracles by situating the conversion of the people into exile before the return and establishment of the new covenant (alone Ba. 2:30 follows it on this point). It is the transposition of a theme which appears in several parts of Deuteronomy: entry into the land of Canaan is conditioned by fidelity to the law, it is a blessing among the others (Dt. 4:1; 6:18; 8:1; 16:20; 11: 8). The return is therefore seen in the same light as the conquest; it will be a new *heilsgeschichte*, an idea which clearly outweighs that of a new covenant in Dt. 30" (my translation). "Il est plus difficile de situer Dt. xxx 1–10, qu'on attribue assez communément à l'édition deutéronomiste du Deutéronome, quand on ne lui assigne pas une date plus tardive. Ce texte est donc très probablement plus récent que Jr. xxxi. S'ensuit-il qu'il en dépende? Ce serait une conclusion beaucoup trop rapide. Les deux textes n'ont que peu de points communs (Dt. xxx 8 et Jr. xxxi 33); Dt. xxx se rapprocherait plutôt de Jr. xxiv (Dt. xxx 3, 4, 9 et Jr. xxiv 6; Dt. xxx 6 et Jr. xxiv 7). Et il se distingue de tous les autres oracles en situant la conversion du peuple en exil, avant le retour et l'établissement de la nouvelle alliance (seul Ba. ii 30 le suit sur ce point). C'est la transposition d'un thème qui apparait dans plusieurs parties du Deutéronome: l'entrée dans le pays de Canaan est conditonnée par la fidélité à la loi, c'est une bénédiction parmi les autres (Dt. iv 1; vi 18; viii 1; xvi 20; xi 8). Le retour est donc vu dans la même optique que la conquête; ce sera une nouvelle «Heilsgeschichte», idée qui l'emporte nettement sur celle de nouvelle alliance dans Dt. xxx." Buis, "La Nouvelle Alliance," 13.

'The fathers have eaten sour grapes, and the children's teeth are set on edge.' But everyone shall die for his own iniquity. Each man who eats sour grapes, his teeth shall be set on edge" (Jer 31:29–30).

In Deuteronomy 29, the sins of an individual set in motion the exile of an entire people. No longer will this be the case in the days to come. Carson rightly points out the radical nature of this claim: it necessarily undermines the entire Mosaic covenant:

> The [Mosaic] covenant structure was profoundly racial and trib-al. Designated leaders—prophets, priests, king, and occasion-ally other leaders such as the seventy elders or Bezalel—were endued with the Spirit, and spoke for God to the people and for the people of God. Thus when the leaders sinned, the entire nation was contaminated, and ultimately faced divine wrath. But the time is coming, Jeremiah says, when this proverb will be abandoned. "Instead," God promises, "everyone will die for his own sin; whoever eats sour grapes—his own teeth will be set on edge" (Jer. 31:30). This could be true only if the entire covenantal structure associated with Moses' name is replaced by another.[55]

In this way, the first oracle sets up the second oracle by subtly sug-gesting the need for a new covenant.

### The Second Oracle: New Covenant, New Heart

The second oracle spans Jeremiah 31:31–37 and contains what I argue is a biblical-theological development of Deuteronomy 30:11–14. In this oracle, Yahweh makes explicit what was implicit in the first oracle: days are coming when Yahweh will establish a new covenant with his people that is "not like the covenant that I made with their fathers" (Jer 31:32). In Jeremiah 31:31–34, Jeremiah relates this prophetic vision of the new covenant, which is described as eternal in poetic terms in 31:35–37. This is the covenant to complete all covenants.

With the book of Deuteronomy in mind, and specifically Deuter-onomy 30:1–14, several inter-canonical connections between these two passages are apparent: (1) the mention of a new covenant; (2) the heart-internalization of the *torah*; and (3) "knowledge" of Yahweh.

---

55. Carson, "Evangelicals, Ecumenism, and the Church," 359–60.

## Newness of the New Covenant

Jeremiah 31:31–34 is the only place in the OT where a covenant is referred to as "new." This passage has drawn a great deal of attention not only from biblical scholars, but also from the New Testament writers themselves. What is "new" in the new covenant? Duhm argues that interpreters should ignore the word "new" and acknowledge that there is nothing new in the new covenant—in fact, everything promised in Jeremiah 31:31–34 is already said to be readily available under the Mosaic covenant. In support of this claim, Duhm turns to a passage significant for the current thesis: Deuteronomy 30:11–14:

> If one does not allow oneself to be blinded by the terms "new covenant," "writing on the heart," then the passage tells us no more about the relation of the individual than what Deuteronomy already considered possible (Dtn 30:11ff) and desirable (Dtn 6:6–8), namely that every man should be in the law at home and faithfully observe it.[56]

As I made clear above, I am unpersuaded by this reading of Deuteronomy 30:11–14. I believe Duhm is correct, however, to point to Deuteronomy 30:11–14 as an interpretive key to Jeremiah 31:31–34, but for the exact opposite reason.

As I argued in chapter 2, Deuteronomy 30:1–14 is rehearsed in the context of a covenant that is to be distinguished from a previously established covenant (Deut 28:69 [ET 29:1]), which has led some to call the covenant at Moab a "new" covenant.[57] This context of a "new" covenant is the first of several touchpoints between Jeremiah 31:31–34 and Deuteronomy 30:1–14. The new covenant Jeremiah 31 describes is contrasted with—"not like" (ב לֹא, Jer 31:32); "no longer" (עוֹד . . . לֹא, Jer 31:34)—the covenant "which [Israel] broke" (Jer 31:32). From Jeremiah's standpoint, the old covenant was broken the day of its institution (Jer 31:32; cf. 7:22–26; 11:7–8) and in fact was in worse shape than what the

---

56. My translation. "Wenn man sich von den Ausdrücken: 'neuer Bund', 'ins Herz schreiben' nicht blenden lässt, so sagt uns die Stelle über das Verhältnis des Einzelnen nicht mehr, als was schon das Deuteronomium für möglich (Dtn 30:11ff) und wünschenswert (Dtn 6:6–8) ansah, dass nämlich jeder im Gesetz zu Hause sein und es treulich befolgen wird." Duhm, *Das Buch Jeremia*, 254–55. Duhm's interpretation is followed by Ludwig, "Shape of Hope: Jeremiah's Book of Consolation," 540ff.

57. Sailhamer, *The Pentateuch as Narrative*, 471.

wilderness generation experienced: "You have done worse than your fathers" (Jer 16:12; cf. 7:26).[58]

The human partners are to blame for this covenant failure, just as Yahweh predicted would happen in Deuteronomy 31:16–22 and Moses echoed in the prologue to his song in 31:26–29. What is introduced in the new covenant in Jeremiah 31:31–34, then, is a remedy to the failing aspects of the old covenant: the *torah* written on the human heart accompanied by a knowledge of Yahweh that is grounded in the unconditional forgiveness of sins. The newness of the new covenant must be explained, at the very least, as a new mechanism whereby the law is able to penetrate the callous heart. As Seebass puts it, this new covenant "kündigt eine radikale anthropogische Erneuerung des Gottesvolkes."[59] Calvin expands on this new aspect of the covenant when he writes,

> As then God has added nothing to the Law as to the substance of the doctrine, we must come, as I have already said, to the form, as Christ was not as yet manifested: God made a new covenant, when he accomplished through his Son whatever had been shadowed forth under the Law. For the sacrifices could not of themselves pacify God, as it is well known, and whatever the Law taught respecting expiation was of itself useless and of no importance. The new covenant then was made when Christ appeared with water and blood, and really fulfilled what God had exhibited under types, so that the faithful might have some taste of salvation. But the coming of Christ would not have been sufficient, had not regeneration by the Holy Spirit been added. *It was, then, in some respects, a new thing, that God regenerated the faithful by his Spirit, so that it became not only a doctrine as to the*

---

58. Calvin concurs: "The circumstance as to the time ought to be noticed, for the memory of a recent benefit ought to be a most powerful motive to obedience. For how base an ingratitude it was for those, who had been delivered by the wonderful power of God, to reject his covenant at a time when they had been anticipated by divine mercy? As then they had made void even at that time the covenant of God, it may with certainty be concluded, that there had been no time in which they had not manifested their impiety, and had not been covenant-breakers." Calvin, *Commentaries on the Book of the Prophet Jeremiah and the Lamentations*, 4:129. So also McKane, *A Critical and Exegetical Commentary on Jeremiah*, 1:172–73; Thompson, *The Book of Jeremiah*, 289.

59. My translation: "announces a radical anthropological renewal of the people of God." Seebass, "Erstes oder Altes Testament?," 33. So also Eichrodt: "The purport of Jer. 31.31ff., even though it does not speak of the spirit, is in effect no different from that of Isa. 32.15ff.; 11.9 or Ezek. 36.26ff., namely a new possibility, created by God himself, of realizing the will of God in human life." Eichrodt, *Theology of the Old Testament*, 2:58n5.

*letter, but also efficacious, which not only strikes the ear, but penetrates into the heart, and really forms us for the service of God.*[60]

## INTERNALIZATION OF THE TORAH

The unique contribution of Jeremiah's vision of the new covenant comes in his description of the relationship between the law and the heart(s) of the covenant people. Jeremiah describes this new covenant: "I will put my law within them, and I will write it on their hearts" (נתתי את־תורתי בקרבם ועל־לבם אכתבנה).

The meaning of these two phrases has been variously understood, the first of which provides the most divergent interpretations. First, should the perfect verb נתתי be rendered in the past tense, "I put," or in the future tense, "I will put"? Adrian Schenker argues that since the verb is a Hebrew perfect, the first reading is to be preferred, which he argues is a reference

---

60. Calvin, *Commentaries on the Book of the Prophet Jeremiah and the Lamentations*, 4:127. Emphasis added. Calvin qualifies his description of the newness of regeneration "in some respects" later when he writes, "A question may however be here moved, Was the grace of regeneration wanting to the Fathers under the Law? But this is quite preposterous. What, then, is meant when God denies here that the Law was written on the heart before the coming of Christ? To this I answer, that the Fathers, who were formerly regenerated, obtained this favor through Christ, so that we may say, that it was as it were transferred to them from another source. The power then to penetrate into the heart was not inherent in the Law, but it was a benefit transferred to the Law from the Gospel. This is one thing. Then we know that this grace of God was rare and little known under the Law; but that under the Gospel the gifts of the Spirit have been more abundantly poured forth, and that God has dealt more bountifully with his Church. But still the main thing is, to consider what the Law of itself is, and what is peculiar to the Gospel, especially when a comparison is made between the Law and the Gospel. For when this comparison ceases, this cannot be properly applied to the Law; but with regard to the Gospel it is said, that the Law is that of the letter, as it is called elsewhere, (Romans 7:6) and this also is the reason why Paul calls it the letter in 2 Corinthians 3:6, 'the letter killeth,' etc. By 'letter' he means not what Origen foolishly explained, for he perverted that passage as he did almost the whole Scripture: Paul does not mean there the simple and plain sense of the Law; for he calls it the letter for another reason, because it only sets before the eyes of men what is right, and sounds it also in their ears. And the word letter refers to what is written, as though he had said, The Law was written on stones, and was therefore a letter. But the Gospel—what is it? It is spirit, that is, God not only addresses his word to the ears of men and sets it before their eyes, but he also inwardly teaches their hearts and minds. This is then the solution of the question: the Prophet speaks of the Law in itself, as apart from the Gospel, for the Law then is dead and destitute of the Spirit of regeneration." Ibid., 4:131. I revisit this quotation by Calvin in the concluding chapter below.

to when Yahweh gave Israel the law, "I put my law in their midst/among them."[61] Gentry notes, however, that when a prophetic perfect is followed by a *waw*-consecutive perfect or imperfect that is not clause-initial, this construction is the "normal pattern for beginning a prophecy in the future tense."[62] In line with this understanding, the LXX renders this verb as a future (δώσω νόμους μου εἰς τὴν διάνοιαν αὐτῶν, LXX Jer. 38:33).[63] As a future-oriented phrase, then, this gift of the law must somehow be distinguished from the gift of the law under the old covenant.

What does it mean that the law will be set within them/in their midst (קרב)? Does this refer to the midst of a crowd or people, such as when the law was put "in the midst" of the people when the tablets were set in ark of the covenant, or does it refer individually to the inward parts of a person? The answer becomes clear when the parallelism in Jeremiah 31:33 is recognized. Hebrew parallelism describes the same reality from two angles:[64] "I will put my law within them/I will write it on their hearts." In this way, the phrases become mutually interpreting.

| Jer 31:33a | Jer 31:33b |
|---|---|
| נתתי | אכתבנה |
| את־תורתי | ‑נה |
| בקרבם | על־לבם |

**Table 11. Parallelism in Jeremiah 31:33**

"I will put"/"I will write" both metaphorically describe the action of internalization with Yahweh as agent. "My law"/"it" both refer to the

---

61. Schenker, *Das Neue am Neuen Bund und das Alte am Alten*, 30.

62. Gentry goes on to cite Num 24:17 as an example of this pattern. Gentry and Wellum, *Kingdom through Covenant*, 506n23.

63. Some Hebrew manuscripts have a *weqatal* verbal form, which implies a future. While the perfect verbal form is probably original, the future context of the pericope would explain the addition of a *waw* and may also explain why the Greek translator would render it with a future verbal form. Rudolph, *Jeremia*, 170; Carroll, *Jeremiah*, 610.

64. In the eleventh century, Ibn Ezra summarized parallelism as "an elegance of style, and in particular a characteristic of the *prophetic* style, to repeat the same thought by means of synonymous words." Cited from Gray, *The Forms of Hebrew Poetry*, 18. For an in-depth treatment of Hebrew parallelism, see Berlin, *The Dynamics of Biblical Parallelism*.

same content to be internalized, namely the *torah*. "Within them"/"on their heart" both metaphorically depict the location of the action: the putting and writing of the law will take place in the inward parts of the covenant people. Each part of this parallelism deserves careful attention.

Under the old covenant arrangement, the law was written on tablets of stone and placed in the ark of the covenant. The people were to read, know, and obey the law—they were to internalize this external word, as Yahweh commands in Deuteronomy 6:6, 9: "[T]hese words that I command you today shall be on your heart. . . . You shall write them on the doorposts of your house and on your gates" (cf. Deut 11:18; 32:46).[65] But by the end of Deuteronomy, it is clear that this command is not enough to enact lasting covenant obedience. The people lack the will to obey and have not internalized the words of Yahweh. In Jeremiah, the same problem persists, so much so that what is revealed to be "on the heart" of the covenant people is not the words of Yahweh but instead their own sin: "The sin of Judah is written with a pen of iron; with a point of diamond it is engraved on the tablet of their heart" (Jer 17:1).[66] This metaphor of writing on the heart seems to function in the following way: what is written on the heart is a kind of script, as it were, that an individual's will follows in order to live and move in the world. In this case, Judah is sinful because the script they are enacting is intermingled with sin. As in Deuteronomy, divine intervention is needed to reverse this state, and this is what is foretold in Jeremiah 31:33: Instead of commanding the people to

---

65. Carr argues that Deut 6:6 and 11:18 are in the background of Jer 31:33 because the author would have memorized the "Deuteronomic texts as part of their formation." "Having memorized the Deuteronomic injunction to 'have the words [God] is commanding in your heart' (Deut 6:6) and 'put [God's] words on your heart and soul' (11:18) they then might easily write in a prophecy from Jeremiah that spoke of how God will 'put my torah in them and write it on their heart' (Jer 31:33). This is a vision of divine education in the book of Jeremiah built on the educational vision in the Deuteronomic utopia and spoken in the Deuteronomic idiom." Carr, *Writing on the Tablet of the Heart*, 148–49. But Meade rightly recognizes that much more than memorization is in view in Deuteronomy: "The people are to place the Torah on the part of them that controls their feelings, reason, desires, and will. Moses envisions nothing less than a people fully constrained and controlled by the Torah from the heart." Meade, "Circumcision of Flesh to Circumcision of Heart," 134.

66. The prophet Zechariah picks up this imagery when he describes the rebellion of the people of Israel in Zech 7:12: "They made their hearts diamond-hard lest they should hear the law and the words that the LORD of hosts had sent by his Spirit through the former prophets." For Zechariah, a diamond-hard heart means a heart not penetrated by the law and the words Yahweh sent through his prophets.

put the law on their heart, Yahweh will set it there himself; in place of the sin that is engraved on their heart, Yahweh will overwrite his own *torah*.[67]

Jeremiah's emphasis on the necessity of divine intervention in the heart tracks with the movement one observes in Deuteronomy. Just as Moses did in Deuteronomy 10:16, Jeremiah exhorts Judah to circumcise their hearts in Jeremiah 4:4: "Circumcise yourselves to the Lord; remove the foreskin of your hearts." The metaphor persists in Jeremiah 9:24, where it is no longer an exhortation but instead an indictment.

As was the case in Deuteronomy, what Israel needs is a circumcised heart. This is surely in the background of Jeremiah 31:33 in Yahweh's promise to put the law within them and to write (כתב) it on their hearts.[68] The divine surgeon's scalpel, in cutting away the impeding foreskin, will leave behind the divine decree, which will finally enable obedience. As Wells puts it,

> The metaphor of writing on the heart is used to describe the inclinations of people. Judah's sin is "written . . . on the tablet of her heart" (כתובה . . . על־לוח לבם) because she is predisposed to sin (17:1). The promise to write Torah in the heart (31:33) is therefore a promise to reorient Israel's will so that she is inclined to obey.[69]

67. So also Weinfeld: "Jeremiah proclaims that in the future the covenant would be written on the heart and not engraved, as before, on tables of stone. In other words, it would not be enforced from without through learning and indoctrination which could be forgotten and put out of mind (cf. Dtn 4:9–10–'Lest you forget . . . and they depart from your heart . . . and that they may teach their children') but would be implanted in a man's heart so that it would not depart from the heart and would not be forgotten." Weinfeld, "Jeremiah and the Spiritual Metamorphosis of Israel," 26.

68. Contra von Rad, who seems to reject the notion that Deuteronomy and Jeremiah share the perspective of Israel's inability to communion with God without divine intervention: "Jeremiah speaks of a new covenant, while Deuteronomy preserves the old one and goes to the limits of theological possibility as it extends its force to apply to contemporary conditions—the final period of the Monarchy. The difference highlights the crucial feature in the prophetic teaching; for Jeremiah places his entire confidence in the expectation of a new saving act with which Jahweh is to eclipse the Sinai covenant: but Deuteronomy hopes that Jahweh is now to give effect to the promises of the old covenant. Here is a remarkable and deep distinction which must be linked, as we have already seen, with the fact that for Deuteronomy the question of Israel's obedience had not yet become a problem, whereas Jeremiah and Ezekiel take Israel's total inability to obey as the very starting-point of their prophecy." Von Rad, *Old Testament Theology*, 2:270. Instead, as has been shown in the chapter prior and above, Jeremiah and Deuteronomy both seem to share an equally pessimistic view of man's inability to obey apart from divine intervention.

69. Wells, *Grace and Agency*, 44.

Elsewhere, Jeremiah describes this eschatological action as receiving a new heart, one equipped to know Yahweh (Jer 24:7; cf. Deut 29:3 [ET 29:4]), and the gift of a singular heart, wherein the fear of Yahweh is placed (Jer 33:39–40).

Jeremiah hints earlier in the book at a coming change in Israel's relationship with the law under the old covenant in Jeremiah 3:16–17:

> And when you have multiplied and been fruitful in the land, in those days, declares the LORD, they shall no more say, "The ark of the covenant of the LORD." It shall not come to mind or be remembered or missed; it shall not be made again. At that time Jerusalem shall be called the throne of the LORD, and all nations shall gather to it, to the presence of the LORD in Jerusalem, and they shall no more stubbornly follow their own evil heart. (Jer 3:16–17)

The significance of the ark of the covenant is twofold: the ark of the covenant represented the presence of God and housed a copy of the covenant documents, the Pentateuch (Deut 31:26).[70] But under the new covenant arrangement, the house of the covenant is the covenant individual. In Weinfeld's words,

> If we deny any need of the ark of the covenant we naturally deny any need of the tables of the covenant. And indeed in the prophetic context of the rebirth of Israel and of its being sown anew in its land (Jer 31:26ff.), Jeremiah proclaims that in future [sic] the covenant would be written on the heart and not engraved, as before, on tables of stone. In other words, it would not be enforced from without through learning and indoctrination which could be forgotten and put out of mind (cf. Dtn 4:9–10— Lest you forget . . . and lest they depart from your heart . . . and that they may teach their children") but would be implanted in

---

70. So also Weinfeld: "This view of Jeremiah concerning the ark has its roots in the Book of Deuteronomy which was discovered at that time and whose ideology Jeremiah undoubtely [sic] supported, being perhaps even active in the covenant of Josiah made on that Book (see Jer 11:1–11). An extremely compromising attitude towards the ark is adopted by the Book of Deuteronomy, according to which the sole function of the ark is to safeguard the tables of the covenant (Dtn 10:1–5). Of the ark-cover and the cherubim, which impart to the ark the character of a chariot of God or a throne of the LORD, there is no hint. The principal importance of the ark lies in the fact that the tables and the book of the Law are kept in it (Dtn 31:26). . . . In addition to serving as the throne of God, the ark was also a receptacle for the tables of the covenant between God and Israel." Weinfeld, "Jeremiah and the Spiritual Metamorphosis of Israel," 25–26.

a man's heart so that it would not depart from the heart and would not be forgotten.[71]

If the above analysis is correct, what is the *torah* that is given and written on the heart in Jeremiah 31:33? Is it coterminous with the law given at Sinai? Or is there a new or different element to the *torah* to be inscribed on the heart of Israel in the new covenant arrangement?

In the book of Jeremiah, the word *torah* (תורה) is used ten times outside of Jeremiah 31:33. In the first occurrence, there appears to exist the possibility of a conceptual distance between knowing the law and knowing Yahweh: "The priests did not say, 'Where is the LORD?' Those who handle the law (תורה) did not know me" (Jer 2:8). Jeremiah makes clear, however, that mishandling the law lies at the root of their apostasy: the people have neglected the law by perniciously twisting the law and posturing with the law instead of heeding its instruction:

> How can you say, "We are wise, and the law (תורה) of the LORD is with us"? But behold, the lying pen of the scribes has made it into a lie. (Jer 8:8)

> Then they said, "Come, let us make plots against Jeremiah, for the law (תורה) shall not perish from the priest, nor counsel from the wise, nor the word from the prophet." (Jer 18:18)

In the majority of the occurrences in the book of Jeremiah, *torah* (תורה) is closely associated with the voice and person of Yahweh himself:

> . . . they have not paid attention to my words; and as for my law (תורה), they have rejected it. (Jer 6:19)

> Because they have forsaken my law (תורה) that I set before them, and have not obeyed my voice or walked in accord with it. (Jer 9:12 [ET 9:13])

> Because your fathers have forsaken me, declares the LORD, and have gone after other gods and have served and worshiped them, and have forsaken me and have not kept my law (תורה). (Jer 16:11)

> If you will not listen to me, to walk in my law (תורה) that I have set before you. (Jer 26:4)

> But they did not obey your voice or walk in your law (תורה). They did nothing of all you commanded them to do. (Jer 32:23)

---

71. Weinfeld, "Jeremiah and the Spiritual Metamorphosis of Israel," 26.

It is because you made offerings and because you sinned against the LORD and did not obey the voice of the LORD or walk in his law (תורה) and in his statutes and in his testimonies that this disaster has happened to you, as at this day. (Jer 44:23)

In the book of Jeremiah, as it is in the book of Deuteronomy, to listen to the *torah* is to listen to Yahweh; to obey the *torah* is to obey Yahweh. The *torah* is that which was "set (נתן) before you and before your fathers" (Jer 44:10); but it is also the same *torah* that is associated with the words of the prophets, Jeremiah among them, who were sent to Israel:

You shall say to them, "Thus says the LORD: If you will not listen to me, to walk in my law (תורה) that I have set before you, and to listen to the words of my servants the prophets whom I send to you urgently, though you have not listened, then I will make this house like Shiloh, and I will make this city a curse for all the nations of the earth." (Jer 26:4–6)

Accordingly, the *torah* in the book of Jeremiah can be summarized as the word of Yahweh, which was given to Israel at Sinai, inscripturated in the Pentateuch, and expanded to include the words and writings of Yahweh's inspired emissaries, the prophets, sent to speak the words of Yahweh to the people of Yahweh. Yahweh "set" (נתן) this *torah* (תורה) "before" (פנה) the people for them to heed and obey (Jer 9:12 [ET 9:13]; 26:4; 44:10) under the old covenant. But in the new covenant described in Jeremiah 31:33, Yahweh promises to "set" (נתן) his *torah* (תורה) "within" (קרב) them, writing it on their hearts to obey it. Human mediation will no longer be necessary: the Word will be its own mediator as Yahweh will implant it on the human heart. In sum, the newness of the new covenant is anthropological, not theological. That is to say, there is no change in the divine person(s) or demands, but a change in the human person. This is how Calvin describes the newness of the new covenant:

He afterwards says, I will put my Law in their inward parts. By these words he confirms what we have said, that the newness, which he before mentioned, was not so as to the substance, but as to the form only: for God does not say here, "I will give you another Law," but I will write my Law, that is, the same Law, which had formerly been delivered to the Fathers. He then does not promise anything different as to the essence of the doctrine, but he makes the difference to be in the form only.[72]

72. Calvin, *Commentaries on the Book of the Prophet Jeremiah and the Lamentations*, 4:131–32.

The inter-canonical connection between Jeremiah 31:33 and Deuteronomy 30:11–14 is perhaps most clear in Jeremiah's description of the new location of the *torah* in the new covenant: it will be "within" (קרב) the new covenant people, written "on their heart." BDB explains that the word קרב connotes the idea of "midst," and can refer to the midst of a city (Gen 18:24), a land (Gen 45:6), a people (Deut 18:18), or an individual (Jer 23:9).[73] Were this phrase not in parallel construction with לב in Jeremiah 31:33, it would be difficult to determine whether Yahweh is promising to set the *torah* in the midst of the covenant people, as he did at Sinai, or whether he is promising a more radical setting, namely the law in the midst of the covenant individual. But the parallelism points toward the latter reading. Yahweh will set the law *within* them by writing it *on their heart.* That the individual is in view is evidently how both the LXX translator and the author of Hebrews understood this phrase, as they both render קרב with διάνοια, or "mind" (cf. LXX Jer 38:33; Heb 8:10; 10:16).

What is to be made of the singular לב in Jeremiah 31:33? Is this the collective "heart" of the people, as Shead suggests,[74] or does this refer to the individual heart of the covenant individual? If one heeds the cues of both the LXX and the author of Hebrews, this "heart" should be understood to refer to the heart of the covenant individual, as both render לב with the plural καρδίας, or "hearts."[75]

Brueggemann summarizes the significance of this internalization of the *torah* in the individuals of the covenant people:

> [T]the commandments will not be an external rule which invites hostility, but now will be an embraced, internal identity-giving mark so that obeying will be as normal and as readily accepted as breathing and eating. All inclination to resist, refuse, or disobey will have evaporated, because the members of the new community of covenant are transformed people who have

73. BDB, s.v. "קרב."

74. Shead finds significance in the singular לב arguing that "[i]n the new covenant God will overwrite an original sinful text with his own words, and he will write it on their 'heart,' singular. That is, he will write it not only inwardly, but universally." Shead, *A Mouth Full of Fire*, 198.

75. Gentry argues that the Greek translation in the LXX pluralizes לב "according to the demands of Greek." That is, singular לב is understood by the Hebrew reader to sometimes refer to a plurality of "hearts," but the Greek reader would not be used to making the same interpretive judgment in Greek, which distinguishes more readily between singular and plural "heart." Gentry and Wellum, *Kingdom through Covenant*, 518.

rightly inclined hearts. There will be easy and ready community between God and reconstituted Israel.[76]

If Yahweh's promise to set the *torah* within Israel and to write it on their hearts represents a new relationship with the law, as Brueggemann articulates above, what is to be made of a reading of Deuteronomy 30:11–14 that understands this internalization to be a present reality on the plains of Moab? If a present reading of Deuteronomy 30:11–14 is correct, Israel already had the word within them at Moab, "in their mouth and in their heart," for them "to do it." It seems to me that this reading would considerably reduce the newness of the act of internalization of the law described in Jeremiah 31:33.

If, however, Deuteronomy 30:11–14 is understood to be linked to the future promise of heart circumcision in 30:1–10, as I have argued in chapter 2 above, then what is found in Jeremiah 31:33 is actually an expanded description of the same reality foretold in Deuteronomy 30:11–14.[77]

In Deuteronomy 30:11–14, Moses speaks of a commandment that is not too difficult or too wonderful *because* (כי) it is a word that is "exceedingly near" (קרוב)—that is, "in the mouth and in the heart (לבב) to do it." Hence, when Jeremiah writes of Yahweh setting the *torah* "within them" (קרב) and writing it on their heart (לב) in Jeremiah 31:33, the thematic and verbal parallels between Deuteronomy 30:1–14 and Jeremiah 30–31 mentioned above warrant an exploration into the possibility of intentional verbal parallels between these two texts.

---

76. Brueggemann, *A Commentary on Jeremiah*, 293.

77. Interestingly, some commentators link Jer 31:33 to Deut 30:11–14 without extended comment. So Thompson, "The heart as a writing material is spoken of in 17:1 in relation to sin. There are parallels of a kind in Deut. 6:6; 11:18; 30:14. But there could be no obedience and no recognition of Yahweh's sovereignty as long as the covenant was externalized. It needed to touch the life deeply and inwardly in mind and will." Thompson, *The Book of Jeremiah*, 581. Fretheim recognizes a connection between Deut 30:14 and Jer 31:33, but he argues that Deut 30:14 is the old covenant corollary to the new covenant described in Jer 31:33. Yet he still links Deut 30:14 to 30:6, which he seems not to recognize as a future, new covenant reality. "The law remains a key point of continuity between the old and the new; but the law will no longer be an external code; it will be written upon the heart. In view of this promise, many commentators speak of the interiorization of this covenant compared to other covenants. Yet, the language of texts such as Deuteronomy 30:6 and 30:14 speak of a similar internal reality for older covenantal understandings. The difference seems only to be that such people will no longer need to be taught via the written Torah." Fretheim, *Jeremiah*, 443.

In Deuteronomy 30:14, the "word," which I argued above is best described as the "eschatological *torah*" of Yahweh, is described as "exceedingly near" (קרוב). The word used in Deuteronomy 30:14 for "near," קרוב, is an adjective built from the verbal form קָרַב, which means "to come near, to approach."[78] In Deuteronomy, the word is described as "exceedingly near" because it is an internal word—in the mouth and in the heart. Nearness cannot exceed internalization, hence the phrase "exceedingly near." Consequently, when Jeremiah describes Yahweh setting the law within Israel using קֶרֶב—a noun built from the same verbal form קָרַב found in Deuteronomy 30:14—the verbal parallel may be more than a coincidence. Jeremiah is describing how the word, the *torah*, will come to be "exceedingly near," "in the heart," the same reality described in Deuteronomy 30:14. Yahweh is planning a heart intervention very much like the description of the heart circumcision foretold in Deuteronomy 30:6. In the new covenant, Yahweh will set the *torah* "within" (קֶרֶב, Jer 31:33) the covenant individual himself—making it exceedingly "near" (קרוב, Deut 30:14)—and will write it *on* his heart (Jer 31:33), which permanently places the *torah in* the heart.[79]

In this way, there is direct continuity between the vision of Jeremiah in the Book of Consolation and the prophetic description of the new covenant in Deuteronomy 30.[80] Both locate the old covenant's failure at

---

78. BDB, s.v. "קרב."

79. Significantly, Ezekiel's vision of the new covenant describes this same divine internal intervention using the same root קרב. But instead of the torah or word that is placed within (קרב) the new covenant individual, it is the Spirit of Yahweh himself: "And I will give you a new heart, and a new spirit I will put within (קרב) you. And I will remove the heart of stone from your flesh and give you a heart of flesh. And I will put my Spirit within (קרב) you, and cause you to walk in my statutes and be careful to obey my rules" (Ezek 36:26–27). In the following chapter, Ezekiel restates this promise, but in place of קרב he uses the preposition ב: "And I will put my Spirit within (ב) you, and you shall live, and I will place you in your own land. Then you shall know that I am the LORD; I have spoken, and I will do it, declares the LORD" (Ezek 37:14). This lends credence to the individual interpretation of קרב advocated above in Jeremiah, and it also sets up an interesting parallel between Jer 31 and Ezek 36: The gift of the Spirit and the gift of the law written on the heart appear to be two sides of the same eschatological coin.

80. Contra Sprinkle in his chapter "Deuteronomic and Prophetic Restoration," where he argues, following Brueggemann, that there are two opposing strands of restoration traditions in the OT, the Deuteronomic and Prophetic. Sprinkle, *Paul & Judaism Revisited*, 38–67. Sprinkle cites Potter positively, who writes that Jeremiah's intentional use of Deuteronomic language is "a deliberate contrast to Deuteronomy, not a complement to it, or a restatement of it." Potter, "The New Covenant in Jeremiah xxxi 31–34," 350.

the level of the sinful heart, and both locate the solution at the level of divine intervention in the heart, which takes the form of an internalization of the words of the covenant, the eschatological *torah*.[81] This reading of Jeremiah and Deuteronomy also relieves the tension between Deuteronomy 30:1–10, Deuteronomy 30:11–14, and Jeremiah 31:33 that is potentially created when interpreters read Deuteronomy 30:11–14 as a positive assertion of the Israelites' present relationship to the law on the plains of Moab. This tension is summarized by Scalise in his commentary on Jeremiah: "In spite of assurances that 'this commandment' is not hidden in heaven or in a distant country and that no messenger is needed to retrieve it because it is 'in your [sg] mouth and in your heart' (30:11–14), it is still 'written in the book of the law' (30:10)."[82]

My interpretation of Jeremiah 31:33 and the description of the internalized *torah* as it relates to Deuteronomy 30:11–14 is consciously contrary to interpretations like the one offered by Carroll, who argues, "If fulfilment of the new covenant expectation must be sought, let it be found in the achievements of the Pharisees, who helped to create the spiritual way of life of a very practical but deeply internalized rabbinical religion."[83] Carroll goes on to cite Ellis Rivkin positively, who says, "Internalization is the only road to salvation."[84] This will be unconvincing to the Christian who takes seriously Jesus' condemnation of the Pharisees. Bright offers a more compelling description of what the fulfillment of Jeremiah 31:31–34 looks like:

81. This interpretation recognizes continuity and not discontinuity between the messages of Jeremiah and Deuteronomy, contra Potter, who says, "The whole point of these verses is that they are a deliberate contrast to Deuteronomy, not a complement to it, or a restatement of it. . . . It should first of all be noticed that these verses are different from their three closest parallels, namely Jer. xxiv 7; Deut. xxx 6, vi 4–9. Jer. xxiv 7 reads 'I will give them a heart to know that I am Yahweh', and Deut. xxx 6 'Yahweh your God will circumcise your heart and the heart of your offspring, so that you will love Yahweh your God with all your heart and with all your soul.' There is no guarantee that this will be successful since v.17 of the same chapter can admit the possibility of the heart turning away. In neither passage is there any mention of God writing on the heart." Potter, "The New Covenant in Jeremiah xxxi 31–34," 350–51. In this sense, Duhm is correct to conclude that Jeremiah offers no new vision over against the one offered in the book of Deuteronomy, but not in the sense that he argues. Contra Duhm, both Jeremiah and Deuteronomy envision a new relationship with Yahweh via a new relationship with the law. Duhm, *Das Buch Jeremia*, 254ff.

82. Keown, Scalise, and Smothers, *Jeremiah 26–52*, 133–34.

83. Carroll, *From Chaos to Covenant*, 225.

84. Rivkin, *A Hidden Revolution*, 310.

> We must follow Jeremiah's word ahead to the gospel, for it is to
> the gospel that it points us and drives us; and until it has driven
> us there it has not discharged its function. We hear Jeremiah's
> word, ". . . I will make a new covenant . . ."—and that is promise.
> We also hear the word, "This cup is the new covenant in my
> blood"—and that is fulfillment.[85]

I would simply add to Bright's comment the observation that this promise and fulfillment has a textual ancestor in Deuteronomy 30:1–14—not in the way Carroll posits textual ancestry, which is one of "critical dialogue," but in the theologically congruent, organically developed sense one can observe elsewhere in the OT.[86]

My understanding is closer to von Rad's description of the meaning of the internalized *torah* in Jeremiah 31:33:

> If God's will ceases to confront and judge men from outside
> themselves, if God puts his will directly into their hearts, then,
> properly speaking, the rendering of obedience is completely
> done away with, for the problem of obedience only arises when
> man's will is confronted by an alien will. Now however, the pos-
> sibility of such a confrontation has ceased to exist, for men are
> to have the will of God in their heart, and are only to will God's
> will. What is here outlined is the picture of a new man, a man
> who is able to obey perfectly because of a miraculous change of
> his nature.[87]

---

85. Bright, "Exercise in Hermeneutics: Jeremiah 31:31–34," 613.

86. Carroll's argument is bound up in the complicated source-critical argument of trying to discern the various textual histories he detects in Jeremiah including from the prophet himself, the Deuteronomists, and other layers of redactional authorship: "Deuteronomistic influence must be acknowledged in the passage, but in view of the fact that the Deuteronomists do not themselves at any point in their writings propose a new covenant, not even in the late piece on the restoration of Israel in Deut. 30:1–10, it must be questioned whether they are responsible for this addition to the cycle. . . . I would regard the relation between 31.31–34 and the Deuteronomistic strand in the tradition to be one of critical dialogue. The Deuteronomists believed that the covenant had been broken and therefore had become inoperable. Late additions to their work allow for the possibility of Yahweh's restoration of the nation and the divine circumci- sion of its mind after it has turned back to him (Deut. 30.1–10). But of a new covenant the Deuteronomists know nothing." Carroll, *Jeremiah*, 613.

87. Von Rad, *Old Testament Theology*, 2:217.

### KNOWLEDGE OF YAHWEH

Whether the internalization of the *torah* and its inscription on the heart results in true knowledge of Yahweh or vice versa, Jeremiah's statement in 31:34 echoes Deuteronomy 29:3 [ET 29:4]: "And no longer shall each one teach his neighbor and each his brother, saying, 'Know the LORD,' for they shall all know me, from the least of them to the greatest, declares the LORD." Whereas the people possessed a heart that did not "know" under the old covenant (Deut 29:3 [ET 29:4]), Yahweh promises to give them a heart "to know" (Jer 31:34; cf. Jer 24:7) in the new covenant, a whole heart that fears Yahweh (cf. Jer 32:39). Invoking the covenant formula, "And I will be their God, and they shall be my people" (Jer 31:33b), Yahweh further grounds the new covenant in his forgiveness: "For I will forgive their iniquity, and I will remember their sin no more" (Jer 31:34b).[88] And in Jeremiah 31:35–37, the eternal nature of this new covenant is established: Yahweh's intervention in the heart will result in a lasting relationship that will not need to be replaced.

### *Third Oracle: The Expanse of the New Covenant*

The third oracle in Jeremiah 31:38–40 is the most enigmatic and the least clearly related to Deuteronomy 30:1–14, but the overall significance of this oracle is clear: an everlasting city will be built in the new covenant, and even those places thought to be irredeemable and unholy under the old covenant—"the whole valley of the dead bodies and the ashes, and all the fields as far as the brook Kidron, to the corner of the House Gate toward the east"—will be "sacred to the LORD" (Jer 31:40).

### Jeremiah's Deuteronomic Prophecy

Jeremiah had made a study of the human heart and the human condition throughout his ministry, and he had come to understand that the only hope for true change for humanity must come from without, namely divine attention to man's innermost being. Von Rad describes Jeremiah's view of man's predicament:

---

88. See Shead's helpful discussion on the unprecedented nature of this forgiveness. Shead, *A Mouth Full of Fire*, 200–204.

Jeremiah gained an ever increasing insight into man's actual condition, and for this reason he did not unthinkingly demand that man should follow a road on which he would again inevitably come to grief. His appeals to return increasingly emanate "from God's decision to save." They urge the nation to settle for what God has promised to do for it. . . . [Jeremiah] constantly reflected on the problem of man; that is to say, he reflected on the question of what must come about in man as man if God is to receive him into a new communion with himself. If God is again gracious to him, how can he in any way stand before him as man without once again coming to grief because of his heart's opposition to God? The answer which Jeremiah received to this question was the promise that God would himself change the human heart and so bring about perfect obedience.[89]

Reflecting on Jeremiah 31, Calvin similarly writes,

Jeremiah shows here the difference between the law and the Gospel, for the Gospel brings with it the grace of regeneration. Its doctrine, therefore, is not that of the letter; rather, it penetrates into the heart and reforms all the inner faculties, so that we are obedient to the righteousness of God.[90]

In the final analysis, it is clear that the prophet Jeremiah was just as much a student of the Pentateuch as he was a student of the human heart. One could describe Jeremiah 31:31–33, then, as a sprout growing up from the seed of Deuteronomy 30:1–14. This plant will flower in Romans 10, to which I will turn in the next chapter. But before doing so, in the next section I take up the final place in the OT where God's law on the heart is mentioned: the Psalter.

## Deuteronomy 30:11–14 and the Book of Psalms

There are three passages in the Psalter where the internalization of the *torah* appears to be described: Psalm 37:30–31; 40:8; and 119:11, quoted below respectively:[91]

89. Von Rad, *Old Testament Theology*, 2:217.

90. Calvin, *Commentaries on the Book of the Prophet Jeremiah and the Lamentations*, 4:188.

91. The connection between these three passages is recognized by Mays, who says, "Three times in the Psalter we hear of the person on whose mind and emotions torah is, as it were, imprinted." Mays, "The Place of the Torah-Psalms in the Psalter," 9.

The mouth of the righteous utters wisdom,
    and his tongue speaks justice.

The law of his God is in his heart;
    his steps do not slip. (Ps 37:30–31)

I delight to do your will, O my God;
    your law is within my heart (Ps 40:8)

I have stored up your word in my heart,
    that I might not sin against you. (Ps 119:11)

According to Mays, the internalization of the *torah* mentioned in these three passages is the result of prolonged, earnest *torah*-study:

> How does one come to be able to praise and pray and act out of the center of torah? Three times in the Psalter we hear of the person on whose mind and emotions torah is, as it were, imprinted. "I am concerned to do your will; your torah is inside me" (40:9); "Your word I have stored up in my mind" (119:11); "The mouth of the righteous recites wisdom and his tongue speaks what is right. The instruction of his God is in his mind" (37:30–31). How is it that the instructing word has been incorporated in the very structure of consciousness? By a kind of study mentioned in the context of two of these quotations and in all three of the torah psalms. It is a kind of study that proceeds orally; it rehearses and repeats. It searches the instruction of God by reciting in receptivity until the matter becomes part of the thinking and willing and doing.[92]

But William S. Plumer offers a helpful caveat on the heart-posture necessary for the divine word to work its course within a man:

> It is a good thing to read God's word much. It is also well to commit much of it to memory. The history of the church furnishes many bright examples of great skill in Scripture. Yet not wit and memory, but the heart, is the chest to keep it in. Neither hearing, nor reading, nor reciting the holy Scriptures will save us from false ways, unless with the heart we cordially embrace whatever they teach us. To this work we ought to be greatly stimulated.[93]

92. Mays, "The Place of the Torah-Psalms in the Psalter," 9.
93. Plumer, *Studies in the Book of Psalms*, 1028.

My argument below will be to insist on the close connection between this internalization of the *torah* in the book of Psalms with the divine gift of heart renovation associated with the identity of the promised coming of the righteous one and the new covenant.

## Reading the Psalms as a Book

In the early twentieth century, the works of Hermann Gunkel[94] and Sigmund Mowinckel[95] set a trend of form-critical, atomistic interpretation of the Psalter that led away from reading the Psalter as a book and emphasized instead reading the individual psalms apart from their surrounding context.[96] But ever since Gerald Wilson published his 1985 study, *The Editing of the Hebrew Psalter*, in which he followed the canonical cues of his mentor Brevard Childs, the field of Psalms studies has gone through a kind of Copernican revolution as scholars are increasingly reading the psalms according to the unification of the book, especially attempting to trace the logic of the five books of the Psalms: Psalms 1–41 (Book I); 42–72 (II); 73–89 (III); 90–106 (IV); and 107–50 (V).[97] The assumption of a logical and even narratival unity undergirds the analysis below. Of the psalms under investigation, two belong to Book I (Pss 37 and 40) and one belongs to Book V (Ps 119) of the Psalter.

94. Gunkel, *Einleitung in die Psalmen die Gattungen der religiösen Lyrik Israels*.

95. Mowinckel, *Psalm Studies*.

96. The heading of this subsection is the title of Whybray's book, *Reading the Psalms as a Book*.

97. For a detailed rehearsal of the development in the study of the composition and arrangement of the Psalter that took place from Gunkel to Wilson, see Whybray, *Reading the Psalms as a Book*, 15–35, and Cole, *Psalms 1–2*, 1–45. Although Whybray in the end rejects an "all-embracing structure for the book as a whole," his treatment of the discussion is stimulating. I agree with Robert Cole's criticism of Whybray's approach when he says, "To state it baldly, Whybray is arguing that when choosing between traditional form criticism and the canonical approach to the Psalms, the canonical approach is invalid because it does not follow form-critical categories!" Cole, *Psalms 1–2*, 32. Exciting work is being done in this field, the kind of which can be seen in McCann, *The Shape and Shaping of the Psalter*.

## "The Law of God Is in His Heart"

The first appearance of the internalization of the *torah* in the Psalter occurs in Psalm 37.[98] This psalm is an acrostic poem associated with David (לדוד, Ps 37:1). In it, the fates of the righteous—a word that occurs in both the singular and plural [(צדיק(ים)]—and the evildoers/ wrongdoers/wicked—words that also occur in the singular and plural —are contrasted. The righteous one(s) is/are encouraged to persevere in trusting Yahweh (37:3a) and to cultivate (רעה, lit. "shepherd") faith-fulness (37:3b) in spite of the actions of evildoers through a series of imperatives and statements about divine recompense and retribution. The righteous one(s) is/are at once exhorted as well as described in Psalm 37—and it is the description of the righteous that contains our *torah*-internalization metaphor below.

Psalm 37 begins with a series of second-person imperatives that continue through to verse 11, from the "א" stanza to the "ג" stanza. In 37:12–24, from "ז" to "מ," the psalmist moves to a third-person descrip-tion that contrasts the wicked and the righteous. Throughout this section, references to the righteous are singular, with an exception in the second half of the "ט" stanza in 37:17b, which describes a cohort of righteous ones who are also referred to in the plural as blameless in the following "י" stanza (37:18–19).

At the beginning of this section in the "ז" stanza, there is a verbal and thematic connection to Psalm 2 in Psalm 37:12–13:[99]

---

98. Here we are translating תורה as law but to refer to the word of Yahweh. Kraus's cautions are correct when he says, "From the outset the issues are stated wrongly if תורה (*torah*) is translated 'law.' . . . [It] is 'instruction' . . . the gracious expression of the will of Yahweh as experienced by the individual." Kraus, *Theology of the Psalms*, 161.

99. In Cole's estimation, as we will see below, Pss 1 and 2 belong together as the gateway to the Psalter. "Psalms 1 and 2 were not read as two disparate Torah and royal psalms respectively in the final redaction of the Psalter; rather, both depict the ideal Joshua-like warrior and king who through divinely given authority vanquishes his en-emies. From this eschatological perspective the Psalter opens and sets the tone for all subsequent psalms." Cole, "An Integrated Reading of Psalms 1 and 2," 88.

| | |
|---|---|
| The wicked plots against the righteous and gnashes his teeth at him, | The kings of the earth set themselves, and the rulers take counsel together, |
| but the LORD (אדון) laughs (חקש) at the wicked, | against the LORD and against his Anointed, saying, |
| for he sees that his day is coming. (Ps 37:12–13) | "Let us burst their bonds apart and cast away their cords from us." |
| | He who sits in the heavens laughs (חקש); |
| | the LORD (אדון) holds them in derision. (Ps 2:2–4) |

This verbal connection encourages the reader to understand the plot of the wicked against the righteous one in Psalm 37:12–13 in light of the scheming of the kings and rulers of the earth who take counsel together against the LORD and his anointed in Psalm 2:4. As a result, the righteous one in Psalm 37:12 is closely identified with the LORD in 37:13, which is in turn related to the identity of the LORD in Psalm 2:4.

In 37:21, the psalmist switches back to describing a singular righteous one, who "is generous and gives." Interestingly, the following stanza includes a masculine singular pronoun with an unclear antecedent, which is typically taken in translations to be a referent to Yahweh: "those blessed by the LORD (מברכיו) shall inherit the land, but those cursed by him (מקלליו) shall be cut off" (37:22).[100] This antecedent, however, could more readily be referring to the righteous one in 37:21 who is "generous and gives"—an intriguing reading that would naturally flow out of an association of the righteous one(s) and the man in Psalms 1 and 2.

In Psalm 37:25–26—the "נ" stanza—the psalmist briefly switches to first-person pronouns to relate his experience seeing the prosperity of the righteous (sg.)—a pattern that is repeated in the "ר" stanza in Psalm 37:35–36, where the psalmist describes the futility of the wicked one (sg.) who attains power only to lose it when he dies.

The "ס" stanza in Psalm 37:27–29 returns to the 2nd person singular imperative with the exhortation, "Turn away from evil and do good; so shall you (2ms) dwell forever" (Ps 37:27), a promise grounded in Yahweh's love of justice and commitment to his saints (37:28). This is followed by

---

100. The ESV, NIV and RSV render the masculine singular pronoun in Ps 37:22 with "the LORD," while the ASV, NASB, and CSB translate it "Him" (note the capitalization) and the KJV "him."

a universal maxim about the righteous ones (pl.): they "shall inherit the land and dwell upon it forever" (37:29).

The "internalized *torah*" passage is located in the "פ" stanza. The psalmist returns to describing a singular righteous one whose mouth "utters wisdom" and whose tongue "speaks justice" (Ps 37:30). Here is a second connection in Psalm 37 to Psalms 1–2.[101] The righteous one of Psalm 37:30 "utters" (הגה) wisdom, the same verbal form that describes the blessed man who meditates (הגה) day and night on the *torah* in Psalm 1:2.[102] It is this righteous one who has the *torah* internalized: "The law (תורה) of his God is in his heart (לב); his steps do not slip" (37:31). How is the *torah* of his God in his heart? Is it the result of rote memorization by the righteous? Or is it referring to, as Johannes Bugenhagen argues, the "spirit of life written on their hearts by God, according to the prophet Jeremiah"?[103] While these two options are not mutually exclusive, Hans-Joachim Kraus contends that "[i]t cannot be denied that Ps. 40:7–8 and Ps. 37:30–31 refer to the effects of the 'new covenant' which had been promised, especially in Jer. 31:31–34."[104] The answer to this question may in part depend on the identification of the blessed man in Psalm 1, which I consider in the summary of this section below. For now, I simply note the close connection between the righteous one whose heart houses the *torah* of his God with the blessed man in Psalms 1–2.

### "Your Law Is within My Heart"

Psalm 40 is the penultimate psalm in Book I. Like Psalm 37, it is associated with David (לדוד, Ps 40:1). In 40:2–4 (ET 40:1–3), the psalmist relays in a first-person account a sequence of events that runs from trouble to tranquility: he patiently called out to Yahweh for help and was heard (Ps 40:2 [ET 40:1]); Yahweh responded by rescuing him from the

---

101. See n. 34 in this chapter.

102. So also Cole: "The Hebrew verbal root הגה, usually translated "mediate" [sic, "meditate"], is closely associated with verbs of remembering (זכר), musing (חיש) and speaking (דבר). . . . Within the Psalter, this root is often found in first-person singular speech. Psalm 37.30–31 refers to the righteous one in language reminiscent of Ps. 1:2: חכמה יהגה צדיק פי בלבו אלהיו תורת (Ps. 37:30a, 31a)." Cole, *Psalms 1–2*, 62.

103. Speaking of Ps 37:31, Bugenhagen continues, "The impious and hypocrites have it only in books; they only have it, but they do not speak it from the heart." Selderhuis, *Psalms 1–72*, 299.

104. Kraus, *Theology of the Psalms*, 162.

pit of "roaring" (waters?[105] 40:3a [ET 40:2a]); Yahweh set his feet on firm ground, securing his steps (40:3b [ET 40:2b]; cf. אשור in Ps 37:31); Yahweh put a new song of praise in his mouth (note the actor is Yahweh, the action is "giving/setting" [נתן], and the location of the action is in the mouth [פה], 40:4a [ET 40:3a]); and on account of this public rescue, many see, fear, and trust in Yahweh (40:4b [ET 40:3b]). This near-death experience brings about new life which begets new life for many.[106]

In Psalm 40:5 (ET 40:4), the psalmist uses language that recalls the opening of the Psalter in Psalm 1:1, "Blessed is the man who makes the LORD his trust"—but instead of the blessed איש of Psalm 1, the psalmist uses another word for man, גבר. The verbal root for "trust" (מבטח) in 40:5 serves to lace it to the verse prior: the blessed man in Psalm 40:5 is revealed to be the one who sees Yahweh's rescue and responds the way it is designed to function: he makes Yahweh his trust (מבטח, 40:5a [ET 40:4a], cf. בטח in 40:4b [ET40:3b]). This one does not turn back toward the Rahabites (רהבים)[107] or the apostatizing liars. Resuming the first-person perspective and speaking on behalf of a plurality, the psalmist praises Yahweh in response to his wondrous deeds and purposes toward his people, which he declares are too many to recount (40:5b [ET 40:4b]).

Psalm 40:7–9 (ET 40:6–8) contains the metaphor of the internalization of the *torah*. The psalmist begins this section by stating that Yahweh's delight (חפץ) is not in sacrifice (זבח) or offering (מנחה); Yahweh does not ask for burnt offering (עלה) or sin offering (חטאה). Instead, what Yahweh desires is a reality that he creates: open ears that result in a *torah*-filled heart that delights in God's will.[108] In the midst of this evaluation of sac-

---

105. See BDB, s.v. "שָׁאוֹן" for "pit of roaring" waters.

106. Brueggemann likewise notes the significance of what is "new": "The phrase, 'new song,' is a sign of new orientation. The new situation of well-being requires a break with old liturgical claims and practices. Perhaps the phrase originally referred to the public commissioning of a new song for a fresh public occasion such as a new year. Here it is used to say that life has begun anew for this person, and it requires new lyrical speech to match the gift." Brueggemann, *The Message of the Psalms*, 128. So also Mays: "The psalmist sees his deliverance as one more example of the innumerable wonders by which the LORD has preserved his people; the salvation of the psalmist is set within the continuity of salvation history of Israel." Mays, *Psalms*, 167.

107. The plural for רהב is a hapax-legomenon. Elsewhere it occurs in the singular and is associated with Egypt (Isa 30:7) or refers to a symbolic sea monster (cf. Job 26:12).

108. Calvin rightly understands the psalmist to be contrasting the sacrificial system with heart obedience: "I have no doubt that David, under the four different kinds of sacrifices which he here enumerates, comprehends all the sacrifices of the law. His

rifice, whether it is to contrast Yahweh's gift of "hearing" with ceremonial sacrifice or to root his insight into Yahweh's true desires in the divine gift he has received, the speaker interjects in an almost parenthetical aside "ears you have dug for me."[109] Then (אז), at this divine action—the significance of which I explore below—the speaker relays his response to Yahweh's gift: "Behold, I have come." The direct quotation may stop here, or more probably it continues on to encompass the text through the end of 40:9 (ET 40:8):[110]

> Behold, I have come;
>> in the scroll of the book it is written of me:
> I delight to do your will, O my God;
>> your law is within my bowels. [Ps 40:8–9 (ET 40:7–8)]

The referent of the "scroll of the book" as well as the contents of what is written in this scroll are very difficult to ascertain. This could be an internal reference to another psalm where the psalmist's delight is written down (cf. Ps 119:16, 24, 35, 92). Calvin argues this book could be the "secret book of God" that records the will of God to give to some the gift of the "inward and effectual teaching of the Spirit."[111] Craigie thinks it is a reference to the instructions found in Deuteronomy 17:14–20 for the king to write a copy of the *torah* to keep with him throughout his reign.[112] Still other interpreters argue that it is a reference to an earlier prophetic text in the Pentateuch, perhaps Genesis 3:15. Though it is not necessary to determine the referent of the "scroll of the book" for the following interpretation, I tend to agree with Calvin. Whatever the case may be,

---

meaning, to express it in a few words, is, that God requires not mere ceremonies of those who serve him, but that he is satisfied only with sincerity of heart, with faith and holiness of life." Calvin, *Commentary on the Book of Psalms*, 2:98–99.

109. My translation. The LXX renders the Hebrew phrase אזנים כרית לי with ὠτία δὲ κατηρτίσω μοι, which in the book of Hebrews changes to σῶμα δὲ κατηρτίσω μοι—perhaps interpreting this gift of new "ears" as a synecdoche for a (re)creation of the whole self.

110. The quotation of this psalm in the book of Hebrews indicates that the author took the quotation to include Ps 40:9 (ET 40:8), as he includes the phrases "to do your will" and "in the scroll of the book it is written of me," though he switches the order of these. See Jobes, "Rhetorical Achievement in the Hebrews 10 'Misquote' of Psalm 40," 387–96 for a detailed look at the differences between Ps 40 and its quotation in Heb 10, which Jobes expands to explain the possible rationale behind such differences in Jobes, "The Function of Paronomasia in Hebrews 10:5–7," 181–91.

111. Calvin, *Commentary on the Book of Psalms*, 102.

112. Craigie, *Psalms 1–50*, 315.

the phrase "in the scroll of the book it is written of me" in Psalm 40:8 (ET 40:7) is governed by the passive participle כָּתוּב, which, as a verbless clause, indicates offline or background material[113] and could allow Psalm 40:8–9 (ET 40:7–8) to be read continuously: "Behold, I have come to do your will, O my God; I delight (in) your law within my bowels." It seems that this is closer to how the author of Hebrews renders it in Hebrews 10:5–7 and may better reflect his interpretation.[114]

The *torah* in Psalm 40:9b (ET 40:8b) is said to be "in the midst of my inward parts" (בתוך מעי), the second half of a couplet which begins, "I delight (חפץ, cf. Yahweh's חפץ in Ps 40:7 [ET 40:6]) to do your will, O my God" (Ps 40:9a [ET 40:9a]). This one delights (חפץ) in his God's will out of a heart filled with the *torah*; "his delight (חפץ) is in the law of the LORD" (Ps 1:2). It is as though the digging out (circumcision? cf. Jer 6:10) of the ears results in the right response to God's will and *torah*: a canal opened to the heart through which divine instruction can penetrate to the very seat of the will of man, the heart.

The result of this internalized *torah* is an externalized, proclaimed righteousness: The speaker tells of the glad news of "righteousness" (צדק) to a great congregation (Ps 40:10 [ET 40:9]). He does not conceal in his heart this "righteousness," which belongs to Yahweh (צִדְקָתְךָ). Instead he freely speaks of it to the congregation: a righteousness filled out by Yahweh's faithfulness (אמונה), salvation (העושׁת), steadfast love (חסד), and truthfulness (אמת, Ps 40:11 [ET 40:10]).

What then of the overall movement of the first half of Psalm 40? The psalmist describes a rescue in the form of a kind of watery rebirth, which results in many trusting in Yahweh (Ps 40:1–2 [ET 40:1–3]). Then he zooms out the lens, as it were, to offer a universal maxim corresponding to this particular situation: the blessed man is the one who trusts in Yahweh who multiplies grace to his own (40:3–4 [ET 40:4–5]). In 40:5 (ET 40:6), the psalmist moves to describe how man is properly to relate with Yahweh. The speaker has come to know through divine intervention—the divine gift of "new" ears—the right way to relate to Yahweh:

---

113. Van Wolde, "The Verbless Clause and Its Textual Function," 330.

114. This is, self-admittedly, a difficult reading and would require the *waw* in Ps 40:9b (ET 40:8b) to be read as a ב. It could, however, be compatible with the LXX translation: "τότε εἶπον Ἰδοὺ ἥκω, ἐν κεφαλίδι βιβλίου γέγραπται περὶ ἐμοῦ, τοῦ ποιῆσαι τὸ θέλημά σου, ὁ θεός μου, ἐβουλήθην καὶ τὸν νόμον σου ἐν μέσῳ τῆς κοιλίας μου," with the "καὶ" being understood as an emphatic. I make this suggestion humbly as in wrestling with how the author of Hebrews understands Ps 40:6–8 when he cites it in Heb 10:5–7.

not sacrifice *per se*, but doing and delighting in God's will, which wells up from an internalization of the *torah*. The result of this is the revelation of Yahweh's righteousness to the great congregation.

Many interpreters note that the language of Psalm 40 is related to the development of the new covenant ideal in Isaiah, Jeremiah, and Ezekiel. For example, Mays connects the description of the individual in Psalm 40 with the exilic prophecies of Isaiah, Jeremiah, and Ezekiel:

> This profile and the language in which it is sketched have important connections with exilic prophecy. In the prophecies of Jeremiah and Ezekiel there are promises of a people of the LORD who have the LORD's *torah* in their heart (Jer. 31:31–34; Ezek. 36:25–28). The prophet of Isaiah 40–55 was called to bring tidings of righteousness (*sedeq*; compare Isa. 40:9; 41:27; 52:7 with Ps. 40:9). He describes one group he addressed as a people who know the LORD's saving righteousness and in whose heart was his *torah* (Isa 51:7).[115]

In the sections above, I engaged Jeremiah 31:31–34 and Isaiah 51:7 and suggested that a common root of these texts—especially Jeremiah 31:31–34—is Deuteronomy 30:1–14. Brueggemann likewise points to several new covenant texts that draw from the same vein of Psalm 40:

> The sense of the middle part of verse 6 is a bit obscure, but the emphasis seems to be on hearing and obeying God rather than on sacrifice. Verse 6 is one of the texts often taken to express a negative view of sacrifice. That emphasis combined with verse 8 is reminiscent of the prophecies of a new covenant written on the heart in Jer 31:31–34 and Ezek 36:26–28. The psalm could well reflect concerns also found in exilic prophetic traditions in Jeremiah, Ezekiel, and Isaiah 40–55.[116]

While Brueggemann proposes that Psalm 40 is reminiscent of Jeremiah 31:31–34 and Ezekiel 36:26–29, insinuating a later date for Psalm

---

115. Mays, *Psalms*, 169.

116. Brueggemann and Bellinger, *Psalms*, 197. He continues in another place, "Yahweh does not want more conventional religion; that belongs to the old world of fatigue. Those habitual practices are not condemned, but they are recognized as irrelevant. So what does the one with the 'new song' do? He engages in new obedience, an embrace of the torah which is not burden but delight.... This speaker has the torah in his "guts." That is exactly where Jeremiah promised the torah would be." Brueggemann, *The Message of the Psalms*, 129.

40, I suggest that both traditions are drawing on and developing a previous text tradition, Deuteronomy 30:1–14.

According to Keil and Delitzsch, Psalm 40 points to the in-breaking of the new covenant into the old among the people of Israel:

> That the Tôra is to be written upon the tables of the hearts is even indicated by Deuteronomium, Deut. vi. 6, cf. Prov. iii. 3, vii. 3. This reception of the Tôra into the inward parts among the people hitherto estranged from God is, according to Jer. xxxi. 33, the characteristic of the new covenant. But even in the Old Testament there is among the masses of Israel "a people with My law in their heart" (Isa. li. 7), and even in the Old Testament, "he who hath the law of his God in his heart" is called righteous (Ps. xxxvii. 31). As such an one who has the Tôra within him, not merely beside him, David presents himself on the way to the throne of God.[117]

Keil and Delitzsch rightly recognize the new covenant undertones to Psalm 40. Is the internalized *torah* a present reality in the heart of the psalmist, as Keil and Delitzsch argue, or is it a forward-looking silhouette expecting fulfillment at the coming of the Messiah? This question will be put off until the conclusion, but in turning to the final "internalized *torah*" passage in the Psalter, it is sufficient to reflect on the new covenant milieu that several commentators identify in Psalm 40. I would simply want to graft these inner-biblical observations onto the root of the new covenant imagery identified above: Deuteronomy 30:1–14.

## "I Have Stored Up Your Word in My Heart"

Psalm 119 contains the final instance of a description of an internalized *torah* in the Psalter. F. Hossfeld notes that Psalm 119:11 is reminiscent of Deuteronomy 30:14 when he writes,

> In v. 10, the petitioner looks back at his life thus far and emphasizes his efforts to seek YHWH's will in the various situations of his life, and he seeks YHWH for help, so that he may not stray from the right way of life. Verse 11 even intensifies this, adopting formulations from Deut 6:6; 30:14; Jer 31:33 (the Torah is "written on the heart," or "in the heart," so that it can be kept): the petitioner makes the word of God that has been given to him

---

117. Keil and Delitzsch, *Biblical Commentary on the Old Testament*, 12:40.

the guiding principle of his thought and will, so that he may not miss the way of life to which he has been directed.[118]

This psalm is distinct, however, from the other two psalms in that it appears to reveal *how* the *torah* is internalized: instead of a mere assertion that the divine word has been internalized, the psalmist is said to have himself "stored" it there. What is more, it is not explicitly the *torah* (תורה) that is said to be stored in the heart, but divine speech (אמרה). There is good internal evidence in Psalm 119, however, that אמרה is a synonym for תורה (cf. Ps 119:97–104, the "מ" strophe, where several synonyms for תורה throughout this psalm are gathered together interchangeably: תורה, 119:97; מצוה, 199:98; עדות, 119:99; פקודם, 119:100; דבר, 119:101; משפט, 119:102; אמרה, 119:103). Psalm 119 is situated near the center of Book V. On a narratival/logical reading of the Psalter, Book V follows up the exilic theme of Book IV with the theme of life after exile.[119] Mays makes an intriguing observation about the placement of Psalm 119 in the final form of the Psalter:

> Is it fortuitous that both 18 and 118 are subject to an eschatological rereading? There are features of content and motif that suggest an intentional pairing. In the case of 18 and 19, both begin with a cosmic theophany which reveals the power of God (18:8–16 and 19:2–7). Psalm 18 says that the way of God is perfect and the word of the LORD is pure (v 31) and Psalm 19 says that the instruction of the LORD is perfect and the commandment of the LORD is pure (v 8, 9). Psalm 118 tells of the salvation of a rejected righteous one which vindicates the faith of the righteous. Psalm 119 is a prayer for salvation by the righteous who are rejected on account of faithfulness to torah. These are only illustrations of the connecting features to be found. In all three cases, the purpose of the pairing seems to be the provision of an eschatological context for a piety based in torah.[120]

Does the final form of the Psalter situate the "piety based in torah" described in Psalm 119 in an "eschatological context"? This question is in the background of the following analysis.

Psalm 119 is a giant acrostic—twenty-two strophes with eight stanzas apiece that each begin with a corresponding letter of the Hebrew

118. Hossfeld et al., *Psalms 3*, 266–67.

119. Cf. Ps 107, the psalm that opens Book V, which is about the ingathering from exile of God's people from the four corners of the world (cf. Ps 107:3).

120. Mays, "The Place of the Torah-Psalms in the Psalter," 11.

alphabet sequentially.[121] Psalm 119:11, which contains the description of the internalized *torah*, occurs in the second strophe, "ב":

> I have stored up your word in my heart,
> that I might not sin against you.

Psalm 119:2 contains the following macarism that echoes the opening of Psalm 1: blessed (אשרי) are those "who seek [Yahweh] with their whole heart." The psalmist declares in 119:10 that he has done just that: "With my whole heart I seek you." In Psalm 119:11, the psalmist says that he has "hidden" or "treasured" (צפן) Yahweh's word in his heart (לב), indicating he is someone who has paid close attention to these words and heeded their significance (cf. Prov 2:1; 7:1), probably memorizing them and meditating on them after the pattern of Psalm 1 and the instructions of Deuteronomy 6:6. This is exactly what he asserts in Psalm 119:97: "Oh how I love your law! It is my meditation all the day" (cf. Ps 1:2). The psalmist exemplifies the right response to Yahweh's word: the desire to allow the word of Yahweh to underwrite the thoughts and attitudes of the heart. As Mays comments on Psalm 119,

> The instruction comes from God, but it must become part of the servant of God. It must be gathered into the store of the heart, the mind and mentality with which one thinks and wills (v. 11). The heart itself must be converted from all else (v. 36). The word is reason and opportunity for the human heart to be whole (vv. 2, 10, 34, 58, 69, 145).[122]

Relating to Yahweh must include seeking him with a whole heart that is formed by the *torah*; the very existence of a person must be defined and influenced by his word. In Wilson's words,

> Ps 119 emphasizes the primacy of the law in man's relationship to YHWH. This relationship is viewed as primarily one of

---

121. It has been suggested that Ps 119 is a chiasm in Hossfeld et al., *Psalms 3*, 262.
A. *Strophe pair 1–2* (vv. 1–16): programmatic opening (theme and hermeneutical horizon)
  B. Strophes 3–6 (vv. 17–48): lament-petition-trust
    C. Strophes 7–10 (vv. 49–80): retrospect (negatively dominated)
      D. *Strophe pair 11–12* (vv. 81–96): dramatic center (powerlessness and the omnipotence of Torah)
    C'. Strophes 13–16 (vv. 97–128): retrospect (positively dominated)
  B'. Strophes 17–20 (vv. 129–60): petition-lament-petition
A'. *Strophe pair 21–22* (vv. 161–76): summary (assurance of salvation and praise)

122. Mays, *Psalms*, 385.

*individual* approach and access through the appropriation of and obedience to *Torah*, a concept shared with Ps 1. . . . How are those who fear YHWH to relate to him? They must enter "the gate of righteousness" by keeping his law and incorporating it into their very existence.[123]

The man described in Psalm 119 understands the importance and significance of the internalized *torah*, and he has taken earnest steps to, as Wilson says, "incorporat[e] it into [his] very existence." But is his heart renovation by the *torah* complete insofar as he has stored it in his heart? Or is he still anticipating heart change when he cries out to Yahweh later in Psalm 119:32, "I will run in the way of your commandments when you enlarge my heart!" Is the blessed man of Psalm 119 related to the blessed man of Psalm 1? I return to this question below.

## The Blessed Man of Psalms 1 and 2

In his book *Psalms 1–2: Gateway to the Psalter*, Robert Cole argues that the first two psalms in the Psalter act as a kind of lens through which the rest of the book should be read. These two psalms present the blessed man, Yahweh's messiah (מָשִׁיחַ, Ps 2:2), as a conglomerate archetype who overshadows the rest of the Psalter. He is prophet, priest, and king—a second Moses and a second Joshua—and throughout the Psalter his identity is alluded to and developed by the psalmist.[124] Cole's summary of the significance of the man in the opening two psalms—the blessed man in Psalm 1 who is revealed to be the Son of Yahweh in Psalm 2—deserves quotation in full:

> Psalms 1 and 2, in spite of being discrete and self-contained texts, together open and introduce the Psalter with an integrated and unified message. Psalm 1 announces by its opening phrase אַשְׁרֵי־הָאִישׁ a focus on the blessed man, whose conduct is entirely blameless and separate from the wicked. The first half of the psalm (vv. 1–3) is devoted to a full description of this man, including his abstention from wickedness on the one hand and his dedication to the instruction of Yhwh on the other, the latter a trait of righteous kings. Then in v. 3 is found an extensive description of his future establishment in the eschatological garden sanctuary (thus a priestly figure), concluding with an

123. Wilson, *The Editing of the Hebrew Psalter*, 223–24.
124. Cole, *Psalms 1–2*, 59n52; 63n71, n73.

affirmation of his absolute and unqualified success in every endeavor. This lengthy and pointed focus on one *mam* identifies
it as the primary topic of the psalm. Since the psalm opens the
book as a whole it also has implications for the message of the
entire work.

By contrast, the ultimate destiny of the wicked is depicted
in the second half of Psalm 1. As opposed to the ultimate and
eschatological destiny of the man in v. 3, they and their way of
life will suffer utter and ultimate destruction without participation in the final resurrection of the righteous at the judgment.
*The single blessed man opening the psalm is now joined by a com-
pany of righteous suggesting the possibility of participation in his
benefits.* The second psalm will point the way to that privilege.

Psalm 2 opens with a further description of the wicked,
now identified as rebellious nations and their rulers who plot
against Yhwh and his messiah, not wanting to serve them. A
response comes from the heavenly figure, seated and laughing,
who can be identified as the faultless man from Psalm 1 and who
did not participate in the session nor the scorn of the wicked.
His laughter turns to anger in 2.5, which will be illustrated in
v. 9 and named again in v. 12. His heavenly session is explained
in v. 6 followed by his father-son relationship with Yhwh in v.
7, and finally his received inheritance of all nations throughout
the world in v. 8. The following v. 9 illustrates the power he will
wield to bring his unruly inheritance into submission. Finally,
vv. 10–12 warn the earth's rulers to submit to Yhwh and the son
or they will be destroyed, repeating and affirming the promise
of 1.6. *For those who trust in the son of God there is promised
participation in the very blessings ascribed to him from the opening of Psalm 1 to the end of Psalm 2.*[125]

As noted above, connections to Psalms 1 and 2 are present in each
of the three passages where internalization of the *torah* appears in the
Psalter. In his chapter devoted to the exegesis Psalm 1, Cole recognizes
these connections to Psalms 1 and 2 in Psalms 37, 40, and 119 as well. In
fact, Cole cites all three psalms under investigation in this section within
the span of two pages where he describes how the blessed man of Psalms
1 and 2 appears in later psalms:

> Another example of "all-day meditation" on the torah of the
> LORD is Ps. 119.97, מה אהבתי תורתך כל היום היא שיחתי, which
> words would certainly qualify as those uttered by the man of Ps.

---

125. Cole, *Psalms 1–2*, 140–41. Emphasis added.

1.1. Psalm 119 is an example on a substantial scale of uninterrupted devotion to the torah.[126]

Near the conclusion of Book I is another expression of *delight* in God's will and *his torah* (Ps. 40:9 . . . חפצתי ותורתך . . .) by an individual speaker identified as David in the superscription. This would appear to constitute another inclusio across the initial division of the Psalter, and also suggest that the flawless man described in Psalm 1 is given voice through Psalm 40.[127]

The Hebrew verbal root הגה, usually translated "mediate" [sic, meditate], is closely associated with verbs of remembering (זכר), musing (שיח) and speaking (דבר). . . . Within the Psalter, this root is often found in first-person singular speech. Psalm 37.30–31 refers to the righteous one in language reminiscent of Ps. 1:2: פי צדיק יהגה חכמה . . . תורת אלהיו בלבו (Ps. 37:30a, 31a).[128]

If Cole is correct, and the exegetical observations offered above stand, then perhaps the psalmist's description of internalized *torah* are meant to be read in light of the identity of the blessed man in Psalm 1 and 2, a practice the psalmist encourages through his textual allusions in these psalms in Psalms 37, 40, and 119.

Cole is not the first to suggest an eschatological interpretation of the psalms that speak of the internalized *torah*. Reflecting on Psalm 40 in his *Church Dogmatics*, Karl Barth suggests a similar interpretation, focusing not on the identity and referent of the righteous one, but on the heart experience of the psalmist in relation to the (yet-future) new covenant:

Who is the man who can take to himself the words of Ps. 40:8f.: "Then said I, Lo, I am come; in the roll of the book is written what I must do. I delight to do thy will, O my God: yea, thy law is within my heart"? To be sure, this was said by a member of the later Jewish Church, but in what dimension was he thinking, in what hidden sense—pointing up and away from himself—was he speaking, unless we are to take it that he was most strangely puffed up and self-deceived? . . . The Psalmist was no doubt speaking of himself, but in so doing he obviously did not focus his gaze upon the place to which he finally addressed that prayer. In these verses we have an almost verbal reminiscence of the well-known promise of Jer. 31:31ff. concerning the new

126. Cole, *Psalms 1–2*, 60.

127. Cole, *Psalms 1–2*, 61.

128. Cole, *Psalms 1–2*, 62.

covenant of the last day. When and as God establishes this new covenant, it will come to pass that "I will put my law in their inward parts and in their heart will I write it." The subject is obviously what Jer. 32:39 speaks of as "another heart," and Ezek. 11:19; 36:26 as the promised "new spirit"—the future I that lives and works only by the grace of God and that is promised to the Israelite by the grace and Word of God."[129]

According to Barth, the psalmist in Psalm 40

speaks as a member of that people of the last time which will be a people of doers of the Law, in the words used by Paul in Rom. 2:13f. to describe this people as the fulfilment of all these promises. . . . When the Psalmist looks in this direction, and comes to speak of himself, as it were, from this standpoint, he can speak only in this way.[130]

In the concluding chapter below, I will revisit the potential implications of such a reading, but for now it will be sufficient to say that where a description of the internalized *torah* appears in Psalms 37, 40 and 119, there is evidence to suppose the internalized *torah* is part of a new reality, a new way of relating to the *torah*, that is not the typical experience of Israel under the old covenant. To the contrary, the experience of the internalized *torah* instead everywhere seems to mark out the individual from among his compatriots. The extent to which this was experienced by the faithful under the old covenant is a question that will be taken up in the concluding chapter.

---

129. Barth, *Church Dogmatics*, 2/2:604. Kraus, agreeing with Barth, writes, "[I]t is worthwhile to ask what meaning texts such as Deut. 30:11–14 and Jer. 31:31–34 have for our understanding of תורה (*torah*). It cannot be denied that Ps. 40:7–8 and Ps. 37:30–31 refer to the effects of the "new covenant" which had been promised, especially in Jer. 31:31–34. . . . If we leave aside the problems of translation involved in Ps. 40:7–8, Barth's explanation points up the concrete context with all the clarity that could be desired. The promise of a new covenant was a source of strength for the times that followed, and in that light and under its influence individual Israelites began to participate in the mystery of that which was new. The joy in תורה (*torah*) is ultimately to be seen in this light, which also gave new effectiveness to the Deuteronomic correlation of 'covenant' and 'instruction.'" Kraus, *Theology of the Psalms*, 162.

130. Barth, *Church Dogmatics*, 2/2:604.

## Chapter Summary

In the books of Isaiah and Jeremiah and in the Psalter are several texts that develop the theme of the internalized *torah*. To what extent this internalized *torah* is eschatologically related to the new covenant is apparent in varying degrees and may reflect further development within the canon: the Psalter seems to present the possibility of the experience of the internalized *torah* in the life of the psalmist, albeit apparently contextualized in relation to the blessed man, while the books of Isaiah and Jeremiah seem to locate this reality squarely in the hope of the new covenant. The next chapter considers how Paul appropriates Deuteronomy 30:11–14 and its canonical development in his letter to the Romans.

# — 4 —

# Deuteronomy 30:11–14 in Paul's Letter to the Romans

THE BOOK OF DEUTERONOMY plays a prominent role in Paul's argument in his letter to the church at Rome. In fact, it is the most referenced OT text in the book of Romans after only Isaiah and the Psalter. In frequently returning to Deuteronomy, Paul follows a similar pattern found in the rest of the NT.[1] As demonstrated in table 12 below,[2] Paul quotes or

---

1. As stated in the introduction to *Deuteronomy in the New Testament*, "It is well known that in the early Christian writings that have been collected in the New Testament, the Psalms, Isaiah and Deuteronomy are the most widely used Old Testament books, to judge from quotations, allusions, and other references." Menken and Moyise, *Deuteronomy in the New Testament*, 1.

2. Table 12 is adapted with modifications from Lincicum, *Paul and the Early Jewish Encounter with Deuteronomy*, 119. Lincicum rightly rejects the inclusion of what Hays would call an "echo," but he inexplicably labels the allusions he examines "echoes" and the echoes he rejects, "allusion." I have changed the table to better reflect the definitions of allusion and echo Hays offers, which he quotes partly from Hollander: "The concept of allusion depends both on the notion of authorial intention and on the assumption that the reader will share with the author the requisite 'portable library' to recognize the source of the allusion; the notion of echo, however, finesses such questions: 'echo is a metaphor of, and for, alluding, and does not depend on conscious intention.'" Hays, *Echoes of Scripture in the Letters of Paul*, 29; Hollander, *The Figure of Echo: A Mode of Allusion in Milton and After*, 64. With Lincicum I am excluding the allusion proposed by some to Deut 4:7–8 in Rom 3:1–2. Contra Lincicum, I am also excluding the allusion to Deut 10:17 in Rom 2:11.

alludes to the book of Deuteronomy in every major section in his letter to the Romans to pursue his thesis: the apocalypse of the righteousness of God in the gospel he proclaims (Rom 1:16–17).[3]

Not only is the book of Deuteronomy integral to Paul's argument in Romans, but the passage under consideration in this study, Deuteronomy 30:11–14, lies at the very heart of Paul's argument in the book of Romans. According to Mark Seifrid, Romans 10:5–13, which contains Paul's citation of Deuteronomy 30:12–14, is "hermeneutically the most significant of the entire letter."[4]

| Rom 2:28–29 | Deut 30:6 | Allusion; cf. also Deut 29:28(29) |
|---|---|---|
| Rom 7:7 | Deut 5:21 | Explicit quotation, cf. also Exod 20:17 |
| Rom 10:6 | Deut 8:17/9:4 | Allusion, mixed citation |
| Rom 10:6–8 | Deut 30:12–14 | Explicit quotation |
| Rom 10:19 | Deut 32:21 | Explicit quotation |
| Rom 11:8 | Deut 29:3(4) | Explicit quotation; cf. also Isa 29:10 |
| Rom 12:19 | Deut 32:35 | Explicit quotation |
| Rom 13:9 | Deut 5:17–19, 21 | Explicit quotation |
| Rom 15:10 | Deut 32:43 | Explicit quotation |

**Table 12. Citations and allusions to Deuteronomy in Romans**

N. T. Wright calls Romans 10:5–13 "structurally the heart" of chapters 9–11,[5] chapters that interpreters increasingly are recognizing to be central in Paul's letter to the Romans as a whole.[6] Wright suggests that

3. Schreiner notes that "[v]irtually all scholars acknowledge that these verses [Rom 1:16–17] are decisive for the interpretation of Romans." Schreiner, *Romans*, 58. Hamilton is representative in summarizing these verses as the "theme of the letter—the righteousness of God revealed in the gospel." Hamilton, *God's Glory in Salvation through Judgment*, 449.

4. Seifrid, "Romans," 652.

5. Wright, *Paul and the Faithfulness of God*, 1163.

6. For a defense of the centrality of Rom 9–11, see Baur, *Paul the Apostle of Jesus Christ*, 315–41; Stendahl, *Paul among Jews and Gentiles, and Other Essays*, 4; Beker, *Paul the Apostle*, 87.

the structure of Romans 9–11 is chiastic, which would place Paul's citation of Deuteronomy 30:12–14 in Romans 10:6–8 at the vital center of
the chiasm:[7]

What is it that Paul finds in Deuteronomy that compels him to return again and again to this book to make his argument, especially at the
apex of his argument in Romans 9–11? And what is it about Deuteronomy
30:11–14 particularly that attracts Paul to cite it at such a crucial place in
his argument? I am convinced, in line with what I argued in the previous
chapters, that what Paul finds in Deuteronomy, specifically in the concluding chapters 29–32—precisely 30:1–14—is the announcement of a new
redemptive act of God which anticipated the very gospel he was entrusted
to proclaim throughout the world—an act that Paul has come to realize
was initiated in the redemptive mission of Christ, the new covenant.

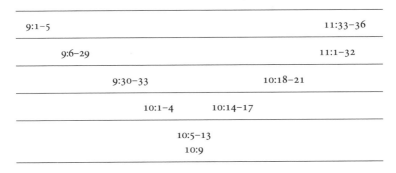

Figure 8. N. T. Wright's chiastic structure of Romans 9–11

## The End of Deuteronomy and the Heart of Romans

In Romans 9–11, Paul is essentially responding to the question, Has
God's word failed in spite of his promises to Israel?[8] In response, Paul

7. Wright, *Paul and the Faithfulness of God*, 1163. Wright refers to the "remarkably careful, almost artistic, structure of [Rom 9–11]. The closest thing I know to this
elsewhere in Paul might be 1 Corinthians 15, but that was only fifty-eight verses, and
this is ninety." Wright, 1161.

8. Schreiner summarizes the question Paul is answering in Rom 9–11: "If the Jews
and Gentiles are both equally indicted in sin and have equal access to salvation through
Christ, and if the blessings of the OT people of God are in the possession of the church
(righteousness, reconciliation, sonship, the gift of the Spirit, the ability to keep the law,
the promise of future salvation), then what does one make of the OT promises made

rehearses Israel's story in order to demonstrate that neither God nor his word has changed. Yahweh can be trusted to keep his promises. Paul's burden is to show that the OT bears witness to—albeit at times in ways hard to discern apart from the light of Christ—the very gospel Paul proclaims and the gospel fruit Paul's ministry has produced. Thus, in rehearsing "Israel's story"[9] in Romans 9–11, Paul can do no better than to turn to Deuteronomy 30 (and 32), which foretells of a promised hope in spite of Israel's failure. Wright explains the significance of these chapters in Deuteronomy for Paul's argument:

> Some of the prophets had spoken of a coming great reversal, when the story would come back with a bang, the world would be turned the right way up, God would reveal his currently well-hidden faithfulness. Maybe, even, the Messiah would appear. Sometimes those prophecies spoke of covenant renewal, with the heart being softened and Torah at last obeyed in a new way. Sometimes they included the remarkable passages in Isaiah about the servant who would be a light to the nations. Sometimes they offered explanations—often cryptic, often powerful—for why the present Israel was in such dire straits. Sometimes all these lines of thought ran back to the Pentateuch: to the great single (if complex) story of Abraham, of the Exodus, of Moses, of Moses' own prophecies at the end of Deuteronomy.[10]

As I will argue below, Paul turns to "Moses' own prophecies at the end of Deuteronomy" at a pivotal point in his letter because he understands the latter days (אחרית הימים, Deut 4:30) to have dawned in his day, ushering in the fulfillment of Deuteronomy 30. With Wright, I suggest that Paul's pivot to Deuteronomy 30 in Romans 10 is

> about the fulfillment of Deuteronomy 30: in other words—though this is almost always missed by the commentators!—*covenant*

---

to Israel qua Israel? Have the promises simply been transferred to the church and is ethnic Israel left outside? If God's promises to Israel have not come to fruition, then how can one be sure that the great promises made to the church in Rom. 8 will be fulfilled? How could a righteous God transfer his promises from Israel to the church? The fundamental issue in Rom. 9–11, then, is not the place of Israel, though that is a crucial issue. The primary question relates to the faithfulness and righteousness of God. Is the God who made these saving promises to Israel faithful to his pledges?" Schreiner, *Romans*, 470–71. So Johnson, "The Faithfulness and Impartiality of God," 215.

9. Wright argues convincingly that Rom 9–11 is Paul's retelling of Israel's story in a new way. Wright, *Paul and the Faithfulness of God*, 1159.

10. Wright, *Paul and the Faithfulness of God*, 1159.

*renewal and the end of exile.* It is all about God's righteousness revealed in the good news of the Messiah for the benefit of all who believe.[11]

To pursue Paul's understanding of the book of Deuteronomy in this chapter, and specifically his citation and interaction with Deuteronomy 30:11–14, I begin at the center of the chiasm suggested by Wright in Romans 9–11. I then zoom out the lens to see how the book of Deuteronomy functions in Paul's argument in Romans 9–11, and then zoom out once more to view the deuteronomic shape of the letter as a whole. This complete, I attempt to reconstruct how Paul read the message of Deuteronomy in light of the revelation of God's righteousness in the gospel, "the power of God for salvation to everyone who believes" (Rom 1:16).

## Deuteronomy 30:11–14 in Romans 10

Paul quotes Deuteronomy 30:12–14 alongside Leviticus 18:5 in Romans 10:5–8 to ground (γάρ) his assertion in 10:4 that "Christ is the τέλος[12] of the law for righteousness to everyone who believes."[13] This statement itself grounds (γάρ) Paul's discussion in 9:30—10:3, where he contrasts Israel's failure to attain righteousness in spite of their zealous pursuit of the law with the Gentile's attainment of righteousness by faith.[14] This sets up Paul's contrast between two kinds of righteousness in 10:5–8: the righteousness-by-law in Leviticus 18:5 and the righteousness-by-faith in Deuteronomy 30:12–14. After exploring the text form of Paul's use of Deuteronomy 30:12–14, I will attempt to trace out how this quotation and righteousness dichotomy fits in Paul's larger argument.

---

11. Wright, *Paul and the Faithfulness of God*, 1164.

12. See the discussion below for the meaning of τέλος in Rom 10:4.

13. Emphasis added. So Cranfield, *Romans*, 2:550; Schreiner, *Romans*, 550.

14. Seifrid argues, "10:4 is an explanation of what precedes, namely the failure of the Jews in spite of their zeal (10:2,3). Verses 2, 3 are themselves a recapitulation of Israel's failure as it is described in 9:31–33, separated only by Paul's heartfelt expression of concern." Seifrid, "Paul's Approach to the Old Testament in Romans 10:6–8," 8. In this sense, Käsemann is correct to call Rom 9:30–33 "the thesis developed and established in chapter 10." Käsemann, *Commentary on Romans*, 276. So Seifrid, "Paul's Approach to the Old Testament in Romans 10:6–8," 5.

## Text Form Analysis: Deuteronomy 30:12–14 in Romans 10:6–8

Paul quotes Deuteronomy 30:12–14 in Romans 10:6–8 with an atypical introduction formula as the speech content of the "righteousness [that comes] from faith" (ἡ ἐκ πίστεως δικαιοσύνη).[15] It is first necessary to examine the text form of this quotation before grappling with Paul's meaning in citing this text.

The verbal and structural parallels between Romans 10:6–8 and Deuteronomy 30:12–14 leave little doubt that Paul is quoting from the book of Deuteronomy in this passage.[16] In addition to Deuteronomy 30:12–14, Paul inserts at the beginning of the citation the phrase μὴ εἴπῃς ἐν τῇ καρδίᾳ σου, which occurs twice in LXX Deuteronomy in 8:17 and 9:4. The contexts of both passages provide an intriguing background to Paul's message about faith righteousness. Below, Romans 10:6–8 is set alongside LXX and MT Deuteronomy 8:17, 9:4, and 30:12–14. Verbal parallels are underlined with a solid line and verbal correspondences are underlined with a dashed line:

---

15. For a thorough defense of the presence of a quotation in Rom 10:6–8 as opposed to a "rhetorically construed paraphrase," see Waters, *The End of Deuteronomy in the Epistles of Paul*, 163–66.

16. Contra Sanday and Headlam, *A Critical and Exegetical Commentary on the Epistle to the Romans*, 287–88; Davies, *Paul and Rabbinic Judaism*, 153–55.

| Rom 10:6–8 | LXX Deut 8:17/9:4 | MT Deut 8:17 |
|---|---|---|
| ἡ δὲ ἐκ πίστεως δικαιοσύνη οὕτως λέγει, Μὴ εἴπῃς ἐν τῇ καρδίᾳ σου, Τίς ἀναβήσεται εἰς τὸν οὐρανόν; τοῦτ᾽ ἔστιν Χριστὸν καταγαγεῖν· ἤ, Τίς καταβήσεται εἰς τὴν ἄβυσσον; τοῦτ᾽ ἔστιν Χριστὸν ἐκ νεκρῶν ἀναγαγεῖν. ἀλλὰ τί λέγει; <br><br> Ἐγγύς σου τὸ ῥῆμά ἐστιν <br><br> ἐν τῷ στόματί σου καὶ ἐν τῇ καρδίᾳ σου, <br><br> τοῦτ᾽ ἔστιν τὸ ῥῆμα τῆς πίστεως ὃ κηρύσσομεν. | μὴ εἴπῃς ἐν τῇ καρδίᾳ σου <br><br> **LXX Deut 30:12–14** <br><br> οὐκ ἐν τῷ οὐρανῷ ἄνω ἐστὶν λέγων Τίς ἀναβήσεται ἡμῖν εἰς τὸν οὐρανὸν καὶ λήμψεται αὐτὴν ἡμῖν; καὶ ἀκούσαντες αὐτὴν ποιήσομεν. οὐδὲ πέραν τῆς θαλάσσης ἐστὶν λέγων Τίς διαπεράσει ἡμῖν εἰς τὸ πέραν τῆς θαλάσσης καὶ λήμψεται ἡμῖν αὐτήν; καὶ ἀκουστὴν ἡμῖν ποιήσει αὐτήν, καὶ ποιήσομεν. ἔστιν σου ἐγγὺς τὸ ῥῆμα σφόδρα ἐν τῷ στόματί σου καὶ ἐν τῇ καρδίᾳ σου καὶ ἐν ταῖς χερσίν σου αὐτὸ ποιεῖν. | ואמרת בלבבך <br><br> **MT Deu 9:4** <br><br> אל־תאמר בלבבך <br><br> **MT Deut 30:12–14** <br><br> לא בשמים הוא לאמר מי יעלה־לנו השמימה ויקחה לנו וישמענו אתה ונעשנה <br><br> ולא־מעבר לים הוא לאמר מי יעבר־לנו אל־עבר הים ויקחה לנו וישמענו אתה ונעשנה <br><br> כי־קרוב אליך הדבר מאד בפיך ובלבבך לעשתו |

## Textual Discrepancies

A side-by-side comparison of Deuteronomy 8:17/9:4 and 30:12–14 and Paul's quotation of this text in Romans 10:6–8 reveals a number of discrepancies, including a number of textual additions, omissions, and adaptations. The first of Paul's textual interactions with Deuteronomy in Romans 10:6–8 is presented below with verbal parallels underlined:

| Rom 10:6 | LXX Deut 8:17/9:4 | MT Deut 8:17 |
|---|---|---|
| ἡ δὲ ἐκ πίστεως δικαιοσύνη οὕτως λέγει, Μὴ εἴπῃς ἐν τῇ καρδίᾳ σου, Τίς ἀναβήσεται εἰς τὸν οὐρανόν; τοῦτ᾽ ἔστιν Χριστὸν καταγαγεῖν· | μὴ εἴπῃς ἐν τῇ καρδίᾳ σου <br><br> **LXX Deut 30:12** <br><br> οὐκ ἐν τῷ οὐρανῷ ἄνω ἐστὶν λέγων Τίς ἀναβήσεται ἡμῖν εἰς τὸν οὐρανὸν καὶ λήμψεται αὐτὴν ἡμῖν; καὶ ἀκούσαντες αὐτὴν ποιήσομεν. | ואמרת בלבבך <br><br> **MT Deu 9:4** <br><br> אל־תאמר בלבבך <br><br> **MT Deut 30:12** <br><br> לא בשמים הוא לאמר מי יעלה־לנו השמימה ויקחה |

In Romans 10:6, Paul begins quoting not in Deuteronomy 30:11, which obviously heads the passage under investigation in this study, but instead with a phrase that occurs in both LXX Deuteronomy 8:17 and 9:4. This is then followed by a phrase from the middle of Deuteronomy 30:12. Instead of starting at the beginning of 30:12, Paul has replaced the introductory phrase οὐκ ἐν τῷ οὐρανῷ ἄνω ἐστὶν λέγων with an introductory personification: the righteousness that comes by faith (ἡ ἐκ πίστεως δικαιοσύνη), which speaks the words of Deuteronomy 8:17 and 9:4 in concert with phrases from Deuteronomy 30:12–14. This is the first of a series of textual omissions wherein Paul seems to leave out the notion of "doing" and "commandment" from Deuteronomy 30:11–14—more on this below.[17]

In this near-verbatim quotation from Deuteronomy 30:12, Paul omits ἡμῖν as well as the rest of phrase, καὶ λήμψεται αὐτὴν ἡμῖν; καὶ ἀκούσαντες αὐτὴν ποιήσομεν—again leaving out any notion of "doing" from this verse. After this amalgamation from Deuteronomy 8:17/9:4 and 30:12, Paul inserts the first of three explanatory comments headed by the phrase τοῦτ' ἔστιν that are interspersed throughout his interaction with Deuteronomy 30:12–14 in Romans 10:6–8.

Paul's second textual interaction with Deuteronomy 30:12–14 is in Romans 10:6–8, this time with verbal *correspondences* underlined with a dashed line:

| Rom 10:7 | LXX Deut 30:13 | MT Deut 30:13 |
|---|---|---|
| ἤ, Τίς καταβήσεται εἰς τὴν ἄβυσσον; τοῦτ' ἔστιν Χριστὸν ἐκ νεκρῶν ἀναγαγεῖν. | οὐδὲ πέραν τῆς θαλάσσης ἐστὶν λέγων Τίς διαπεράσει ἡμῖν εἰς τὸ πέραν τῆς θαλάσσης καὶ λήμψεται ἡμῖν αὐτήν; καὶ ἀκουστὴν ἡμῖν ποιήσει αὐτήν, καὶ ποιήσομεν. | ולא־מעבר לים הוא לאמר מי יעבר־לנו אל־עבר הים ויקחה לנו וישמענו אתה ונעשנה |

In Romans 10:7, Paul transforms the text of Deuteronomy 30:13 from a hypothetical question about journeying across the sea into a hypothetical question about journeying down to the abyss (ἄβυσσος)—a transformation whose significance we will examine below. As he did in the first textual interaction with Deuteronomy 30:12–14, Paul economizes

---

17. So Badenas, "Paul deletes all the expressions of Deut 30.12–14 which refer directly to the observance of the law." Badenas, *Christ the End of the Law*, 125.

this quotation by employing only the middle phrase from Deuteronomy 30:13, albeit through the aforementioned transformation. By omitting the beginning and end of Deuteronomy 30:13, Paul again leaves out the concept of "doing" as well as the first-person plural ἡμῖν.[18] This is followed by the second of three comments headed by τοῦτ᾽ ἔστιν.

Paul's final textual interaction with Deuteronomy 30:12–14 in Romans 10:6–8 is below with verbal parallels underlined:

| Rom 10:8 | LXX Deut 30:14 | MT Deut 30:14 |
|---|---|---|
| ἀλλὰ τί λέγει; | <u>ἔστιν σου ἐγγὺς τὸ ῥῆμα</u> σφόδρα | כִּי־קָרוֹב אֵלֶיךָ הַדָּבָר מְאֹד בְּפִיךָ |
| <u>Ἐγγύς σου τὸ ῥῆμά ἐστιν</u> <u>ἐν τῷ στόματί σου καὶ</u> <u>ἐν τῇ καρδίᾳ σου,</u> | <u>ἐν τῷ στόματί σου καὶ ἐν τῇ</u> <u>καρδίᾳ σου</u> | וּבִלְבָבְךָ לַעֲשֹׂתוֹ |
| τοῦτ᾽ ἔστιν τὸ ῥῆμα τῆς πίστεως ὃ κηρύσσομεν. | καὶ ἐν ταῖς χερσίν σου αὐτὸ ποιεῖν. | |

In Romans 10:8, Paul introduces a quote from Deuteronomy 30:14 that nearly matches the LXX verbatim with the phrase, ἀλλὰ τί λέγει; which most likely refers back to the personified righteousness-by-faith. This interrogative interjection serves, as Dunn suggests, to re-ground his appeal in "an authoritative text."[19] Paul's quotation of Deuteronomy 30:14 has four slight deviations from the LXX: (1) he eliminates the modifier σφόδρα (MT מְאֹד); (2) he follows the word order of the MT over against the order of the LXX by fronting ἐγγύς and demoting the copulative verb (which does not occur in the MT); (3) he leaves out the phrase καὶ ἐν ταῖς χερσίν σου, which occurs in LXX Deuteronomy 30:14 but has no correlative in the MT; and (4) he shortens the verse to exclude αὐτὸ ποιεῖν after the pattern already observed above. Paul follows up this last quote from Deuteronomy with his final explanatory commentary headed again by τοῦτ᾽ ἔστιν.

18. A comparison of LXX Deut 30:12 and 30:13 with MT 30:12 and 30:13 reveals a duplication of the ποιέω in 30:13 that makes little sense in light of the identical phrasing of MT 30:12 and 30:13.

19. Dunn, "'Righteousness from the Law' and 'Righteousness from Faith,'" 218.

## Exegetical and Theological Meaning in Paul's Text Form

The textual analysis above can be summed up into five significant hermeneutical moves by Paul that deserve our attention: (1) personifying righteousness-by-faith as speaking the Deuteronomy quote amalgamation; (2) text splicing Deuteronomy 8:17/9:4 and 30:12–14; (3) orienting textual referents through clarifying commentary; (4) transforming the quests in Deuteronomy 30:12–13; and (5) omitting law observance from Deuteronomy 30:12–14. If choice implies meaning,[20] then exegetical and theological meaning surely abounds in this dense passage which we will attempt to unpack.

### *Personifying Righteousness-by-Faith*

In Romans 10:5, Paul introduces an OT quotation from Leviticus 18:5 with the phrase, "Moses writes the righteousness which comes from the law" (Μωϋσῆς γράφει τὴν δικαιοσύνην τὴν ἐκ [τοῦ] νόμου). Directly following, Paul introduces a correlating concept in 10:6 (δέ) through a new speaking agent, ἡ ἐκ πίστεως δικαιοσύνη. What is this faith righteousness? And why is it personified speaking?[21]

Throughout his letter, and especially in chapters 9–10, Paul has constructed, as Waters puts it, "two mutually exclusive clusters of concepts": "righteousness // law // works // striving // one's own, and righteousness // faith // not by works // not by striving // from God."[22] We could extend Waters' observation to the whole book of Romans: ἔργον // πίστις (Rom 3:27–28; 4:1–5; 9:30–32; 10:4) νόμος // χάρις/πίστις (3:21–26; 4:13–15; 5:20–21; 6:14–15; 10:5–8) νόμος/γράμμα // πνεῦμα (7:4–6). Consequently, the righteousness-by-faith that speaks in Romans 10:6 should be associated with this second concept cluster, which is contrasted with the law elsewhere in the book of Romans. For example, in Romans 4, where Paul cites Yahweh's promise to Abraham that he would be heir of the world, Paul says the promise was not mediated (communicated?) to

---

20. See Runge's helpful discussion under the heading "Choice Implies Meaning" in Runge, *Discourse Grammar of the Greek New Testament*, 5–7.

21. According to Bates, Paul's quotation of Deuteronomy in Rom 10:6–8 provides the "clearest example of prosopological exegesis in Paul." Bates, *The Hermeneutics of the Apostolic Proclamation*. While I find Bates' work helpful, I think Paul finds OT precedent in Deuteronomy for this personification that better explains this introduction.

22. Waters, *The End of Deuteronomy in the Epistles of Paul*, 180.

him through the law (νόμος). Instead, Paul says that it came through the righteousness of faith (διὰ δικαιοσύνης πίστεως, Rom 4:13). Thus, in Romans 10:6, one should not be surprised that the ἡ ἐκ πίστεως δικαιοσύνη speaks in opposition to τὴν δικαιοσύνην τὴν ἐκ [τοῦ] νόμου in 10:5. But why is righteousness-by-faith personified? Some have suggested that this unusual introductory formula is evidence that Paul does not intend to quote Moses.[23] But Schreiner responds that (1) an OT quotation in Romans 10:5 sets the reader up to expect an OT quote in 10:6–8; (2) λέγει acts as an introduction formula elsewhere in Romans (9:15, 17, 25; 10:11, 16, 19, 20, 21; 11:2, 4, 9); and, most definitively, (3) Paul would not need to interject explanatory commentary (τοῦτ' ἔστιν) throughout 10:6–8 if he intended merely to access phrases rhetorically and wasn't intending to interact with the text.[24]

In contrast with the citation formula Paul uses in Romans 10:5 to introduce Leviticus 18:5 with Moses as the subject, it may be that Paul personifies righteousness-by-faith to introduce Deuteronomy 30:12–14 in order to "highlight the difference between the old covenant and the new."[25] Accordingly, Paul emphasizes the fact that "the Torah itself speaks of the righteousness of faith."[26] That is, this text in Deuteronomy 30:12–14 specifically bears witness to the righteousness-by-faith available in the new covenant that has been inaugurated in the mission of Christ.

*Text-Splicing Deuteronomy 8:17/9:4 and Deuteronomy 30:12–14.*

The first words attributed to the personified righteousness-by-faith come not from Deuteronomy 30:11–14 but from Deuteronomy 8:17/9:4. Why does Paul begin this way? Francis Watson answers that Paul does so to obscure the original meaning of Deuteronomy 30:11–14:

> Paul attaches the phrase, "Do not say in your heart" to his quotation from Deuteronomy 30 in order to conceal the fact that, in

23. So Longenecker: "It may be that by such an introduction Paul was endeavoring more to alert us to a proverbial employment of biblical language than to identify a biblical quotation." Longenecker, *Biblical Exegesis in the Apostolic Period*, 114.

24. Schreiner, *Romans*, 556.

25. Schreiner, *Romans*, 556.

26. Das, *Paul, the Law, and the Covenant*, 260. Das notes that this corresponds with Paul's argument in Rom 3:27—4:25 and 9:30–33.

its literal sense, it speaks unambiguously of the righteousness of the law.[27]

Kyle Wells offers a different reason for the omission of Deuteronomy 30:11:

> One can see why Paul opens his quotation by omitting a statement from Deuteronomy 30:11 about the accessibility of the commandment and replaces it with an allusion to Deuteronomy 8:17 and 9:4. Philo bears witness that, at least for some Jews, Deuteronomy 30:11–14 incontrovertibly establishes the competence of human agents to fulfil Torah (*Praem.* 80; *Virt.* 183; *Prob.* 69).[28]

Richard Hays has argued persuasively via the concept of metalepsis[29] to explain why Paul substitutes Deuteronomy 8:17/9:4 for 30:11 in Romans 10:5.[30] Paul intends to weave the surrounding context of Deuteronomy 8 and, especially, 9 into the speech content of the righteousness of faith. In this way, Paul brings to bear through an economy of expression the message of these two chapters in Deuteronomy, which "warns them against the presumption of their own righteousness and reminds these 'stiffnecked' people that the initiative in deliverance and covenant-making is [God's], not theirs."[31]

---

27. Watson, *Paul and the Hermeneutics of Faith*, 339.

28. Wells, *Grace and Agency in Paul and Second Temple Judaism*, 271–72.

29. Metalepsis "places the reader within a field of whispered or unstated correspondences" in the surrounding context of the text quoted or alluded to. Hays, *Echoes*, 20. Hays is responsible for introducing into biblical academics the concept of metalepsis, which he borrows from Hollander, *The Figure of Echo*. Encountering this aspect of Hays's work was paradigm-shifting in my own thinking, and in some ways it undergirds the present study. The evangelical interpreter must proceed with caution, however, in deploying this concept of metalepsis, as often its use is paired with the postmodern idea of intertextuality—a concept cited positively by Hays—which is colored not a little by notions of a reader-response hermeneutic. This hermeneutic is baked into Hays's definition of an "echo" (see n. 2 above) and by definition mutes the voice and intent of the original author in search for echoes of texts that did not influence the author's meaning—and therefore should not influence our understanding of the author's meaning.

30. Although Hays is in agreement with Watson that the substitution does "serve the negative purpose of deleting material uncongenial to Paul's case." Hays, *Echoes*, 78. But it is not the material *itself* that is uncongenial to Paul's case. Instead, along with Wells, I argue that it is an easy *misreading* of the material that is uncongenial to his case.

31. Hays, *Echoes*, 79.

In the context of Deuteronomy 8:17, Moses is warning Israel against a kind of self-dependent, forgetful pride that would portray God's deliverance and provision to be the result of Israel's own strength and ingenuity instead of what they really are: unilateral, gracious acts of God. Moses warns Israel in Deuteronomy 8:17–18,

> Beware lest you say in your heart, "My power and the might of my hand have gotten me this wealth." You shall remember the Lord your God, for it is he who gives you power to get wealth, that he may confirm his covenant that he swore to your fathers, as it is this day.[32]

But it is the context of Deuteronomy 9 that is particularly relevant to Paul's point in Romans 10. In this chapter, Moses warns Israel against considering their own righteousness (MT, צדקה; LXX δικαιοσύνη) to be the cause of God's deliverance and provision:

> Do not say in your heart, after the Lord your God has thrust them out before you, "It is because of my righteousness (MT, צדקה; LXX δικαιοσύνη) that the Lord has brought me in to possess this land," whereas it is because of the wickedness of these nations that the Lord is driving them out before you. Not because of your righteousness (MT, צדקה; LXX δικαιοσύνη) or the uprightness of your heart are you going in to possess their land, but because of the wickedness of these nations the Lord your God is driving them out from before you, and that he may confirm the word (דבר) that the Lord swore to your fathers, to Abraham, to Isaac, and to Jacob. Know, therefore, that the Lord your God is not giving you this good land to possess because of your righteousness, for you are a stubborn people. (Deut 9:4–6)[33]

---

32. MT Deut 8:17 begins with a *weqatal* verb (בלבבך אמרת) making it grammatically related to a series of verbs that begins in 8:11. A better translation would be, "Then you will say in your heart . . . ." But LXX Deut 8:17 renders this phrase with a negated imperative, matching the translation in LXX Deut 9:4, μὴ εἴπῃς ἐν τῇ καρδίᾳ σου. In MT Deut 9:4, there actually is a negated imperative (בלבבך אל־תאמר), which makes better sense of LXX Deut 9:4 and likely explains the rendering in LXX Deut 8:17 as an intentional or perhaps even unintentional synthetization by the translator.

33. LXX Deut 9:4–6 differs slightly from the MT, in particular its rendering of the word (דבר) which Yahweh swore to Abraham as a covenant (διαθήκην) in 9:5: μὴ εἴπῃς ἐν τῇ καρδίᾳ σου ἐν τῷ ἐξαναλῶσαι κύριον τὸν θεόν σου τὰ ἔθνη ταῦτα ἀπὸ προσώπου σου λέγων Διὰ τὰς δικαιοσύνας μου εἰσήγαγέν με κύριος κληρονομῆσαι τὴν γῆν τὴν ἀγαθὴν ταύτην, ἀλλὰ διὰ τὴν ἀσέβειαν τῶν ἐθνῶν τούτων κύριος ἐξολεθρεύσει αὐτοὺς πρὸ προσώπου σου. οὐχὶ διὰ τὴν δικαιοσύνην σου οὐδὲ διὰ τὴν ὁσιότητα τῆς καρδίας σου σὺ εἰσπορεύῃ κληρονομῆσαι τὴν γῆν αὐτῶν, ἀλλὰ διὰ τὴν ἀσέβειαν τῶν ἐθνῶν τούτων κύριος

By quoting the first part of this passage in Romans 10:6, it is hard not to think that Paul aims for the reader to import, as Hays suggests, its larger context and the warning against trusting in one's own righteousness or seeking to establish one's own righteousness as the basis for Yahweh's favor. This is the very thing Paul had accused the Jews of doing just a few verses prior in Romans 10:1–3:

> Brothers, my heart's desire and prayer to God for them is that they may be saved. For I bear them witness that they have a zeal for God, but not according to knowledge. For, being ignorant of the righteousness of God, and seeking to establish their own, they did not submit to God's righteousness.

In addition to the warning not to consider Israel's own righteousness as commendable, there is another feature to the context of Deuteronomy 9:4 that may serve to undergird Paul's argument in Romans 10, especially in light of his argument in chapters 9–11. In Deuteronomy 9:5, Moses reminds Israel that Yahweh acts graciously toward them because of the word (MT דבר; LXX διαθήκη, "covenant"; cf. Rom 9:6) that he swore to Abraham, Isaac, and Jacob. (Cf. Rom 4:13, "For the promise to Abraham and his offspring that he would be heir of the world did not come through the law but through the righteousness of faith.") Paul's understanding of the righteousness based on faith comes with a web of associations—God's fidelity to his unfailing word being one of them.

### Clarifying Commentary

The commentary Paul intersperses throughout his citation of Deuteronomy 30:12–14 has caused the most consternation amongst interpreters

---

ἐξολεθρεύσει αὐτοὺς ἀπὸ προσώπου σου καὶ ἵνα στήσῃ τὴν διαθήκην αὐτοῦ, ἣν ὤμοσεν τοῖς πατράσιν ὑμῶν, τῷ Αβρααμ καὶ τῷ Ισαακ καὶ τῷ Ιακωβ. καὶ γνώσῃ σήμερον ὅτι οὐχὶ διὰ τὰς δικαιοσύνας σου κύριος ὁ θεός σου δίδωσίν σοι τὴν γῆν τὴν ἀγαθὴν ταύτην κληρονομῆσαι, ὅτι λαὸς σκληροτράχηλος εἶ. "Do not say in your heart, when the LORD your God drives these nations out before you, 'Because of my righteousness the LORD has brought me in to inherit this good land, but because of the ungodliness of these nations the LORD will drive them out before you. Not because or your righteousness nor because of the holiness of your heart will you go in to inherit their land, but because of the ungodliness of these nations the LORD will destroy them from before you and in order to establish his covenant which he swore with you fathers, Abraham and Isaac and Jacob. And you will know today it is not because of your righteousness the LORD your God gives you this good land to inherit, for you are a stiff-necked people." My translation.

seeking to unravel this text.[34] How can Paul make this text, which most interpreters understand to be about Israel's ability to obey the command delivered to Israel at Moab, speak of Christ, his mission, and the gospel? Is this not bold-faced revisionism?[35] In what sense does Paul understand Deuteronomy 30:12–14 to speak of Christ's incarnation ("that is, to bring Christ down," Rom 10:6b), resurrection ("that is, to bring Christ up from the dead," 10:7b) and the proclamation of the gospel ("that is, the word of faith that we proclaim," 10:8b)?

My contention is that the key to understanding Paul's hermeneutical maneuvers in Romans 10:6–8 is found at the intersection of two concepts: Paul's statement in Romans 10:4 declaring Christ the τέλος of the law—remember that Romans 10:5–8 grounds (γάρ) 10:4, which in turn grounds the previous section—and the new covenant context of Deuteronomy 30:1–14 I have argued for in the chapters above.[36]

Paul's declaration that Christ is the τέλος of the law in Romans 10:4 has been variously understood. Most commonly, interpreters take τέλος to mean either "end" or "goal."[37] Seifrid charts a compelling *via media*:

34. Many interpreters appeal to the Jewish interpretive practice of *pesher* to explain Paul's interspersed commentary in Rom 10:6–8. Cf. Jewett and Kotansky, *Romans*, 625. But Seifrid notes that his commentary has more similarities to the Greek style. Seifrid, "Paul's Approach to the Old Testament in Romans 10:6–8," 29–34. Regardless of the particular interpretive practice Paul is drawing on, what is more important is the "how" and "why" of this textual reorientation to his purposes in Rom 10:6–8.

35. So Watson: "The nearness of the word means that 'you can do it', and the decision whether or not to obey it is essentially a choice between 'life and good' on the one hand, and 'death and evil' on the other. It is this focus on 'the commandment' that Paul suppresses at the outset. The Deuteronomy text must be rewritten so that it testifies to the righteousness of faith, and *against* the righteousness of the law as articulated in the Leviticus citation . . . in its literal sense, [Deuteronomy 30:12–14] speaks unambiguously of the righteousness of the law." Watson, *Paul and the Hermeneutics of Faith*, 338–38. Similarly Hays: "The choice of Deut. 30:12–14, with its blunt insistence on doing the commandments, is daring and perhaps deliberately provocative. It would not be easy to find another text in the Old Testament that looks less promising for Paul's purposes. . . . His subversive exegesis commands our attention," Hays, *Echoes*, 79.

36. As Schreiner notes, "A careful analysis of Deut. 29–30 reveals that Paul's hermeneutical approach is grounded in the narrative structure of Deuteronomy itself." Schreiner, *Romans*, 557.

37. I am in basic agreement with Badenas' summary of the meaning of τέλος in Rom 10:4: "It is extremely difficult to ascertain from contextual evidence whether Paul intended more than one meaning. It seems more reasonable, therefore, to stay within the margin of latitude allowed by context and the philological research on parallels. A dynamic translation like 'the law points to (or intends) Christ . . .' is faithful and broad enough to accommodate the semantically essential content of τέλος without

To understand τέλος to contain both a temporal and a teleological sense fits the broader outlines of Pauline theology . . .
[W]ithin the Pauline epistles there are a variety of expressions,
some indicating that the law is in some sense terminated (Rom
6:14, 15; 7:4; Gal 2:19; 1 Cor 9:20); others indicating that the
law continues or is established (Rom 3:31; 13:8; the many OT
citations). This . . . argues against interpreting τέλος in a purely
teleological or purely temporal sense in Rom 10:4. It is best to understand 10:4 in a manner which allows for both continuity and
discontinuity. This may be expressed by rendering 10:4: Christ is
the culmination of the law (i.e., the mosaic law, the whole of the
Scriptures) resulting in righteousness for all who believe.[38]

Christ culminates all that the law initiates and, in that sense, stands
as the herald as well as the very embodiment of the "eschatological *torah*." The redemption foretold in the OT finds not only its catalyst but
also its climax in Christ.[39] In this sense, Paul understands Deuteronomy

---

discarding the related nuances of 'purpose', 'goal', 'climax', or 'fulfillment', and without
going beyond what the text allows in the definition of its precise shade of meaning. . . .
Paul proceeds to quote Scripture in a way intended to prove that the Christ event is the
*aboutissement* of the whole Torah." Badenas, *Christ the End of the Law*, 147–48. Cf. Seifrid, "Romans," 653–54. For a thorough summary of the various positions interpreters
take on the meaning of τέλος in Rom 10:4, see Cranfield, *Romans*, 2:516–18; Schreiner, "Paul's View of the Law in Romans 10:4–5," 113–24. Though Schreiner rejects
Badenas's interpretation of τέλος, opting instead for "end," he states that "the primary
fault ascribed to the Jews in 10:3 is not salvation-historical but anthropological. They
refused to submit themselves to God's righteousness because they were ignorant of it
and attempted to establish their own. . . . Paul does not make a global statement on
the relationship between gospel and law here. Instead, his point is an experiential one.
'Christ is the end of using the law for righteousness for everyone who believes.'" Schreiner, *Romans*, 547. Moo emphasizes a salvation-historical disjunction in the meaning of τέλος. "As Christ consummates one era of salvation history, so he inaugurates a
new one. In this new era, God's eschatological righteousness is available to those who
believe; and it is available to everyone who believes." Moo, *The Epistle to the Romans*,
641. Augustine's interpretation of τέλος as "end" is more anthropological: "This then is
the sole distinction, that the very precept, 'Thou shalt not covet,' and God's other good
and holy commandments, they attributed to themselves; whereas, that man may keep
them, God must work in him through faith in Jesus Christ, who is 'the end of the law
for righteousness to every one that believeth.' That is to say, every one who is incorporated into Him and made a member of His body, is able, by His giving the increase
within, to work righteousness. It is of such a man's works that Christ Himself has said,
'Without me ye can do nothing.'" Augustine, *De spir. et litt.*, 29.50 (*NPNF* 1/5:105).

38. Seifrid, "Paul's Approach to the Old Testament in Romans 10:6–8," 10.

39. I came to this description independently of Wright, *The Climax of the Covenant*. My interpretation of Rom 10:5–8 differs substantially from Wright's, but it is
also corroborated in part by some of his important observations, as catalogued below.

30:12–14 to be "about" Christ—for Christ is its τέλος. But it is necessary to go one step further to fully understand Paul's appeal to Deuteronomy 30:12–14 in Romans 10:6–8, namely Paul's understanding of this passage in its original context.

Paul finds exegetical and biblical warrant for his use of Deuteronomy 30:11–14 in the OT context and development I traced in prior chapters. This is the root and growth that Paul perceived to be flowering in the message of the righteousness of faith. I have argued that in the original context of Deuteronomy, Deuteronomy 30:11–14 grounds the optimism regarding Israel's capacity to obey in the restoration that Yahweh promises after exile in 30:1–10. "This command" is not too difficult or too hard—not in heaven or across the sea requiring human (or even prophetic?) effort to retrieve it—because the "word" is in the mouth and in the heart to do it in the context of the restoration promised in Deuteronomy 30:1–10, which points forward to a new covenant. Christ has inaugurated this new covenant.[40] Therefore, Paul clarifies with his commentary ("that is . . .") how he reads this passage, which turns out to be the reason he was attracted to Deuteronomy 30:11–14 to explain the message of the righteousness-by-faith in the first place: Moses originally spoke of a future fulfillment in Deuteronomy 30:1–14, a restoring of fortunes that would include heart circumcision and the internalized *torah*, and Paul perceived this to be a present reality in Christ's advent. Wells similarly explains Paul's hermeneutic in Romans 10:6–8:

> On Paul's reading strategy Deuteronomy 30:11–14 stands true not because possession of the commandments proves that Torah can be fulfilled, but because Moses' prophetic word in Deuteronomy 30:1–10 has been eschatologically realised in the Christ event. Since God is now circumcising hearts by bringing people into union with Christ through the proclamation of the gospel, Paul can insist: "the word *is* [eschatologically now] near you, in your mouth and in your heart." Paul's interpretation provides a direct polemic against an Israelite-priority reading of Deuteronomy 30:1–14 and any attempt to usher in the Messianic age through Law-keeping. God's apocalypse renders the human quest for salvation futile and senseless.[41]

40. Eckstein posits a new covenant textual "web" (Isa 51; Jer 31; Ezek 36) in Paul's use of Deut 30:12–14 in Rom 10:6–8, but he does not think this is what the original context of Deut 30:11–14 referred to. Instead, Paul's understanding is "entgegen der ursprünglichen Intention." Eckstein, "'Nahe Ist Dir das Wort,'" 216–20.

41. Wells, *Grace and Agency*, 272.

Further on, Wells writes, "Deuteronomy 30:11–14 bespeaks a situation wherein humans are made competent agents through the liberating work of Christ."[42]

When Paul articulates the message of the righteousness of faith, his aim is to ground it in the witness of the OT—specifically Deuteronomy 30:11–14—to demonstrate its continuity with the OT, as well as to show its τέλος is Christ.

But Paul does not just want to declare *that* Deuteronomy 30:1–14 is fulfilled in Christ, but *how* Deuteronomy 30:1–14 is fulfilled in Christ. Through a dense, canonically-informed economy of expression which weaves together both citation and commentary, Paul packs a great deal of meaning via this christological substitution, what Lincicum refers to as "transformative deixis":[43] Christ not only *brings about* the fulfillment of Deuteronomy 30:11–14, but he *is* the fulfillment of Deuteronomy 30:11–14. For Paul, Christ's mission—his incarnation and resurrection functioning as a kind of synecdoche for his birth, life, death, and resurrection—is both the message *and* the content of the righteousness of faith, as well as the grounds, inauguration, and guarantee of the new covenant reality prefigured in Deuteronomy 30:1–14. In his mission as the τέλος of the *torah*, Christ mediates the *torah* in a way that Moses never could: Christ both fulfills its requirements perfectly and bears the curses due those who fail to do so, and he gives the Spirit who inscribes the *torah* in the heart, a reality Moses said would come by Yahweh's initiation after exile in Deuteronomy 30:1–14. Coxhead explains Paul's theological substitution of Christ in the place of the "commandment" in Deuteronomy 30:12–14:

> For Paul, the simple fact of the matter is that Christ is eschatological torah and vice versa. Paul sees Christ as being the whole fullness of deity (Col 2:9), the supreme revelation of God, hence, the embodiment of torah. Thus, the Mosaic, yet "non-Sinaitic" torah hinted at in Deut 30:11–14 is none other than Jesus Christ himself. Christ fulfils the law of Moses and transforms it at the same time. Paul's point in Rom 10:6, therefore, is that Jesus Christ is the fulfillment of Deut 30:12. In the new covenant age of the restoration of Israel, torah comes down out of heaven

---

42. Wells, *Grace and Agency*, 274.

43. Lincicum, *Paul and the Early Jewish Encounter with Deuteronomy*, 156.

without any human intermediary, being incarnate in Christ, who is the Word/Law of God become flesh.[44]

The ease of *torah* obedience foretold in Deuteronomy 30:11–14, which takes place through *torah* internalization, i.e., heart circumcision (Deut 30:6; Rom 2:24–25), is fulfilled by the obedience of faith in the gospel of Christ, who both perfectly embodies and obeys the *torah* (cf. Rom 5:19). And by virtue of a Spirit-enabled union-by-faith (cf. Rom 6:3–5; 8:2), Christ communicates the *torah* to the heart of the believer, transferring both righteousness (of faith) *and* motivating *torah* obedience.

This may help to explain the logic behind an earlier statement made by Paul in Romans 8:3–4. With the dawn of the new covenant in the mission of Christ, the righteous requirement of the law (cf. "this commandment" of Deuteronomy 30:11–13[45]) is "fulfilled in us" who believe in Christ:

> For God has done what the law, weakened by the flesh, could not do. By sending his own Son in the likeness of sinful flesh and for sin, he condemned sin in the flesh, in order that the righteous requirement of the law might be fulfilled in us, who walk not according to the flesh but according to the Spirit. (Rom 8:3–4)

The righteous requirement of the law is fulfilled in the believer because it is in their mouths and in their hearts by faith in Christ, who enables them to do it—precisely because it is fulfilled in Christ, who sees that it is fulfilled the believer.[46]

By citing Deuteronomy 30:11–14, Paul militates against those who would read this passage as providing grounds for the ability to establish one's own righteousness through the obedience of "this commandment."

---

44. Coxhead, "Deuteronomy 30:11–14 as a Prophecy of the New Covenant in Christ," 316. I would add to Coxhead's quote the qualification that though this "eschatological torah" be "non-Sinaitic," the content has not changed, only the form. Wells offers a similar explanation: "Paul substitutes Christ for *the commandments* because the word of the gospel is God's eschatologically revealed will, which has drawn near. . . . God's eschatological Torah is the Gospel which is put on the mouths and written on the hearts of Christian believers." Wells, *Grace and Agency*, 273.

45. As John Davies points out, the singular מצוה "sums up the whole of what is required of Israel as one obligation[:] . . . a commitment of love and loyalty to the LORD." Davies, "The Heart of the Old Covenant," 36.

46. I am in agreement with Schreiner, who argues against interpreters who see in Rom 8:4 merely a reference to forensic righteousness instead of a reference to the obedience of the believer. Schreiner, *Romans*, 397–408. It is possible, however, with my interpretation to see both present in Rom 8:4 and 10:6–8.

There is only one fulfillment of this passage, and it is to be found in Christ and his mission. This is one step beyond what Lincicum suggests when he writes,

> What prompts [Paul] to the transformation of the text we see here? Part of the answer may in fact lie in a global construal of Deuteronomy. If one asks, "What is Deuteronomy fundamentally about?" one could do worse than to answer: the Torah. But already within the horizon of Deuteronomy itself we find a certain identification of God with Torah (e.g., Deut 4:7–8). What is more, the whole thrust of Deuteronomy tells against a legalistic interpretation of the law. So for Paul to identify the "word" of Deuteronomy with Christ simply extends (and to a certain extent radicalizes) a trajectory already begun within Deuteronomy itself.[47]

To be sure, Paul roots his interpretation of Deuteronomy 30:12–14 in a "global construal of Deuteronomy." But he does so not through vague associations, as if any law text might undergo this kind of christological transformation,[48] but by tapping into the very narrative flow of the message of the book of Deuteronomy itself. This is slightly different from Lincicum's suggestion of a "trajectory," which would refer to a message *implied* by the book of Deuteronomy. The book's message itself entices Paul toward the context of Deuteronomy 30 to ground the message of the righteousness-by-faith.[49]

The christological substitution in Romans 10:6–7 is not the only hermeneutical clarification in Paul's citation of Deuteronomy 30:12–14. Paul also relates the "word" of Deuteronomy 30:14 to the gospel he proclaims in Romans 10:8. In so doing, Paul communicates how righteousness-by-faith comes to the individual. "The word is near you, in your mouth and

47. Lincicum, *Paul and the Early Jewish Encounter with Deuteronomy*, 157.

48. I would argue that this is the mistake interpreters like Cranfield, following Barth, make when they argue that Paul's use of Lev 18:5 is christological as well. Cf. Cranfield, *Romans*, 2:521–22; Barth, *Church Dogmatics*, 2/2: 245.

49. Via takes a similar approach, stating that "Paul was consciously drawn to a particular item in his historical tradition—Deuteronomy—because both Deuteronomy and the shape of Paul's own theological expression were already generated by the same genre-structure." Via, *Kerygma and Comedy in the New Testament*, 57–66. What Via means here is that Paul—at times both consciously and subconsciously—appealed to Deuteronomy because of that book's shape and theological message, its structure, witnessed to the same righteousness Paul proclaims is present in Christ's mission. But Via does not cite directly Deut 30:1–10 and states that Paul misread 30:14, conclusions incompatible with the thesis of the current study.

in your heart," as it comes through "the word of faith" that Paul and the apostles proclaim (Rom 10:8b). This word of faith, the gospel, communicates the internalized *torah* "in [the] mouth and in [the] heart." Paul's change in referent from "Christ" to "the word of faith" follows exactly the change in referent from "commandment" to "word" in Deuteronomy 30:11–14. The commandment is made "not too difficult" in the mission of Christ (Rom 10:6–7; Deut 30:12–13), and the internalization of the "word" comes through apprehending and believing the "word of faith" about Christ's mission (Rom 10:8; Deut 30:14), which Christ speaks through his apostles.[50] In this way, Paul declares the reality Moses spoke of on the plains of Moab—the internalization of the *torah*—to be present in the transforming power of the proclamation of the good news that Christ Jesus has come into the world to save sinners and was raised for their justification (Rom 4:25).

Paul's interspersed commentary in Romans 10:6–8 acts to orient the promise contained in Deuteronomy 30:12–14 to the gospel Paul proclaims, and in so doing he declares it to be fulfilled in Christ. Though Frank Thielman rejects a future timeframe interpretation in Deuteronomy 30:12–14, he nevertheless understands Paul's reading to be dependent on Deuteronomy 30:1–10 and therefore properly eschatological. As Thielman observes,

> Although the focus in [Deut 30:11–14] is back on the present, the preceding paragraphs have shown that the obedience Moses urges on Israel will happen only after Israel's failure to keep the covenant and God's gracious intervention to circumcise their hearts (v. 6). Because Paul believes that this eschatological era has dawned with the coming of the gospel, he is able to make "the righteousness that comes by faith" speak the language of this passage. The Mosaic law has been transformed into the gospel, and in this form Deuteronomy 30:11–14 has become a reality for believers in a way that it never was for Israel.[51]

50. Mark Seifrid helpfully pointed out to me in a seminar that Paul understands those who hear the gospel from those sent to proclaim it as hearing directly from Christ in Rom 10:14: "How are they to believe whom they have not heard?" (πῶς δὲ πιστεύσωσιν οὗ οὐκ ἤκουσαν;).

51. Thielman, *Paul & the Law*, 210. Cf. Schreiner, who writes, "The christological focus in Rom. 10:6–8 indicates that Paul read the OT text in light of the arrival of Jesus the Messiah. A careful analysis of Deut. 29–30 reveals that Paul's hermeneutical approach is grounded in the narrative structure of Deuteronomy itself. . . . Israel will return to the LORD following exile, after he has circumcised their hearts and removed the hardness that has prevented them from keeping the Torah (30:6). It is likely Paul would have seen this prophecy fulfilled with the coming of Christ." Schreiner, *Romans*, 557.

But with Coxhead, I would want to suggest that there is not merely contextual but also grammatical warrant outlined above in chapter 2 for Paul's appeal to Deuteronomy 30:12–14.

> Instead of saying . . . that the context of Deut 29–30 legitimizes Paul's interpretation of Deut 30:11–14, we should say that the text of Deut 30:11–14 *both* contextually *and* grammatically looks forward to a future fulfillment, and that Paul saw Jesus as the fulfillment of this important text.[52]

By applying Deuteronomy 30:12–14 to Christ, Paul not only proclaims that this text has its τέλος in Christ—Deuteronomy 30:1–14 is a present reality in Paul's proclamation of the gospel—but how: Christ's mission has brought about the internalization of the eschatological *torah*.[53]

### Transforming the Quests in Deuteronomy 30:12–13.

If Paul's christological application of Deuteronomy 30:12–14 is rightly understood above, the relationship between hypothetical quests in Deuteronomy 30:12–13 and Romans 10:6–8 is easier to grasp. In Deuteronomy 30:12, a hypothetical (prophetic?) quest up to heaven to retrieve the commandment—perhaps meant to evoke Moses' journey up Sinai to retrieve the law—is not necessary: "not in heaven saying, 'Who will ascend to heaven for us and bring it to us, that we may hear it and do it?'" In Deuteronomy 30:13, a hypothetical (prophetic?) quest across the sea to retrieve the commandment—perhaps meant to evoke Israel's crossing of the Red Sea under Moses' leadership[54]—is not necessary: "neither beyond the sea saying, 'Who will go across the sea for us and bring it to us, that we may hear it and do it?'" These prophetic journeys are rendered unnecessary because of the proximity of the word through the eschatological circumcision of the heart in Deuteronomy (Deut 30:1, 6, 14).

In Romans 10:6–8, Paul declares this to be the message of the righteousness of faith: the quests in Deuteronomy 30:12–13 are unnecessary

---

52. Coxhead, "Deuteronomy 30:11–14," 312.

53. Achtemeier corroborates the eschatological aspect of this reading of Rom 10:6–8 when he writes, "The substance of verse 6–8 are taken from Deuteronomy 30:12–14, a passage in which Moses assures the Israelites that God's law is truly accessible to them. It is not remote, or isolated. *When Moses described the law in those terms, Paul implies, Moses was describing the reality of the law which has now been realized in Christ.*" Achtemeier, *Romans*, 169. Emphasis added.

54. See chapter 2 above.

because Christ has descended in the incarnation and has been brought up in the resurrection. These hypothetical quests have their τέλος in Christ's mission. A symbolic correlation between the sea and the abyss/death is well established in the OT as well as in Jewish writings[55] and provides very natural footing for Paul to transform the quest across the sea in Deuteronomy 30:13 into a quest down to the abyss in Romans 10:7.[56] The old covenant was inaugurated when Moses went up "into heaven" to retrieve the law for the people after he had led them across the Red Sea. The new covenant was inaugurated when Christ descended from heaven in the incarnation (Rom 10:6) and was raised again from the dead (10:7).

Yahweh has raised up a prophet like Moses and placed words in his mouth (Deut 18:15–19) that demand the obedience of faith (Rom 1:5) stemming from the good news about the Christ, which communicates the word in the mouth and in the heart and fulfills the *torah*. Thus the righteousness of faith bears witness to the fact that Christ has already come in the incarnation and has already risen from the dead and ascended to the right hand of the Father. All human effort is eclipsed in this divine act that makes one "alive to God in Christ Jesus" (6:11) and able to "walk in newness of life" (6:4). In short, Christ's incarnation, life, death, and resurrection bring near the מצוה in the דבר of the gospel and effect the circumcision of the heart (cf. 2:29), which in turn fulfills the righteous requirements of the *torah* (8:3–4) in the obedience brought about by faith (1:5; 16:26).

55. Although Jewish writings such as Philo and Baruch form an interesting foil to compare Paul's citation of Deut 30:12–14 in Rom 10:6–8 to, I am not convinced they form the primary background for understanding Paul's use of Deut 30:12–14. I have argued above and will continue to argue below that the primary background is the OT, especially the immediate context of Deut 30. Contra Dunn, "'Righteousness from the Law' and 'Righteousness from Faith,'" 218; Bekken, *The Word Is Near You*, 19–23. Cf. Seifrid, "Romans," 657–58. For a thorough engagement with and systematic rejection of the possible interpretive traditions behind Paul's quotation of Deut 30:12–14, see Seifrid, "Paul's Approach to the Old Testament in Romans 10:6–8," 17–34.

56. Schreiner gives the example of LXX Jonah 2:4 where Jonah is thrown into the heart of the sea (καρδίας θαλάσσης), which immediately after is referred to as the abyss (ἄβυσσος, Jonah 2:6). Schreiner, *Romans*, 559. Some commentators, like Dunn, point to *Targum Neofiti* as providing historical precedent for Paul's transformation: "Nor is the law beyond the Great Sea, that one should say: Would that we had one like Jonah the prophet who would descend into the depths of the Great Sea and bring up the law for us." Dunn, *Romans 9–16*, 605–6. The comparison of Christ's death with Jonah three days in the belly of the whale (Matt 12:40) coupled with the NT association of baptism with crossing the sea and Christ's death (cf. 1 Cor 10:2; Rom 6:3) reveals that the inter-canonical connections are rife with associative meaning.

## Omitting Law Observance from Deuteronomy 30:12–14.

If the explanation above helps shed light on what Paul intends in his mixed citation of Deuteronomy 8:17/9:4 and Deuteronomy 30:12–14, then it is a simpler task to understand why he seems to leave out phrases that have to do with observance of the law. In Deuteronomy 30:12–14, no less than three times does the phrase "to do" crop up in the MT, and it appears four times in the LXX:

---

| | |
|---|---|
| לא בשמים הוא לאמר מי יעלה־לנו השמימה ויקחה לנו וישמענו אתה <u>ונעשנה</u>: | οὐκ ἐν τῷ οὐρανῷ ἄνω ἐστὶν λέγων Τίς ἀναβήσεται ἡμῖν εἰς τὸν οὐρανὸν καὶ λήμψεται αὐτὴν ἡμῖν; καὶ ἀκούσαντες <u>αὐτὴν ποιήσομεν</u>. |
| ולא־מעבר לים הוא לאמר מי יעבר־לנו אל־עבר הים ויקחה לנו וישמענו אתה <u>ונעשנה</u>: | οὐδὲ πέραν τῆς θαλάσσης ἐστὶν λέγων Τίς διαπεράσει ἡμῖν εἰς τὸ πέραν τῆς θαλάσσης καὶ λήμψεται ἡμῖν αὐτήν; καὶ ἀκουστὴν ἡμῖν ποιήσει αὐτήν, καὶ <u>ποιήσομεν</u>. |
| כי־קרוב אליך הדבר מאד בפיך ובלבבך <u>לעשתו</u> | ἔστιν σου ἐγγὺς τὸ ῥῆμα σφόδρα ἐν τῷ στόματί σου καὶ ἐν τῇ καρδίᾳ σου καὶ ἐν ταῖς χερσίν σου <u>αὐτὸ ποιεῖν</u>. |

---

One obvious reason Paul does not include observance of the law in Romans 10:6–7 is because Paul applies this text to Christ, which makes "doing" no longer fit the context. But why does he exclude αὐτὸ ποιεῖν in 10:8? The contextual answer is that the proper response to the "word of faith that we proclaim" is confession and belief, not "doing." But at a deeper level, this is exactly how the *torah* is "done"—by the obedience of faith, which unites the believer to the one whose obedience has "done" the law—which requires perfect obedience—securing justification (cf. Rom 2:13; 5:19) and fulfilling the righteous requirement in the confessing believer (8:4). In this way, it is not Paul's ultimate aim to remove any notion of law obedience from Deuteronomy 30:12–14. Instead, he establishes law obedience in the only way that is life-giving: on the priority of faith and the *torah* internalized by divine gift apart from human effort, which motivates the obedience (out) of faith. Wright explains the larger picture of what Paul intends:

> [Deuteronomy 30] presumes that Israel has been sent into exile and is now going to turn to YHWH from the heart, and proceeds to explain what it really means to "do" the law and so to

"live." This life-giving "doing" will be a matter, not of a struggle to obey an apparently impossible law, but of heart and mouth being renewed by God's living "word." It will not be a matter of someone else teaching it to them as from a great distance. Verse 14, significantly, omits even the mention of "hearing" the commandment; it will be inside them, in their mouth and heart. We cannot but think of Jer 31:33-34: In the restoration after the exile, the people will not need to be taught the commandments, because they will be written on their hearts. And this cannot but remind us of Rom 2:25-29, a passage that Paul is about to echo in 10:9-10. It should be clear already that Paul has the context, and overall meaning, of Deuteronomy 30 firmly in mind. This is anything but a clever prooftext taken out of context.[57]

For Paul, God has fulfilled Deuteronomy 30:1-14 in Christ, and the obedience brought about by faith stems from a circumcised heart that is written over with the *torah* by the Spirit.

To further understand Paul's meaning in quoting Deuteronomy 30:12-14 in Romans 10:6-8, I turn now to examine this quotation in the larger context of Romans 9-11. After this, I zoom out further to explore its meaning in light of the message of Paul's letter to the Romans as a whole.

## Deuteronomy 30:11-14 in Romans 9-11

Recent studies and commentaries on Romans have recovered the importance of Romans 9-11 to the message of the letter as a whole, rightly rejecting the view that these chapters constitute a kind of addendum or afterthought[58]—a view typified in C. H. Dodd's suggestion that Romans

57. Wright, "The Letter to the Romans," 659-60. Though Wright reads Paul's citation of Lev 18:5 in Rom 10:5 as continuous with instead of contrary to the message of the righteousness of faith in 10:6-8, I think his contextual reading of Deut 30:12-14 in Rom 10:6-8 is correct—disagreements over the so-called New Perspective on Paul, righteousness, justification, and the law notwithstanding.

58. Cranfield writes, "A superficial reading of the epistle might easily leave one with the impression that chapters 9 to 11 are simply an excursus which Paul has included under the pressure of his own deep personal involvement in the matter of Israel's destiny but which is without any real inner relatedness to the main argument of Romans. But a closer study reveals the fact that there are very many features of chapters 1 to 9 which are not understood in full depth until they are seen in the light of chapters 9 to 11." Cranfield, *Romans*, 2:445.

9–11 was an old sermon of Paul's that made its way into later editions of the letter.[59]

In these chapters, Hays rightly points out that the

> density of scriptural citation and allusion increases dramatically in these chapters, as Paul seeks to show that Israel's unbelief, though paradoxical, is neither unexpected nor final. As Paul read Scripture, he finds not only manifold prefigurations of God's mercy to the Gentiles but also promises of Israel's ultimate restoration.[60]

The book of Deuteronomy plays a prominent role in this scriptural "density" in Romans 9–11. Four of the seven explicit quotations from the book of Deuteronomy in Paul's letter to the Romans occur in Romans 9–11. Two of these quotations we have already addressed extensively above (Deut 8:17/9:4; 30:12–14 in Rom 10:6–8). The other two, Deuteronomy 32:21 in Romans 10:19 and Deuteronomy 29:3 [ET 29:4] in Romans 11:8, occur at pivotal points in Paul's argument in Romans 9–11 and help to fill out Paul's understanding of the book of Deuteronomy in light of the gospel.

The overall structure of Romans 9–11 can be laid out as follows, which I will walk through consecutively below.[61]

> 9:1–5: Paul's anguish at Israel's current unbelief
> > 9:6–29: Has God's word failed? No, God's electing purposes have always distinguished between an Israel within Israel and intended Gentile inclusion: (cf. LXX Isaiah 40:7–8)
> > > 9:30—10:4: Gentiles have been made righteous by faith in Christ while Israel, trying to establish their own righteousness, has stumbled on Christ, the climax of the law

---

59. Dodd, *The Epistle of Paul to the Romans*, 161–63.

60. Hays, *Echoes*, 64.

61. I have modified slightly the chiasm suggested by N. T. Wright in part due to insight gained from the section divisions suggested in Hamilton, *God's Glory in Salvation through Judgment*, 450–51. This structure is similar to the one offered by Hays, *Echoes*, 64.

9:1–15 Lament over Israel.
  9:6–29: Has God's word failed? Defense of God's elective purpose.
    9:30—10:21: Paradox: Israel failed to grasp the word of faith attested by God in Scripture
  11:1–32: Has God abandoned his people? No, all Israel will be saved.
11:33–36: Doxological conclusion.

10:5–13: Two kinds of righteousness: The righteousness
that comes by the law requires perfection to live; the righteousness that comes by faith is a gift made possible by the
mission of Christ

10:14–21: Faith comes by hearing the word of Christ, which
the Gentiles have believed and beckons Israel to belief

11:1–32: Has God rejected his people? No, God's electing purposes
include a Jewish remnant, inclusion of the Gentiles, and Israel's
eschatological belief

11:33–36: Paul rejoices in spite of Israel's current unbelief

## Paul's Anguish at Israel's Current Unbelief (Rom 9:1–5)

At the apex of Paul's presentation of the gospel—the revelation of the righteousness of God (Rom 1–2) in the mission of Christ (3–6) through the
ministry of the Spirit (7–8)—he aims to demonstrate how he can claim
that this gospel was "promised beforehand through [God's] prophets in
the holy Scriptures" (1:2)—with a special view toward explaining why the
Jews, who had access to these holy Scriptures, currently reject this gospel.
Paul wants to prove that the word of God has not failed (Rom 9:6; cf. Isa
40:7–8). On the contrary, it is confirmed. This is one reason why these
chapters are more laden with OT citations than the rest of the book.[62]

## God's Word Has Not Failed (Rom 9:6–29)

Has Paul's gospel resulted from the failure or the fulfillment of God's
word (Rom 9:6; cf. Isa 40:7–8)? In order to answer the implicit charge
that God's word has failed in the failure of the Jews to believe in Christ,
Paul rewinds back to the beginning of Israel's history to the patriarchs (cf.
Rom 9:5), specifically, to Abraham, to demonstrate that God's word has
not failed, but been fulfilled. As N. T. Wright suggests,

> [I]f we treat the Pentateuch as containing, in both history and
> prophecy, the full story of the people of God, we could plausibly
> suggest that what Paul is doing in 9.6–10.13 is *telling the Torah's*
> *own story of Israel*, from the call of Abraham through to the . . .
> *telos*, the "goal," the "end" in the sense of the "moment when,

62. According to Ciampa, "Romans has the greatest density of biblical quotations
of all the books of the New Testament, with 7.2 verses per quotation." Ciampa, "Deuteronomy in Galatians and Romans," 99.

with the covenant renewed, Israel would finally be established as God's people."[63]

Paul intends to retell Israel's history in light of God's purposes in Christ. He goes to great lengths to prove that these purposes were present all along in Israel's scriptures so that he might show how their scriptures testify to the gospel of God and, in reality, the triumph of God's word.[64] In this historical rehearsal, Paul shows that God's word is confirmed, not contradicted, by the gospel he has proclaimed in Romans 1–8.

Paul begins his argument in this section by pointing out that God's people have always consisted of a "true Israel" that must be distinguished from Israel (cf. Rom 2:28–29). The true Israel is a community created by faith in God's word and promise. The true children of Abraham are those who have true faith, not merely those who are physically descended from him (9:7; cf. 4:11–12). God's electing purposes are effected through a word of promise (ἐπαγγελίας ὁ λόγος, 9:9; cf. αἱ ἐπαγγελίαι in Rom 9:4), a word that makes Isaac a child of God and not Ishmael (9:7–8), Jacob a child of God and not Esau (9:9–13). Paul anticipates a logical objection: If in God's electing purposes he shows mercy to some and not others, does this mean there is unrighteousness (ἀδικία) in his character (9:14)? Paul answers this rhetorical question emphatically by turning to the next phase of Israel's history, the ministration of Moses (9:15–18). God's electing purposes to show mercy and compassion, which are aspects of his character Yahweh revealed to Moses (9:15), depend not on human will or running (τρέχω, 9:16; cf. 9:30–33; 11:7)—a concept that becomes relevant in 9:30—10:4—but on the will and mercy of God (9:16–29).

Here Paul anticipates another logical objection: Does God's irresistible will in his electing purposes make him inconsistent when he finds mankind blameworthy? Paul grounds his retort in another subsequent phase of Israel's history. By employing a metaphor about the potter and the clay, Paul alludes to the pre-exilic prophetic ministries of Isaiah and Jeremiah (9:20–24; cf. Isa 9:16; 45:9; 64:8; Jer 18:1–6; 19:1–13) in order to head off this arrogant notion at the pass, as it were, via appeal to the Creator/creature distinction. Sticking with the prophetic ministrations, Paul then trots out direct citations from the prophets Hosea (Rom 9:25–26; cf.

---

63. Wright, *Paul and the Faithfulness of God*, 1172.

64. Although this section is, properly speaking, about the righteousness of God, a sub-theme could be traced through the efficacy of the divine word(s) (ὁ λόγος τοῦ θεοῦ, Rom 9:6; ἐπαγγελίας ὁ λόγος, 9:9; ῥῆμα τῆς πίστεως, 10:8; ῥήματος Χριστοῦ, 10:17; τὰ ῥήματα αὐτῶν [οἱ οὐρανοί], 10:18).

Hosea 2:23; 1:10) and Isaiah (Rom 9:27–29; cf. Isa 10:22–23; 1:9) to remind his interlocutor that God's *modus operandi* and intentions throughout Israel's history have always been to create a people according to his
mercy, not according to their merit or identity. God does this in order
to show his power and glory (Rom 9:23) among Israel and the nations,
which results in the nations becoming "sons of the living God" alongside
those "sons of Israel" who "will be saved" (9:27). Yes, to Israel belongs
"the adoption, the glory, the covenants, the giving of the law, the worship, . . . the promises [and] the patriarchs" (9:4–5); yes, from Israel is the
Christ descended (9:5); but apart from God's mercy, they "would have
been like Sodom and become like Gomorrah" (9:29)—a quotation from
Isaiah 1:9 which echoes the prophetic chapters of Deuteronomy where
Moses foretells of Israel's future destruction "like Sodom and Gomorrah"
due to their disobedience (Deut 29:22 [ET 29:23]).

In this way, Paul rehearses in Romans 9:1–29 Israel's history up to
the exile—a history foretold by Moses in Deuteronomy 4, 29, and 32—
and shows how the gospel he proclaims confirms the revelation of God's
saving purposes in Israel's scriptures. This is the theological half, if it can
be so neatly divided—an appeal to God's elective mercy, will, and saving
power—of the answer to Paul's original burden in Romans 9:6: Has God's
word failed? The anthropological half comes in 9:30ff.[65]

## Righteous Gentiles, Unrighteous Israelites (Rom 9:30—10:4)

In Romans 9:30, Paul continues his argument to answer the rhetorical
charge that God's word has failed because of the failure of Israel in rejecting the Christ (cf. Rom 9:6ff).[66] Having previously answered this charge
with an explanation of the doctrine of God's elective purposes (9:6–29),
Paul answers from another perspective by highlighting Israel's disobedience in their failure to submit to God's righteousness, which has been

---

65. Schreiner puts this theological-anthropological shift in terms of God's election and the gospel: "Paul wants to investigate further the implications of what he has
just stated, that God has elected many Gentiles unto salvation while choosing only a
remnant of Jews. Now he contemplates the exclusion of Israel, which is his primary
concern, and the inclusion of the Gentiles from the perspective of the Gospel." Schreiner, *Romans*, 535.

66. Noting the string of γὰρ conjunctions in Rom 10:2, 3, 4, 5, 10, 11, 12a, 12b, and
13, N. T. Wright comments, "his is as tightly linked a chain as any in Paul's writings."
Wright, "The Letter to the Romans," 652.

revealed in Christ (10:3–4). The Gentiles, who did not pursue[67] righteousness, achieved the "righteousness that comes by faith" (δικαιοσύνην δὲ τὴν ἐκ πίστεως), whereas the Jews, who ran after the "law for righteousness" (νόμον δικαιοσύνης),[68] did not achieve the righteousness that is testified to in the law.[69] What then is the failure of the Jews? Is it the manner in which they pursued the law—by faith and not by works? Or is it that they pursued after the law when they should have been pursuing after righteousness? According to Hays, "the problem is that [the Jews] pursue[d] obedience not *ek pisteos* (through faith) but *ex ergon* (through works)."[70] Hays grounds his reading in Romans 9:32, διὰ τί; ὅτι οὐκ ἐκ πίστεως ἀλλ' ὡς ἐξ ἔργων. Any interpretation of this verse must supply not only the missing verb but also the direct object of the verb. Hays supplies "pursue" and "the law" where one could just as easily supply "pursue" and "righteousness," so that 9:32 would read as follows, "Why? Because they did not *pursue righteousness* by faith but as by works." This would mean that Romans 9:31 should be translated, "Israel who pursued a law that would lead to righteousness did not succeed in reaching *that righteousness* in the law."[71] This understanding seems to comport better with Romans 11:7, where Paul writes that "Israel failed to obtain what it was seeking. The elect obtained it, but the rest were hardened." The elect obtained righteousness—not the law.

If this reading is correct, Paul probably intends in Romans 9:30–33 to allude to the context of Isaiah 51:1ff, where the prophet Isaiah addresses "you who pursue righteousness, you who seek the LORD" (οἱ διώκοντες τὸ δίκαιον καὶ ζητοῦντες τὸν κύριον, LXX Isa 51:1).[72] As noted

---

67. Paul probably means to continue to use the race imagery he has already established in Rom 9:16 in explaining the faith of the Gentiles over-against the failure of Israel.

68. For a defense of reading the genitival construction νόμον δικαιοσύνης to mean "law for righteousness," see Schreiner, *Romans*, 537.

69. I am here in agreement with Schreiner, who writes "It seems probable that δικαιοσύνην is the object of the verb ἔφθασεν and that εἰς νόμον is a predicate accusative." Oddly, though, he does not develop this point further in his commentary, later stating that Israel failed to attain the law. Schreiner, *Romans*, 538. Schreiner is more clear on this point in another article on the same passage: Schreiner, "Israel's Failure to Attain Righteousness in Romans 9:30—10:3," 212–13.

70. Hays, *Echoes*, 75.

71. Contra the ESV, which reads "Israel who pursued a law that would lead to righteousness did not succeed in reaching that law."

72. This allusion is confirmed by Wagner, who writes, "In describing the Gentiles

in the previous chapter, the ones whom Isaiah addresses in 51:1ff who "pursue righteousness" are a collective that "fears the LORD and obeys the voice of his servant" (51:10), the servant identified with the Christ. This is this people "in whose heart is my law" (51:7). Contrast this with the priests of Jeremiah's day who, though they "handle (חפש, 'are experts in')[73] the law," rejected the divine word through the mouth of the prophet and did not think to ask, "Where is the LORD?" (Jer 2:8). These priests typify a pursuit after the law which does not obtain righteousness (cf. Rom 11:7).

With Isaiah 51:1ff in the background, Paul locates Israel's failure in the *goal* of their pursuit as well as the manner in which they pursued it.[74] All along their goal should have been Christ and his righteousness (cf. 10:4), not the law as a goal unto itself.[75] As Seifrid puts it, "the goal of the law lies beyond the law"[76]—which is essentially what Paul means in Romans 10:4: "Christ is the τέλος (end/goal/fulfillment/climax) of the law for righteousness to everyone who believes."[77]

Paul further fleshes out Israel's failure in a composite Isaianic quotation found in Romans 9:33 from Isaiah 28:16 and 8:14.[78] Continuing with the race imagery, Paul allows Isaiah to make his argument for him when he writes that Israel has stumbled over the stone of stumbling that Yahweh placed in Zion.[79] In their zealous pursuit of the law, they neglected the weightier matters of the law, namely God, the Christ, and

---

as 'those not pursuing righteousness,' Paul takes up a description of Israel employed by Isaiah, οἱ διώκοντες τὸ δίκαιον (Isa 51:1), and turns it on its head." Wagner, *Heralds of the Good News*, 122.

73. BDB, s.v. "תָּפַשׂ."

74. For a sustained support of this reading, see Sprinkle, *Law and Life*, 176. Sprinkle seems to suggest that pursuit of any kind is antithetical to the gospel. Thus, he seems to agree with Käsemann who argues that "live" should be the verb inserted into Rom 9:32. Käsemann, *Commentary on Romans*, 277.

75. Earlier in the letter, Paul clearly states that God has manifested his righteousness "apart from the law" in Rom 3:21. Therefore, the Jews who continue to pursue the law for righteousness are ignorant of God's righteousness. To further support this reading, there is possibly an allusion to the text of LXX Isa 51:1ff and the idea of the pursuit of righteousness (or the righteous one) in Rom 9:30—10:4.

76. Seifrid, "Romans," 652.

77. For a comprehensive look at the interpretive options available in Rom 10:4, see Schreiner, "Paul's View of the Law in Romans 10," 113–24.

78. For a comparison of a similar composite citation of these texts in 1 Pet 2:6, see Jewett and Kotansky, *Romans*, 612–14.

79. A few verses later, Paul restates this quotation from Isa 28:16 in Rom 10:11 where he makes clear the referent is Jesus (cf. 10:9).

his righteousness. In their ignorance, they rejected the righteousness of God—the righteousness that comes by faith (Rom 9:30; 10:6–8)—and sought to "establish their own" righteousness—the righteousness that is based on the law (9:31; 10:5).

In what way did Israel seek to establish their own righteousness? If the texts Paul quotes from and alludes to in the surrounding passages are a good indication of his thought stream in Romans 9–11, then the looming composite quotation in Romans 10:6–8 provides a compelling background for what "establishing" or "making to stand" one's own righteousness looks like. As I noted above, in Deuteronomy 9:4ff, Moses warns Israel against thinking it is because of their own righteousness that Yahweh will give them the promised land. In fact, in the context, he emphatically reminds them of their unrighteousness when he tells them in Deuteronomy 9:6, "you are a stubborn people." This is the way Israel sought to establish their own righteousness: they tried to rely on a righteousness that is from the law based on works of the law. In so doing, they failed to recognize, as Paul models in Romans 7:10, that they will never measure up to the demands of this law that promises life. Their righteousness does not meet the standards of the law. They have also failed to recognize that God has manifested his righteousness apart from the law (χωρὶς νόμου), which, paradoxically, is the very thing to which the Law and the Prophets bore witness (Rom 3:21).

What is more, this is how it has always been. Abraham was justified by faith *before* the law was given (cf. Rom 4:1–25; Gal 3:17). Israel has no salvation (Rom 10:1) because they attempted to establish their own righteousness *on the basis of the law* while being ignorant of God's righteousness revealed *apart from the law* in the gospel through faith in Jesus Christ (10:2–3; cf. 1:16–17; 3:21). They are not in pursuit of the true τέλος of the law—Christ and his righteousness (10:4)—to whom the law was pointing all along, and thus are ignorant of God, even though they are zealous for him (10:2). Seifrid sums up Israel's failure:

> [I]n 10:4 Paul identifies Christ as the goal (*telos*) of the law. He brings righteousness for all who believe. God's revealed righteousness is found in him and given through him. Paul's naming Christ as the goal of the law obviously takes up his preceding image of running a course (9:30–31; cf. 9:16). It is thus Christ who is the cause of Israel's failure: he is the "stone of stumbling" that the LORD promised to place in Zion (9:30–33; Isa. 28:16 [with 8:14]). He has been set in the path of the false pursuit of

the law, bringing both judgment and salvation. In a fresh act of salvation beyond the law, the LORD has set this stone in Zion. The path of Scripture, and indeed of the law itself, leads from Sinai to Zion and ends there. As the goal of the law, Christ is the message of Scripture.[80]

80. Seifrid, "Romans," 653–54. My interpretation of Deut 30:11–14 would work just as well with a salvation-historical reading of Rom 10:4ff that sees Christ as the "end" of the law, i.e., bringing to close the cultic provisions of the old covenant, as represented by Hamilton: "'Before faith came' Leviticus 18:5 meant that the one who by faith kept the Mosaic Covenant would live. Now that 'faith has come,' the Mosaic covenant is no longer in force, it has served its salvation-historical purpose, with the result that anyone who seeks to live by it must keep all of its regulations flawlessly since its sacrifices are now abolished." Hamilton, "The One Who Does Them Shall Live by Them," 12. Similarly Moo: "Paul is implying that Christ is the 'end' of the law (he brings its era to a close) and its 'goal' (he is what the law anticipated and pointed toward)." Moo, *The Epistle to the Romans*, 641. Cf. Schreiner, who writes, "It is certainly the case that a salvation-historical shift is taught in the Pauline letters to the effect that the Mosaic covenant is no longer in force. Thus no theological objection to this exegesis can be maintained. Moreover, the text implies a salvation-historical shift, for faith in Christ is the means of salvation. Nonetheless, the primary fault ascribed to the Jews in 10:3 is not salvation-historical but anthropological." Schreiner, *Romans*, 547. Cf. also Calvin: "In order to instruct the people in the doctrine of repentance, it was necessary for [Moses] to teach what manner of life was acceptable to God; and this he included in the precepts of the law. That he might also instil [sic] into the minds of the people the love of righteousness, and implant in them the hatred of iniquity, promises and threatenings were added; which proposed rewards to the just, and denounced dreadful punishments on sinners. It was now the duty of the people to consider in how many ways they drew curses on themselves, and how far they were from deserving anything at God's hands by their works, that being thus led to despair as to their own righteousness, they might flee to the haven of divine goodness, and so to Christ himself. This was the end or design of the Mosaic dispensation. But as evangelistic promises are only found scattered in the writings of Moses, and these also somewhat obscure, and as the precepts and rewards, allotted to the observers of the law, frequently occur, it rightly appertained to Moses as his own and peculiar office, to teach what is the real righteousness of works, and then to show what remuneration awaits the observance of it, and what punishment awaits those who come short of it. . . . Paul indeed thus reasons,—'Since no man can attain the righteousness prescribed in the law, except he fulfils strictly every part of it, and since of this perfection all men have always come far short, it is in vain for any one to strive in this way for salvation: Israel then were very foolish, who expected to attain the righteousness of the law, from which we are all excluded.'" Calvin, *Romans*, 385–87. Moo recognizes this interpretation of is integral to the Reformation: "Central to the Reformers' teaching about salvation was their distinction between 'law' and 'gospel.' 'Law' is whatever God commands us to do; 'gospel' is what God in his grace gives to us. The Reformers uniformly insisted that human depravity made it impossible for a person to be saved by doing what God commands; only by humbly accepting, in faith, the 'good news' of God's work on our behalf could a person be saved. This theological 'law'/'gospel' antithesis is at the heart of [Romans 10:5–8], as Paul contrasts the

To summarize the context of Romans 9:30—10:4 before getting to Paul's OT citations in 10:5–8: Israel has failed because they pursued the law by works instead of pursuing Christ and his righteousness by faith (Rom 9:30–32). They stumbled over the rock in Zion, Christ Jesus, and failed to believe in him (9:33). Instead, they ignorantly tried to establish their own righteousness while rejecting the righteousness of God in Christ, which is the whole point (τέλος) of the law they were pursuing (10:1–4).

## Two Kinds of Righteousness (Rom 10:5–13)

The rival experiences of the Jews and Gentiles in succeeding and failing to attain righteousness in Romans 9:30—10:4 (the failure of the Jews to attain righteousness from the law and the success of the Gentiles to attain the righteousness by faith) sets up the contrast we find in Romans 10:5–13 between these two kinds of righteousness. In this passage, Paul does not, as some have argued,[81] claim that the righteousness based on

---

righteousness that is based on 'doing' the law (v. 5) with the righteousness that is based on faith (vv. 6–13). Significantly, Paul finds this distinction in the OT itself, manifesting his concern to prove that the gospel that has proved a stumbling block for so many Jews and a foundation stone for so many Gentiles is in continuity with the OT." Moo, *The Epistle to the Romans*, 644. Moo goes on in his commentary to articulate a similar interpretation to the one Calvin rejects in the quotation above when Moo says that Paul is (partly) refuting a Jewish misinterpretation of Lev 18:5. But this understanding of Lev 18:5 is not new with Calvin and the Reformers. On the contrary, it is well grounded in the early church fathers as represented by Chrysostom's commentary on Rom 10:5. "What he means is this. Moses showeth us the righteousness ensuing from the Law, what sort it is of, and whence. What sort is it then of, and what does it consist in? In fulfilling the commandments. 'He that doeth these things,' he says, 'shall live by (or in), them.' (Lev. xviii. 5.) And there is no other way of becoming righteous in the Law save by fulfilling the whole of it. But this has not been possible for any one, and therefore this righteousness has failed them." Chrysostom, *Hom. Rom.*, 16 (NPNF 1/11:473). See also Augustine: "The righteousness of the law is proposed in these terms,—that whosoever shall do it shall live in it; and the purpose is, that when each has discovered his own weakness, he may not by his own strength, nor by the letter of the law (which cannot be done), but by faith, conciliating the Justifier, attain, and do, and live in it. For the work in which he who does it shall live, is not done except by one who is justified. His justification, however, is obtained by faith; and concerning faith it is written, 'Say not in thine heart.'" Augustine, *De spir. et litt.*, 29.51 (NPNF 1/5:105).

81. Interpreters who understand Paul's citation of Lev 18:5 and Deut 30:12–14 in Rom 10:5–8 as a synthesis include Cranfield, *Romans*, 2:520–26; Wright, "The Letter to the Romans," 658–64; Hays, *Echoes*, 76–83; Wagner, *Heralds of the Good News*, 160; Kaiser, "Leviticus 18:5 and Paul" 19–28. I have attempted to gather the best evidence set forth by these interpreters in favor of this view. (1) Paul's audience would have

the law and the righteousness based on faith are one and the same. Instead, it is most natural to read Romans 10:5–8 as Paul's effort to further ground (γάρ, Rom 10:5) in the Scriptures his previous assertion about the two pursuits after righteousness—seeking righteousness based on works and the law or seeking righteousness based on faith and grace.[82]

---

understood Moses to be the author of Deuteronomy and Leviticus, so it would not make sense for Paul to pit Moses against Moses, and it would be out of character for Paul to set one passage of Scripture against another. (2) In Deut 30:16, a mere two verses after the ones cited by Paul, Moses says something very similar to what is found in Lev 18:5, "If you obey the commandments of the LORD your God . . . you shall live." Therefore, if Paul quotes Deuteronomy against Leviticus, opponents could easily appeal to the context of Deuteronomy to refute him. (3) The γάρ . . . δέ conjoining the two citations does not have to be contrastive, but Paul can and does use these as a correlative in the near context of Rom 10:10. (4) "Doing the law" in the context of Leviticus does not imply a legalistic perfectionism but instead recognizes that the law makes provision for the atonement for sin, which necessitates faith in God and his Messiah. Thus Paul has redefined "doing" as "believing/trusting" in what God has done in Christ, which corresponds to the message of the Deuteronomy citation. (5) Some argue that the one who does the law in Lev 18:5 refers to Christ in Rom 10:5, who perfectly fulfills the law, which is the intended message of the Deuteronomy quotation. Since the presence of a synthesis between the two OT citations in Rom 10:5–8 remains unconvincing in my view, below is a brief response to each of the arguments above. (1) Perhaps Paul is indeed uncomfortable with the appearance of setting Moses against Moses, which would explain his strange introduction to the Deuteronomy quotation, "the righteousness of faith speaks in this manner." Paul does not seem to have a problem pitting Scripture "against itself" elsewhere (cf. Gal 3:11–12), and this hermeneutical move might be better explained by another reading. (2) Many interpreters fail to take into account the placement of Deut 30:12–14 in its original context, which takes place *after* the promise of heart circumcision in Deut 30:6. (3) Δέ, while not *always* encoded to express contrast, is often used to do so. (See Steven Runge's helpful discussion that corrects the notion that δέ is always contrastive, contra BDAG. Runge, *Discourse Grammar of the Greek New Testament*, 28–36.) (4) Against the notion that "doing" is positive for Paul in his quotation of Lev 18:5, Doug Moo rightly notes, "Faith and believing on the one hand and works and doing on the other are one of the most pervasive contrasts in the Pauline letters." Moo, *Romans*, 646. (5) The interpretation that sees Christ as the one who does the law in the citation of Lev 18:5 in Rom 10:5 would place Paul in conflict with himself in Gal 3:12 where he cites this text differently. Again Moo, "While not impossible, a difference between the two [uses of Leviticus 18:5] would be unlikely because the texts have a great deal in common." Moo, *Romans*, 647.

82. Interpreters who argue for antithesis in Rom 10:5–8 include Dunn, *Romans 9–16*, 602; Hamilton, *God's Glory in Salvation through Judgment*, 111–14.; Moo, *Romans*, 645–50; Schreiner, *Romans*, 551–54; Seifrid, "Romans," 652–60; Sprinkle, *Law and Life*, 172; Watson, *Paul and the Hermeneutics of Faith*, 332. So also Calvin: "To render it evident how much at variance is the righteousness of faith and that of works, he now compares them; for by comparison the opposition between contrary things appears more clear." Calvin, *Romans*, 385. I have enumerated the evidence cited by interpreters in favor of antithesis: (1) In Rom 9:30, Paul contrasts the Gentiles who attain

In Romans 10:5–8, Paul cites two OT texts that bear witness to two types of righteousness: Leviticus 18:5 and "the righteousness that is based on the law," and our text in Deuteronomy 30:12–14, which is the message of "the righteousness based on faith." To make his point, Paul turns to the

---

"the righteousness that is by faith" with the Jews who pursue the "law of righteousness" and do not attain it. Immediately following this in 10:2–3, Paul declares that the Jews are ignorant of the "righteousness of God" and instead they have tried to establish their own righteousness, failing to submit to God's righteousness. Therefore, in the immediate context, Paul is contrasting two types of righteousness. He contrasts the "righteousness that is by faith" vs. pursuing "the law for righteousness" in 9:30–32, and "God's righteousness" vs. "their own righteousness" in 10:2–3. This would lend naturally to identifying a contrast between "the righteousness that is from the law" and "the righteousness of faith" in 10:5–8. (2) For Paul, "doing the law" and "works" are related concepts (cf. Rom 3:20), a view that finds support in LXX Exod 18:20: "And you shall proclaim to them the decrees of God and his law, and you shall show them the ways in which they shall walk, and the works which they shall do (τὰ ἔργα ἃ ποιήσουσιν)." So Watson, *Paul and the Hermeneutics of Faith*, 332. Thus when Paul cites Lev 18:5, he does so to recall Rom 9:32 and the Jews who were in pursuit not "by faith" but "by works." As Preston Sprinkle writes, "'Doing' the law belongs to the same field of ideas as various other terms that Paul opposes in Rom 9–11. For instance, 'works' (9:12, 32; 11:6), 'running' (9:16), 'seeking' (10:3, 20; 11:7), 'ascending' (10:6), and 'descending' (10:7) are all terms of human endeavor which stand antithetically to 'election' (9:11), 'calling' (9:12), 'mercy' (9:16), 'not pursuing' (9:30), 'faith' (9:32), 'submitting' (10:3), 'confessing' (10:9, 10), 'believing' (10:9, 10; cf. 9:33; 10:11), and 'grace' (11:6), terms which emphasise God's initiative, or human response to God's prior action." Sprinkle, *Law and Life*, 172. Lev 18:5 speaks of "the man who does them," where Paul quotes Deut 30:12–14 and purposefully omits any reference to "doing." (3) Dunn writes, "When Paul sets righteousness ἐκ πίστεως alongside righteousness ἐκ something else, with δέ as the linking word, he obviously intends his readers to understand a contrast between the two phrases." (cf. Rom 4:15; 9:30, 32; Gal 3:10–12.) Dunn, *Romans 9–16*, 602. (4) Within the argument of his letter to the Romans, Paul speaks of God's righteousness being established *apart* from the law (Rom 3:21–22). The law holds a man captive and must be died to (7:6) for "the very commandment that promised life (cf. Lev 18:5) proved to be death" (Rom 7:10). Therefore, to speak of "the righteousness that is from the law" positively would be for Paul to go against his established argument in the rest of Romans (cf. Rom 4:13–14). (5) Outside of Romans, in Gal 3:11–12, Paul contrasts Lev 18:5 with Hab 2:4 to make the point that "no one is justified by the law" for "the law is not of faith" (ὁ δὲ νόμος οὐκ ἔστιν ἐκ πίστεως). Additionally, in Phil 3:9 Paul can say that he does not have a righteousness that is from the law (δικαιοσύνην τὴν ἐκ νόμου) but rather that his righteousness is from God and it depends on faith (τὴν ἐκ θεοῦ δικαιοσύνην ἐπὶ τῇ πίστει). Therefore, outside of the book of Romans, there is warrant for seeing a law-faith antithesis in Paul's thought, especially with regard to justification and righteousness. (6) The introductions are strikingly different—Moses "writes" while the righteousness of faith "speaks"—perhaps setting up a letter/Spirit antithesis which is present elsewhere in Pauline theology (cf. Rom 2:29; 7:6).

Pentateuch, the Law itself, to demonstrate that the *torah* points beyond itself for righteousness. Calvin explains why:

> [Paul] refers not now to the oracles of the Prophets, but to the testimony of Moses, and for this reason—that the Jews might understand that the law was not given by Moses in order to detain them in a dependence on works, but, on the contrary, to lead them to Christ. He might have indeed referred to the Prophets as witness; but still this doubt must have remained, "How was it that the law prescribed another rule of righteousness?" He then removes this, and in the best manner, when by the teaching of the law itself he confirms the righteousness of faith.[83]

In short, Paul's aim is to show how the law itself bears witness to the righteousness of faith—the very place his opponents would have turned to counteract his message.[84]

Paul first turns to Leviticus 18:5 to highlight the rigorous demands of the law in order to attain life.[85] How does the law prescribe life? "Mo-

---

83. Calvin, *Romans*, 385–86.

84. Lang argues that the reason why Paul turns again to the Pentateuch is because his Jewish opponents would have understood the Pentateuch, not the Prophets and the Writings, to be decisive. "Wenn dieser Verheißungszusammenhang richtig gesehen ist und in der Sache der neue Bund so stark im Blickfeld steht, dann wird die häufig nicht gestellte Frage unausweichlich, warum Paulus gerade Dtn 30 als Schriftbeleg für Glaubensgerechtigkeit herangezogen und nicht mit der prophetischen Heilsverheißung und dem neuen Bund argumentiert hat. Allerdings ist sich der Apostel dessen voll bewußt, daß für die jüdischen Ausleger vor allem die Tora beweiskräftig ist, während die Propheten und Hagiographen als deren Auslegung verstanden werden." Lang, "Erwägungen Zu Gesetz Und Verheissung in Römer 10,4–13," 594–95.

85. At first glance, the text form of Lev 18:5 seems to be the most straight forward of the two OT passages cited in Rom 10:5–8. Paul appears to quote LXX Lev 18:5, which is close to a word-for-word rendering of MT Lev 18:5, almost verbatim in Rom 10:5. Paul inserts an αὐτά in place of the relative pronoun ἅ, which in the context of LXX Leviticus refers back to "all my commandments and all my judgments" (πάντα τὰ προστάγματά μου καὶ πάντα τὰ κρίματά μου). Paul also nominalizes the participle ποιήσας, which as Seifrid argues may represent an attempt to reflect the text of the MT. Seifrid, "Romans," 655. The αὐτά, however, has no clear antecedent in the context of Rom 10, which has led to variations in the manuscript evidence. Two significant variations appear in Rom 10:5, but both have been dismissed by Bruce Metzger as scribal emendations that were probably made to make the text more readable: "Apart from several more or less insignificant variations, there are two main readings which differ as to the position of ὅτι and the construction of δικαιοσύνην. With ὅτι immediately before ὁ ποιήσας the sentence runs, 'For Moses writes concerning the righteousness [accusative of specification] which is of the law, that "the man who does them shall live in them."'" Moving ὅτι earlier to follow γράφει has the effect of extending the quotation

ses writes about the righteousness that is based on the law that the person who does the commandments shall live by them."[86] Calvin sees embedded in this verse not only the promise of eternal life—not merely life in the land[87]—but also the demand for perfection inherent in it:[88]

> The passage is taken from Lev. xviii. 5, where the LORD promises eternal life to those who would keep his law; for in this sense, as you see, Paul has taken the passage, and not only of temporal life, as some think. Paul indeed thus reasons—"Since no man can attain the righteousness prescribed in the law, except he fulfils strictly every part of it, and since of this perfection all men have always come far short, it is in vain for any one to strive in this way for salvation: Israel then were very foolish, who expected to attain the righteousness of the law, from which we are all excluded." See how from the promise itself he proves, that it

---

and making δικαιοσύνην the object of ποιήσας. A majority of the Committee preferred the former sequence. . . . As for the variations involving αὐτά and αὐτοῖς, the omission of the former and the substitution of αὐτῇ for the latter appear to be scribal emendations, prompted because the context contains no antecedent to which the plural may refer." Metzger, *A Textual Commentary on the Greek New Testament*, 524. This is the only place in Paul's letters where Paul introduces a Scripture citation by the present tense γράφει. Also unique to this citation is the description of the content of the quotation, summarized as τὴν δικαιοσύνην τὴν ἐκ [τοῦ] νόμου. For a detailed examination of the variations in this text, see the discussion in Sprinkle, *Law and Life*, 165–67.

86. For a thorough engagement and defense of this translation of Rom 10:5 in light of the significant textual variant related to the position of ὅτι, see Moo, *The Epistle to the Romans*, 643n1.

87. Contra Kaiser, "Leviticus 18:5," 19–28.

88. Other interpreters argue that Paul is making a salvation-historical argument in his appeal to Lev 18:5 in Rom 10:5. On this reading, since Christ is the "end" of the law for righteousness (Rom 10:4), the sacrificial provisions under the old covenant have ceased with the dawn of the new covenant in Christ, which means that perfect obedience is required if one would look to the law for righteousness *now that Christ has come*. Regardless of which reading is taken, Schreiner is right to summarize Paul's point when he writes, "the attempt to obtain righteousness by the law is futile. Israel under the law only ended up in exile." Schreiner, *Romans*, 556.

can avail us nothing, and for this reason, because the condition is impossible. What a futile device it is then to allege legal promises, in order to establish the righteousness of the law! For with these an unavoidable curse comes to us; so far is it, that salvation should thence proceed.[89]

Many have noted an allusion to Leviticus 18:5 earlier in Paul's letter to the Romans in Romans 7:10: "The very commandment that promised life (ζωή, Rom 7:10) proved to be death to me" (cf. "the person who does [them] shall live (ζάω) by them (Rom 10:5; Lev 18:5).[90] In Romans 7:7ff, Paul writes about the function of the law that Calvin highlights in the quotation above—consciousness of transgression—while still defending the holiness, righteousness, and goodness of the law (Rom 7:12).[91] The "righteousness that is based on the law" demands perfection for eternal life, and sin deceives the sinner by leading him astray of the commandment

89. Calvin, *Romans*, 387. Calvin goes on to write, "The more detestable on this account is the stupidity of the Papists, who think it is enough to prove merits by adducing bare promises. 'It is not in vain,' they say, 'that God has promised life to his servants.' But at the same time they see not that it has been promised, in order that a consciousness of their own transgressions may strike all with the fear of death, and that being thus constrained by their own deficiency, they may learn to flee to Christ." In his day, Jonathan Edwards countered an Arminian reading of this text that argued, much as the NPP does today, "law" in Romans 10:5–8 refers to ceremonial and not moral demands. "By the apostle's saying, the righteousness of the law is described thus, he that doth these things, shall live in them; but the righteousness of faith saith thus, plainly intimates that the righteousness of faith saith otherwise, and in an opposite manner. Besides, if these words cited from Moses are actually said by him of the moral law as well as ceremonial, as it is most evident they are, it renders it still more absurd to suppose them mentioned by the apostle, as the very note of distinction between justification by a ceremonial obedience, and a moral sincere obedience, as the Arminians must suppose." Edwards, "Justification by Faith Alone," 634–35.

90. Cf. Jewett and Kotansky, *Romans*, 452. Fitzmyer, *Romans*, 468. Moo sees a connection between Paul's citation of Lev 18:5 in Rom 10:5 and Rom 7:10: "Paul does think that the law embodies, in its very nature, the principle that perfect obedience to it would confer eternal life (see 2:13 and 7:10). It may be this principle that Paul intends to enunciate here via the words of Lev. 18:5." Moo, *The Epistle to the Romans*, 648.

91. So also Augustine: "For there was need to prove to man how corruptly weak he was, so that against his iniquity, the holy law brought him no help towards good, but rather increased than diminished his iniquity; seeing that the law entered, that the offence might abound; that being thus convicted and confounded, he might see not only that he needed a physician, but also God as his helper so to direct his steps that sin should not rule over him, and he might be healed by betaking himself to the help of the divine mercy; and in this way, where sin abounded grace might much more abound,—not through the merit of the sinner, but by the intervention of his Helper." Augustine, *De spir. et litt.*, 6.9 (*NPNF* 1/5:86).

while blinding him to the extent of his transgression. The law is good because it illumines the discrepancy in spite of sin's delusion (7:13); but the righteousness which the law offers is unattainable because of our sin.[92]

Thus, when Paul turns to Leviticus 18:5 in Romans 10:5, he does so in order to conclude one leg of his argument that has been building from the very first chapter of the letter. That is, running after righteousness based on the law by works of the law is futile. Set in contrast to this, however, is the righteousness of God, which Paul has also been speaking about from the beginning (Rom 1:16–17). It is a gift from God, a righteousness that stems from *faith* (3:22), by *grace* (3:24), through the mission of *Christ* (3:25), applied by the *Spirit* (8:2). And this is the only way for sinful man to truly "do the law" and thus be justified (2:13). To prove this point, Paul does not turn to the Prophets or the Writings, as if their witness was opposed to that of the Law. Instead, he stays within the Pentateuch to demonstrate that the Scriptures have borne witness to the righteousness-by-faith all along, the gift-righteousness testified about in Deuteronomy 30:1–14.[93]

As I argued in chapter 2 above, Deuteronomy 30:12–14 occurs in the context of the return from exile Moses promised *in spite* of the inevitable disobedience of Israel. At this return, this "restoring of fortunes," Yahweh will circumcise their hearts by implanting the word in their mouth and in their hearts so that they might "do it." This divinely initiated act of grace—a new covenant act of grace—transforms the inner disposition of man through no effort of his own, which is the very thing Paul highlights in Romans 10:6–8 in contrast to the law-righteousness in Romans 10:5. Wells neatly explains the significance of this contrast:

92. See Augustine: "There is, of course, nothing said figuratively which is not to be accepted in its plain sense, when it is said, 'Thou shall not covet;' but this is a very plain and salutary precept, and any man who shall fulfil it will have no sin at all. The apostle, indeed, purposely selected this general precept, in which he embraced everything, as if this were the voice of the law, prohibiting us from all sin, when he says, 'Thou shalt not covet;' for there is no sin committed except by evil concupiscence; so that the law which prohibits this is a good and praiseworthy law. But, when the Holy Ghost withholds His help, which inspires us with a good desire instead of this evil desire (in other words, diffuses love in our hearts), that law, however good in itself, only augments the evil desire by forbidding it." Augustine, *De spir. et litt.*, 4.6 (*NPNF* 1/5:85).

93. Contra Knox, who writes "It is hard to see why Paul should have chosen for use a passage for whose clear original meaning he must substitute a meaning almost the exact opposite." Knox, "The Epistle to the Romans," 557. Hays says something similar when he writes, "It would not be easy to find another text in the Old Testament that looks less promising for Paul's purposes." Hays, *Echoes*, 79.

Whereas Leviticus 18:5 speaks of covenant obedience to a Mosaic code that remains under the power of Sin (Rom 7:7–13), Deuteronomy 30:11–14 bespeaks a situation wherein humans are made competent agents through the liberating work of Christ. Doing the righteous things of Torah remains a dead end because such activity lies outside God's saving agency. If this assessment is correct, then it is erroneous to assume that Paul is not really interpreting Deuteronomy 30:11–14 in Romans 10:6–8. Nor is he rewriting a passage that he finds distasteful and at cross-purposes with his own theology. Nor is it altogether accurate to conclude that Paul blatantly and intentionally ignores the original context and meaning of Deuteronomy 30. To be sure, Paul *has* rewritten various features of Deuteronomy 30:11–14; but he has done so according to his understanding of what God's apocalypse has now revealed those verses to foretell.[94]

Paul recognizes that in the mission of Christ, God has acted decisively and brought about the fulfillment of Deuteronomy 30:11–14, which is a continuation of the new covenant themed "restoration of fortunes" in 30:1–10, in those who believe in him. Those who have faith in Christ have circumcised hearts that house the obedience-of-faith-motivating *torah*. Badenas notes a connection to heart circumcision in Paul's citation of Deuteronomy 30:12–14:

> The fact that Paul sees as characteristic of the new dispensation the circumcision of the heart (Rom 2.29), and that this is precisely stated in Deut 30.6 . . . makes it easier to understand why has he [sic] chosen this chapter as anticipatory of righteousness by faith. The fact that the promised "circumcision of the heart" was understood as messianic prophecy (Jer 31.33; 32.39–40; Ezek 11.19–20; 36:26–27) explains that Paul could use [Deut 30.11–14] as one of those most clearly pointing towards the NT.[95]

In my view, this is a better reading than the one offered by Watson, who sees two opposing threads in the ending of Deuteronomy and argues that Deuteronomy 30 conveys a return program that is "a matter of appropriate *human* action, beginning with confession and determined by the law," while Deuteronomy 32 conveys a return program that is "a matter of definitive, unsurpassable *divine* saving action, which reorients

94. Wells, *Grace and Agency*, 274–75.
95. Badenas, *Christ the End of the Law*, 130.

human action toward itself and so represents a breach with the law."[96]
Watson's reading of Deuteronomy 30 leads him to conclude that

> the non-Christian Israel of [Paul's] own day is characterized
> by the ever-renewed attempt to enact the return to the Law by
> zealous practice of the Law's works. This is the theological pro-
> gramme of Deuteronomy 30, and, from a Pauline perspective,
> its failure is confirmed by the simple fact that God has chosen
> to act differently.[97]

Against Watson's interpretation, I agree with Ciampa who states that
"[i]t seems unlikely, however, that Paul finds two opposing abstract and
static approaches to redemption in Scripture, two contradictory voices,
one of which must be rejected and the other upheld."[98] I think Ciampa's
explanation of Paul's turn to Deuteronomy 30:12–14 is helpful:

> [T]here are enough hints to suggest that in Paul's view God has
> fulfilled the theological programme of Deuteronomy 30 *through
> Christ himself*, and that has brought about significant implications
> for understanding how the realities of curse and blessing, death
> and life, disobedience and obedience, sin and righteousness are
> conceived in light of the good news of Christ's achievement.[99]

My position is close to how John Gill wrestles with what Paul saw in
Deuteronomy 30:12–14 for his purposes in Romans 10:

> Moses himself is not speaking of the law only, but either of the
> whole word of God, both law and Gospel; or particularly of the
> Gospel, which holds forth those special blessings and promises

96. Watson, *Paul and the Hermeneutics of Faith*, 464.

97. Watson, 473.

98. Ciampa, "Deuteronomy in Galatians and Romans," 116. This conclusion is
drawn as well by Whittle, *Covenant Renewal and the Consecration of the Gentiles in
Romans*, 52–57. In an argument very similar to the current thesis, Whittle argues that
"Paul rewrites the text of Deuteronomy 30:11–14 not because he thinks [Torah obedi-
ence] is humanly possible but because of its significance as the key covenant-renewal
text, and because of its proximity to the affirmation of the divine activity. Righteousness by Faith gives this grace-enabled obedience and covenant renewal a Christological interpretation so that Deuteronomy 30 actually becomes the story of what God has
done in Christ. In this renewal it is not Torah commandments that are in view but a
confession of faith and belief in one's heart. Paradoxically, however, the result is that
law's fulfilment is indeed a real possibility, but only for those in Christ, in whom law
finds its eschatological fulfilment on the basis of faith's obedience." Whittle, *Covenant
Renewal and the Consecration of the Gentiles in Romans*, 55.

99. Ciampa, "Deuteronomy in Galatians and Romans," 117.

of grace, pardon of sin, and circumcision of the heart, which are mentioned in the context, as what should be bestowed upon the people of the Jews in the latter days; and so is rightly applied by the apostle to the then dispensation, and is to be understood of the Gospel; which was nigh both in the ministration of it, by the apostles, to Jews and Gentiles, and in the application and experience of it; it was not only *in the mouth* of the preachers, but also of the hearers of it, by a hearty and sincere confession; and *in their hearts*, being attended with the power of God, and received in the love of it, was truly believed in, and cordially embraced.[100]

I quote Olshausen's interpretation of Paul's use of Deuteronomy 30:12–14 in Romans 10:6–8 to allow room for the development of his argument, which I am sympathetic with:

The connexion in Deut. xxx. is as follows:—In ch. xxix., Moses had threatened the people with ejection from the land of promise, in case of unfaithfulness, but afterwards, in ch. xxx., foretells that they will return to themselves, and will at last be gathered again by God into the land of their fathers. . . . The passage is unmistakably Messianic; it points to the circumcision of the heart—to a state in which man will be able truly to love God and to keep the commandments. The only difficulty is from xxx. 11, which says . . . *the commandment which I command thee to-day;* which seems to refer the passage to the law of the Old Testament, and not to faith. But if we consider that the law is by no means wanting in the New Testament—that it is only regarded as no longer something merely outward, but as inward—as the voice of the eternal Word in the heart of man (John xii. 50), nay, that this reception of divinity into itself is the very essence of the New Testament, and of the life of faith which belongs to it—it will be clear how the apostle might with perfect justice, interpret those words of the Old Testament as applicable to the relation of the New. . . . The course of thought, therefore, in Paul, takes this form. "The Scripture saith of the righteousness of the law, that whoever shall fashion himself conformably to the law which meets him from without shall live; but this no man can do; consequently no man attains life thus; all that he can attain by this way is the knowledge of sin (iii. 20). But, in the New Testament, he hath, by the operation of the Spirit, the law within himself; it is written on his heart; therefore he need no longer

---

100. Gill, *Exposition of the Old and New Testaments*, 8:520.

seek it from afar, but only become aware of this treasure within him, and follow the power of the Spirit."[101]

Wright further elaborates on how Paul's incorporation of Deuteronomy 30 into his argument in Romans points to the fulfillment of the new covenant promises in Christ:

> Paul's basic claim about Deuteronomy 30 is that the great change in Israel's fortunes which that chapter describes—or, as many of his contemporaries would have said, prophesies—is precisely what has come about through Jesus the Messiah. Deuteronomy 30 comes, as we have remarked before, at the turning-point of Israel's prophetic history, the moment for which so many were waiting during much of the second-temple period, and the moment for which Paul's own narrative in Romans 9.26–29 was implicitly waiting as well. In fact, if we treat the Pentateuch as containing, in both history and prophecy, the full story of the people of God, we could plausibly suggest that what Paul is doing in 9.6–10.13 is *telling the Torah's own story of Israel,* from the call of Abraham through to the . . . *telos,* the "goal," the "end" in the sense of the "moment when, with the covenant renewed, Israel would finally be established as God's people." . . . Through the Messiah the prophecies have come true, the covenant has been re-established, exile is over, God himself has acted to unveil his faithfulness to his promises, and God's people are now able . . . to keep Torah from the heart.[102]

Although Wright sees in Romans 10 merely a "pattern" of Messiah "coming from God to Israel enabling them to be God's people in a new way," his conclusion is very similar to the thrust of my argument that

> Paul is using Deuteronomy 30 to say: Ah, but in the enabling promise of covenant renewal, God himself holds out a new way of 'doing the law', a way which will be "in your mouth and in your heart," a way which will come from God himself in the form of his 'word', and which will enable you to "do" it.[103]

---

101. By this last phrase, "become aware of this treasure within him," Olshausen reveals that he conceives of the word of God as eternally present in all people, which they must be awakened to and turn toward, which is faith. But it is my argument that the word only comes accompanied by the Spirit in the heart of man at the preaching and believing of the gospel. Olshausen, *Biblical Commentary on the New Testament,* 4:106–7.

102. Wright, *Paul and the Faithfulness of God,* 1172. Emphasis original.

103. Wright, *Paul and the Faithfulness of God,* 1173. Wright reasons elsewhere,

The interpreters quoted above all share one thing in common: they argue for the significance of the context of Deuteronomy 30:1–10 to unlocking Paul's use of Deuteronomy 30:12–14 in Romans 10:6–8.[104] Paul Barker's conclusion is a concise summary of the position I have attempted to defend:

> [W]e find that Paul's understanding of Deuteronomy 30 is not contrived or misconstrued but rather he understands the passage properly. This supports our thesis that 30:11–14 is dependent on 30:1–10 and therefore grounds Israel's capacity to obey the law

---

"[Rom 10.5–8] is regularly regarded as an arbitrary piece of exegesis on Paul's part, choosing to treat Leviticus 18 as a statement of a pre-Christian view of Torah and its accomplishment and Deuteronomy 30 as a 'Christian' view of its fulfillment. But . . . I suggest that this is actually unwarranted. Paul's whole theme thus far has been the covenant purpose of God. He has traced it from Abraham, Isaac and Jacob (9.6–13) through Moses and the prophets to the exile (9.14–29), and has now stated that it has reached its climax in the Messiah. What more natural move than that he should now draw on a classic Old Testament passage (Deuteronomy 30) which, certainly from a first-century perspective, would inevitably be read as a prophecy of return from exile, that is, of the renewal of the covenant, to express that which results from the climatic work of the Messiah? This is further supported by the clear 'new covenant' overtones of Joel 3.5 (quoted in 10.13) and Isaiah 52.7 (10.15)." Wright, *The Climax of the Covenant*, 245.

104. Lang likewise argues that the context of Deut 30:1–10, which he acknowledges has similarities to Jer 31:33ff and 32:39–41, is hermeneutically significant for Paul's choice of this text in Rom 10:5–8. "Nun ist zu beachten, daß 30,10 den zusammenfassenden Abschluß des Verheißungsabschnitts 30,1–9 bildet, in dem der Blick in die Zukunft geht und der „in der Stilform einer prophetischen Weissagung" ganz in die Nähe von Jer 31,33ff und 32,39–41 führt. Wenn also Paulus dieses Gebot (V. 11) mit dem als Verheißung verstandenen nahen Wort (V. 14) verbunden sieht und wenn kurz vorher gesagt ist, daß Gott sich an dem durch Gottes Eingreifen zum Gehorsam umgekehrten Volk wieder freuen wird, „wie er sich über deine Väter gefreut hat" (V. 9), dann kann man ihm m.E. schwerlich vorwerfen, daß er die Aussage-Intention des Textes bewußt verfälsche, so sehr wahr ist, daß Paulus das Alte Testament vom Standort des Christusgeschehens her auslegt." Lang, "Erwägungen Zu Gesetz Und Verheissung in Römer 10,4–13," 594–95. Schreiner, while rejecting the prophetic reading of Deut 30:11–14, presents a similar argument. "A careful analysis of Deut. 29–30 reveals that Paul's hermeneutical approach is grounded in the narrative structure of Deuteronomy itself. In Deut. 27:1—29:1 the blessings and curses for obedience and disobedience are rehearsed. As the narrative unfolds in Deut. 29–30 it becomes apparent that Israel will certainly experience the curse and be thrust out of the land (30:1). The LORD has withheld his grace from the Israel of Moses' day so that they cannot comprehend or perceive what God has done in their midst (29:3–4). Israel will return to the LORD following exile, after he has circumcised their hearts and removed the hardness that has prevented them from keeping the Torah (30:6). It is likely that Paul would have seen this prophecy fulfilled with the coming of Christ." Schreiner, *Romans*, 557.

in the circumcision of the heart by Yahweh. We have rejected the view that 30:11–14 stands in temporal contrast to 30:1–10. Rather it describes the consequences of the circumcision of the heart. It therefore denies human capacity to fulfil the covenant demands. It is not a statement that the law is easy to fulfil. Nor is the law's accessibility due to revelation. Being in the mouth and heart is not a reference to memorisation or recital. Rather, v14 is a statement of the effect of the circumcision of the heart in v6. Ultimately, the fulfilment is the work of God, in Christ, as Paul argues in Romans 10:4. Thus the optimism of 30:11–14 derives from the hope of God's gracious, and future, work.[105]

To further draw out how the gospel Paul proclaims relates to the message of the righteousness-by-faith, Paul explains how an individual comes to obtain this righteousness in Romans 10:9–13: it is through a (divinely placed, as Deut 30:12–14 reminds us) heart-faith and mouth-confession that comes in response to the word of faith proclaimed by the apostles (Rom 10:8), which is one and the same with the word of (about/from) Christ (cf. 10:17). Christ communicates his righteousness to the faith-full through the proclamation of the gospel (10:9–13).

## Faith Comes by Hearing the Word of Christ

In Romans 10:14–21, Paul turns again to the question of Israel's failure to attain the righteousness of faith (cf. Rom 9:30—10:4) with a series of interlocking rhetorical questions in 10:14–15a whose logic Cranfield summarizes:

> They can only call upon Christ in the sense of v.12 and 13, if they have already believed on Him; they can only believe on Him, if they have heard Him (speaking to them through the message about Him); they can only hear Him, if someone proclaims the message; the message can only be proclaimed, if God commissions someone to proclaim it.[106]

The generic 3rd plural in Romans 10:14 most likely refers back not to Israel specifically, but to Jews and Greeks (cf. Rom 10:12), the indiscriminate "everyone" to whom the exhortation to call on the name of the LORD goes out (10:13). But Israel is currently part of those who have

---

105. Barker, *The Triumph of Grace in Deuteronomy*, 198.
106. Cranfield, *Romans*, 2:533–34.

not "obeyed the gospel" (Rom 10:16a), which entails faith, as the citation from Isaiah 53:1 in Romans 10:16 makes clear, specifically belief in the word of God's messengers: "Lord, who has believed what he has heard from us?" (10:16b). Paul then summarizes the logical progression of the string of rhetorical questions in 10:14–15a: faith comes from hearing the word of Christ (10:17). In 10:18, Paul anticipates another potential question. Maybe those who haven't obeyed the gospel, a group that includes Israel, have failed to attain the righteousness of faith because they haven't heard its message, the word of Christ (10:18)? But Paul emphatically declares in 10:18ff that, indeed, they have heard, and it is their failure to understand what they have heard that is the problem, just as Moses and Isaiah foretold.

To defend his claim, Paul cites Psalm 19:4,[107] Deuteronomy 32:21, and Isaiah 65:1—one each from the Law, the Prophets, and the Writings. Though Israel has heard, they did not "understand" (γνώσκω) what they heard, right in line with what Moses predicted would happen (cf. Deut 32:28–29). This even though they had the special revelation of the message of the righteousness of faith embedded in the Scriptures all along.

### Jealous of Those Who Are Not a Nation

Paul's quotation of Deuteronomy 32:21 in Romans 10:19 is the third of four textual interactions with Deuteronomy 30 in chapters 9–11. Paul roots Israel's failure to understand in God's divine plan from the beginning, which Moses laid out fully in Deuteronomy 32. In response to the disobedience that flows from Israel's failure to understand (cf. Rom 10:19a; Deut 32:28–29), Yahweh tells Israel through Moses, "I will make you jealous of those who are not a nation; with a foolish nation I will make you angry" (Rom 10:19b; Deut 32:21). Paul sharpens the original rebuke in Deuteronomy by changing the 3rd person plural pronouns to 2nd person plural pronouns.[108] Israel's disobedience to the gospel leads to the inclusion of "those who are not a nation," "a foolish nation," namely the Gentiles (cf. Rom 9:22–26; 11:11–24). In turning to Deuteronomy

107. This citation is difficult, but a detailed explanation of Paul's use of Ps 19:4 in Rom 19:18 is beyond the scope of this project.

108. Watson's suggestion as to why Paul changes these pronouns is intriguing: "Paul's substitution of 'you' for 'them' (MT, LXX) may suggest that the generation has now arrived for whom the Song was once written. Watson, *Paul and the Hermeneutics of Faith*, 447n60.

32, Paul again reinforces his reading of the Pentateuch as pointing forward to his proclamation of the gospel while also advancing his retelling of Israel's history, which he grounds partly in the narrative structure of Deuteronomy itself. Deuteronomy 29–32 is being fulfilled, the restoring of fortunes has arrived, and the nations are being included at the expense of Israel's (temporary) disobedience, just as Deuteronomy 32 predicted. Stanley is right to observe that Deuteronomy 32:21 "actually foreshadows the position that Paul will develop in fuller terms throughout the whole of chapter 11."[109]

Paul concludes this section in Romans 10:14–21 with two consecutive texts from the last chapter of Isaiah that likewise foretell the reality Paul observes in his day: the Gentiles have found Yahweh whom they did not seek (Isa 65:1; Rom 10:20; cf. Rom 9:30), while Israel remains disobedient and contrary in spite of Yahweh's persistence (Isa 65:2; Rom 10:21).

## Has God Rejected His People?

Paul's fourth and final interaction with the book of Deuteronomy in Romans 9–11 takes place in Romans 11:1–32, where Paul continues to defend Yahweh against the charge that his word has failed with the failure of Israel to obey the gospel. Paul continues his argument by pointing out that a remnant of believing Jews is even now present—he himself, an Israelite, is evidence of this fact (Rom 11:1–5)! This preservation of a remnant is in accord with God's electing purposes, which have always maintained that salvation comes by grace alone (Rom 11:5–6). This is how the righteousness they are seeking eludes unbelieving Israel (Rom 10:7; cf. 9:31–32): they have been hardened (ἐπωρώθησαν), a passive verb which Paul indicates should be understood as a divine passive by following it up with a mixed citation from Isaiah 29:10 and Deuteronomy 29:3 (ET 29:4):

> As it is written,
>> "God gave them a spirit of stupor,
>>> eyes that would not see
>> and ears that would not hear
>>> down to this very day." (Rom 11:8)

The phrase "spirit of stupor" comes directly from LXX Isaiah 29:10, while the rest of the citation, "God gave . . . eyes that would not see and

109. Stanley, *Paul and the Language of Scripture*, 144.

ears that would not hear, down to this very day"—a trope that later prophets would pick up frequently (Isa 6:9–10; 43:8; Jer 5:21; Ezek 12:2)—is a
modification of Deuteronomy 29:3 (ET 29:4) to fit Paul's context:

| Rom 11:8 | LXX Deut 29:3 | MT Deut 29:3 |
|---|---|---|
| Ἔδωκεν αὐτοῖς ὁ θεὸς πνεῦμα κατανύξεως, | καὶ οὐκ ἔδωκεν κύριος ὁ θεὸς ὑμῖν καρδίαν εἰδέναι καὶ ὀφθαλμοὺς βλέπειν καὶ ὦτα ἀκούειν ἕως τῆς ἡμέρας ταύτης. | ולא־נתן יהוה לכם לב לדעת ועינים לראות ואזנים לשמע עד היום הזה |
| ὀφθαλμοὺς τοῦ μὴ βλέπειν | | |
| καὶ ὦτα τοῦ μὴ ἀκούειν, | | |
| ἕως τῆς σήμερον ἡμέρας | | |

In Deuteronomy 29:3 (ET 29:4), the negation (οὐκ) functions with
the verb, stating that Yahweh has still not given Israel "hearts to know
or eyes to see or ears to hear" up to this day.[110] In his citation, Paul shifts
the negation (μή) to function with the infinitives βλέπειν and ἀκούειν in
order to make clear the logical corollary: by not giving them ears that
hear and eyes that see, "God gave them . . . eyes that would not see and
ears that would not hear." The answer given in Deuteronomy to this dilemma comes, as I argued in chapter 2, in Deuteronomy 30:1–14 with
the divine gift of heart circumcision, which is exactly where Paul turns in
Romans 10 to meet the challenges presented in the impossibility of the
righteousness of the law. In this way, Paul again signals how he reads the
Pentateuch, especially Deuteronomy, in light of Christ's mission. Waters
refers to this as "another instance of Paul's eschatological reading of Deut
27–30."[111] As Lincicum argues,

> [T]he main thrust of Paul's citation is to establish divine inten-
> tion in Israel's unbelief. Here it is crucial to recall the context of
> Deuteronomy 29. The chapter is a résumé and re-establishment
> of the covenant, together with a sure prediction of Israel's fail-
> ure to keep it. The curses have just been enunciated in Deuter-
> onomy 27–28, and are assumed to be on the brink of a terrible
> realization in Israel's history. The εὐλογία is not mentioned at
> all in Deuteronomy 29; it has simply faded from view, not to

110. See chapter 2 above for a defense of this reading of "to this day" in Deut 29:3
(ET 29:4).

111. Waters, *The End of Deuteronomy in the Epistles of Paul*, 205.

be reintroduced until 30:1. Deut 29:3 LXX thus functions as a guarantee that Israel's failure is not beyond God's providential outworking. In this way, perhaps paradoxically, the ground is prepared for the restoration which is detailed in 30:1–10, a restoration that is arguably divinely initiated.[112]

In his divine plan, Yahweh has delayed his promise to Israel because of their unbelief. Then through a citation from Psalm 69:22–23 (Rom 11:9–10), Paul indicates that Israel in her present condition occupies the same situation as the enemies of King David: opposing and rejecting God's anointed.

Paul's final response in Romans 11:11–32 to the apparent failure of God's word with respect to his people in Romans 9–11 is to express hope for Israel's future in the divine plan, which, according to Seifrid, has a "Deuteronomic sequence."[113] Hamilton summarizes Paul's message here concisely: "Israel has not stumbled so as to fall. Remarkably, Israel has been hardened for the full number of the Gentiles to come in. Once that has happened, Israel will be saved."[114]

## Paul Rejoices in Spite of Israel's Current Unbelief

Paul closes out Romans 9–11 in doxology, praising Yahweh for the unfathomable riches, knowledge, and wisdom of his judgements and ways (Rom 11:33). After traversing the depths of the revelation of God's unfolding plan in these chapters, Paul can only stand back and with Isaiah and Job declare,

> For who has known the mind of the Lord,
>    or who has been his counselor?
> Or who has given a gift to him
>    that he might be repaid?
> (Rom 11:34–35; cf. LXX Isa 40:13; Job 41:3a [ET 41:11a])[115]

Paul's closing statements in Romans 11:33–36 serve to recall his opening in Roman 9:1–5 and punctuate the chiastic construction of

---

112. Lincicum, *Paul and the Early Jewish Encounter with Deuteronomy*, 148.

113. Seifrid, *Christ, Our Righteousness*, 168.

114. Hamilton, *God's Glory in Salvation through Judgment*, 451.

115. For a comparison of Paul's text form to the LXX and MT, see Cranfield, *Romans*, 2:590–91; Jewett and Kotansky, *Romans*, 718–21. For a summary of how interpreters have understood Paul's text form, see Moo, *The Epistle to the Romans*, 742–43.

Romans 9–11. Eulogizing (Rom 9:5) and glorifying (11:36) God in Christ has been Paul's ultimate aim in these chapters, a task he considers never complete (εἰς τοὺς αἰῶνας, ἀμήν, Rom 9:5; 11:36; cf. 1:25).

## The Deuteronomic Shape of Paul's Gospel in His Letter to the Romans

There are five additional textual interactions with the book of Deuteronomy in Paul's letter to the Romans outside of the four we assessed in Romans 9–11 (see table 16 above). These texts serve to further fill out a picture of how Paul understood and applied the book of Deuteronomy in his communication of his gospel, the revelation of God's righteousness for all who believe.

### The Law Written on the Circumcised Heart

In Romans 2:25–29, Paul explicitly alludes to the circumcision of the heart in terms that recall Deuteronomy 30:6. The surrounding context suggests that the narrative flow of Deuteronomy 29–32 was very much in the mind of Paul when he wrote this passage, especially in light of how frequently he returns to this section in Deuteronomy throughout his letter to the Romans (Deut 30:6 in Rom 2:28–29; Deut 30:12–14 in Rom 10:6–8; Deut 32:21 in Rom 10:19; Deut 29:3(4) in Rom 11:8; Deut 32:35 in Rom 12:19; Deut 32:43 in Rom 15:10).

Paul seems to be responding in Romans 2:25 to an unstated but reasonably anticipated protest from his (rhetorical) Jewish interlocutor. A Jew might question Paul's prior assertion that Jews can be objects of God's wrath and Gentiles can be objects of God's mercy.[116] One might

---

116. In Rom 2:17ff, Paul addresses the Jew directly: "you bear the name Jew." He accuses them of hypocrisy; they have not practiced what they claim to be so excellent at teaching others, which results in God's name being blasphemed among the Gentiles (Rom 2:24; cf. Eze 36:20ff). Perhaps the most shocking statement in Rom 1:1—2:24—at least from a Jewish standpoint—is Paul's indictment of the Jews in the group who will be subjected to God's wrath. In Rom 2:8–9, Paul writes that those who are selfishly ambitious, disobedient to the truth, and obedient to unrighteousness will receive wrath and indignation (Rom 2:8). Every soul of man who works evil, *the Jew first* and also the Greek, will receive tribulation and distress (2:9). And perhaps the second most shocking statement follows quickly on its heels—those who do good will receive glory and honor and peace, the Jew first *and also the Greek* (2:10). According to Paul's gospel, the disobedient Jew will experience the wrath and indignation

respond, "Are we Jews not marked out as the people of God? Do we not bear the sign of the covenant in our circumcision?" (cf. Rom 3:1).[117] Up to this point in the letter, Paul has not mentioned circumcision. But by mentioning it in verse 25, Paul probably has in mind addressing this potential protest. To this hypothetical question, Paul responds in 2:25 that circumcision is indeed of value (ὠφελέω),[118] "profit in terms of

---

of God *alongside* the disobedient Gentile, and the obedient Gentile will receive glory and honor *alongside* the obedient Jew. Paul elaborates on these two propositions—that Jews can be objects of God's wrath and Gentiles can be objects of God's mercy—in the rest of chapter 2, including in the section under consideration in 2:25–29. This is why the section on heart circumcision, exegetically speaking, is grounding (γάρ, 2:25) the previous section.

117. C. K. Barrett notes that Jews would have considered their circumcision as a type of "effective shield against God's wrath." Barrett, *A Commentary on the Epistle to the Romans*, 57.

118. With the use of ὠφελέω, Paul culminates an allusion to LXX Jer 7:4, 8ff, where Paul finds the Jews of Jeremiah's day participating in unfounded boasting just as he observed in his fellow countrymen. Berkley states, "[Paul] relies in part again on Jer 7:4, 8, where a marker of relationship with God was rendered worthless because of disobedience." Berkley, *From a Broken Covenant to Circumcision of the Heart*, 146. In Jer 7:4 and 8, Jeremiah warns against confidence (πείθω, cf. Jer 7:4, 8; Rom 2:19) in the deceptive words, "The temple of the LORD, the temple of the LORD, the temple of the LORD." These words are of no value (ὠφελέω, LXX Jer 7:8; cf. Rom 2:25) because the Jews have broken the law—they have murdered, committed adultery (μοιχάω, LXX Jer 7:9; cf. Rom 2:22), stolen (κλέπτω, cf. Jer 7:9; Rom 2:22), and have turned the temple into a den of robbers (LXX Jer 8:11; cf. "do you rob temples?" in Rom 2:22). Their confidence is found to be groundless in light of their many transgressions. Perceiving an allusion to Jer 7 in this passage enriches Paul's rhetoric. Just as Jeremiah warned his contemporaries that putting confidence in the temple is of no value (ὠφελέω) on account of their many transgressions against the law, in Rom 2:25 Paul warns his contemporaries that putting confidence in physical circumcision is of no value (ὠφελέω) because of the very same type of transgressions that Jeremiah observed in his day. Further, both the temple and the sign of circumcision were visible signs of covenantal relationship with God, and both signs tempted the Jews into false assurance when in fact what the signs were supposed to signify—the presence of God and devotion to God, respectively—were conspicuously absent. The circumcision of Paul's contemporaries has become uncircumcision (ἡ περιτομή σου ἀκροβυστία γέγονεν)—has been nullified—on account of their transgressions. Thus they have become like the Jews of Jeremiah's day mentioned above in Jer 9:25, who though circumcised were uncircumcised of heart. They are no better than the uncircumcised Egyptians, Edomites, Ammonites, and Moabites, which is exactly Paul's point in Rom 2. Jews do not stand on higher ground than Gentiles in the judgment simply because they possess the law or because they possess the sign of circumcision. What these Jewish possessions were meant to effect—law obedience and covenantal loyalty—is what actually matters in the judgment according to Paul's gospel.

salvation," as Schreiner renders it,[119] but only if one practices (πράσσω) the law (νομός).[120]

In Romans 2:26, it follows (οὖν) for Paul that if one's failure to keep the law can *disqualify* someone from covenant blessing in spite of their physical circumcision, then succeeding in keeping the law can *qualify* someone even if they are not circumcised (e.g., a Gentile). "If an uncircumcised man keeps (φυλάσσω) the righteous requirements of the law (τὰ δικαιώματα τοῦ νόμου)," Paul asks, "then will not his uncircumcision be reckoned (λογισθήσεται) as circumcision?" Who is it that wields the power to reckon circumcision to the uncircumcised? The passive infinitive λογισθήσεται should be read as a divine passive: it is the same one who wields the power to reckon righteousness to the unrighteous (Rom 4:5).[121]

In Romans 2:27, Paul states that the one who is uncircumcised according to his "outward form" (φύσις) but nevertheless fulfills the law

119. Schreiner, *Romans*, 138.

120. Paul uses πράσσω here synonymously with ποιέω elsewhere (cf. Rom 10:5) in reference to perfect obedience. So Schreiner, 138. "The covenant signified by circumcision does not and cannot save, for only perfect obedience would qualify and no one can obey to such an extent." I am using the term "perfect obedience" to refer to the kind of obedience that no mere man has or ever will live up to (Rom 3:23).

121. But what of the uncircumcised man? How is it that Paul can say that he keeps the righteous requirements of the law? The phrase "keeps the righteous requirements of the law" (τὰ δικαιώματα τοῦ νόμου φυλάσσῃ) in Rom 2:26 is best interpreted in parallel with the phrase "fulfilling the law" (τὸν νόμον τελοῦσα) in 2:27 (cf. Rom 10:4). The fact that δικαίωμα is used instead of νόμος may point away from interpreting the phrase synonymously with "practicing the law" (νόμον πράσσῃς) in 2:25, which I have argued above is the same as "doing the law," or perfect obedience, by which no man will be justified (3:20). Instead, Paul seems to distinguish in Romans between the legal demands of the law (ποιέω νόμον, ἔργων νόμου, cf. 3:20, 28) and the righteous requirements of the law (δικαίωμα, cf. 1:32, 2:26; 5:16, 18; 8:4). Even though the Gentile has not performed the legal demands of the law—he is uncircumcised, after all—he has kept the righteous requirements of the law (loving God in Christ, cf. Deut 6:4–5) by the regenerating power of the Spirit in his circumcised heart (2:29) which produces faith in (3:22) and union with (6:3) the one who has fulfilled the law completely. Jesus made the same distinction as he summed up the law in the righteous requirements of loving God and loving your neighbor (Matt 22:37–40, cf. Mic 6:8). In the previous section in Rom 2:14, the Gentile Christian "does the things of the law (τὰ τοῦ νόμου ποιῶσιν)." The phrase "things of the law" probably points forward to the righteous requirements (δικαίωμα) identified in 2:26. It is not insignificant that in Ezek 36:26–27, the same word is used to describe the promise that Yahweh, with the gift of a new Spirit, will cause his people to walk in his statues (δικαίωμα) and keep (φυλάσσω) his judgments, to do them (ποιέω, LXX Ezek 36:27). Therefore, the one who is uncircumcised yet keeps the righteous requirements of the law in Rom 2:26 demonstrates that, for him, the law (νόμος) has been internalized—he has been circumcised of heart.

(τὸν νόμον τελοῦσα) will judge the one who is a transgressor of the law. The word φύσις appears here for the second time in chapter 2, the first being in 2:14. In both contexts, I suggest that a better translation is "outward form" instead of "naturally" or "by nature."[122] In Romans 2:14, Paul describes Gentiles who do not have the law by nature (φύσις)[123] but nevertheless do the things of the law (τὰ τοῦ νόμου ποιῶσιν). By so doing, these Gentiles demonstrate that the "work"[124] of the law is "written on their hearts" (Rom 2:15; cf. Jer 31:33). The linguistic parallels between this verse and Jeremiah 31:33 point toward the view that these Gentiles are regenerate Gentile Christians and not merely Gentiles who have and obey the natural law.[125] The Gentile Christian in 2:14 does not have the law in outward form (φύσις), i.e. he is not circumcised, but he still does the righteous requirements of the law. Likewise, in 2:27, the Gentile who is uncircumcised in "outward form" (φύσις) but who nevertheless fulfills the law, demonstrates that in him dwells the signification of the sign. The signification of circumcision is present in his real devotion to God (for Paul, πίστις) and the sign of the letter of the law is significantly fulfilled in his obedience to do the righteous requirements of the law—the obedience of faith (1:5; 16:26).

This is why Paul goes on to explain in 2:28–29 that being a Jew is not a matter of outward appearances (φανερός), nor is circumcision a matter of fleshly appearances (φανερός). Instead, Jewishness is hidden

---

122. Contra the ESV, NIV, and NASB, which all render it "naturally."

123. I find Gathercole's argument for taking φύσις with the leading clause and not the trailing one, as most translations do, to be persuasive. Gathercole, "A Law unto Themselves: The Gentiles in Romans 2.14–15 Revisited," 35–37. Below I argue that this phrase ἔθνη τὰ μὴ νόμον ἔχοντα φύσει refers to those Gentiles who are not physically circumcised—the law has not "marked" their outward form or nature, which is a logical conclusion of how Gathercole understands φύσις, as not having the law "by birthright."

124. Cranfield explains why the word ἔργον is singular, not plural. "We understand τὸ ἔργον τοῦ νόμου in 2.15 as 'the work which the law requires', and take Paul's meaning here to be that the eschatological promise of Jer. 31.33 that God would write his law in the hearts of his people is being fulfilled in the Gentiles who have believed in Christ. The use of the singular may be explained as intended to bring out the essential unity of the law's requirements, the fact that the plurality of commandments is no confused and confusing conglomeration but a recognizable and intelligible whole." Cranfield, "'The Works of the Law' in the Epistle to the Romans," 94.

125. For a thorough defense of a Gentile Christian reading of Rom 2:14–15, see Gathercole, "A Law unto Themselves." Augustine famously switched from a *lex naturalis* reading to a Gentile Christian reading of Rom 2:14–15. Gathercole, "A Conversion of Augustine: From Natural Law to Restored Nature in Romans 2:13–16," 147–72.

(κρυπτός), and circumcision is a matter of the heart by the (indwelling) Spirit and not the (external) letter. In this external/internal (φανερός/ κρυπτός) dichotomy is an allusion to a very significant text that we have already referred to earlier, a context that functions as the headwaters of the metaphor of heart circumcision: Deuteronomy 29–30.[126]

Deuteronomy 29:28 (ET 29:29) is the "meta-comment" that bridges chapters 29 and 30.[127] "The secret things (κρυπτός) are for the LORD our God, but the things revealed (φανερός) are for us and our sons forever to do all the words of this law." Directly after this text, Moses speaks of heart circumcision, which Yahweh promises to effect after the exile (Deut 30:1–14). Paul is almost certainly drawing upon these textual headwaters by mentioning heart circumcision in Romans 2:28–29:

> For no one is a Jew who is merely one outwardly (φανερός), nor is circumcision outward (φανερός) and physical (σάρξ). But a Jew is one inwardly (κρυπτός), and circumcision is a matter of the heart (καρδία), by the Spirit (πνευμα), not by the letter (γραμμά).[128]

Heart circumcision—true Jewishness—is so defined by Paul: it is an act of God, by the Spirit, in the inward heart; it is not an act of men, by the letter, in the outward flesh. And the praise of the "true Jew" is from God—not men—an eternal reward that will be distributed "on the day when God judges the secrets (κρυπτός) of men according to my Gospel through Christ Jesus" (Rom 2:16). In context, the "secrets" (κρυπτός) are the states of men's hearts, that is, whether or not one is truly faith-full to Yahweh in his Son from a circumcised heart.[129]

---

126. So Berkley, *From a Broken Covenant to Circumcision of the Heart*, 153. "Paul takes this passage [Deut 29:29], in conjunction with the nearby mention of heart circumcision (30:6), as evidence of the fact that God looks upon what is unseen: the secrets (Rom 2:16), the inward heart (2:28–29)."

127. Gentry, "The Relationship of Deuteronomy to the Covenant at Sinai," 51.

128. Paul alludes to Deut 29–30 while also drawing on the two major new covenant passages of the OT, Jer 31 and Ezek 36, with a γραμμά/πνευμα antithesis. According to Paul, the problem with the old covenant is not the law (Rom 7:7). The problem with the old covenant is that the law remains external and stands over against the sinner in condemnation (2 Cor 3:9). The law lacks the mechanism to enable obedience, which can only happen through a circumcised heart indwelt by the Spirit. Paul finds in the new covenant promise the missing mechanism: internalization of the law (Rom 2:15; Jer 31:33) by the gift of the Spirit (Ezek 36:26–27) who enables obedience to the law.

129. Waters writes, "If Paul broaches language of Deuteronomic restoration at Rom 2:29, he does so in a setting where Israel's failings are very much in view. This

## "You Shall Not Covet"

In Romans 7:7 and 13:9, Paul quotes the tenth commandment, "You shall not covet," which is found in both Exodus 20:17 and Deuteronomy 5:21.[130] According to Lincicum, this commandment

> comes to epitomize for Paul both the goodness of the law and its powerlessness, helpful and holy in identifying sin, but in that very identification providing a vehicle for sin to hijack in order to provoke humanity without the Spirit to deadly transgression—a picture of Israel's history *in nuce*.[131]

For Paul, the tenth commandment stands as a convenient synecdoche for the sum of the law's demands. This commandment is conducive for Paul's purposes because in its original form, it addresses itself to the oft-neglected interior aspect of sin and obedience in the law. As a synecdoche for the whole law, Paul equates it with the command that offers life in exchange for obedience (Rom 7:10; cf. Lev 18:5). But as Paul makes clear, when the law meets sin in a man's heart, what is inevitably produced is disobedience leading to death (Rom 7:8–12). Paul's exegetical association of the Deuteronomic Decalogue in Romans 7:7—which is a summary in its own right of the Mosaic and natural law—with the unachievable life-giving law which produces death in man in Romans 7:10 is telling. Apart from the divine intervention of the Spirit in the heart, the holy, righteous, and good commandment (Deut 5:21) yields only deadness.

But as Paul states elsewhere in his letter to the Romans, the very same commandment (Deut 5:21) that meets the Spirit dwelling in the circumcised heart, on which the selfsame law is inscribed, is not a threat but an exhortation toward fulfilling the whole law in love (cf. Rom 13:8–10).

---

setting is not unlike that of Rom 10:6–8, in which Israel's failure to respond positively to the Christian gospel, we observed, serves as a crucial backdrop to Paul's argument and exposition of Scripture. Further study might consider the significance of this allusion to Deut 30 so early in Romans to the argument of the epistle as a whole." Waters, *The End of Deuteronomy in the Epistles of Paul*, 253. While there is much more work to be done here, I have attempted to show how Paul's allusion to Deut 30 in Rom 2:28–29 comports with his reading of Deut 30:12–14 in Rom 10:6–8.

130. An argument could be made for the priority of Deuteronomy's Decalogue in Paul's thought, as his second interaction with the Decalogue in Rom 13:9a follows Deuteronomy rather than Exodus in order, but Paul probably did not have a strong bifurcation in his mind between the law in Exodus and Deuteronomy.

131. Lincicum, *Paul and the Early Jewish Encounter with Deuteronomy*, 125.

The difference between Paul's use of Deuteronomy 5:21 in Romans 7:7 and in 13:8–9 has everything to do with the absence or presence of Christ and his Spirit. As Paul writes in Romans 8:3–4,

> For God has done what the law, weakened by the flesh, could not do. By sending his own Son in the likeness of sinful flesh and for sin, he condemned sin in the flesh, in order that the righteous requirement of the law might be fulfilled in us, who walk not according to the flesh but according to the Spirit.

The right approach to the things Moses commanded on the plains of Moab, things which include the Decalogue, is through the divine promise of heart-renovation in Deuteronomy 30:1–14.

## Singing the Song of Moses

Paul twice accesses the Song of Moses in Deuteronomy 32 outside of Romans 9–11, both times in explicit quotation, and both times in Romans 12–15. These chapters are, as Mark Reasoner puts it, a "picture of how the new covenant community of Jew and Gentile is to live now (12:1—15:6) in light of their spectacular destiny (15:8–12)."[132] By appealing to Deuteronomy 32 to fill out this picture, Paul shares one more insight into how he reads the eschatological promises of Deuteronomy 32, which involves the eschatological inclusion of the Gentiles. So Waters: "The people of God . . . are now assumed to include Jew *and* Gentile."[133]

In Romans 12:14–21, Paul presents a Christian *lex talionis*. Christians are not to repay evil for evil (Rom 12:17) and are never to avenge themselves, leaving instead the recompense of wrongdoing to God's wrath (12:19; cf. Lev 19:18). It is here that Paul quotes Deuteronomy 32:35, "Vengeance is mine; I will repay." Hence, Paul identifies the Christian community with God's people whom he will avenge in the eschaton.

The first half of the Song of Moses in Deuteronomy 32 rehearses God's kindness to Israel in their national ascendency, and it foretells their decline and fall due to wickedness in spite of God's goodness toward them (Deut 32:1–20). Just as Israel provoked Yahweh, he will likewise provoke them to jealousy with those who are not his people, and he will afflict Israel to the point of death as a nation (32:21–27). But the song takes a positive turn in 32:28ff, where Yahweh promises vindication for

132. Reasoner, "The Theology of Romans 12.1–15.13," 294.

133. Waters, *The End of Deuteronomy in the Epistles of Paul*, 222. Emphasis original.

his people (עַם) "when he sees that their power is gone" (32:36). At this juncture in Deuteronomy 32, an ambiguity exists as to the identity of this "people." Paul interprets this ambiguity expansively to include the nation(s) who are no people (בְּלֹא־עָם, 32:21). By appealing to Deuteronomy 32:21 at just this point, Paul again signals where he understands himself to be ministering in the narrative timeline laid forth in the book of Deuteronomy. What is more, Paul realizes that this timeline includes a redefinition of the people of God. As Waters argues,

> Paul has continued to read Deut 32 as a text that regulates the behavior of his churches, whom he conceives to be the people of God. . . . [His] reading continues to be eschatological and christological, since Christ remains the standard by which Paul assesses the identity of the people of God.
>
> At both Rom 9–11 and Rom 12, then, Paul appeals to Deut 32 in order to establish certain claims concerning divine activity that serves as the foundation for his audience's *extra*ecclesial relations.[134]

Paul's final citation of the Song of Moses (Deut 32) in Romans 15:10 is perhaps the more intriguing. In this section, Paul grounds the gospel he proclaims and his Gentile mission in the warp and woof of the Scriptures—a task he has been about since the beginning of the letter (Rom 1:2)—with a string of OT quotations. As Seifrid comments, "Paul derives his understanding of the mission of the Messiah from Scripture."[135] Paul understands that in Christ's mission, the Song of Moses is coming to fulfilment where it is written, "Rejoice, O Gentiles, with his people" (15:10; Deut 32:43).[136]

In the original context of Deuteronomy 32:43, it is not explicit why the גוים are exhorted to rejoice, especially since it comes directly after Yahweh's promise to vanquish the enemies of his people. Is it because they

---

134. Waters, *The End of Deuteronomy in the Epistles of Paul*, 222, 223.

135. Seifrid, "Romans," 688.

136. MT: הַרְנִינוּ גוֹיִם עַמּוֹ. Cranfield notes that this "is an exact quotation of part of LXX Deut 32.43. It is an express summons to the Gentiles to rejoice together with God's own people." Cranfield, *Romans*, 2:746. The discrepancy between the MT and LXX is explained by Ciampa: "The Hebrew consonants for 'people' (עַמּוֹ) can also be read as 'with' and the LXX has given the word a 'double reading', incorporating both potential meanings, so that the Hebrew 'his people' (עַמּוֹ) has been read 'with his people'. Ciampa, "Deuteronomy in Galatians and Romans," 114. See also Wagner, *Heralds of the Good News*, 316.

are amazed at Yahweh's faithfulness to Israel? Or is it because they are included among those children whom Yahweh avenges (Deut 32:43b)? By citing Deuteronomy 32:43 in this string of OT texts, which serve to prove the purpose of Christ's mission is, in part, "that the Gentiles might glorify God for his mercy" (Rom 15:9), Paul once again reveals his own understanding of his mission and place in salvation history. Deuteronomy 32:43 foreshadows the inclusion of the Gentiles in the people of God, which is fulfilled in the mission of Christ and the proclamation of the gospel which they have believed. As Seifrid argues,

> Paul cites the single statement in the Song of Moses that holds out hope of salvation for the Gentiles: there is salvation for them, too, in the salvation of God's people. This promise of salvation, spoken by Moses in the narrative of the Song, is now spoken to the Gentiles by the risen Christ. Judgment has been passed. The Messiah now invites them to salvation.[137]

In Deuteronomy 32, as in the rest of the book of Deuteronomy, especially chapters 29–32, Paul sees the gospel he proclaims about Christ's mission prefigured. As evangelist to the Jew and the Greek, he deftly wields the book of Deuteronomy in order to precisely and persuasively demonstrate how it bears witness to the gospel he proclaims.

## Chapter Summary

With the foregoing analysis before us, I am now in a position to summarize Paul's view of Deuteronomy in general as well as his appeal to Deuteronomy 30:12–14 in particular. In Romans 10:6–8, Paul turns to Deuteronomy 30:12–14 for the message of the righteousness of faith. This turn is better understood within Paul's entire understanding of the book of Deuteronomy, which is formed in no small part by the narrative progression of the end of the book in Deuteronomy 29–32.

Francis Watson summarizes Paul's use of Deuteronomy in the following way:

> [T]he non-Christian Israel of his own day is characterized by the ever-renewed attempt to enact the return to the law by zealous practice of the law's works. This is the theological programme of Deuteronomy 30, and, from a Pauline perspective, its failure is confirmed by the simple fact that God has chosen to

137. Seifrid, "Romans," 689.

act differently. As a read of Deuteronomy, Paul's advice to other readers . . . is simply to *keep reading*—not to come to a halt at the end of chapter 30, but to read on into chapter 32. There, Moses sees that God's saving action will be manifested in a different form and on a different basis to what he has previously imagined. Israel must learn this from and with the Gentiles; but also from and with Moses, retracing his own movement beyond the conditional logic of the blessing and the curse to a final insight into the unconditional basis of divine saving action.[138]

But contra Watson, as I have attempted to demonstrate in the previous chapters as well as in this one, the theological program of Deuteronomy 30 is not, as Watson asserts, "a matter of appropriate *human* action" as opposed to the "matter of definitive, unsurpassable *divine* saving action" found in the theological program set out by the Song of Moses in Deuteronomy 32. Instead, these two chapters sing harmony as they *both* bear witness to the promise of God's saving initiative, which Paul understands to be fulfilled in Christ. Roy Ciampa's summary of what Paul sees in Deuteronomy 30 is similar to my conclusions above:

> Although Paul hardly spells it out in Romans . . . we would argue that there are enough hints to suggest that in Paul's view God has fulfilled the theological programme of Deuteronomy 30 *through Christ himself*, and that has brought about significant implications for understanding how the realities of curse and blessing, death and life, disobedience and obedience, sin and righteousness are conceived in light of the good news of Christ's achievement.[139]

But I would want to go one step beyond Ciampa and assert that Paul has, essentially, "spelled it out" through his constant and careful recourse to the book of Deuteronomy in order to declare that in Christ, the restoration foretold in Deuteronomy 30 has begun, the Song of Moses is being fulfilled, and God has granted what he commands (cf. Deut 10:16; 30:6; Rom 2:24–25; 10:6–8) through the mission of Christ apprehended by faith and sealed with the gift of the Spirit.

---

138. Watson, *Paul and the Hermeneutics of Faith*, 473.

139. Ciampa, "Deuteronomy in Galatians and Romans," 117.

— 5 —

# Conclusion

As the survey in chapter one revealed, the various approaches to Paul's quotation of Deuteronomy 30:12–14 in Romans 10:6–8 are as divergent as they are diverse. In some ways, this passage serves as a Rorschach test for an interpreter's views of the law, the gospel, and the relationship between the OT and the NT. The main contention of this book has been to show that the experience of which Moses speaks in Deuteronomy 30:11–14 in reality describes the divine act of writing the law on the human heart in order to motivate obedience, an act that is part and parcel with the divine promise of heart circumcision in 30:6.

Chapter 1 surveyed the various approaches taken by interpreters trying to understand Paul's use of Deuteronomy in Romans 10:6–8 in the history of interpretation. Of the four approaches surveyed—Metaphorical/Allegorical, Jewish-Exegetical, Analogical/Typological, and Canonical-Contextual—the Canonical-Contextual approach seemed to me most promising.

Chapter 2 examined Deuteronomy 30:11–14 in the context of the book of Deuteronomy, specifically in light of the book's literary structure, narrative flow, and thematic development. In this chapter, I suggested that Deuteronomy 30:11–14 is grammatically related to 30:1–10, which would relate 30:11–14 to the divine promise of heart circumcision associated with the post-exilic restoration of God's people. I also argued that

Deuteronomy 30 hints at the necessity of a new covenant, a theme that is developed in the rest of the OT.

Chapter 3 took up instances in the OT where the text seemed to describe "God's law on the heart," which I argued is related to the experience described in Deuteronomy 30:14. In this chapter, I argued that the prophet Jeremiah and, to a lesser extent, Isaiah, pick up on the seedling promise found in Deuteronomy 30:1–14, which is, as it were, rooted in the context of a (re)new(ed) covenant in Deuteronomy 30, and they cultivate it in new contexts with new promises of a new covenant. I also argued that the Psalter likewise seems to relate the experience of the internalized *torah* to the new covenant through the identity of the blessed man in Psalms 1 and 2.

Chapter 4 examined Paul's use of Deuteronomy 30:12–14 in Romans 10:6–8 within the immediate context of his argument in chapters 9–11, and then as it relates to his interaction with the book of Deuteronomy throughout his letter to the Romans. In this chapter, I argued that what attracted Paul to Deuteronomy 30:12–14 is the new covenant context of Deuteronomy 30:1–14, which he understands to be inaugurated in the mission of Christ. Paul cites Deuteronomy 30:12–14 specifically in order to call attention to the flowering of this deuteronomic restoration, which was nurtured by the Prophets and the Writings, in the mission of Christ. This is the message of the righteousness-by-faith: Christ's life, death, and resurrection inaugurates the new covenant, and those who believe the good news of what Christ has accomplished have this word, this eschatological *torah*, in their hearts.

If this is the case, one consequence of the internalized, eschatological *torah* being so closely related to the new covenant is a contrast between the *externality* of the law under the old covenant and the *internality* of the law in the new covenant. In his treatise "On the Spirit and the Letter," Augustine makes this distinction when he argues that the law written on the heart is a feature of the new covenant:

> As then the law of works, which was written on the tables of stone, and its reward, the land of promise, which the house of the carnal Israel after their liberation from Egypt received, belonged to the old testament, so the law of faith, written on the heart, and its reward, the beatific vision which the house of the spiritual Israel, when delivered from the present world, shall perceive, belong to the new testament.[1]

1. Augustine, *De spir. et litt.*, 24.41 (*NPNF* 1/5:100).

Augustine goes on to elaborate on the difference between the old and new covenants, including the necessity of the work performed by the Holy Spirit:

> When the prophet [Jeremiah] promised a new covenant ... he simply called attention to this difference, that God would impress His laws on the mind of those who belonged to this covenant, and would write them in their hearts, whence the apostle drew his conclusion,—"not with ink, but with the Spirit of the living God; not in tables of stone, but in fleshy tables of the heart;" and that the eternal recompense of this righteousness was not the land out of which were driven the Amorites and Hittites, and other nations who dwelt there, but God Himself. ... By the law of works, then, the LORD says, "Thou shalt not covet:" but by the law of faith He says, "Without me ye can do nothing;" for He was treating of good works, even the fruit of the vine-branches. It is therefore apparent what difference there is between the old covenant and the new,—that in the former the law is written on tables, while in the latter on hearts; so that what in the one alarms from without, in the other delights from within; and in the former man becomes a transgressor through the letter that kills, in the other a lover through the life-giving spirit. We must therefore avoid saying, that the way in which God assists us to work righteousness, and "works in us both to will and to do of His good pleasure," is by externally addressing to our faculties precepts of holiness; for He gives His increase internally, by "shedding love abroad in our hearts by the Holy Ghost, which is given to us."[2]

To paraphrase Augustine, under the old covenant, people encounter the law externally as a threat; under the new covenant, people encounter the law planted internally by the Spirit as a love-enabled motivation for obedience.

One of the implications of this dichotomy begs the question, Was the internalized *torah* experienced by old covenant believers? This question is a kind of summary of the questions I proposed and then postponed in chapter 3 above with respect to the identity of those in Psalms 37, 40, and 119 who appear to have the law internalized, as well as the description of the people in whose heart is Yahweh's law in Isaiah 51. Calvin may be able to help us here.

---

2. Augustine, *De spir. et litt.*, 25.42 (*NPNF* 1/5:100–101).

Like Augustine, Calvin understands heart circumcision and the internalized law, which he summarizes succinctly with the theological concept of regeneration, to be features of the new covenant:

> The new covenant then was made when Christ appeared with water and blood, and really fulfilled what God had exhibited under types, so that the faithful might have some taste of salvation. But the coming of Christ would not have been sufficient, had not regeneration by the Holy Spirit been added. It was, then, in some respects, a new thing, that God regenerated the faithful by his Spirit, so that it became not only a doctrine as to the letter, but also efficacious, which not only strikes the ear, but penetrates into the heart, and really forms us for the service of God.[3]

Although Calvin identifies regeneration to be a new covenant feature, he nevertheless argues that old covenant believers experienced this reality:

> Was the grace of regeneration wanting to the Fathers under the Law? But this is quite preposterous. What, then, is meant when God denies here that the Law was written on the heart before the coming of Christ? To this I answer, that the Fathers, who were formerly regenerated, obtained this favor through Christ, so that we may say, that it was as it were transferred to them from another source. The power then to penetrate into the heart was not inherent in the Law, but it was a benefit transferred to the Law from the Gospel. This is one thing. Then we know that this grace of God was rare and little known under the Law; but that under the Gospel the gifts of the Spirit have been more abundantly poured forth, and that God has dealt more bountifully with his Church.[4]

In these passages, Calvin and Augustine aid the drawing of a conclusion. With Calvin, it is possible to insist that heart circumcision and law internalization, which I have suggested are inseparable concepts above (cf. Deut 30:6, 11–14), are in fact features of the new covenant, while at the same time not denying their accessibility to old covenant believers. In this way, descriptions of the internalized law encountered in the OT (e.g., Ps 37:31; 40:8; 119:11) point toward a kind of proleptic experience for OT believers of the new covenant that is finally inaugurated in Christ.

While this study has focused on Paul's quotation of Deuteronomy 30:12–14 in Romans 10:6–8, further research is needed to flesh out a

3. Calvin, *Commentaries on the Book of the Prophet Jeremiah and the Lamentations*, 4:131.

4. Calvin, *Commentaries on the Book of the Prophet Jeremiah and the Lamentations*, 4:133.

biblical-theological understanding of the internalized *torah* in the rest of the NT (cf. 2 Cor 3; Heb 8–10). It is also yet to be seen how this study might undergird or help to further define new covenant theology from a systematic standpoint.

For now, I conclude with these singular reflections from Augustine's "On the Spirit and the Letter" on the new covenant reality described by Paul as the righteousness that comes by faith:

> [B]y the law of works, God says to us, Do what I command thee; but by the law of faith we say to God, Give me what Thou commandest. Now this is the reason why the law gives its command—to admonish us what faith ought to do, that is, that he to whom the command is given, if he is as yet unable to perform it, may know what to ask for; but if he has at once the ability, and complies with the command, he ought also to be aware from whose gift the ability comes.[5]

> What then is God's law written by God Himself in the hearts of men, but the very presence of the Holy Spirit, who is "the finger of God," and by whose presence is shed abroad in our hearts the love which is the fulfilling of the law, and the end of the commandment? Now the promises of the Old Testament are earthly; and yet it contains such precepts of righteousness as we are even now taught to observe, which were especially expressly drawn out on the two tables without figure or shadow: for instance, "Thou shalt not commit adultery," "Thou shalt do no murder," "Thou shalt not covet," "and whatsoever other commandment is briefly comprehended in the saying, Thou shall love thy neighbour as thyself." Nevertheless, whereas as in the said Testament earthly and temporal promises are, as I have said, recited, and these are goods of this corruptible flesh (although they prefigure those heavenly and everlasting blessings which belong to the New Testament), what is now promised is a good for the heart itself, a good for the mind, a good of the spirit, that is, an intellectual good; since it is said, "I will put my law in their inward parts, and in their hearts will I write them," —by which He signified that men would not fear the law which alarmed them externally, but would love the very righteousness of the law which dwelt inwardly in their hearts.[6]

To God be the glory. Amen.

---

5. Augustine, *De spir. et litt.*, 13.22 (*NPNF* 1/5:92).

6. Augustine, *De spir. et litt.*, 21.36 (*NPNF* 1/5:98).

# Bibliography

Achtemeier, Paul J. *Romans*. Interpretation. Atlanta: John Knox Press, 1985.

Aejmelaeus, Anneli. "Function and Interpretation of כי in Biblical Hebrew." *Journal of Biblical Literature* 105, no. 2 (1986) 193–209.

Badenas, Robert. *Christ the End of the Law: Romans 10.4 in Pauline Perspective*. Journal for the Study of the Old Testament: Supplement Series 10. Sheffield: JSOT, 1985.

Baltzer, Klaus. *Deutero-Isaiah: A Commentary on Isaiah 40–55*. Translated by Margaret Kohl. Hermeneia. Minneapolis: Fortress, 2001.

Bandstra, Barry L. "The Syntax of Particle 'Ky' in Biblical Hebrew and Ugaritic." PhD diss., Yale University, 1982.

Barclay, John M. G. *Paul and the Gift*. Grand Rapids: Eerdmans, 2015.

Barclay, William. *The Letter to the Romans*. Philadelphia: Westminster, 1975.

Barker, Paul A. *The Triumph of Grace in Deuteronomy: Faithless Israel, Faithful Yahweh in Deuteronomy*. Milton Keynes, UK: Paternoster, 2004.

Barrett, C. K. *A Commentary on the Epistle to the Romans*. Black's New Testament Commentaries. London: A & C Black, 1957.

Barth, Karl. *Church Dogmatics*. Edited by G. W. Bromiley and T. F. Torrance. Edinburgh: T. & T. Clark, 1957.

Bates, Matthew W. *The Hermeneutics of the Apostolic Proclamation: The Center of Paul's Method of Scriptural Interpretation*. Waco, TX: Baylor University Press, 2012.

Baur, Ferdinand Christian. *Paul the Apostle of Jesus Christ: His Life and Works, His Epistles and Teachings*. Peabody, MA: Hendrickson, 2003.

Beale, G. K. *The Erosion of Inerrancy in Evangelicalism: Responding to New Challenges to Biblical Authority*. Wheaton, IL: Crossway, 2008.

———. *Handbook on the New Testament Use of the Old Testament*. Grand Rapids: Baker, 2012.

———. *A New Testament Biblical Theology: The Unfolding of the Old Testament in the New*. Grand Rapids: Baker, 2011.

Bekken, Per Jarle. *The Word Is Near You: A Study of Deuteronomy 30:12–14 in Paul's Letter to the Romans in a Jewish Context*. Beihefte zur Zeitschrift für die Neutestamentliche Wissenschaft 144. New York: de Gruyter, 2007.

Berkley, Timothy W. *From a Broken Covenant to Circumcision of the Heart: Pauline Intertextual Exegesis in Romans 2:17–29*. Atlanta: Society of Biblical Literature, 2000.

Berlin, Adele. *The Dynamics of Biblical Parallelism*. 2nd ed. The Biblical Resource Series. Grand Rapids: Eerdmans, 2008.

Beuken, Wim. "The Main Theme of Trito-Isaiah, 'the Servants of YHWH.'" *Journal for the Study of the Old Testament* 15, no. 47 (1990) 67–87.

Biddle, Mark E. *Deuteronomy*. Smyth & Helwys Bible Commentary. Macon, GA: Smyth & Helwys, 2003.

Black, Matthew. "The Christological Use of the Old Testament in the New Testament." *New Testament Studies* 18 (1971) 1–14.

Blenkinsopp, Joseph. *Isaiah 40–55: A New Translation with Introduction and Commentary*. The Anchor Bible Commentary. New York: Doubleday, 2002.

———. *Isaiah 56–66: A New Translation with Introduction and Commentary*. The Anchor Bible Commentary. New York: Doubleday, 2003.

Bozak, Barbara A. *Life Anew: A Literary-Theological Study of Jeremiah 30–31*. Rome: Editrice Pontificio Istituto Biblico, 1991.

Braulik, Georg. "Die Ausdrücke für 'Gesetz' im Buch Deuteronomium." *Biblica* 51, no. 1 (1970) 39–66.

———. "The Destruction of the Nations and the Promise of Return: Hermeneutical Observations on the Book of Deuteronomy." *Verbum et Ecclesia* 25, no. 1 (2004) 46–67.

———. *Deuteronomium II: 16,18–34,12*. Würzburg, Germany: Echter, 1992.

———. "Gesetz Als Evangelium: Rechtfertigung Und Begnadigung Nach Der Deuteronomischen Tora." *Zeitschrift Für Theologie Und Kirche* 79, no. 2 (1982) 127–60.

———. *The Theology of Deuteronomy: Collected Essays of Georg Braulik*. Translated by Ulrika Lindbald. North Richland Hills, TX: BIBAL, 1994.

Brettler, Marc Zvi. "Predestination in Deuteronomy 30.1–10." In *Those Elusive Deuteronomists: The Phenomenon of Pan-Deuteronomism*, edited by Linda S. Schearing and Steven L. McKenzie, 171–88. Journal for the Study of the Old Testament: Supplement Series 268. Sheffield, UK: Sheffield Academic Press, 1999.

Bright, John. "Book of Jeremiah: Its Structure, Its Problems, and Their Significance for the Interpreter." *Interpretation* 9, no. 3 (1955) 259–78.

———. "Exercise in Hermeneutics: Jeremiah 31:31–34." *Interpretation* 20, no. 2 (1966) 188–210.

Brown, Francis, S. R. Driver, and Charles A. Briggs, eds. *A Hebrew and English Lexicon of the Old Testament: With an Appendix Containing the Biblical Aramaic: Based on the Lexicon of William Gesenius as Translated by Edward Robinson*. Oxford: Clarendon, 1955.

Brueggemann, Walter. *A Commentary on Jeremiah: Exile and Homecoming*. Grand Rapids: Eerdmans, 1998.

———. *Deuteronomy*. Abingdon Old Testament Commentaries. Nashville: Abingdon Press, 2001.

———. *The Message of the Psalms: A Theological Commentary*. Minneapolis: Augsburg, 1984.

Brueggemann, Walter, and W. H. Jr. Bellinger. *Psalms*. New Cambridge Bible Commentary. New York: Cambridge University Press, 2014.

Buis, Pierre. "La Nouvelle Alliance." *Vetus Testamentum* 18, no. 1 (1968) 1–15.

Cairns, Ian. *Word and Presence: A Commentary on the Book of Deuteronomy*. Grand Rapids: Eerdmans, 1992.

Calvin, John. *Commentaries on the Book of the Prophet Jeremiah and the Lamentations*. Translated by John Owen. 5 vols. Grand Rapids: Baker, 1996.

———. *Commentaries on the Epistle of Paul the Apostle to the Romans*. Translated by John Owen. *Calvin's Commentaries*. Grand Rapids: Baker, 1996.

———. *Commentaries on the Four Last Books of Moses: Arranged in the Form of a Harmony*. Translated by Charles William Bingham. 4 vols. Grand Rapids: Eerdmans, 1950.

———. *Commentary on the Book of Psalms*. Translated by James Anderson. Grand Rapids: Eerdmans, 1949.

———. *Commentary on the Book of the Prophet Isaiah*. Translated by William Pringle. Grand Rapids: Eerdmans, 1948.

———. *Sermons on Deuteronomy*. Carlisle, PA: Banner of Truth Trust, 1987.

Carr, David McLain. *Writing on the Tablet of the Heart: Origins of Scripture and Literature*. New York: Oxford University Press, 2005.

Carroll, Robert P. *From Chaos to Covenant: Uses of Prophecy in the Book of Jeremiah*. London: SCM, 1981.

———. *Jeremiah: A Commentary*. The Old Testament Library. Philadelphia: Westminster, 1986.

Carson, D. A. "Evangelicals, Ecumenism, and the Church." In *Evangelical Affirmations*, edited by Kenneth S. Kantzer and Carl F. H. Henry, 359–60. Grand Rapids: Zondervan, 1990.

Carson, D. A., Peter T. O'Brien, and Mark A. Seifrid, eds. *Justification and Variegated Nomism*. 2 vols. Wissenschaftliche Untersuchungen zum Neuen Testament. Grand Rapids: Baker Academic, 2001.

Cazelles, Henri. "Jeremiah and Deuteronomy." In *A Prophet to the Nations*, edited by Leo G. Perdue and Brian W. Kovacs, 89–111. Winona Lake, IN: Eisenbrauns, 1984.

Childs, Brevard S. *Biblical Theology of the Old and New Testaments: Theological Reflection on the Christian Bible*. Minneapolis: Fortress, 1993.

———. *Introduction to the Old Testament as Scripture*. Philadelphia: Fortress, 1979.

———. *Isaiah*. Old Testament Library. Louisville, KY: Westminster John Knox, 2001.

Christensen, Duane L. *Deuteronomy 1:1—21:9*. Rev. ed. Nashville: Thomas Nelson, 2001.

Chrysostom. *Homilies on the Acts of the Apostles and the Epistle to the Romans*. Edited by Philip Schaff and Henry Wace. Vol. 11. 28 vols. *A Select Library of Nicene and Post-Nicene Fathers of the Christian Church*. Edinburgh: T. & T. Clark, 1956.

Ciampa, Roy E. "Deuteronomy in Galatians and Romans." In *Deuteronomy in the New Testament*, edited by M. J. J. Menken and Steve. Moyise, 99–117. Library of New Testament Studies 358. London: T. & T. Clark, 2007.

Clines, David J. A., ed. *The Dictionary of Classical Hebrew*. Sheffield, UK: Sheffield Academic Press, 1993.

Cole, Robert Luther. "An Integrated Reading of Psalms 1 and 2." *Journal for the Study of the Old Testament* 26, no. 4 (2002) 75–88.

———. *Psalms 1–2: Gateway to the Psalter*. Hebrew Bible Monographs 37. Sheffield, UK: Sheffield Phoenix, 2013.

Coxhead, Steven R. "Deuteronomy 30:11–14 as a Prophecy of the New Covenant in Christ." *Westminster Theological Journal* 68, no. 2 (2006) 305–20.

Craigie, Peter C. *The Book of Deuteronomy.* 2nd ed. Grand Rapids: Eerdmans, 1976.

———. *Psalms 1–50.* Word Biblical Commentary. Nashville: Word, 1983.

Cranfield, C. E. B. *A Critical and Exegetical Commentary on the Epistle to the Romans.* 2 vols. The International Critical Commentary. London: T. & T. Clark, 2004.

———. "'The Works of the Law' in the Epistle to the Romans." *Journal for the Study of the New Testament* 43 (1991) 89–101.

Currid, John D. *A Study Commentary on Deuteronomy.* Webster, NY: Evangelical, 2006.

Das, A. Andrew. *Paul, the Law, and the Covenant.* Peabody, MA: Hendrickson, 2001.

Davies, John A. "The Heart of the Old Covenant." In *Evangelism and the Reformed Faith, and Other Essays Commemorating the Ministry of J. Graham Miller,* 33–40. Sydney: Presbyterian Church of Australia, 1980.

Davies, W. D. *Paul and Rabbinic Judaism.* London: SPCK, 1955.

De Vries, Simon John. *Yesterday, Today, and Tomorrow: Time and History in the Old Testament.* London: SPCK, 1975.

Dempster, Stephen G. *Dominion and Dynasty: A Biblical Theology of the Hebrew Bible.* New Studies in Biblical Theology 15. Downers Grove, IL: InterVarsity, 2003.

Dodd, C. H. *The Epistle of Paul to the Romans.* Moffatt New Testament Commentary. London: Hodder and Stoughton, 1949.

Driver, S. R. *A Critical and Exegetical Commentary on Deuteronomy.* Edinburgh: T. & T. Clark, 1902.

———. *A Treatise on the Use of the Tenses in Hebrew and Some Other Syntactical Questions.* Eugene, OR: Wipf & Stock, 2004.

Duhm, Bernhard. *Das Buch Jeremia.* Tübingen: Mohr Siebeck, 1903.

Dunn, James D. G. "The New Perspective on Paul (1983)." In *The New Perspective on Paul,* 2nd ed., 99–120. Grand Rapids: Eerdmans, 2007.

———. "'Righteousness from the Law' and 'Righteousness from Faith': Paul's Interpretation of Scripture in Rom 10:1–10." In *Tradition and Interpretation in the New Testament: Essays in Honor of E. Earle Ellis for His 60th Birthday,* edited by Gerald Hawthorne and Otto Betz, 216–28. Grand Rapids: Eerdmans, 1987.

———. *Romans 9–16.* Word Biblical Commentary. Dallas, TX: Word, 1988.

Eckstein, Hans-Joachim. "'Nahe Ist Dir das Wort': Exegetische Erwägungen zu Röm 10:8." *Zeitschrift für die Neutestamentliche Wissenschaft* 79 (1988) 204–20.

Edwards, Jonathan. "Justification by Faith Alone." In *The Works of Jonathan Edwards,* edited by Edward Hickman, vol. 1, 622–54. Carlisle, PA: Banner of Truth Trust, 2005.

Eichrodt, Walther. *Theology of the Old Testament.* Translated by J. A. Baker. 2 vols. Old Testament Library. Philadelphia: Westminster, 1961.

Elman, Yaakov. "Moses Ben Nahman / Nahmanides (Ramban)." In *Hebrew Bible/Old Testament: From the Beginnings to the Middle Ages (Until 1300),* 416–33. Göttingen: Vandenhoeck & Ruprecht, 2000.

Feldmeier, Reinhard, and Hermann Spieckermann. *God of the Living: A Biblical Theology.* Waco, TX: Baylor University Press, 2011.

Fitzmyer, Joseph A. *Romans: A New Translation with Introduction and Commentary.* The Anchor Bible Commentary. New York: Doubleday, 1993.

———. "The Use of Explicit Old Testament Quotations in Qumran Literature and in the New Testament." *New Testament Studies* 7 (1961) 297–333.

Fohrer, Georg. *Das Alte Testament: Einführung in die Bibelkunde und Literatur des Alten Testaments und in Geschichte und Religion Israels.* Gütersloh, Germany: Gütersloher Publishing House, 1977.

Follingstad, Carl M. "Deictic Viewpoint in Biblical Hebrew Text: A Syntagmatic and Paradigmatic Analysis of the Particle כי." PhD diss., SIL International, 2001.

Fretheim, Terence E. *Jeremiah.* Smyth & Helwys Bible Commentary. Macon, GA: Smyth & Helwys, 2002.

Gathercole, Simon J. "A Conversion of Augustine: From Natural Law to Restored Nature in Romans 2:13–16." In *Engaging Augustine on Romans: Self, Context, and Theology in Interpretation,* edited by Daniel Patte and Eugene TeSelle, 147–72. Harrisburg, PA: Trinity, 2003.

———. "A Law unto Themselves: The Gentiles in Romans 2.14–15 Revisited." *Journal for the Study of the New Testament* 24, no. 85 (2002) 27–49.

Gaugler, Ernst. *Der Epheserbrief.* Zurich: EVZ, 1966.

Gentry, Peter J. "The Literary Macrostructures of the Book of Isaiah and Authorial Intent." In *Bind up the Testimony: Explorations in the Genesis of the Book of Isaiah,* edited by Daniel I. Block and Richard L. Schultz, 227–53. Peabody, MA: Hendrickson, 2015.

———. "The Relationship of Deuteronomy to the Covenant at Sinai." *The Southern Baptist Journal of Theology* 18, no. 3 (2014) 35–57.

———. "The Septuagint and the Text of the Old Testament." *Bulletin for Biblical Research* 16, no. 2 (2006) 193–218.

———. "The Text of the Old Testament." *Journal of the Evangelical Theological Society* 52, no. 1 (2009) 19–45.

Gentry, Peter J., and Stephen J. Wellum. *Kingdom through Covenant: A Biblical-Theological Understanding of the Covenants.* Wheaton, IL: Crossway, 2012.

Georgi, Diete. *The Opponents of Paul in Second Corinthians: A Study of Religious Propaganda in Late Antiquity.* Philadelphia: Fortress, 1986.

Gill, John. *Exposition of the Old and New Testaments.* 9 vols. Paris, AR: The Baptist Standard Bearer, 1989.

Godet, Frederic Louis. *Commentary on Romans.* Grand Rapids: Kregel, 1977.

Grant, Robert M. *The Letter and the Spirit.* London: SPCK, 1957.

Gray, George Buchanan. *The Forms of Hebrew Poetry: Considered with Special Reference to the Criticism and Interpretation of the Old Testament.* The Library of Biblical Studies. New York: Hodder and Stoughton, 1972.

Gross, Walter, Hubert Irsigler, and Theodor Seidl, eds. *Text, Methode und Grammatik: Wolfgang Richter zum 65. Geburtstag.* St. Ottilien, Germany: EOS, 1991.

Guest, Steven Ward. "Deuteronomy 26:16–19 as the Central Focus of the Covenantal Framework of Deuteronomy." PhD diss., The Southern Baptist Theological Seminary, 2009.

Gunkel, Hermann. *Einleitung in die Psalmen die Gattungen der religiösen Lyrik Israels.* Handkommentar zum Alten Testament. Göttingen: Vandenhoeck and Ruprecht, 1933.

Hamilton, James M. *God's Glory in Salvation through Judgment: A Biblical Theology.* Wheaton, IL: Crossway, 2010.

———. *God's Indwelling Presence: The Holy Spirit in the Old & New Testaments.* NAC Studies in Bible & Theology. Nashville: B. & H. Academic, 2006.

———. "N.T. Wright and Saul's Moral Bootstraps: Newer Light on 'the New Perspective.'" *Trinity Journal* 25, no. 2 (2004) 139–55.

———. "The One Who Does Them Shall Live by Them: Leviticus 18:5 in Galatians 3:12." *The Gospel Witness*, August 2005, 10–12.

———. "The Seed of the Woman and the Blessing of Abraham." *Tyndale Bulletin* 58, no. 2 (2007) 253–73.

———. "The Skull Crushing Seed of the Woman: Inner-Biblical Interpretation of Genesis 3:15." *The Southern Baptist Journal of Theology* 10, no. 2 (2006) 30–54.

———. "Still *Sola Scriptura*: An Evangelical Perspective on Scripture." In *The Sacred Text: Excavating the Texts, Exploring the Interpretations, and Engaging the Theologies of the Christian Scriptures*, edited by Michael F. Bird and Michael Pahl, 215–40. Gorgias Précis Portfolios 7. Piscataway, NJ: Gorgias, 2010.

———. *With the Clouds of Heaven: The Book of Daniel in Biblical Theology*. New Studies in Biblical Theology 32. Downers Grove, IL: InterVarsity, 2014.

Hanson, Anthony Tyrrell. *Studies in Paul's Technique and Theology*. London: SPCK, 1974.

Hays, Richard B. *The Conversion of the Imagination: Paul as Interpreter of Israel's Scripture*. Grand Rapids: Eerdmans, 2005.

———. *Echoes of Scripture in the Letters of Paul*. New Haven: Yale University Press, 1989.

Holladay, William L. *Jeremiah 1: A Commentary on the Book of the Prophet Jeremiah, Chapters 1–25*. Hermeneia. Philadelphia: Fortress, 1986.

———. *The Root שׁוּב in the Old Testament with Particular Reference to Its Usages in Covenantal Contexts*. Leiden: Brill, 1958.

Hollander, John. *The Figure of Echo: A Mode of Allusion in Milton and After*. Berkeley: University of California Press, 1981.

Hossfeld, Frank-Lothar, Erich Zenger, Linda M. Maloney, and Klaus Baltzer. *Psalms 3: A Commentary on Psalms 101–150*. Hermeneia. Minneapolis: Fortress, 2011.

Huddleston, Neal A. "Deuteronomy as Mischgattung: A Comparative and Contrastive Discourse Analysis of Deuteronomy and Ancient Near Eastern Treaty Traditions." PhD diss., Trinity International University, 2015.

Jewett, Robert, and Roy D. Kotansky. *Romans: A Commentary*. Edited by Eldon Jay Epp. Hermeneia. Minneapolis: Fortress, 2007.

Jobes, Karen H. "Rhetorical Achievement in the Hebrews 10 'Misquote' of Psalm 40." *Biblica* 72, no. 3 (1991) 387–96.

———. "The Function of Paronomasia in Hebrews 10:5–7." *Trinity Journal* 13, no. 2 (1992) 181–91.

Johnson, E. Elizabeth. "The Faithfulness and Impartiality of God." In *Pauline Theology*, Vol. 3, edited by David M. Hay and E. Elizabeth Johnson, 211–39. Minneapolis: Fortress, 1995.

Kaiser, Jr., Walter C. "Leviticus 18:5 and Paul: Do This and You Shall Live (Eternally?)." *Journal of the Evangelical Theological Society* 14, no. 1 (1971) 19–28.

Käsemann, Ernst. *Commentary on Romans*. Translated by G. W. Bromiley. Grand Rapids: Eerdmans, 1980.

———. *Perspectives on Paul*. London: SCM, 1971.

Keil, Carl Friedrich, and Franz Delitzsch. *Biblical Commentary on the Old Testament*. Grand Rapids: Eerdmans, 1900.

Keown, Gerald L., Pamela J. Scalise, and Thomas G. Smothers. *Jeremiah 26–52*. Word Biblical Commentary. Waco, TX: Word, 1995.

Kirk, K. E. "The Epistle to the Romans." In *The Clarendon Bible*, edited by T. H. Robinson. Oxford: Clarendon, 1955.

Klein, Ernest. *A Comprehensive Etymological Dictionary of the Hebrew Language for Readers of English.* New York: Macmillan, 1987.

Kline, Meredith G. *Treaty of the Great King: The Covenant Structure of Deuteronomy.* Grand Rapids: Eerdmans, 1963.

Klink, Edward W., and Darian R. Lockett. *Understanding Biblical Theology: A Comparison of Theory and Practice.* Grand Rapids: Zondervan, 2012.

Knox, John. "The Epistle to the Romans: Introduction and Exegesis." In *The Interpreter's Bible,* Vol. 9, edited by G. A. Buttrick, 353–668. Nashville: Abingdon, 1951.

Köhler, Ludwig, Walter Baumgartner, M. E. J Richardson, Johann Jakob Stamm, Benedikt Hartmann, G. J Jongeling-Vos, and L J. de Regt. *The Hebrew and Aramaic Lexicon of the Old Testament.* New York: Brill, 1994.

Kraus, Hans-Joachim. *Theology of the Psalms.* Minneapolis: Fortress, 1992.

Labuschagne, C. J. *Deuteronomium.* Vol. 3. Nijkerk, Netherlands: Callenbach, 1997.

Lagrange, Marie-Joseph. *Saint Paul: Épitre aux Romains.* Paris: Librairie Victor Lecoffre, 1922.

Lang, Friedrich Gustav. "Erwägungen zu Gesetz und Verheissung in Römer 10,4–13." In *Jesus Christus als die Mitte der Schrift: Studien zur Hermeneutik des Evangeliums,* edited by Hans-Joachim Eckstein and Hermann Lichtenberger, 579–602. Berlin: de Gruyter, 1997.

Lenchak, Timothy A. *Choose Life! A Rhetorical-Critical Investigation of Deuteronomy 28,69–30,20.* Rome: Editrice Pontificio Istituto Biblico, 1993.

Lessing, R. Reed. *Isaiah 40–55.* Concordia Commentary. Saint Louis: Concordia, 2011.

Lincicum, David. *Paul and the Early Jewish Encounter with Deuteronomy.* Tübingen: Mohr Siebeck, 2010.

Link, Peter Jackson. "A Composition Criticism of Deut 28:69—30:20: An Analysis of the Pericope's Intentional Repetition as a Part of the Pentateuch with the Pentateuch, the Prophets and the Writings." PhD diss., Southeastern Baptist Theological Seminary, 2012.

Lohfink, Norbert. "Der Bundesschluss im Land Moab: Redaktionsgeschichtliches zu Dt 28:69—32:47." *Biblische Zeitschrift* 6, no. 1 (1962) 32–56.

———. "Dtn 28,69—Überschrift Oder Kolophon?" *Biblische Notizen* 64 (1992) 40–52.

———. "Der Neue Bund im Buch Deuteronomium?" *Zeitschrift für Altorientalische und Biblische Rechtsgeschichte* 4 (1998) 100–125.

———. *Das Hauptgebot: Eine Untersuchung Literarischer Einleitungsfragen zu Dtn 5–11.* Rome: Editrice Pontificio Instituto Biblico, 1963.

———. *Höre, Israel! Auslegung von Texten aus dem Busch Deuteronomium.* Die Welt der Bibel: Kleinkommentare zur Heiligen Schrift 18. Düsseldorf, Germany: Patmos, 1965.

Lohfink, Norbert, and Erich Zenger. *The God of Israel and the Nations: Studies in Isaiah and the Psalms.* Collegeville, MN: Liturgical, 2000.

Longacre, Robert E. *The Grammar of Discourse.* 2nd ed. Topics in Language and Linguistics. New York: Plenum, 1996.

Longenecker, Richard N. *Biblical Exegesis in the Apostolic Period.* Grand Rapids: Eerdmans, 1974.

———. *The Epistle to the Romans: A Commentary on the Greek Text.* New International Greek Testament Commentary. Grand Rapids: Eerdmans, 2016.

Ludwig, Theodore M. "Shape of Hope: Jeremiah's Book of Consolation." *Concordia Theological Monthly* 39, no. 8 (1968) 526–41.

Lundbom, Jack R. *Deuteronomy: A Commentary.* Grand Rapids: Eerdmans, 2013.

———. *Jeremiah: A New Translation with Introduction and Commentary*. The Anchor Bible Commentary. New York: Doubleday, 1999.

Lunde, Jonathan. "An Introduction to Central Questions in the New Testament Use of the Old Testament." In *Three Views on the New Testament Use of the Old Testament*, edited by Jonathan Lunde and Kenneth Berding, 7–44. Grand Rapids: Zondervan, 2008.

Luther, Martin. *Lectures on Deuteronomy*. Vol. 9. *Luther's Works*. Translated by Jaroslav Pelikan. St. Louis: Concordia, 1968.

———. *Lectures on Romans*. Translated by Wilhelm Pauck. Philadelphia: Westminster, 1961.

Mastnjak, Nathan. *Deuteronomy and the Emergence of Textual Authority in Jeremiah*. Forschungen zum Alten Testament 2, 87. Tübingen: Mohr Siebeck, 2016.

Mayes, A. D. H. *Deuteronomy*. Greenwood, SC: Attic, 1979.

Mays, James Luther. "The Place of the Torah-Psalms in the Psalter." *Journal of Biblical Literature* 106, no. 1 (1987) 3–12.

———. *Psalms*. Interpretation. Louisville, KY: John Knox, 1994.

McCann, J. Clinton. *The Shape and Shaping of the Psalter*. The Library of Hebrew Bible/ Old Testament Studies 159. Sheffield: JSOT, 1993.

McConville, J. G. *Deuteronomy*. Downers Grove, IL: InterVarsity, 2002.

———. *Grace in the End: A Study in Deuteronomic Theology*. Grand Rapids: Zondervan, 1993.

———. *Judgment and Promise: An Interpretation of the Book of Jeremiah*. Winona Lake, IN: Eisenbrauns, 1993.

McKane, William. *A Critical and Exegetical Commentary on Jeremiah*. 2 vols. International Critical Commentary. Edinburgh: T. & T. Clark, 1986.

McNamara, Martin. *Targum Neofiti 1: Deuteronomy*. Collegeville, MN: Liturgical, 1997.

Mead, James K. *Biblical Theology: Issues, Methods, and Themes*. Louisville, KY: Westminster John Knox, 2007.

Meade, John D. "Circumcision of Flesh to Circumcision of Heart: The Typology of the Sign of the Abrahamic Covenant." In *Progressive Covenantalism: Charting a Course between Dispensational and Covenantal Theologies*, edited by Stephen J. Wellum and Brent E. Parker, 127–58. Nashville: B. & H. Academic, 2016.

———. "Circumcision of the Heart in Leviticus and Deuteronomy: Divine Means for Resolving Curse and Bringing Blessing." *The Southern Baptist Journal of Theology* 18, no. 3 (2014) 59–85.

Mendenhall, George E. "Covenant Forms in Israelite Tradition." *The Biblical Archaeologist* 17, no. 3 (1954) 50–76.

Menken, M. J. J., and Steve. Moyise, eds. *Deuteronomy in the New Testament*. Library of New Testament Studies 358. London: T. & T. Clark, 2007.

Merrill, Eugene H. *Deuteronomy*. New American Commentary. Nashville: B. & H., 1994.

Metzger, Bruce M. *A Textual Commentary on the Greek New Testament*. 2nd ed. Stuttgart: United Bible Societies, 2002.

Meyer, Jason C. *The End of the Law: Mosaic Covenant in Pauline Theology*. New American Commentary Studies in Bible & Theology. Nashville: B. & H., 2009.

Meyers, Carol L., and Eric M. Meyers. *Haggai, Zechariah 1–8: A New Translation with Introduction and Commentary*. The Anchor Bible Commentary. New York: Doubleday, 1987.

Millar, J. G. *Now Choose Life: Theology and Ethics in Deuteronomy.* New Studies in Biblical Theology. Leicester, UK: Apollos, 1998.

Miller, Cynthia L. "Pivotal Issues in Analyzing the Verbless Clause." In *The Verbless Clause in Biblical Hebrew: Linguistic Approaches,* edited by Cynthia L. Miller, 3–18. Linguistic Studies in Ancient West Semitic. Winona Lake, IN: Eisenbrauns, 1999.

Moo, Douglas J. *The Epistle to the Romans.* The New International Commentary on the New Testament. Grand Rapids: Eerdmans, 1996.

———. "Paul's Universalizing Hermeneutic in Romans." *The Southern Baptist Journal of Theology* 11, no. 3 (2007) 62–90.

Moo, Douglas J., and Andrew D. Naselli. "The Problem of the New Testament's Use of the Old Testament." In *The Enduring Authority of the Christian Scriptures,* edited by D. A. Carson, 702–46. Grand Rapids: Eerdmans, 2016.

Morales, L. Michael. *Who Shall Ascend the Mountain of the Lord?: A Biblical Theology of the Book of Leviticus.* New Studies in Biblical Theology 37. Downers Grove, IL: InterVarsity, 2015.

Motyer, J. A. *The Prophecy of Isaiah: An Introduction & Commentary.* Downers Grove, IL: InterVarsity, 1993.

Mowinckel, Sigmund. *Psalm Studies.* Translated by Mark E. Biddle. 2 vols. Society of Biblical Literature: History of Biblical Studies. Atlanta: Society of Biblical Literature, 2014.

———. *Zur Komposition des Buches Jeremia.* Kristiania, Norway: J. Dybwad, 1914.

Muilenburg, James. "The Book of Isaiah: Chapters 40–66 (Exegesis)." In *The Interpreter's Bible,* Vol. 5, edited by G. A. Buttrick, 422–776. Nashville: Abingdon, 1951.

———. "The Linguistic and Rhetorical Usages of the Particle Ky in the Old Testament." *Hebrew Union College Annual* 32 (1961) 135–60.

Muraoka, T. *Emphatic Words and Structures in Biblical Hebrew.* Jerusalem: Magnes, 1985.

Murray, John. *The Epistle to the Romans: The English Text with Introduction, Exposition, and Notes.* Vol. 2. Grand Rapids: Eerdmans, 1959.

Myers, Jacob M. "Requisites for Response: On the Theology of Deuteronomy." *Interpretation* 15, no. 1 (1961) 14–31.

Nachmanides. *Commentary on the Torah.* Translated by Charles Ber Chavel. New York: Shilo, 1971.

Nelson, Richard D. *Deuteronomy: A Commentary.* Louisville, KY: Westminster John Knox, 2002.

Newman, Barclay M., and Philip C. Stine. *A Handbook on Jeremiah.* UBS Handbook Series. New York: United Bible Societies, 2003.

Nicholson, Ernest W. *Deuteronomy and Tradition.* Philadelphia: Fortress, 1967.

North, Christopher R. *The Second Isaiah.* Oxford: Clarendon, 1964.

———. *The Suffering Servant in Deutero-Isaiah: An Historical and Critical Study.* 2nd edition. London: Oxford University Press, 1956.

Nygren, Anders. *Commentary on Romans.* Philadelphia: Muhlenberg, 1949.

Olshausen, Hermann. *Biblical Commentary on the New Testament.* Translated by A. C. Kendrick. New York: Sheldon, Blakeman, & Co., 1857.

Orlinsky, Harry M., and Robert G. Bratcher. *A History of Bible Translation and the North American Contribution.* Atlanta: Society of Biblical Literature, 1991.

Oswalt, John N. *The Book of Isaiah: Chapters 40–66.* The New International Commentary on the Old Testament. Grand Rapids: Eerdmans, 1998.

Otto, Eckart. *Deuteronomium*. 4 vols. Herders Theologischer Kommentar zum Alten Testament. Freiburg, Germany: Herder, 2012.

Plumer, William S. *Studies in the Book of Psalms: Being a Critical and Expository Commentary, with Doctrinal and Practical Remarks on the Entire Psalter*. Philadelphia: J. B. Lippincott, 1866.

Poole, Matthew. *Annotations upon the Holy Bible*. Vol. 1. New York: Robert Carter and Brothers, 1853.

Potter, H. D. "The New Covenant in Jeremiah xxxi 31–34." *Vetus Testamentum* 33 (1983) 347–57.

Poulsen, Frederik. *God, His Servant, and the Nations in Isaiah 42:1–9: Biblical Theological Reflections after Brevard S. Childs and Hans Hübner*. Tübingen: Mohr Siebeck, 2014.

Rad, Gerhard von. *Deuteronomy*. Philadelphia: Westminster, 1966.

———. *Old Testament Theology*. New York: Harper, 1962.

Rashi. *Pentateuch with Targum Onkelos, Haphtaroth and Prayers for Sabbath and Rashi's Commentary*. Translated by M. Rosenbaum and Abraham Maurice Silbermann. London: Shapiro, Valentine & Co., 1946.

Reasoner, Mark. "The Theology of Romans 12.1—15.13." In *Pauline Theology III: Romans*, edited by D. M. Hay and E. E. Johnson. 287–99. Minneapolis: Fortress, 1997.

Rendsburg, Gary A. "A New Look at Pentateuchal HW." *Biblica* 63, no. 3 (1982) 351–69.

Rendtorff, Rolf. *The Covenant Formula: An Exegetical and Theological Investigation*. Edinburgh: T. & T. Clark, 1998.

Revell, E. J. "Thematic Continuity and the Conditioning of Word Order in Verbless Clauses." In *The Verbless Clause in Biblical Hebrew: Linguistic Approaches*, edited by Cynthia L. Miller, 297–320. Linguistic Studies in Ancient West Semitic. Winona Lake, IN: Eisenbrauns, 1999.

Rhyne, C. Thomas. "*Nomos Dikaiosynēs* and the Meaning of Romans 10:4." *The Catholic Biblical Quarterly* 47 (1985) 486–99.

Ridderbos, J. *Deuteronomy*. Grand Rapids: Regency Reference Library, 1984.

Rivkin, Ellis. *A Hidden Revolution*. Nashville: Abingdon, 1978.

Robertson, A. T. *Word Pictures in the New Testament*. Vol. 4. Nashville: Broadman, 1930.

Rofé, Alexander. "The Covenant in the Land of Moab." In *A Song of Power and the Power of Song: Essays on the Book of Deuteronomy*, edited by Duane L. Christensen, 269–80. Winona Lake, IN: Eisenbrauns, 1993.

Rudolph, Wilhelm. *Jeremia*. Edited by Otto Eissfeldt. Handbuch Zum Alten Testament 12. Tübingen: Mohr, 1947.

Runge, Steven E. *Discourse Grammar of the Greek New Testament: A Practical Introduction for Teaching and Exegesis*. Lexham Bible Reference Series. Peabody, MA: Hendrickson, 2010.

Sæbø, Magne, ed. *Hebrew Bible/Old Testament: The History of Its Interpretation: From the Renaissance to the Enlightenment*. Vol. 2. Göttingen: Vandenhoeck & Ruprecht, 2008.

Sailhamer, John. *The Meaning of the Pentateuch: Revelation, Composition, and Interpretation*. Downers Grove, IL: InterVarsity, 2009.

———. *The Pentateuch as Narrative: A Biblical-Theological Commentary*. Grand Rapids: Zondervan, 1992.

Sanday, W., and Arthur C. Headlam. *A Critical and Exegetical Commentary on the Epistle to the Romans*. 5th ed. International Critical Commentary. Edinburgh: T. & T. Clark, 1902.

Sanders, E. P. *Paul and Palestinian Judaism: A Comparison of Patterns of Religion*. Philadelphia: Fortress, 1977.

Schenker, Adrian. *Das Neue am Neuen Bund und das Alte am Alten: Jer 31 in der Hebräischen und Griechischen Bibel, von der Textgeschichte zu Theologie, Synagoge und Kirche*. Göttingen: Vandenhoeck & Ruprecht, 2006.

Schmidt, Hans Wilhelm. *Der Brief des Paulus an die Römer*. Berlin: Evangelische Verlagsanstalt, 1962.

Schoors, Anton. "The Particle Ki." In *Remembering All the Way: A Collection of Old Testament Studies*, edited by Bertil Albrektson, 240–76. Leiden: Brill, 1981.

Schreiner, Thomas R. "Israel's Failure to Attain Righteousness in Romans 9:30—10:3." *Trinity Journal* 12, no. 2 (1991) 209–20.

———. *The King in His Beauty: A Biblical Theology of the Old and New Testaments*. Grand Rapids: Baker, 2013.

———. "Paul's View of the Law in Romans 10:4–5." *Westminster Theological Journal* 55 (1993) 113–35.

———. *Romans*. Baker Exegetical Commentary on the New Testament. Grand Rapids: Baker, 1998.

Schultz, Richard L. "The Origins and Basic Arguments of the Multi-Author View of the Composition of Isaiah: Where Are We Now and How Did We Get Here?" In *Bind up the Testimony: Explorations in the Genesis of the Book of Isaiah*, edited by Daniel I. Block and Richard L. Schultz, 7–31. Peabody, MA: Hendrickson, 2015.

Seebass, Horst. "Erstes oder Altes Testament?" In *Die Einheit der Schrift und die Vielfalt des Kanons*, edited by John Barton and Michael Wolter, 27–44. Berlin: de Gruyter, 2003.

Seifrid, Mark A. *Christ, Our Righteousness: Paul's Theology of Justification*. New Studies in Biblical Theology 9. Downers Grove, IL: InterVarsity, 2000.

———. "Paul's Approach to the Old Testament in Romans 10:6–8." *Trinity Journal* 6, no. Spring (1985) 3–37.

———. "Romans." In *Commentary on the New Testament Use of the Old Testament*, edited by G. K. Beale and D. A. Carson, 607–94. Grand Rapids: Baker Academic, 2007.

Selderhuis, H. J. *Psalms 1–72*. Reformation Commentary on Scripture. Downers Grove, IL: InterVarsity, 2015.

Shead, Andrew G. *A Mouth Full of Fire: The Word of God in the Words of Jeremiah*. New Studies in Biblical Theology 29. Downers Grove, IL: Apollos, 2012.

Sprinkle, Preston M. *Law and Life: The Interpretation of Leviticus 18:5 in Early Judaism and in Paul*. Wissenschaftliche Untersuchungen zum Neuen Testament. Tübingen: Mohr Siebeck, 2007.

———. *Paul & Judaism Revisited: A Study of Divine and Human Agency in Salvation*. Downers Grove, IL: InterVarsity, 2013.

Stanley, Christopher D. *Paul and the Language of Scripture: Citation Technique in the Pauline Epistles and Contemporary Literature*. Society for New Testament Studies Monograph Series 74. Cambridge: Cambridge University Press, 1992.

Starling, David I. *Hermeneutics as Apprenticeship: How the Bible Shapes Our Interpretive Habits and Practices*. Grand Rapids: Baker, 2016.

Stendahl, Krister. *Paul among Jews and Gentiles, and Other Essays*. Philadelphia: Fortress, 1976.

Strickland, Wayne G. "The Inauguration of the Law of Christ with the Gospel of Christ: A Dispensational View." In *The Law, the Gospel, and the Modern Christian: Five Views*, edited by Wayne G. Strickland, 229–79. Grand Rapids: Zondervan, 1993.

Suggs, M. Jack. "'The Word Is Near You': Romans 10:6–10 within the Purpose of the Letter." In *Christian History and Interpretation: Studies Presented to John Knox*, edited by W. R. Farmer, C. F. D. Moule, and R. R. Niebuhr, 289–312. Cambridge: Cambridge University Press, 1967.

Thielman, Frank. *Paul & the Law: A Contextual Approach*. Downers Grove, IL: InterVarsity, 1994.

Thompson, J. A. *Deuteronomy: An Introduction and Commentary*. The Tyndale Old Testament Commentaries. London: InterVarsity, 1974.

———. *The Book of Jeremiah*. The New International Commentary on the Old Testament. Grand Rapids: Eerdmans, 1980.

Tigay, Jeffrey H. *Deuteronomy* = דברים: *The Traditional Hebrew Text with the New JPS Translation*. Philadelphia: Jewish Publication Society, 1996.

Tov, Emanuel, and F. H. Polak. *The Parallel Aligned Text of the Greek and Hebrew Bible*. CATSS database. Dir. by R.A. Kraft and E. Tov, 2005. BibleWorks. v. 9.

Turner, Kenneth J. *The Death of Deaths in the Death of Israel: Deuteronomy's Theology of Exile*. Eugene, OR: Wipf & Stock, 2011.

Unterman, Jeremiah. *From Repentance to Redemption: Jeremiah's Thought in Transition*. Journal for the Study of the Old Testament: Supplement Series 54. Sheffield, UK: Sheffield Academic Press, 1987.

Vanhoozer, Kevin. "Christ and Concept: Doing Theology and the 'Ministry' of Philosophy." In *Doing Theology in Today's World: Essays in Honor of Kenneth S. Kantzer*, 99–145. Grand Rapids: Zondervan, 1991.

Vanoni, Gottfried. "Der Geist und der Buchstabe: Überlegungen zum Verhältnis der Testamente und Beobachtungen zu Dtn 30, 1–10." *Biblische Notizen* 14 (1981) 65–98.

Via, Dan Otto. *Kerygma and Comedy in the New Testament: A Structuralist Approach to Hermeneutics*. Philadelphia: Fortress, 1975.

Vollmer, Hans Arthur. *Die Alttestamentlichen Citate bei Paulus: Textkritisch und Biblisch-Theologisch Gewürdigt Nebst Einem Anhan. Über das Verhältnis des Apostels zu Philo*. Freiburg, Germany: Mohr Siebeck, 1895.

Vos, Geerhardus. *Biblical Theology: Old and New Testaments*. Grand Rapids: Eerdmans, 1948.

Wagner, J. Ross. *Heralds of the Good News: Isaiah and Paul "in Concert" in the Letter to the Romans*. Supplements to Novum Testamentum. Leiden: Brill, 2002.

Waters, Guy P. *The End of Deuteronomy in the Epistles of Paul*. Wissenschaftliche Untersuchungen zum Neuen Testament. Tübingen: Mohr Siebeck, 2006.

Watson, Francis. *Paul and the Hermeneutics of Faith*. London: T. & T. Clark, 2004.

Weinfeld, Moshe. "Jeremiah and the Spiritual Metamorphosis of Israel." *Zeitschrift für die Alttestamentliche Wissenschaft* 88 (1976) 17–56.

Wellhausen, Julius. *Israelitische und Jüdische Geschichte*. Berlin: Georg Reimer, 1904.

Wells, Kyle B. *Grace and Agency in Paul and Second Temple Judaism: Interpreting the Transformation of the Heart*. Supplements to Novum Testamentum 157. Boston: Brill, 2015.

Westerholm, Stephen. *Perspectives Old and New on Paul: The "Lutheran" Paul and His Critics*. Grand Rapids: Eerdmans, 2004.

Wevers, John William. *Notes on the Greek Text of Deuteronomy*. Atlanta: Scholars, 1995.

Whittle, Sarah. *Covenant Renewal and the Consecration of the Gentiles in Romans.* Society for New Testament Studies Monograph Series 161. New York: Cambridge University Press, 2015.

Whybray, R. N. *Reading the Psalms as a Book.* Journal for the Study of the Old Testament: Supplement Series 222. Sheffield, UK: Sheffield Academic Press, 1996.

Wilson, Gerald Henry. *The Editing of the Hebrew Psalter.* Society of Biblical Literature Dissertation Series 76. Chico, CA: Scholars, 1985.

Wolde, Ellen von. "The Verbless Clause and Its Textual Function." In *The Verbless Clause in Biblical Hebrew: Linguistic Approaches,* edited by Cynthia L. Miller, 321–36. Linguistic Studies in Ancient West Semitic. Winona Lake, IN: Eisenbrauns, 1999.

Wolff, Hans Walter. *Anthropology of the Old Testament.* Philadelphia: Fortress, 1974.

Work, Telford. *Deuteronomy.* Brazos Theological Commentary on the Bible. Grand Rapids: Brazos, 2009.

Wright, Christopher J. H. *Deuteronomy.* New International Biblical Commentary. Peabody, MA: Hendrickson, 1996.

Wright, N. T. *The Climax of the Covenant: Christ and the Law in Pauline Theology.* Edinburgh: T. & T. Clark, 1991.

———. "The Letter to the Romans." In *The New Interpreter's Bible,* Vol. 10, edited by Leander E. Keck, 393–770. Nashville: Abingdon, 1994.

———. *Paul and the Faithfulness of God.* London: SPCK, 2013.

# Ancient Document Index

## OLD TESTAMENT

### Genesis

| | |
|---|---|
| 3:15 | 59, 141 |
| 9:9 | 59 |
| 12:7 | 59 |
| 13:15 | 59 |
| 13:16 | 59 |
| 14:2 | 71n114 |
| 15:5 | 59 |
| 15:13 | 59 |
| 15:18 | 59 |
| 17:7 | 59 |
| 17:8 | 59 |
| 17:9 | 59 |
| 17:10 | 59 |
| 17:12 | 59 |
| 17:19 | 59 |
| 18:24 | 128 |
| 19:37 | 39 |
| 20:5 | 71n114 |
| 26:33 | 39 |
| 32:33[32] | 39 |
| 38:25 | 71n114 |

| | |
|---|---|
| 45:6 | 128 |
| 47:26 | 39 |
| 48:15 | 39 |

### Exodus

| | |
|---|---|
| | 207n130 |
| 10:6 | 39, 39n25 |
| 13:9 | 22 |
| 17:8–13 | 104n28 |
| 18:20 LXX | 187n82 |
| 19:1–25 | 42 |
| 20:6 | 40 |
| 20:17 | 207 |
| 24:12 | 111 |
| 31:18 | 111 |

### Leviticus

| | |
|---|---|
| | 186n81 |
| LXX | 188n85 |
| 11:39 | 71n114 |
| 13:10 | 71n114 |
| 13:21 | 71n114 |
| 16:31 | 71n114 |
| 18 | 196n103 |

**Leviticus** (*cont.*)

| | |
|---|---|
| 18:5 | 3, 3n13, 14, 20n87, 156, 161, 162, 171n48, 176n57, 184n80, 185n80, 185n81, 186n81, 187, 187n82, 188, 188n85, 189, 189n88, 190, 190n90, 191, 192, 207 |
| 18:5 LXX | 188n85 |
| 18:5 MT | 188n85 |
| 19:18 | 208 |
| 20:17 | 71n114 |
| 21:9 | 71n114 |
| 26:41 | 46n42, 109 |

**Numbers**

| | |
|---|---|
| 5:13 | 71n114 |
| 5:14 | 71n114 |
| 22:30 | 39 |
| 22:38 | 101 |
| 24:17 | 101n20, 122n62 |

**Deuteronomy**

| | |
|---|---|
| | 3, 4, 5, 7, 9, 13, 18, 18n76, 20n82, 25, 28, 30, 31, 32, 32n8, 37, 37n18, 39, 40, 41, 43n35, 45, 50n48, 59n71, 62n83, 84, 86, 86n151, 87, 89, 91, 105, 105n30, 105n31, 106, 108, 109, 111, 112, 112n45, 113, 114, 116, 116n54, 123, 124n68, 125n70, 127, 130, 131, 131n81, 152, 152n1, 153, 154, 156, 157, 161n21, 163, 168, 171, 171n49, 172n51, 177, 180, 186n81, 196n104, 199, 200, 202, 207n130, 209, 211, 212 |
| 1:1–2 | 29 |
| 1:1–3:29 | 33, 35 |
| 1:1–4:4 | 33 |
| 1:1–4:44 | 32, 34, 37, 40, 48 |
| 1:1–5 | 31 |
| 1:1ff | 33 |
| 1:3 | 29 |
| 1–3 | 35n12, 86n151 |
| 1:4 | 32, 47 |
| 1:4–3:18 | 29 |
| 1:6–3:20 | 31n5 |
| 1:6–4:44 | 31 |
| 1:8 | 59n71 |
| 1:21 | 40, 89 |
| 1:28 | 40 |
| 1:30 | 89 |
| 1:31 | 89 |
| 1:32 | 40, 89 |
| 1:34 | 89 |
| 2:22 | 39 |
| 3:14 | 39 |
| 3:14–17 | 29 |
| 3:18–4:28 | 29 |
| 4 | 18, 50, 51, 86n151, 180 |
| 4:1 | 117n54 |
| 4:1–28 | 33, 35 |
| 4:6 | 78 |
| 4:7–8 | 152n2, 171 |
| 4:9–10 | 124n67, 125 |
| 4–11 | 35n12 |
| 4:11 | 74 |
| 4:13 | 48 |
| 4:15–31 | 49 |
| 4:16–18, 23, 25 | 49 |
| 4:19 | 49 |
| 4:23 | 48, 49 |
| 4:25 | 49 |
| 4:26 | 49 |
| 4:27 | 49 |
| 4:28 | 49 |
| 4:29 | 46, 49, 112, 113 |

| | |
|---|---|
| 4:29–31 | 29, 30, 30n3, 33, 35, 49, 56 |
| 4:30 | 49, 58, 155 |
| 4:31 | 48, 49, 59 |
| 4:32–40 | 29, 30 |
| 4:32–44 | 33, 35 |
| 4:34 | 38 |
| 4:36 | 73–74 |
| 4:37 | 59n71 |
| 4:39 | 58, 76 |
| 4:40 | 81 |
| 4:41–49 | 29 |
| 4:45—11:32 | 31 |
| 4:45—26:19 | 34, 35 |
| 4:45—28:2 | 34 |
| 4:45—28:68 | 37 |
| 4:45—28:68 [ET 29:1] | 32 |
| 4:45ff | 33 |
| 4:46–47 | 33, 47 |
| 5 | 86n151 |
| 5:1—26:19 | 29 |
| 5:1–33 | 42 |
| 5:2–3 | 48 |
| 5:10 | 88 |
| 5:17–19 | 153 |
| 5:21 | 153, 207, 208 |
| 5:22 | 42 |
| 5–26 | 38n22 |
| 5:27 | 42, 74 |
| 5:27–32 | 43n37 |
| 5:28 | 42 |
| 5:29 | 41–42, 43, 46, 50, 59, 87 |
| 5:31 | 44 |
| 6 | 45 |
| 6:1 | 43, 44, 45 |
| 6:1–3 | 43, 43n37, 44, 88 |
| 6:2 | 43, 44, 45 |
| 6:2, 6 | 81 |
| 6:3 | 43, 44 |
| 6:3 LXX | 43n37 |
| 6:4 | 44 |
| 6:4–5 | 37, 43, 43n35, 44, 45, 46, 59, 84, 88, 204n121 |
| 6:4–9 | 40, 131n81 |
| 6:5 | 41, 45, 46, 60 |
| 6:6 | 45, 45n39, 75, 81, 87, 93n2, 108n38, 112, 123, 123n65, 129n77, 144, 146 |
| 6:6–7 | 22 |
| 6:6–8 | 119, 119n56 |
| 6:9 | 123 |
| 6–11 | 86n151 |
| 6:12–15 | 75 |
| 6:18 | 117n54 |
| 6:25 | 44 |
| 7:9 | 88 |
| 7:11 | 44, 81 |
| 7:16 | 78 |
| 7:17 | 50n48 |
| 7:19 | 38 |
| 8 | 9, 47n44, 163 |
| 8:1 | 81, 117n54 |
| 8:2 | 38 |
| 8:3 | 47n44 |
| 8:7 | 78 |
| 8:11 | 81, 164n32 |
| 8:17 | 8, 50n48, 153, 157, 161, 162, 163, 164, 175, 177 |
| 8:17 LXX | 157, 158, 159, 164n32 |
| 8:17 MT | 158, 164n32 |
| 8:17–18 | 164 |
| 9 | 9, 164 |
| 9:4 | 8, 50n48, 153, 157, 161, 162, 163, 165, 175, 177 |
| 9:4 LXX | 157, 158, 159, 164n32 |
| 9:4 MT | 158, 164n32 |
| 9:4–6 | 62n81, 84n147, 86, 86n152, 164 |
| 9:4–6 LXX | 164n33 |
| 9:4ff | 183 |
| 9:5 | 78, 164n33, 165 |
| 9:6 | 183 |
| 9:7 | 47n44 |
| 9–10 | 84n147 |
| 10:1–5 | 125n70 |
| 10:8 | 39 |
| 10:12 | 45, 46, 60 |
| 10:12–13 | 45, 88 |

**Deuteronomy** (*cont.*)

| | |
|---|---|
| 10:12–14 | 2n6 |
| 10:13 | 45, 81 |
| 10:15 | 59n71 |
| 10:16 | 41n32, 45, 46, 59, 75, 93n2, 109, 110, 111, 112, 211 |
| 10:17 | 152n2 |
| 11:1 | 60, 88 |
| 11:4 | 39 |
| 11:8 | 81, 117n54 |
| 11:9 | 59n71 |
| 11:10 | 59n71 |
| 11:13 | 46, 60, 81, 88 |
| 11:16 | 112 |
| 11:18 | 45, 45n39, 112, 123, 123n65, 129n77 |
| 11:22 | 44, 60, 88 |
| 11:22 LXX | 81 |
| 11:27 | 81 |
| 11:28 | 81 |
| 12:1—26:19 | 31, 34 |
| 12–26 | 35n12 |
| 12–28 | 86n151 |
| 13:3 | 88 |
| 13:4 | 46, 60 |
| 13:19 | 81 |
| 14:22 | 59n71 |
| 15:5 | 44, 81 |
| 15–20 | 16 |
| 16:20 | 117n54 |
| 17:1–10 | 31 |
| 17:14–20 | 141 |
| 17:15 | 89n158 |
| 17:20 | 44 |
| 18 | 101, 103n24 |
| 18:15–19 | 89, 174 |
| 18:15–20 | 74 |
| 18:16–17 | 89 |
| 18:18 | 101, 103n24, 128 |
| 19:9 | 44, 45, 60, 81, 88 |
| 20:1 | 78 |
| 21:35 | 208 |
| 22:9 | 59n71 |
| 26:16 | 46 |
| 27:1 | 81 |
| 27:1–4 | 29 |
| 27:1–26 | 34 |
| 27:1—28:14 | 35 |
| 27:1—29:1 | 196n104 |
| 27:4 | 81 |
| 27:5–7a | 29 |
| 27:7b–8 | 29 |
| 27:9–10 | 29 |
| 27:10 | 81 |
| 27:11–26 | 29, 31 |
| 27–28 | 200 |
| 27–30 | 35n12, 200 |
| 28 | 29, 36, 36n15, 49, 51 |
| 28:1 | 81 |
| 28:1–14 | 34 |
| 28:1–68 | 35 |
| 28:1–69 [ET 29:1] | 31 |
| 28:13 | 81 |
| 28:14 | 81 |
| 28:15 | 60, 81 |
| 28:15–24 | 49 |
| 28:15–68 | 34, 49–50 |
| 28:25 | 49 |
| 28:27 | 49 |
| 28:29 | 49 |
| 28–29 | 84n147 |
| 28:29b–31 | 49 |
| 28:32, 41, 68 | 49 |
| 28:33 | 49 |
| 28:35 | 49 |
| 28:36 | 49 |
| 28:38 | 59n71 |
| 28:41 | 49 |
| 28:45 | 60 |
| 28:46 | 59n71 |
| 28:47 | 49 |
| 28:49–52 | 49 |
| 28:52 | 49 |
| 28:53–57 | 49 |
| 28:58 | 60 |
| 28:59 | 59n71, 72 |
| 28:60–61 | 49 |
| 28:64 | 49 |
| 28:64–68 | 61 |
| 28:65 | 50 |
| 28:65–67 | 49 |
| 28:65–68 | 46 |

28:68        49, 50
28:69 [ET 29:1]   33, 35, 35n13, 36,
        83, 89, 119
28:69 [ET 29:1]—29:8 [ET 29:9] 34,
        35
28:69 [ET 29:1]—30:2    34
28:69 [ET 29:1]—30:10   83n147
28:69 [ET 29:1]—30:20   33, 34
28:69 [ET 29:1]—34:12   32
28:69—29:3 [ET 29:1–4]   47
28:69—30:20   36n17
28:69ff [ET 29:1ff]   37
29    35, 36, 36n15, 40,
    50, 51, 51n50, 90,
    118, 180, 194, 200,
    206
29:1 [ET 29:2]—30:20   31
29:1–2, 4–7 [ET 29:2–3, 5–8]   47
29:1–2 [ET 29:2–3]   38
29:1–8   29
29:3   39n26, 41
29:3 [ET 29:4]   18, 22, 38, 39, 40,
    42, 43, 45, 46, 47,
    56, 59, 83, 84,
    86n151, 91, 109,
    110, 125, 133, 153,
    177, 199, 200,
    200n110, 202
29:3 LXX   200, 201
29:3 MT   200
29:3–4   196n104
29:4   18
29:4 [ET 29:5]   47
29:5 [ET 29:6]   47
29:6 [ET 29:7]   33, 47
29:6–7   39
29:7 [ET 29:8]   90
29:8 [ET 29:9]   47
29:9 [ET 29:10]—28 [ET 29:29]   34,
    35
29:9–14 [ET 29:10–15]   47
29:9—30:1–10   29
29:10 [ET 29:11]   47–48
29:11 [ET 29:12]   48, 48n46
29:12 [ET 29:13]   83
29:15–27 [ET 29:16–27]   49
29:15–27 [ET 29:16–28]   50–51
29:16–19   62

29:17–18 [ET 29:18–19]   50n48
29:17–20 [ET 29:18–21]   83
29:17–27 [ET 29:18–28]   83
29:17a [ET 29:18a]   50, 52
29:17b–18 [ET 29:18b–19] 50, 51, 52
29:18 [ET 29:19]   108, 109, 110
29:19 [ET 29:18]   53
29:20 [ET 29:21]   51
29:20–29   56n64
29:21–27 [ET 29:22–28]   83
29:22 [ET 29:23]   51, 180
29:24 [ET 29:25]   60–61
29:24–25 [ET 29:25–26]   51
29:26–27 [ET 29:27–28]   52
29:27   60
29:27 [ET 29:26]   53
29:27 [ET 29:28]   61, 90
29:28   51n50
29:28 [ET 29:28]   51
29:28 [ET 29:29]   53, 206
29:28 LXX   53n56
29:29   52n53, 63n86,
    206n126
29:29 [ET 29:28]   51
29–30   20n81, 21, 37,
    37n18, 48,
    53, 53n56, 83,
    172n51, 173,
    196n104, 206,
    206n128
29–32   4, 154, 199, 202,
    210
30   4, 8, 9, 10, 11, 12,
    15, 16, 17, 18, 21,
    22, 23n93, 35, 36,
    42, 43, 48n45, 51,
    53, 54, 102, 113,
    117n54, 130, 155,
    162, 171, 174n55,
    175, 176, 188n84,
    192, 193, 194, 195,
    196n103, 198,
    206, 207n129,
    210, 211, 213
30:1   56, 57, 58n66, 61,
    76, 81, 86n151,
    90, 173, 196n104
30:1–2   54

**Deuteronomy** (*cont.*)

| | |
|---|---|
| 30:1–3 | 116 |
| 30:1–9a | 61 |
| 30:1–10 | 4, 16, 17n73, 22, 24n95, 27, 27n2, 28, 30, 30n3, 36, 36n14, 36n15, 54, 55, 55n63, 56, 58, 58n68, 62, 62n81, 63, 63n86, 64, 64n87, 65, 69, 70, 73, 77, 77n129, 79, 79n136, 80, 81, 81n141, 82, 82n146, 83, 84, 84n147, 87, 88, 108, 115, 116n54, 117n54, 129, 131, 132n86, 168, 171n49, 172, 192, 196, 196n104, 197, 201, 212 |
| 30:1–14 | 26, 34, 35, 47, 54, 55n63, 56, 57, 64, 65, 79, 82, 91, 104, 105, 107, 108, 115, 115n50, 116, 118, 119, 129, 132, 133, 134, 143, 144, 154, 166, 168, 169, 173, 176, 191, 200, 206, 208, 213 |
| 30:1a | 57, 58 |
| 30:1a–7 | 61 |
| 30:1b | 57, 58 |
| 30:1ff | 69 |
| 30:2 | 46, 55, 56, 57, 58, 73, 80n138, 81, 81n141, 82, 88, 90, 115 |
| 30:2–10 | 86n151 |
| 30:3 | 54n59, 57, 58, 58n67, 59, 113, 114, 115, 117n54 |
| 30:3–4 | 54 |
| 30:3–7 | 84n147 |
| 30:4 | 57, 58, 117n54 |
| 30:5 | 55, 57, 58, 59, 115 |
| 30:6 | 18, 40, 41n30, 46, 55, 56, 57, 59, 60, 62n83, 75, 79n136, 80, 82, 83, 84n147, 86n151, 88, 90, 93n2, 109, 110, 111, 117n54, 129n77, 130, 131n81, 170, 172, 172n51, 173, 186n81, 192, 196n104, 197, 202, 206n126, 211, 212 |
| 30:6, 11–14 | 215 |
| 30:6, 14 | 61 |
| 30:6, 19 | 59n71 |
| 30:6–8 | 54 |
| 30:7 | 57, 60 |
| 30:8 | 57, 60, 73, 81, 81n141, 82, 84n147, 90, 117n54 |
| 30:8–10 | 116 |
| 30:9 | 54, 55, 57, 59, 64, 65, 66, 73, 80n138, 117n54 |
| 30:9–10 | 22 |
| 30:9–14 | 65, 69 |
| 30:9a | 61 |
| 30:9b | 57 |
| 30:9b–10 | 61, 64, 69 |
| 30:10 | 36n14, 54, 55, 56, ᵀᵀ, 63, 64, 66, 73, 88, 131 |
| 30:10a | 65 |
| 30:10b | 65 |
| 30:10f | 69 |
| 30:11 | 25, 44, 57, 62, 62n83, 63n86, 64, 64n87, 64n88, 65, 68, 69, 71, 77, 80, 81, 81n141, 82, 88, 90, 159, 163, 194 |
| 30:11, 14 | 22, 108n38 |
| 30:11–13 | 71, 87, 170 |

| | |
|---|---|
| 30:11–14 | 1, 2n4, 4, 6n22, 8, 14, 16, 17, 18, 19n80, 20n82, 21n89, 22, 23n93, 23n94, 24n95, 24n96, 24n97, 25, 27, 27n2, 28, 30, 35, 36n14, 52n53, 53, 54, 54n58, 55, 56, 61–64, 62n81, 62n83, 63n86, 63n87, 64n87, 64n89, 68, 69, 70, 71, 73, 73n122, 74, 76, 77, 77n129, 78, 79, 79n136, 80, 81, 81n141, 82, 82n146, 83, 83n147, 84, 84n147, 87, 87n153, 87n155, 88, 89, 90, 92, 93, 104, 105, 108, 108n38, 112n45, 118, 119, 128, 129, 129n77, 131, 134, 150, 151, 153, 154, 156, 159, 162, 168, 168n40, 169, 170, 172, 173, 176, 184n80, 192, 193n98, 196, 196n104, 197, 212, 215 |
| 30:11–20 | 36n14, 63 |
| 30:11—31:18 | 29 |
| 30:11a | 71, 72 |
| 30:11b | 71, 72 |
| 30:11b, c, 12, 13 | 71 |
| 30:11c | 71 |
| 30:11ff | 36n14, 119, 119n56 |
| 30:12 | 8n31, 71, 72, 73, 159, 169, 173 |
| 30:12 LXX | 160n18 |
| 30:12 MT | 158, 160n18 |
| 30:12–13 | 161, 172, 173 |
| 30:12–14 | 2–3, 2n4, 3n13, 4, 5, 6, 7, 8n31, 10, 11, 12, 13, 14–15, 16, 17, 18, 18n76, 19, 20, 20n85, 21, 21n89, 22, 23, 25, 50n48, 63n86, 74, 86n152, 91, 153, 154, 156, 157, 159, 159n17, 160, 161, 162, 165, 166, 166n35, 167–68, 168n40, 169, 171, 172, 173, 173n53, 174n55, 175, 176, 176n57, 177, 185n81, 186n81, 187, 187n82, 191, 192, 193, 194, 196, 197, 202, 207n129, 210, 212, 213, 215 |
| 30:12–14 LXX | 158 |
| 30:12–14 MT | 158 |
| 30:12a | 73 |
| 30:12b, 13b | 73 |
| 30:13 | 71, 72, 73, 73n122, 159, 160, 173, 174 |
| 30:13 LXX | 159, 160n18 |
| 30:13 MT | 159, 160n18 |
| 30:13a | 73 |
| 30:13b | 73 |
| 30:14 | 19n79, 22, 56, 57, 61, 64, 64n88, 65, 66, 68, 69, 71, 73, 74n122, 75, 76, 87, 89, 90, 104, 108n38, 129n77, 130, 144, 171, 171n49, 172, 173, 176, 197, 213 |
| 30:14 LXX | 87, 160 |
| 30:14 MT | 160 |
| 30:15 | 82, 82n146 |
| 30:15–16 | 62n83, 80 |
| 30:15–20 | 34, 35 |
| 30:16 | 60, 81, 88, 186n81 |
| 30:19 | 59n71, 60 |

**Deuteronomy** (*cont.*)

| | |
|---|---|
| 30:20 | 31n5, 35, 35n13, 36, 60 |
| 31:1–15 | 34 |
| 31:1—34:12 | 34 |
| 31:14–15 | 29 |
| 31:16–18 | 49, 85 |
| 31:16–21 | 85 |
| 31:16–22 | 29, 120 |
| 31:16–23 | 34 |
| 31:16–29 | 38 |
| 31:16—32:42 | 86n151 |
| 31:19 | 86 |
| 31:19–21 | 85 |
| 31:21 | 59n71 |
| 31:23 | 29 |
| 31:24–27 | 29 |
| 31:24–29 | 49 |
| 31:24–30 | 34 |
| 31:26 | 125, 125n70 |
| 31:26–29 | 39, 85, 120 |
| 31:27 | 39 |
| 31:28–44 | 30 |
| 31:29 | 39 |
| 31:31–34 | 132n86 |
| 31–32 | 84 |
| 31–34 | 31n5, 35n12 |
| 32 | 155, 180, 192, 198–99, 208, 209, 210, 211 |
| 32:1–20 | 208 |
| 32:1–47 | 34 |
| 32:5 | 86 |
| 32:15–43 | 35, 49 |
| 32:21 | 153, 177, 198, 199, 202, 209 |
| 32:21–27 | 208 |
| 32:23 | 86 |
| 32:28–29 | 198 |
| 32:28ff | 208 |
| 32:35 | 153, 202 |
| 32:36 | 86, 209 |
| 32:43 | 86n151, 153, 202, 209, 210 |
| 32:43 LXX | 209n136 |
| 32:43b | 210 |
| 32:45–57 | 30 |

| | |
|---|---|
| 32:46 | 45, 45n39, 123 |
| 33:1–29 | 34 |
| 33:1—34:5a | 30 |
| 33:26 | 86n151 |
| 34:1–12 | 34 |
| 34:1a | 30 |
| 34:4 | 59n71 |
| 34:5b–9 | 30 |
| 34:6 | 39 |
| 34:10 | 30 |
| 34:11–12 | 30 |

**Joshua**

| | |
|---|---|
| | 105n30 |
| 1:8 | 22 |
| 4:23 | 74 |
| 5:13–15 | 104n28 |
| 9:3–27 | 48n45 |

**Judges**

| | |
|---|---|
| | 105n30 |

**1 Samuel**

| | |
|---|---|
| 12:24 | 41n32 |
| 25:37 | 41n32 |

**2 Kings**

| | |
|---|---|
| 22:8 | 106 |
| 22:8–14 | 106n35 |

**Nehemiah**

| | |
|---|---|
| 9:11 | 74 |

**Job**

| | |
|---|---|
| 26:12 | 140n107 |
| 41:3a [ET 41:11a] | 201 |
| 42:10 | 113 |

**Psalms**

| | |
|---|---|
| | 136, 151, 152, 152n1 |
| 1 | 139, 140, 146, 147, 148, 149, 213 |
| 1:1 | 140, 148–49 |

| | |
|---|---|
| 1:1–3 | 147 |
| 1–2 | 137n99, 138, 139 |
| 1:2 | 139, 139n102, 142, 146 |
| 1–2 | 147, 148 |
| 1:2 | 149 |
| 1–2 | 149 |
| 1:3 | 147, 148 |
| 1:6 | 148 |
| 1–41 | 136 |
| 2 | 137, 148, 213 |
| 2:2–4 | 138 |
| 2:4 | 138 |
| 2:5 | 148 |
| 2:6 | 148 |
| 2:7 | 148 |
| 2:8 | 148 |
| 2:9 | 148 |
| 2:10–12 | 148 |
| 2:12 | 148 |
| 14:7 | 113 |
| 18 | 145 |
| 18:8–16 | 145 |
| 18:31 | 145 |
| 19 | 145 |
| 19:2–7 | 145 |
| 19:4 | 198, 198n107 |
| 19:8 | 145 |
| 27:22 | 138n100 |
| 37 | 26, 136, 137, 139, 148, 149, 214 |
| 37:1 | 137 |
| 37:3a | 137 |
| 37:3b | 137 |
| 37:11 | 137 |
| 37:12 | 138 |
| 37:12–13 | 137, 138 |
| 37:12–24 | 137 |
| 37:13 | 138 |
| 37:17b | 137 |
| 37:18–19 | 137 |
| 37:21 | 138, 140 |
| 37:22 | 138 |
| 37:25–26 | 138 |
| 37:27 | 138 |
| 37:27–29 | 138 |
| 37:28 | 138 |
| 37:29 | 139 |
| 37:30 | 139 |
| 37:30–31 | 134, 135, 139, 139n102, 149, 150 |
| 37:30a | 139n102, 149 |
| 37:31 | 75, 91, 92, 139, 139n103, 144, 215 |
| 37:31a | 139n102, 149 |
| 37:35–36 | 138 |
| 40 | 26, 136, 139, 141n110, 143–44, 148, 149, 150, 214 |
| 40:1 | 139 |
| 40:1–2 [ET 40:1–3] | 142 |
| 40:2 [ET 40:1] | 139 |
| 40:2–4 [ET 40:1–3] | 139 |
| 40:3–4 [ET 40:4–5] | 142 |
| 40:3a [ET 40:2a] | 140 |
| 40:4a [ET 40:3a] | 140 |
| 40:4b [ET 40:3b] | 140 |
| 40:5 [ET 40:4] | 140 |
| 40:5 [ET 40:6] | 142 |
| 40:5a [ET 40:4a] | 140 |
| 40:5b [ET 40:4b] | 140 |
| 40:6 | 143 |
| 40:6–8 | 142n114 |
| 40:7 [ET 40:6] | 142 |
| 40:7–8 | 139 |
| 40:7–9 [ET 40:6–8] | 140 |
| 40:8 | 22, 76, 91, 92, 134, 135, 143, 215 |
| 40:8 [ET 40:7] | 142 |
| 40:8–9 [ET 40:7–8] | 141, 142 |
| 40:8f | 149 |
| 40:9 [ET 40:8] | 141, 141n110 |
| 40:9a [ET 40:9a] | 142 |
| 40:9b [ET 40:8b] | 142, 142n114 |
| 40:10 [ET 40:9] | 142 |
| 40:11 [ET 40:10] | 142 |
| 42–72 | 136 |
| 53:6 | 113 |
| 69:22–23 | 201 |
| 73–89 | 136 |
| 78:13 | 74 |
| 81:13 | 109n40 |
| 85:1 | 113 |
| 90–106 | 136 |
| 107 | 145n119 |
| 107:3 | 145n119 |

**Psalms** (*cont.*)

| | |
|---|---|
| 107–50 | 136 |
| 118 | 145 |
| 119 | 26, 136, 144, 145, 146, 147, 148, 149, 214 |
| 119:1–16 | 146n121 |
| 119:2 | 146 |
| 119:10 | 144, 146 |
| 119:11 | 91, 92, 112, 134, 135, 144, 146, 215 |
| 119:15 | 72 |
| 119:16 | 141 |
| 119:17–48 | 146n121 |
| 119:24 | 141 |
| 119:32 | 147 |
| 119:34 | 146 |
| 119:35 | 141 |
| 119:36 | 146 |
| 119:43 | 22 |
| 119:49–80 | 146n121 |
| 119:58 | 146 |
| 119:69 | 146 |
| 119:81–96 | 146n121 |
| 119:92 | 141 |
| 119:97 | 145, 146, 148 |
| 119:97–107 | 145 |
| 119:97–128 | 146n121 |
| 119:98 | 145 |
| 119:99 | 145 |
| 119:100 | 145 |
| 119:101 | 145 |
| 119:102 | 145 |
| 119:103 | 145 |
| 119:129–60 | 146n121 |
| 119:145 | 146 |
| 119:161–76 | 146n121 |
| 126:1 | 113 |

**Proverbs**

| | |
|---|---|
| 2:1 | 146 |
| 3:3 | 93n2, 144 |
| 6:3 | 144 |
| 7:1 | 146 |
| 7:3 | 93n2 |

**Isaiah**

| | |
|---|---|
| | 93n3, 101, 104, 143, 151, 152, 152n1 |
| 1:9 | 180 |
| 1–37 | 94 |
| 1–39 | 93, 95 |
| 2:1–4 | 23 |
| 6 | 104n28 |
| 6:9–10 | 200 |
| 8:14 | 182, 183 |
| 9:16 | 179 |
| 10:15 | 196n103 |
| 10:22–23 | 180 |
| 10:24 | 100n18 |
| 11:2 | 103 |
| 11:9 | 120n59 |
| 28:16 | 182, 182n79, 183 |
| 29:8 | 103 |
| 29:10 | 199 |
| 29:10 LXX | 199 |
| 29:14 | 102 |
| 29:21 | 104n28 |
| 30:7 | 140n107 |
| 32:15 | 103 |
| 32:15ff | 120n59 |
| 37–38 | 94 |
| 38:1—39:8 | 94, 96n12 |
| 38–55 | 94, 96n12 |
| 40 | 94, 94n4 |
| 40:1 | 95n10 |
| 40:1–8 | 103n27 |
| 40:1—41:20 | 96n12 |
| 40:1—42:17 | 96n12 |
| 40:1ff | 95n10 |
| 40:7–8 | 178 |
| 40:7–8 LXX | 177 |
| 40:9 | 143 |
| 40:13 LXX | 201 |
| 40:15–17, 23–24 | 95 |
| 40:18–20 | 95 |
| 40:23–24 | 95 |
| 40–48 | 95 |
| 40–55 | 94, 95, 96, 143 |
| 40–65 | 103n27 |
| 40–66 | 93, 94, 95, 97, 99 |
| 41:2–4 | 95 |

| | | | |
|---|---|---|---|
| 41:8–9, 14 | 95 | 51:1–2 | 98 |
| 41:14 | 95 | 51:1—52:12 | 97n14, 100 |
| 41:26 | 96 | 51:1ff | 100n18, 181, 182 |
| 41:27 | 143 | 51:1ff LXX | 182n75 |
| 41–54 | 97n14 | 51:2–8 | 97 |
| 42:1 | 103 | 51:3 | 97n15, 98 |
| 42:4 | 100n18 | 51:4 | 100n18, 101 |
| 42:5 | 100n18 | 51:4–8 | 98 |
| 42:6 | 100n18, 101, 103 | 51:4a | 97n15 |
| 42:11ff | 100n18 | 51:4b | 97n15 |
| 42:18—44:23 | 96n12 | 51:5 | 97n15, 99, |
| 42:21—42:17 | 96n12 | | 100n18, 101, 102 |
| 43:1–21 | 95 | 51:6 | 97n15 |
| 43:2 | 74 | 51:7 | 75, 91, 92, 93, 97, |
| 43:8 | 200 | | 97n15, 99, 100, |
| 43:18–19 | 94 | | 101, 102, 112, 143, |
| 43:22—44:23 | 96n12 | | 144, 182 |
| 44:3 | 103 | 51:7ff | 100n18 |
| 44:6–9 | 95 | 51:8 | 97n15 |
| 44:21–28 | 95 | 51:9 | 98 |
| 44:24—53:12 | 96n12 | 51:9–11 | 99 |
| 45:1–7 | 95 | 51:9b–10 | 99 |
| 45:4 | 96 | 51:9ff | 99 |
| 45:9 | 179 | 51:10 | 74, 98, 182 |
| 45:20–21 | 95 | 51:11 | 98, 99 |
| 46:1–5 | 95 | 51:12a | 98, 99, 101 |
| 46:12 | 72 | 51:12b | 98, 99, 101 |
| 48:3–5 | 96 | 51:13 | 98, 99, 100 |
| 48:3–8 | 94 | 51:14 | 98, 99, 100, 101 |
| 48:14–16 | 95 | 51:15–16 | 98, 100 |
| 48:20–22 | 95 | 51:16 | 99, 101 |
| 49:1—53:12 | 96n12 | 51:16a | 101 |
| 49:2 | 101 | 51:16b | 101 |
| 49:6 | 100n18 | 51:17 | 98 |
| 49:8 | 101, 103 | 51:17ff | 99 |
| 49–55 | 96 | 51:18 | 98 |
| 50 | 99 | 51:19–20 | 98 |
| 50:4 | 101 | 51:21 | 98 |
| 50:4–9 | 101 | 51:22a | 98 |
| 50:10 | 99, 99n16 | 51:22b–23a | 98 |
| 50:10–11 | 100 | 51:23b | 98 |
| 51 | 26, 98, 99, 102, | 51:23c | 98 |
| | 168n40, 214 | 51–55 | 97n14 |
| 51:1 | 97, 97n15, 99, | 52:7 | 143, 196n103 |
| | 99n16, 100, | 52:13—53:12 | 97n14 |
| | 182n72 | 53 | 95 |
| 51:1, 7 | 99 | 53:1 | 198 |
| 51:1 LXX | 181 | 53:10 | 103 |

**Isaiah** (*cont.*)

| | |
|---|---|
| 54:1–17 | 96n12, 97n14 |
| 54:1—55:13 | 96n12 |
| 55:1–13 | 96n12, 97n14 |
| 56:1 | 104n28 |
| 56:1–8 | 96, 103n26, 104n28 |
| 56:1—59:21 | 104n28 |
| 56:9—57:13 | 104n28 |
| 56:9—59:15a | 103n26 |
| 56–59 | 104n28 |
| 56–66 | 94, 96, 100, 103n26 |
| 57:14–21 | 104n28 |
| 58:1–14 | 104n28 |
| 58:1—59:21 | 104n28 |
| 59:1–15a | 104n28 |
| 59:15b–21 | 103, 103n26, 104n28 |
| 59:20 | 103 |
| 59:20–21 | 104 |
| 59:21 | 101, 102, 103, 103n26, 104, 104n28 |
| 60:1–3 | 96 |
| 60–62 | 103n26 |
| 61:1 | 103 |
| 62:1–12 | 96 |
| 62:2 | 96 |
| 63:1–6 | 103n26 |
| 63:7—66:17 | 103n26 |
| 64:8 | 179 |
| 65:1 | 198, 199 |
| 65:2 | 199 |
| 65:17–25 | 96 |
| 66:18–24 | 103n26 |
| 66:20 | 96 |
| 66:22 | 96 |

**Jeremiah**

| | |
|---|---|
| | 105, 105n30, 105n31, 105n32, 106, 106n34, 106n35, 107, 107n37, 109, 112n45, 113, 114, 123, 124n68, |
| | 125n70, 127, 130, 130n79, 131, 131n81, 134, 143, 151 |
| 1 | 107 |
| 1:1 | 106, 107 |
| 1:9 | 101 |
| 1:10 | 117 |
| 1–25 | 107n37 |
| 1–28 | 108 |
| 2:8 | 126, 182 |
| 2–24 | 107 |
| 2:25 | 112 |
| 3:10 | 41n32 |
| 3:17 | 108, 109, 110 |
| 4:4 | 41n32, 109, 110, 111, 112, 124 |
| 5:2 | 200 |
| 5:23 | 109n40 |
| 6:10 | 109, 142 |
| 6:19 | 126 |
| 7 | 203n118 |
| 7:1 | 107n37 |
| 7:4 | 203n118 |
| 7:8 | 203n118 |
| 7:8 LXX | 203n118 |
| 7:8ff LXX | 203n118 |
| 7:9 LXX | 203n118 |
| 7:22–26 | 119 |
| 7:24 | 108, 109, 110 |
| 7:26 | 120 |
| 8:8 | 126 |
| 8:11 LXX | 203n118 |
| 9:12 [ET 9:13] | 126, 127 |
| 9:13 [ET 9:14] | 108, 109, 110 |
| 9:24–25 [ET 9:25–26] | 109, 110 |
| 9:25 | 203n118 |
| 9:25 [ET 9:26] | 110 |
| 9:25–26 [MT 9:24–25] | 111 |
| 11:1 | 107n37 |
| 11:1–11 | 125n70 |
| 11:7–8 | 119 |
| 11:8 | 108, 109, 110 |
| 13:10 | 108, 109, 110 |
| 13:23 | 112 |
| 16:12 | 108, 109, 110, 120 |
| 17:1 | 123, 124, 129n77 |
| 18:1 | 107n37 |

| | | | |
|---|---|---|---|
| 18:1–6 | 179 | 31:18–20 | 114 |
| 18:12 | 108, 109, 110 | 31:20 | 115 |
| 18:18 | 126 | 31:21 | 115 |
| 19:1–13 | 179 | 31:21–22 | 114 |
| 21:1 | 107n37 | 31:23 | 113 |
| 23:9 | 128 | 31:23–26 | 114, 115 |
| 23:17 | 108, 109, 110 | 31:26 | 116n53 |
| 24 | 117n54 | 31:26ff | 125 |
| 24:6 | 117n54 | 31:27 | 116 |
| 24:7 | 109, 110, 117n54, | 31:27–30 | 114, 117 |
| | 125, 131n81, 133 | 31:27–40 | 116 |
| 24:17 | 131n81 | 31:28 | 117 |
| 25:1 | 107n37 | 31:29–30 | 118 |
| 25–51 | 107 | 31:30 | 118 |
| 26:4 | 126, 127 | 31:31 | 116 |
| 26:4–6 | 127 | 31:31–33 | 91, 108n38, 134 |
| 26:24 | 106n35 | 31:31–34 | 23, 104, 108, 114, |
| 29 | 107, 113 | | 116, 118, 119, 120, |
| 29:3 | 106n35 | | 139, 143, 150 |
| 29:10 | 112 | 31:31–37 | 118 |
| 29:13 | 41n32, 113 | 31:31ff | 120n59, 149 |
| 29:13–14a | 112, 113 | 31:32 | 76, 118, 119 |
| 29:14 | 113 | 31:33 | 75, 117n54, 122, |
| 29–33 | 111 | | 123, 123n65, 124, |
| 30:1 | 107n37, 116n53 | | 126, 127, 128, 129, |
| 30:1–4 | 114, 115 | | 129n77, 130, 131, |
| 30:3 | 115, 116 | | 132, 144, 192, 205, |
| 30:5–11 | 114 | | 205n124, 206n128 |
| 30:10 | 115 | 31:33–34 | 176 |
| 30:11 | 115 | 31:33a | 122 |
| 30:12–17 | 114 | 31:33b | 122, 133 |
| 30:18 | 113, 115 | 31:33ff | 196n104 |
| 30:18—31:1 | 114 | 31:34 | 119, 131, 133 |
| 30:19 | 115 | 31:34b | 133 |
| 30–31 | 113, 116, 129 | 31:35–37 | 114, 118, 133 |
| 30–33 | 107, 107n37, 108, | 31:38 | 116 |
| | 112, 115n50 | 31:38–40 | 114, 133 |
| 31 | 26, 102, 117n54, | 31:40 | 133 |
| | 119, 130n79, 134, | 32:1 | 107n37 |
| | 168n40, 206n128 | 32:23 | 126 |
| 31:2–6 | 114 | 32:39 | 133, 150 |
| 31:7–14 | 114 | 32:39–40 | 192 |
| 31:8 | 115 | 32:39–41 | 196n104 |
| 31:10 | 115 | 32:44 | 113 |
| 31:15–17 | 114 | 33:7 | 113 |
| 31:16 | 115 | 33:11 | 113 |
| 31:17 | 115 | 33:26 | 113 |
| 31:18 | 115, 116 | 33:39–40 | 125 |

**Jeremiah** (*cont.*)
34:1 107n37
34:8 107n37
35:1 107n37
36:8, 19 106n35
36:10–13 106n35
36:19 106n35
38:33 LXX 122, 128
39:14 106n35
40:1 107n37
40:7–8 150
43:3 106n35
44:1 107n37
44:10 127
44:23 127
46–51 107n37
51:64 107
52 107
52:31–34 106n34

**Lamentations**
2:14 113

**Ezekiel**
143
11:19 41n32, 150
11:19–20 192
11:20 41n32
12:2 200
16:53 113
29:14 113
36 130n79, 168n40, 206n128
36:20ff 202n116
36:24–31 58n66
36:25–28 143
36:26 23n94, 41n32, 73n122, 150
36:26–27 23, 103, 130n79, 204n121, 206n128
36:26–28 143
36:26–29 143
36:26ff 120n59
36:27 41n32
36:27 LXX 204n121
37:14 130n79
39:25 113
44:7 109

**Hosea**
105
1:10 180
2:23 180
6:11 113

**Joel**
2:12 41n32
3:1 113
3:5 196n103

**Amos**
9:14 113

**Jonah**
2:4 LXX 174n56
2:6 174n56

**Micah**
6:8 204n121

**Habakkuk**
2:4 187n82

**Zephaniah**
2:7 113
3:20 113

**Zechariah**
7:12 123n66
10:11 74

**Malachi**
2:6–7 22

## DEUTEROCANONICAL BOOKS

4 Ezra      23n93

**Baruch**
     12, 13, 174n55
2:30      117n54
3      23n93

## PSEUDEPIGRAPHA (OLD TESTAMENT)

**Pseudo Philo**
19      23n93

*Testament of Moses*      23n93

## DEAD SEA SCROLLS

4QMMT      23n93

## ANCIENT JEWISH WRITERS

Philo      13, 174n55

*De Praemiis et Poenis*
     12, 13
80      163

*De Virtutibus*
     12
183      163

*Quod omnis probus liber sit*
69      163

## RABBINIC WORKS

Moses ben Nahman (Nahmanides)
RaMBaN      78, 78n132, 88

*Commentary on the Torah*
342      79n134
342–43      88n156

**Rashi**
*Pentateuch with Targum Onkelos, Haphtaroth and Prayers for Sabbath and Rashi's Commentary*
148      52n52

*Targum Neofiti*      12, 74, 174n56

## NEW TESTAMENT

**Matthew**
5:19      76
12:40      174n56
15:18–19      22
22:37–40      204n121

**John**
1:17      17
12:50      194

**Acts**
18:24–28      11

**Romans**
     4, 5, 12, 151, 152, 153, 153n3, 161, 187n82, 213
1:1—2:24      202n116
1–2      178
1:2      178, 209
1:5      174, 205
1–8      179
1–9      176n58
1:16      156
1:16–17      153, 153n3, 183, 191
1:25      202
1:32      204n121

**Romans** (*cont.*)

| | |
|---|---|
| 2 | 205 |
| 2:8 | 202n116 |
| 2:8–9 | 202n116 |
| 2:9 | 202n116 |
| 2:10 | 202n116 |
| 2:11 | 152n2 |
| 2:13 | 191 |
| 2:13f | 150, 175, 190n90 |
| 2:14 | 204n121, 205 |
| 2:14–15 | 205n125 |
| 2:15 | 205, 205n124, 206n128 |
| 2:16 | 206, 206n126 |
| 2:17ff | 202n116 |
| 2:19 | 203n118 |
| 2:22 | 203n118 |
| 2:24 | 202n116 |
| 2:24–25 | 170, 211 |
| 2:25 | 203, 203n116, 203n118, 204n121 |
| 2:25–29 | 53n56, 176, 202, 203n116 |
| 2:26 | 204, 204n121 |
| 2:27 | 204, 204n121, 205 |
| 2:28–29 | 24, 179, 202, 205, 206, 206n126, 207n129 |
| 2:29 | 53n56, 174, 187n82, 192, 204n121, 206n129 |
| 3:1 | 203 |
| 3:1–2 | 152n2 |
| 3–6 | 178 |
| 3:20 | 187n82, 204n121 |
| 3:21 | 182n75, 183, 204n121 |
| 3:21–22 | 187n82 |
| 3:21–26 | 161 |
| 3:22 | 191 |
| 3:23 | 204n120 |
| 3:24 | 191 |
| 3:25 | 191 |
| 3:27—4:25 | 162n26 |
| 3:27–28 | 161 |
| 3:28 | 204n121 |
| 3:31 | 167 |
| 4 | 161 |

| | |
|---|---|
| 4:1–5 | 161 |
| 4:1–25 | 183 |
| 4:5 | 204 |
| 4:11–12 | 179 |
| 4:13 | 162, 165 |
| 4:13–14 | 187n82 |
| 4:13–15 | 161 |
| 4:15 | 187n82 |
| 4:25 | 172 |
| 5:16 | 204n121 |
| 5:18 | 204n121 |
| 5:19 | 170, 175 |
| 5:20–21 | 161 |
| 6:3 | 174n56, 204n121 |
| 6:3–5 | 170 |
| 6:4 | 174 |
| 6:11 | 174 |
| 6:14, 15 | 167 |
| 6:14–15 | 161 |
| 6:15 | 167 |
| 7:4 | 167 |
| 7:6 | 121n60, 187n82 |
| 7:7 | 153, 206n128, 207, 208 |
| 7:7–13 | 192 |
| 7:7ff | 190 |
| 7–8 | 178 |
| 7:8–12 | 207 |
| 7:10 | 183, 187n82, 190, 190n90, 207 |
| 7:12 | 190 |
| 7:13 | 191 |
| 8 | 155n8 |
| 8:2 | 170, 191 |
| 8:3–4 | 170, 174, 208 |
| 8:4 | 170n46, 175, 204n121 |
| 9:1–5 | 154, 177, 178, 201 |
| 9:1–15 | 177n61 |
| 9:1–29 | 180 |
| 9:4 | 179 |
| 9:4–5 | 180 |
| 9:5 | 178, 180, 202 |
| 9:6 | 165, 178, 179n64, 180 |
| 9:6—10:13 | 178, 195 |
| 9:6–13 | 196n103 |
| 9:6–28 | 178 |

| | | | |
|---|---|---|---|
| 9:6–29 | 154, 177, 177n61, 180 | 9:31–33 | 156n14 |
| 9:6ff | 180 | 9:32 | 181, 182n74, 187n82 |
| 9:7 | 179 | 9:33 | 182, 185, 187n82 |
| 9:7–8 | 179 | 10 | 3, 5, 7, 8, 9, 10, 12, 14, 15, 16, 17, 18, 19, 21, 22, 23, 25, 50n48, 86n152, 134, 155, 156, 156n14, 164, 165, 193, 195, 200 |
| 9:9 | 179n64 | | |
| 9:9–13 | 179 | | |
| 9–10 | 161 | | |
| 9–11 | 153, 153n6, 154, 154n7, 154n8, 155, 155n8, 155n9, 156, 165, 176–77, 176n58, 183, 187n82, 198, 199, 201, 202, 209, 213 | | |
| | | 10:1 | 183 |
| | | 10:1–3 | 165 |
| | | 10:1–4 | 154 |
| | | 10:2 | 156n14, 180n66, 183 |
| 9:12 | 187n82 | 10:2–3 | 183, 187n82 |
| 9:14 | 179 | 10:3 | 156n14, 167n37, 180n66, 184n80, 187n82 |
| 9:14–29 | 196n103 | | |
| 9:15 | 162, 179 | | |
| 9:15–18 | 179 | 10:3–4 | 181 |
| 9:16 | 179, 181n67, 183, 187n82 | 10:4 | 2, 8n31, 25, 156, 156n12, 156n14, 161, 166, 166n37, 167, 167n37, 180n66, 182, 183, 189n88, 197, 204n121 |
| 9:16–29 | 179 | | |
| 9:17 | 162 | | |
| 9:20–24 | 179 | | |
| 9:22–26 | 198 | | |
| 9:23 | 180 | | |
| 9:25 | 162 | 10:4–5 | 167n37 |
| 9:25–26 | 179 | 10:4ff | 12, 184n80 |
| 9:26–29 | 195 | 10:5 | 3n13, 161, 162, 163, 176n57, 180n66, 183, 185n80, 186, 186n81, 188n85, 189n86, 190, 190n90, 191, 204n120 |
| 9:27 | 180 | | |
| 9:27–29 | 180 | | |
| 9:29 | 180 | | |
| 9:30 | 180, 183, 186n82, 187n82, 199 | | |
| 9:30—10:3 | 156 | | |
| 9:30—10:4 | 177, 179, 180, 182n75, 185, 197 | 10:5–8 | 10, 20n87, 26, 74, 156, 161, 166, 167n39, 184n80, 185n81, 186, 186n82, 187, 187n82, 188n85, 190n89, 196n103, 196n104 |
| 9:30—10:21 | 177n61 | | |
| 9:30–31 | 183 | | |
| 9:30–32 | 161, 185, 187n82 | | |
| 9:30–33 | 154, 156n14, 162n26, 179, 181, 183 | | |
| 9:30ff | 180 | | |
| 9:31 | 181, 183 | 10:5–10 | 4, 10 |
| 9:31–32 | 199 | | |

**Romans** (*cont.*)

| | |
|---|---|
| 10:5–13 | 1, 2, 3, 153, 154, 178, 185 |
| 10:6 | 13, 24, 153, 158, 161, 162, 165, 169, 174 |
| 10:6–7 | 13, 171, 172, 175 |
| 10:6–8 | 2n4, 3, 6, 7, 13, 15, 19, 20n87, 23, 91, 153, 154, 157, 157n15, 158, 159, 160, 161n21, 162, 166, 166n34, 168, 168n40, 170n46, 172, 172n51, 173, 173n53, 174n55, 176, 176n57, 177, 183, 191, 192, 194, 196, 202, 207n129, 210, 211, 212, 213, 215 |
| 10:6–10 | 24 |
| 10:6–13 | 185n80 |
| 10:6b | 166 |
| 10:7 | 159, 174, 199 |
| 10:7b | 166 |
| 10:8 | 2n4, 13, 24, 160, 172, 175, 179n64, 197 |
| 10:8b | 166, 172 |
| 10:9 | 154, 182n79, 187n82 |
| 10:9–10 | 176 |
| 10:9–13 | 197 |
| 10:10 | 180n66, 186n81, 187n82 |
| 10:11 | 162, 180n66, 182n79, 187n82 |
| 10:11–13 | 13 |
| 10:12 | 197 |
| 10:12a | 180n66 |
| 10:12b | 180n66 |
| 10:13 | 180n66, 197 |
| 10:14 | 172n50, 197 |
| 10:14–15a | 197, 198 |
| 10:14–17 | 154 |
| 10:14–21 | 178, 197, 199 |

| | |
|---|---|
| 10:16 | 24, 162, 198 |
| 10:16a | 198 |
| 10:16b | 198 |
| 10:17 | 13, 179n64, 198 |
| 10:18 | 179n64, 198 |
| 10:18–21 | 154 |
| 10:18ff | 198 |
| 10:19 | 153, 162, 177, 198, 202 |
| 10:19a | 198 |
| 10:19b | 198 |
| 10:20 | 162, 199 |
| 10:21 | 162, 199 |
| 11 | 199 |
| 11:1–5 | 199 |
| 11:1–32 | 154, 177n61, 178, 199 |
| 11:2, 4, 9 | 162 |
| 11:4 | 162 |
| 11:5–6 | 199 |
| 11:6 | 187n82 |
| 11:7 | 179, 181, 182 |
| 11:8 | 153, 177, 199, 200, 202 |
| 11:9 | 162 |
| 11:9–10 | 201 |
| 11:11–24 | 198 |
| 11:11–32 | 201 |
| 11:33 | 201 |
| 11:33–36 | 154, 177n61, 178, 201 |
| 11:34–35 | 201 |
| 11:36 | 202 |
| 12 | 209 |
| 12:1—15:6 | 208 |
| 12:9 | 153 |
| 12:14–21 | 208 |
| 12–15 | 208 |
| 12:17 | 208 |
| 12:19 | 202, 208 |
| 13:8 | 167 |
| 13:8–9 | 208 |
| 13:8–10 | 207 |
| 13:9 | 153, 207 |
| 13:9a | 207n130 |
| 15:8–12 | 208 |
| 15:9 | 210 |
| 15:10 | 153, 202, 209 |

| | |
|---|---|
| 16:26 | 174, 205 |
| 19:18 | 198n107 |
| 30:11–14 | 24 |
| 30:14 | 24 |
| 37 | 150 |
| 40 | 150 |
| 119 | 150 |

## 1 Corinthians

| | |
|---|---|
| 9:20 | 167 |
| 10:2 | 174n56 |
| 15 | 154n7 |
| 15:3–4 | 11 |

## 2 Corinthians

| | |
|---|---|
| 3 | 216 |
| 3:6 | 121n60 |
| 3:9 | 206n128 |

## Galatians

| | |
|---|---|
| 2:19 | 167 |
| 3:10–12 | 187n82 |
| 3:11–12 | 186n81, 187n82 |
| 3:12 | 3n13, 186n81 |
| 3:17 | 183 |

## Philippians

| | |
|---|---|
| 3:9 | 187n82 |

## Colossians

| | |
|---|---|
| 2:9 | 169 |

## Hebrews

| | |
|---|---|
| 8:10 | 128 |
| 8–10 | 216 |
| 10 | 141n110 |
| 10:5–7 | 142, 142n114 |
| 10:16 | 128 |

## 1 Peter

| | |
|---|---|
| 2:6 | 182n78 |

# EARLY CHRISTIAN WRITINGS

## Augustine

| | |
|---|---|
| | 214, 215 |
| "On the Spirit and the Letter" | 216 |
| 4.6 (*NPNF* 2/5:85) | 191n92 |
| 6.9 (*NPNF* 1/5:86) | 190n91 |
| 13.22 (*NPNF* 1/5:92) | 216n5 |
| 21.36 (*NPNF* 1/5:98) | 216n6 |
| 24.41 (*NPNF* 1/5:100) | 213n1 |
| 25.42 (*NPNF* 1/5:100–101) | 214n2 |
| 29.50 (NPNF 1/5:105) | 167n37 |
| 29.51 (*NPNF* 1/5:105) | 185n80 |

## Chrysostom

| | |
|---|---|
| | 18n76, 20n87, 185n80 |
| In epistolam ad Romanos | |
| 1/11:473 | 21n87 |
| 16 (*NPNF* 1/11:473) | 185n80 |

## Justin Martyr

| | |
|---|---|
| | 101n20 |

*Dialogue with Trypho*

| | |
|---|---|
| ANF 1:200 | 101n20 |

# REFORMATION WRITINGS

## Calvin, John

| | |
|---|---|
| | 120, 127, 215 |

*Commentaries on the Book of the Prophet Jeremiah and the Lamentations*

| | |
|---|---|
| 4:127 | 121n60 |
| 4:129 | 120n58 |
| 4:131 | 215n3 |
| 4:131–32 | 127n72 |
| 4:133 | 215n4 |
| 4:199 | 134n90 |

*Commentaries on the Epistle of
Paul the Apostle to the Romans*

|  | 15 |
| 388 | 18n75, 18n76 |

*Commentaries on the Four Last
Books of Moses*

|  | 15 |
| 1:413 | 16n68 |
| 1:X | 16n67 |

*Commentary on the Book of
Psalms*

| 2:98–99 | 141n108 |
| 102 | 141n111 |

*Commentary on the Book of the
Prophet Isaiah*

| 197 | 95n10 |

*Sermons on Deuteronomy*

|  | 15 |
| 1059 | 18n74 |

**Luther, Martin**

|  | 91 |

*Lectures on Deuteronomy*

| 9:278 | 91n162 |
| 278 | 8n31 |

*Lectures on Romans*

| 288 | 8n31 |